# BEYOND FAITH AND INFIDELITY

CURZON SUFI SERIES

Series Editor: Ian Richard Netton

*Reader in Arabic and Islamic Civilization and Thought, University of Exeter*

The *Curzon Sufi Series* attempts to provide short introductions to a variety of facets of the subject, which are inaccessible both to the general reader and the student and scholar in the field. Each book will be either a synthesis of existing knowledge or a distinct contribution to, and extension of, knowledge of the particular topic. The two major underlying principles of the Series are sound scholarship and readability.

ABDULLAH ANSARI OF HERAT
An Early Sufi Master

A.G. Ravan Farhadi

AL-HALLAJ

Herbert W. Mason

PERSIAN SUFI POETRY
An Introduction to the Mystical Use of Classical Persian Poetry

J.T.P. de Brujin

RUZBIHAN BAQLI
Mysticism and the Rhetoric of Sainthood in Persian Sufism

Carl W. Ernst

# BEYOND FAITH AND INFIDELITY

## The Sufi Poetry and Teachings of Maḥmūd Shabistarī

*Leonard Lewisohn*

CURZON PRESS

First published in 1995
by Curzon Press
St John's Studios, Church Road, Richmond
Surrey, TW9 2QA



Typeset by Florencetype Ltd, Stoodleigh, Devon

Printed in Great Britain by
Biddles Limited, Guildford and King's Lynn



*British Library Cataloguing in Publication Data*
A catalogue record for this book is available from the British Library

*Library of Congress in Publication Data*
A catalogue record for this book has been requested

ISBN 0 7007 0343 8

# CONTENTS

# SYSTEM OF TRANSLITERATION

| Consonants | | | |
|---|---|---|---|
| ء | ' | ظ | ẓ |
| ب | b | ع | ' |
| پ | p | غ | gh |
| ت | t | ف | f |
| ث | th | ق | q |
| ج | j | ك | k |
| چ | ch | گ | g |
| ح | h | ل | l |
| خ | kh | م | m |
| د | d | ن | n |
| ذ | dh | ه | h |
| ر | r | و | w |
| ز | z | ی | y |
| ژ | zh | ة | -a (-*at* in construct state) |
| س | s | | |
| ش | sh | | |
| ص | ṣ | | |
| ض | ḍ | | |
| ط | ṭ | | |

| Vowels | | |
|---|---|---|
| Long: | آ | ā |
| | أو | ū |
| | اِی | ī |
| Doubled: | ـِیّ | iyy |
| | ـُوّ | uww |
| Diphthongs: | او | aw |
| | ای | ay |
| Short: | ـَ | a |
| | ـُ | u |
| | ـِ | i |

# ACKNOWLEDGEMENTS

نشان ناشناسی ناسپاسی است
شناسای حق در حق‌شناسی است

*Not to acknowledge any favour is a sign of ignorance.*
*The knowledge of the Truth and cognizance*
*of God is but to give each man his due.*

—Shabistarī, *Garden of Mystery*

Many are the friends, dead and living, absent or present, who have assisted me in this study of that adept in the lore of the *Truth of Certainty*, Maḥmūd Shabistarī and his arcanum of Sufi symbolism, the *Garden of Mystery*, that Parterre of Symbols leading the way into his eternal *Book of Felicity*.

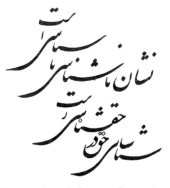

First of all, I would like to acknowledge my gratitude to Dr. Javad Nurbakhsh, Master of the Ni'matu'llāhī Sufi Order, who is also the editor of several of Shabistarī's works, for putting his library of Sufi texts at my disposal during the course of this work. I am grateful to Mehdi Mohaghegh, Professor of Islamic Studies, McGill University, for illuminating comments about Shabistarī's relation to the poet Nāṣir-i Khusraw. I am beholden to Devin DeWeese, Assistant Professor in the Department of Uralic & Altaic Studies at Indiana University, who, with painstaking kindness attempted to elucidate for me Shabistarī's relationship to the Kubrāwiyya. It is equally difficult for me to express the depth of my gratitude to Hermann Landolt, Professor of Islamic Studies, McGill University, Montreal, for his conscientious attention to the Minute Particulars of Shabistarī's spiritual genealogy, and for sharing with me his considerable expertise in this matter. My profound thanks to Carl Ernst, Professor of Religious Studies at the University of North Carolina, who read an early version of chapter eight, kindly offering interesting insights into the relationship of Shabistarī's esoteric ecumenism to the doctrine of 'real infidelity'. I owe a great debt to Dr. Charles Melville, Lecturer in Islamic Studies at Cambridge University, for kindly reviewing and editing several earlier versions of chapter three, thus bringing his vast erudition in mediæval Persian studies to bear upon my analysis of the Mongol period. I would like to acknowledge my gratitude to John Cooper, Lecturer in Persian Studies at Cambridge University, for taking the trouble to look over the final draft of this book, offering me erudite suggestions towards its improvement. I am deeply grateful to Dr. Muhammad Isa Waley, Curator of Persian and Turkish Manuscripts at the British Library in London, who kindly consented to read over several chapters and whose solicitous care for accuracy and truth often ensured that I did not fall into the Slough of Error. I would like to thank Dr. Hossein Ghomshei for contributing many lovely pieces of calligraphy of Shabistarī's poetry to illustrate the text. I am also very indebted to the innate generosity of Manuel Colón, Terry Graham, Neil Johnston and Dr. Peter Lawson for their many selfless kindnesses in perusing chapters of the book and contributing numerous stylistic improvements to the text.

While all contributors to the Curzon Sufi Series (surely a unique venture in the history of Western Islamic Studies) owe a debt to its Editor, Dr. Ian Netton, Head of the Department of Arabic and Islamic Studies at the University of Exeter, for its initiation, I would like thank him not only for his initial encouragement and enthusiasm for this project—as dear to my heart as it is to his—but for having consented to read and review the final draft of this book.

Leonard Lewisohn
London, February 1995

# I

# PERSONALIA
## Temporal and Spiritual

*Of what concern is consanguinity,*
*your ties of blood and lines of pedigree?*
*Set God, the One Reality,*
*before your face and search for harmony.*

### Family & Genealogy

Sa‘d al-Dīn Maḥmūd ibn ‘Abd al-Karīm Yaḥyā Shabistarī[1] was born in the last half of the thirteenth century at Shabistar, a small village northwest of Tabriz, located a few miles inland from Lake Urūmiya in present-day Persian Ādharbāyjān. Very little is known of his life, but he seems to have traveled extensively as is recorded in one of the rare autobiographical passages in his writings:

> I spent a long part of my life studying the science of divine Unity, traveling through Egypt, Turkey, and Arabia, day after day, night after night. Year in and year out, for month on end, like time itself, I trekked through town and country, sometimes burning the midnight oil, sometimes making the moon my bedside lamp.[2]

Although he also enjoyed considerable fame as a religious scholar,[3] no trace of any meetings he might have had with any persons outside his native Ādharbāyjān has survived. Nevertheless, some five hundred years later a dynasty of Sufis in Kirmān laid claim to be both his spiritual and genealogical descendants.[4] One scholar, basing himself on this improbable biographical claim, asserted that Shabistarī married in Kirmān and had several sons.[5] That such a spiritual succession through Shabistarī's family ever actually existed is unlikely for two reasons. 1) According to Ḥāfiẓ Ḥusayn Karbalā'ī Tabrīzī's *Rawḍāt al-jinān,* one of the earliest sources to mention the poet, Shabistarī is quoted as stating that he possessed neither physical nor 'spiritual' (i.e. disciples) offspring.[6] 2) No trace exists in any extant historical account, whether contemporary to the poet or in the following centuries, of his having established an organized initiatic chain *(silsila)* of disciples.

Furthermore, Shabistarī's own works reflect an extremely negative view of hereditary Sufism. He stresses, for instance, in these verses from the *Gulshan-i rāz,* that family and kinship ties carry no spiritual weight whatsoever:

Of what concern is consanguinity,
your ties of blood and lines of pedigree?
Set God, the One Reality,
before your face and search for harmony.[7]
Abandon family and kinship's pedigree!

Whoever makes the plunge into the sea
of Nothingness will find his time
and hours golden coins which cry:
"Then when the Trumpet blows,
no ties of blood or family
upon that Day will last;
of one another they will not ask."[8]
From kinship born of lust there's naught
begot but pride and haughtiness. If lust
were not at work between these folk,
all ties of blood and kin would be
but chimera. Yet once let lust be brought
to play, and see how one becomes
a 'mother' and another is the 'father'.
Who is this 'mother', who this 'father'—
I will not state – because with them you must
behave with reverence. Yet still, you call

a "sister" one who's full of flaws; one ill
in will to you and jealous you proclaim
a "brother." "Son and heir" you name your foe
and enemy, and one estranged from you you say
is "kith and kin!" Of 'aunt' and 'uncle' tell
me now—what gain accrues to you from them
but woe and grief? Those 'friends' of yours
who tread the Path with you are brethren in
mere fun and jest . . . just stop and sit
a moment's breath in earnest on the way
and you will see from them just what I say.
It's just an act, an artifice and fake,
a spell that's cast to tie you down—
Upon the Prophet's soul, I swear
It's all a caricature![9]

In fact, the poet views dynastically inherited Sufism, entailing material advantage disguised as otherworldly spirituality, as a central cause for the decline of genuine Sufism during his own age. The subsequent rise of the Safavid "totalitarian state" (as Roger Savory called it[10]), based on the 'divine right' of certain royal 'spirituals' who had inherited by blood (!) their position of 'Perfect Master', *murshīd-i kāmil,* was to corroborate his tenets on this matter. Hereditary Sufism, which was enhanced by "the disturbed religious climate of the Mongol period" in Jean Aubin's words,[11] is scorned throughout all his poetry. Such self-perpetuating hereditary mysticism or *"dervichisme"* (again Aubin[12]), where religious power was passed down through lineages of 'sacred families' during the Mongol period (as, for instance, in the case of the lineage of Shaykh Ṣafī al-Dīn Ardabilī), was, to Shabistarī (as well as to his eminent contemporary, the Kubrāwī Shaykh 'Alā al-Dawla Simnānī, 659/1261–736/1326[13]) a constant source of vexation, and is featured in his poetry as one of the main causes of the spiritual and cultural decline in his time. Criticizing such narrow-minded family attitudes, Shabistarī laments —

Look! at how the deaf-and-dumb,
  the blind, benighted man's become
the Shepherd; how the knowledge of the Holy Faith
  has fled aloft and gone to heaven!
There's nothing left of benevolence

or gentleness – gone is all reverence,
all peace and tolerance! No man feels vexed
by nescience, nor shame of ignorance.
Now all the world's spirit is in a disarray,
so if you have the wit, survey
the scene and see: a man of hate,
repellent, damned in frame of mind
who chases away his friends and loathes
mankind—he had as father one fair in mind
and meet in virtue . . . now he's renowned
to be a 'Shaykh' supreme! – Remember Khiḍr—
it was who slew the well-omened son,
the one who had a pious father – yet look how you've
become an ass before this 'shaykh', who is
more dense an ass than you, and more a fool
than any ass or mule! And since this 'shaykh' of yours
has not the sense to tell what's good from ill,
nor friend from foe, what chance
he'll clean your heart or know your conscience?
And if you find a son who's got a sign
within that shows his father—fine;
that's "light on light." A heir possessed of acumen,
well-omened, shrewd and wise is like
the choicest fruit which conveys to us
the soul of a tree . . . and yet a man
who cannot tell what's fair from foul
or high from base, how should you hope
that he'll become a 'shaykh'
and leader of the Faith?

Disciplehood in truth is but to learn
the lore of faith and science of religion;
to set alight the lamp of the heart
with the light of Faith. From slag and ash
none has lit a lamp; there is no lore that one can learn
from those who're dead and gone.[14]

The only vaguely credible testimony regarding Shabistarī's descendants is a small notice given by Amīr 'Alī-shīr Nawā'ī[15] of a grandson named "Shaykh 'Abdu'llāh Shabistarī," who purportedly lived in Samarqand, and later, in the early sixteenth century, took up residence at the Ottoman court. Other than this distant relative, nothing further of our poet's wife, children or family ancestors is known.

### Shabistarī's Spiritual Masters and Date of Death

Not one presently available historical source nor the poet's own writings provide any accurate facts concerning Shabistarī's *silsila* affiliations or that of his master, although by sources contemporary to the poet as well as by his own account, we have two names as having been his master: 1) Amīn al-Dīn, 2) Shaykh Bahā' al-Dīn.

#### Amīn al-Dīn

Shabistarī himself describes his "master" in the *Sa'ādat-nāma* as being "Amīn al-Dīn"[16] saying "My Shaykh and Master, Amīn al-Dīn, could really give you good answers. Bless his pure soul. I have never seen another master of his calibre."[17] In his history of Tabriz, Javād Mashkūr mentions a certain Amīn al-Dīn Tabrīzī, which may be the same person mentioned above by the poet in the *Sa'ādat-nāma:*

> Ḥājī Amīn al-Dīn Tabrīzī, also known as "Ḥājī Dada" was adept in Koranic interpretation and *Ḥadīth,* and a master *(ustād)* in the art of poetry. Although usually he used "Amīn" for his penname *(takhalluṣ),* due to the fact that he was a disciple *(murīd)* of Shaykh Nūr al-Dīn Isfarayīnī, he sometimes used "Nūrī" as well. He wrote many *qaṣā'id* in praise of Amīr Shaykh Ḥasan Īlkānī [=Shaykh Ḥasan Buzurk, d. 757/1356], and also spent some years *(rūzigārī)* in Baghdad with his son in the capacity of boon-companion *(munādamat)* of Sultan Uways [d. 776/1375]. At the end of his life he travelled from Baghdad to Tabriz, where he built a garden and busied himself with [religious] instruction, passing away in 758[=1357]. His *Dīwān* comprises 2500 couplets.[18]

Likewise, 'Alī Akbar Dihkhudā describes this same Amīn al-Dīn Tabrīzī in his Dictionary (s.v.) as being "a scholar in the sciences of *ḥadīth* and *tafsīr* as well as a poet," saying that "he wrote many *qaṣā'id* in praise of Shaykh Ḥasan Nūyān and spent some time in Baghdad serving as a boon-companion *(munādim)* to Sultan Uways," also adding that the year of his death was 758/1357.

On the other hand, Muḥammad 'Alī Tarbiyat in his work on the scholars of Tabriz mentions apparently *another* "Amīn al-Dīn Tabrīzī who was one of the students of Shaykh Maḥmūd, who wrote a single sentence commentary on each of the hemistiches of the *Gulshan-i rāz* . . . a copy of which I have seen in the Ma'rifat Library."[19] Not having access to this commentary, I have been unable to ascertain this item.

There is still another person named Amīn al-Dīn who could be taken as one of Shabistarī's masters.[20] Apparently he lived in Tabrīz during the same period. He is mentioned in the *Rawḍāt al-jinān*[21] as "Mawlānā Amīn al-Dīn Bālah," a contemporary of Shaykh Ḥasan Bulghārī (d. 603/1207–693/1294)[22]—whose correspondence with 'Alā' al-Dawla Simnānī is cited by Ibn Karbalā'ī.[23] However, since no further information is forthcoming on this Amīn al-Dīn Bālah cited by Ibn Karbalā'ī, his identity cannot be established satisfactorily.

Muḥammad Lāhījī also mentions an Amīn al-Dīn as Shabistarī's master, albeit with more hesitancy than confidence, in his interpretation of verse 43 in the *Garden of Mystery:*

> Make reply, he said to me:
> in one moment's breath, do it,
> and from this, the entire world shall benefit.[24]

whereon the exegete comments:

> They have said that that "eminent person" who was "experienced" *(kārdīda)* alluded to here, who commanded that the poet make reply to the letter, was the Supreme Shaykh in the world *(Shaykh al-mashāyikh fī'l-'ālam)* Shaykh Amīn al-Dīn, who was the director *(pīr)* and master *(murshid)* of Shaykh Maḥmūd Chabistarī . . . and such an assertion is not far-fetched.[25]

In light of the comments (cited above, page 5) by Javād Mashkūr in his history of Tabrīz about Ḥājī Amīn al-Dīn Tabrīzī's disciplic attachment to Nūr al-Dīn Isfarayīnī (d. 717/1317), it seems fairly conceivable that this "Supreme Shaykh", mentioned here by Lāhījī, is one and the same "al-Ḥājj Amīn al-Dīn 'Abd al-Salām al-Khunjī" whom Hermann Landolt, in his monograph on Isfarayīnī, identifies as "the most important figure among Isfarāyinī's disciples from the point of view of the Kubrāwī Order, since it is through him that the branch of the Order later known under the name *aṭ-ṭarīqa al-isfarāyinīya* is traced back, whereas the branch founded by Simnānī would be designated as *aṭ-ṭarīqa ar-ruknīya.*"[26]

However, before examining in more detail the identities of al-Ḥāj Amīn al-Dīn 'Abd al-Salām al-Khunjī and Ḥājī Amīn al-Dīn Tabrīzī, a brief look at another so-called master of our poet and Shabistarī's date of death is in order.

### Shaykh Bahā' al-Dīn and Shabistarī's Deathdate

Describing the cause of composition of the *Garden of Mystery,* the nineteenth-century historian Riḍā Qulī-Khān Hidāyat represents Shabistarī as answering Mīr Ḥusaynī Harawī's questions "at the behest of his own Shaykh, Bahā' al-Dīn Ya'qūb Tabrīzī."[27] This same "Shaykh Bahā' al-Dīn" is also mentioned by Ibn Karbalā'ī as another of Shabistarī's possible masters in the following passage, which also enables us to approximately calculate the date of the poet's death.

> Above the gravestone of his Worship Shaykh Sa'd al-Dīn Maḥmūd [Shabistarī], is the tomb of a notable by the name of Mawlānā Bahā' al-Dīn (God's mercy be upon him). It is also said that he was also the Shaykh's master *(ustād)* and that they made a pilgrimage together to the House of God [Ka'ba].
>
> It is well known that Mawlānā Sa'd al-Dīn [Shabistarī] made the bequest in his will to 'Bury me at the foot of his Worship Bahā' al-Dīn' (God's mercy be upon him)'. The death of Mawlānā Bahā' al-Dīn occurred in 737 [1336-7], during the reign of Muḥammad Khān, who was one of the sons of Hulākū Khān.[28]

As two contemporary Persian Shabistarī scholars, Ṣamad Muwaḥḥid and Javad Nurbakhsh, have pointed out,[29] it can be deduced solely from this statement that Shabistarī passed away *after* the year 737/1337. On the page following the above-cited passage in the *Rawḍāt al-jinān,* Ibn Karablā'ī provides an even more interesting detail regarding the poet's demise. While Shabistarī was suffering the final death throes, one of his fellow townsman—a Turkish mystic by the name of Bābā Abī Shabistarī—stopped by his residence. Noting that "due to human nature there was some rancour between the two men," Ibn Karbalā'ī recounts:

> Bābā Abī went to pay him a sick-visit. When he left the house, he slammed the door.
>
> [Maḥmūd] Shabistarī remarked, "Bābā Abī has slammed the door. By this gesture, he wished to indicate that the door of my house has been permanently shut, implying that I will not leave behind any sons, whether their genesis be physical or spiritual *(farzand-i ṣūrī yā ma'nawī nīst)*. As a matter of fact, *these will also be his own circumstances,* the truth of which will shortly become manifest, for we will soon encounter one another [in the Hereafter]."
>
> In that same year, or rather in that same month, Bābā Abī died. His death took place on the fifth of Rabī' al-Awwal in the year 740 [=September 11th, 1339][30]

By comparison of the above two passages from the *Rawḍāt al-jinān*, it is obvious that we should reckon the date of Shabistarī's death to be shortly after 1339-40, and not 720/1320 as most Persian *Tadhkira* authors and orientalists such as E.J. Browne[31] have recorded.

Another important point to be gleaned from the above-cited passage in the *Rawḍāt al-jinān* (although it cannot be taken too seriously, since Ibn Karbalā'ī finished his book in 975/1567 – over two hundred years after the poet's death) is that Shabistarī confesses that both he and his jealous rival would die without any physical offspring. If this confession be true, it only amplifies the definitive silence found in credible historical sources concerning, and pointing to the nonexistence of, the poet's family and descendants.

Unfortunately, no other historical sources contemporary to the poet provide any information on the biographical background of Shaykh Bahā' al-Dīn, so any quest for his true hisorical identity at this stage of our research must be relinquished.

We now return to have a closer look at the identity of Amīn al-Dīn Tabrizī (referred to above, page 5) whom Shabistarī had acknowledged as his own teacher.

## Amīn al-Dīn: Shabistarī's Master

The *nisba* "al-Khunjī" in the name Al-Ḥāj Amīn al-Dīn 'Abd al-Salām al-Khunjī, refers, of course, to a village south of Shiraz on the road to the Persian Gulf, as Hermann Landolt observes, and is thus quite far from Tabriz. Rukn al-Dīn Shirāzī in his commentary on the *Fuṣūṣ al-ḥikam* of Ibn 'Arabī (d. 638/1240), completed in 743/1342,[32] also mentions a certain "Ḥājī 'Abd al-Salām—*qaddasa sirruh*, may God hallow his spirit"[33]—whom he encountered "in the town of Khunj, which is among the dependencies of Shiraz."

Two important allusions contained within Rukn al-Dīn's statement above are highly relevant to Shabistarī's spiritual genealogy. The first is that, as this text makes clear—by the conventional formula added to the name of someone deceased: *qaddasa sirruh*—this man died before the book was completed. Furthermore, the fact that the *Nuṣūṣ al-khuṣūṣ* was completed in 1342 demonstrates that this "Ḥājī 'Abd al-Salām", who is "undoubtedly identical with Isfarāyinī's disciple Amīn al-Dīn 'Abd al-Salām," as Hermann Landolt has indicated,[34] must have died some years before this date and therefore cannot be reasonably identified with the Amīn al-Dīn who (according to Javād Mashkūr and 'A. A. Dihkhudā) passed away in 1357.

Although both persons are identified in the sources cited above as being "Ḥājī," and disciples of Shaykh Isfarāyinī, the probability is that they are two entirely different mystics, sharing the same name and the same spiritual master. In conclusion, we may assume that either Amīn al-Dīn, whether hailing from Khunj or Tabriz, may have been Shabistarī's spiritual master, but precisely *who* he was, remains, at the present state of research, a complete enigma.

Lastly, since we know that Shabistarī was in close contact with Shaykh Ismā'īl Sīsī (d. 785/1383 at age 118, an important disciple of Isfarāyinī's celebrated disciple 'Alā' al-Dawla Simnānī), having composed his (now no longer extant) treatise, the *Shāhid-nāma* for one of Shaykh Sīsī's disciples,[35] it is quite likely that he was personally acquainted with Nūr al-Dīn Isfarāyinī as well. Hence, it seems entirely possible that his own spiritual master could have been either eminent disciple of Shaykh Isfarāyinī—"Al-Ḥāj Amīn al-Dīn Tabrīzī" or "Ḥāji Amīn al-Dīn 'Abd al-Salām b. Sahlān al-Khunjī." We may therefore reasonably assume that Shabistarī's spiritual pedigree is of Kubrawī ancestry, even if the question as to which Amīn al-Dīn was his master remains unsolved.

Such speculations do still leave many questions unanswered. Although we may have gained some slight intimacy with his self-professed spiritual director, Amīn al-Dīn, what was Shabistarī's precise relationship to the other Shaykhs of the Kubrawī Order? Who were his own disciples? Unfortunately, these items can only be crudely estimated at present (see below, IV and V).

Given all the biographical confusion which surrounds the identity of Amīn al-Dīn, it is difficult to draw any definite conclusions about his character. One finds an interesting allusion in the *Garden of Mystery* to his apparently tolerant and broad-minded nature in the following verses:

> Be free of shame and name – hypocrisy and notoriety –
> Cast off the dervish frock, tie on the cincture
> and like our master, be inimitable in 'infidelity'
> if man you be: unto a Man commit your heart entirely.[36]

Considered in their proper theosophical context these verses refer to the mystical doctrine of 'real infidelity' *(kufr-i ḥaqīqī)* which is analysed in depth in the final chapter of this book. Here, the poet enjoins his reader to "become like *our master,* inimitable in 'infidelity'" *(chū pīr-i mā shū andar kufr fardī):* that is to say, become inimitable and unique in *kufr,* an individualized 'infidelity' which is the highest degree of faith in Shabistarī's lexicon of esoteric symbolism, signifying "the 'concealing' or 'covering-over' *(kufr)* of multiplicity *(kithrat)* in divine Unity *(waḥdat)."*[37]

One fact about Amīn al-Dīn's personality speaks for itself in these verses. Endowed with the high spiritual trait of being "inimitable in 'infidelity'," he certainly enjoyed an exceptional degree of liberation from the chief bugbear of Persian Sufis: religious conventionalism/blind belief *(taqlīd).* Perhaps the most suggestive indication of the profound spirituality of Shabistarī's teacher is provided by Muḥammad Lāhījī, who, commenting on the last cited couplet above (967), deduced:

"Of course, a master who could have been the spiritual director *(shaykh)* and guide of such a perfect being as the poet would have had to have been the supremely perfect man of his age."[38]

## Notes

1 Sometimes written Chabistarī.

2 See Ṣamad Muwaḥḥid (ed.), *Majmū'a-i āthār-i Shaykh Maḥmūd Shabistarī* (Tehran: Kitābkhāna-i Ṭahūrī 1365 A.Hsh./1986) (Hereafter: MAS), *Sa'ādatnāma,* p. 168, vv. 334-37.

3 MAS, *Gulshan-i rāz,* p. 105, v. 920.

4 Zayn al-Dīn Shīrwānī (Mast 'Alī Shāh), *Riyāḍ al-siyāḥa* (Tehran: 1334 A.Hsh./1955), pp. 89-90; Ma'ṣūm 'Alī Shāh, *Tarā'iq al-ḥaqā'iq,* ed. Muḥammad Ja'far Maḥjūb (Tehran: Kitābfurūshī Bārānī, n.d.), III, p. 733.

5 Muḥammad 'Alī Tarbiyat, *Dānishmandān-i Ādharbāyjān* (Tehran: Maṭab'a Majlis 1314 A.Hsh./1935), p. 335, citing *Riyāḍ al-siyāḥa.*

6 See below, page 8.

7 The poet here contrasts and rhymes *nasab* (familial lineage or descent involving a blood relationship) with *tanāsub* (proportion, symmetry, and harmony), thus underlining the primacy of one's inner spiritual 'harmony' over external family 'connections'. Since, as Shabistarī points out in the next verse, all such blood ties are annulled in the state of 'annihilation in God'—experienced by the gnostic in this world but by ordinary man in the Next—all spiritual merit is determined by the work of the heart *('amal),* rather than hereditary factors based on blood relationships *(nasab)* and or determined by lust *(shawat).* For further elucidation of this fundamental Sufi doctrine, see Muḥammad Lāhījī, *Mafātīḥ al-i'jāz fī sharḥ-i Gulshan-i rāz,* ed. Muḥammad Riḍā Barzgār Khāliqī and 'Iffat Karbāsī, (Tehran: Zawwar 1371 A.Hsh./1992), p. 572ff.

8 Koran XXIII: 101.

9 MAS, *Gulshan-i rāz,* p. 106, vv. 940-951.

10 "Some Reflections on Totalitarian Tendencies in the Safavid State," *Der Islam,* 52 (1976), pp. 226-41.

11 Jean Aubin, "La Propriété Foncière en Azerbaydjan sous les Mongols," in *Le Monde iranien et l'Islam,* IV (1976-77), p. 128.

12 Aubin uses the term "dervichisme"generically to allude to the possibilities for social ascension which various religious organizations enjoyed by masquerading under dervish guise during the Īl-Khānid period: "Most of these organizations," he observes, "were geared overall towards augmenting the temporal benefits of the families of the great founders of an 'Order' *(ṭarīqa),* or of the owners, often of very modest means, of a lodge of Sufis. Spiritual authority and material management was transmited hand in hand, hereditarily, with their morally priveleged status and their ancestry assuring the social position of the inheritors." Jean Aubin, "La Propriété Foncière . . . ," p. 128. On nepotism and family patronage in the Sufi culture of Mongol Iran, also see Marshall Hodgson, *The Venture of Islam,* (Chicago: University of Chicago Press 1977), II, pp. 112, 216-7.

13 The hypocrisy of obtaining material or economic benefits from one's spiritual position, of using one's own publically endowed properties *(waqf)* to advance the social position of one's offspring simply *par*

*obtenir des résultats dès ce monde d'ici-bas,* was well-recognized by Simnānī who relates how, in order to sidestep the possibility of becoming infected with this evil, he deliberately excluded his own family and relatives from acting as trustees to any of the vast properties which he owned and charitably endowed, and, in fact, intentionly overlooked his own sons when appointing spiritual directors for his disciples. See Simnānī's confession in his *Al-'Urwat li'l-ahl al-khalwat wa'l-jalwat,* ed. N.M. Harawī (Tehran: Intishārāt-i Mullā 1362 A.Hsh./1983), pp. 299-301.

14 MAS, *Gulshan-i rāz,* p. 104, vv. 907-18.

15 *Majālis al-nafā'is,* ed. 'Alī Aṣghar Ḥikmat, (Tehran 1323 A.Hsh.), p. 366; Ṣamad Muwaḥḥid, introduction MAS, pp. 4-5.

16 Concerning Amīn al-Dīn, see M.J. Mashkūr, *Tārīkh-i Tabrīz tā payān-i qarn-i nuhum hijrī* (Tehran: Intishārāt-i anjuman-i Āthār-i millī 1352 A.Hsh./1973), p. 766; Ḥāfiẓ Ḥusayn Karbalā'ī Tabrīzī, *Rawḍāt al-jinān va jannāt al-janān,* ed. Ja'far Sulṭān al-Qurrā'ī, (Tehran 1344 A.Hsh./1965; Persian Texts Series No. 20), II, p. 89; 'Azīz Dawlatābādī, *Sukhanvarān-i Ādharbāyjān* (Tabriz 1357 A.Hsh), Vol. 2, pp. 217-19.

17 MAS, *Sa'ādatnāma,* p. 168, vv. 334-343.

18 *Tārīkh-i Tabrīz tā payān-i qarn-i nuhum hijrī,* p. 766. Mashkūr's notice here is based on the *Ṣuḥuf-i Ibrāhīm* mentioned by Muḥammad 'Alī Tarbiyat, *Dānishmandān-i Ādharbāyjān,* p. 53. The *Ṣuḥuf-i Ibrāhīm* was not available to the present writer.

19 *Dānishmandān-i Ādharbāyjān,* p. 336.

20 A hypothesis put forward in a recent edition of *Gulshan-i rāz,* edited by Aḥmad Mujāhid and Muḥsin Kiyānī (Tehran: Chāp-i Bahrām 1371), introduction, p. 3. This new edition, which is accompanied by a *Kashf al-abyāt* and page references to 12 different published *Sharḥ*s according to each verse of the *Gulshan-i rāz,* is a very useful addition to Shabistarī studies.

21 *Rawḍāt al-jinān,* I, p. 154.

22 On Bulghārī, see Javād Mashkūr, *Tārīkh-i Tabrīz,* pp. 776-7.

23 *Rawḍāt al-jinān,* I, pp. 146-154

24 MAS, *Gulshan-i rāz,* p. 68, v. 43.

25 Lāhījī, *Mafātīḥ al-i'jāz,* edited Khāliqī and Karbāsī, p. 34.

26 *Nuruddin Isfarayini: Le Révélateur des mystères: Traité de soufisme,* ed. Hermann Landolt (Paris: Éditions Verdier 1986), p. 29, Introduction.

27 *Tadhkira-yi Riyāḍ al-'arifīn,* ed. Mihr-'Alī Gurkānī (Tehran: Maḥmūdī 1344 A.Hsh.), p. 221.

28 Ibn Karbalā'ī, *Rawḍāt al-jinān,* II, p. 91. On Muḥammad Khān, see E.G. Browne, *A Literary History of Persia* (Cambridge: Cambridge University Press 1956), III, p. 59.

29 MAS, p. 3; *Gulshan-i rāz,* edited by Dr. Javad Nurbakhsh (Tehran: Intishārāt-i khāniqāh-i Ni'matullāhī 1976), p. 6. Dr. Nurbakhsh notes: "To most readers familiar with the verse of the *Gulshan-i rāz* it did appear strange that Shabistarī could have composed this poem when he was only twenty years old. I was also puzzled by this claim until I read the *Rawḍāt al-jinān* of Ibn Karbalā'ī, and came to the conclusion that Ibn Karbalā'ī's version of the poet's deathdate was probably closer to

the truth." *ibid.*

[30] Ḥāfiẓ Ḥusayn Karbalā'ī Tabrīzī, *Rawḍāt al-jinān* II, p. 92.

[31] Browne, *A Literary History of Persia,* (Cambridge: University Press 1956), III, p. 146.

[32] Rukn al-Dīn Mas'ūd Shīrāzī, *Nuṣūṣ al-khuṣūṣ fī tarjumat al-Fuṣūṣ,* ed. Rajab'alī Maẓlūmī (Tehran: 1359 A. Hsh./1980), p. sixteen of Jalāl al-Din Humā'ī's introduction.

[33] *Nuṣūṣ al-khuṣūṣ*, p. 270. I am indebted to Prof. Devin DeWeese for this reference.

[34] Personal communication from Prof. H. Landolt to the author, March 21, 1995.

[35] Zarrīnkūb, *Justujū-yi dar taṣawwuf-i Īrān,* (Tehran: Amīr Kabīr 1357 A.Hsh./1978), p. 319.

[36] *Gulshan-i rāz,* ed. Javad Nurbakhsh (Tehran: Intishārāt-i Khāniqāh-i Ni'matu'llāhī 1976), p. 59; also in MAS, p. 107, vv. 966-7.

[37] *Mafātīḥ al-'ijāz,* ed. Khāliqī & Karbāsī, p. 583: 10.

[38] *Mafātīḥ al-'ijāz,* ed. Khāliqī & Karbāsī, p. 583: 3-4.

# II

# THE LITERARY MILIEU

## Theological and Philosophical Perspectives on Shabistarī's *Oeuvre*

*The folk of this age love song and verse*
*and so we scholars write poetry, of course.*

### *The Garden of Mystery (Gulshan-i rāz)*

Author of two books of mystical poetry and a single theosophical treatise, Shabistarī's fame rests mainly on the *Garden of Mystery* which he composed in December 1317 in rhyming couplets (the *mathnawī* metre of *baḥr-i hazaj)*[39] amounting to about one thousand distichs. This poem was written in response to seventeen queries concerning various intricacies of Sufi metaphysics posed to the Sufi masters of Ādharbāyjān by another great Sufi of his day: Rukn al-Dīn Amīr Ḥusaynī Harawī (d. 718/1318).[40] Composed in a highly symbolic language, and drawing upon the lexicon of several centuries of Persian symbolic poetry, the *Garden of Mystery* sets forth the *dicta* of the Sufis on a variety of themes such as 'Thought' *(fikr)*, 'the Soul' *(nafs)*, Knowledge *(ma'rifat)*, the Multiplicity and Unity of the Realms of Being, the Hierarchial Levels of Being, the Spiritual Voyage *(sayr)* and Methodical Progression on the Sufi Path *(sulūk)*, nearness *(qurb)* and distance from God *(bu'd)*, and the evolution of the soul.[41]

The *Garden of Mystery* was first brought to the attention of Western orientalists by the French travellers Chardin and Bernier who visited Persia in the early 18th century and reported the poem's reputation in learned circles as a "somme théologique."[42] Selected passages from the poem were subsequently translated into Latin in 1821 by Tholuck in his *Sufismus,* later to be followed in 1825 by his translation into German of a third of the poem in his "Blüthensammlung aus der Morgenländischen Mystik."[43] The *Gulshan-i rāz* entered into the mainstream of Western Islamic studies when the Persian text was published in 1838 with a German verse translation by J. von Hammer-Purgstall.[44] In 1880, this same Persian text was revised and collated with several manuscripts omitted by Hammer and republished in England accompanied by an English translation by E.H. Whinfield.[45]

The first critical edition of the *Gulshan-i rāz* in Persian was published in Tehran in 1976 by Dr. Javad Nurbakhsh, the text of which was based on ten different manuscripts.[46] This was followed ten years later by a critical edition of Shabistarī's entire *Collected Works* including the *Gulshan-i rāz,* prepared by Ṣamad Muwaḥḥid.[47] The present study of Shabistarī's writings is based on these two critical editions of his work.

Soon after its composition in the early fourteenth century, Shabistarī's *Garden of Mystery* soared in fame, and by the middle of the sixteenth century close to thirty commentaries had been written upon it by a number of Persian mystics, both renowned and obscure.[48] The greatest commentator on Shabistarī's *Gulshan-i rāz* was undoubtedly Muḥammad Lāhījī (d. 912/1507). Lāhījī's famous commentary, the *Mafātīḥ al-i'jāz fī sharḥ-i Gulshan-i rāz,* evoked this quatrain from his contemporary Jāmī (817/1414–898/1492) who, in the last decade of the fifteenth century, responded to an autographed copy of it sent to him by the author with the following verses:

> Lords of Prayer in their abased neediness
> your Poverty in spirit illuminates,
> Like springtime's green your thoughts
> make glad the *Garden of Mystery.*
> Anyway you may, cast a glance
> at my heart's base copper.
> So from illusion perhaps
> I'll find the road to reality.[49]

Two basic strands of theosophy wind through Lahījī's *Sharḥ-i Gulshan-i rāz:* i) the lyrical Sufism of Rūmi, and ii) the theosophy of Ibn 'Arabī and his followers such as the gnostic poets 'Irāqī and Maghribī.[50] Lāhījī is a visionary theosopher of Shabistarī's own calibre[51] and his exegesis of Shabistarī is steeped in the poetry and theosophy of mediaeval Persian Sufism, being replete with quotations from Shabistarī's other works and ample references to the *Dīwāns* of Rūmī, Maghribī and 'Irāqī, as well as interspersed with the author's personal accounts of dreams, visions and mystical experiences. It is definitely drawn from the same fount of inspiration *(mashrab)* from which Shabistarī's own verse sprung, and thus deserves the fullest attention of all students of Persian Sufism.

The unique element in Shabistarī's *Garden of Mystery* is the extent of its ecstatic, selfless—yet extremely learned—inspiration, an inspiration which derives from the poet's spiritual depths, rather than from his personal genius or muse. It is a poem which seems to be "given rather than made, the utterance rather of the race than of an individual poet,"[52] characteristic of that heaven-sent madness of love *(furor amatoris)* described by Plato in the *Phaedrus,* which alone qualifies a poet's work for immortality. At the same time, the poet makes use of a very precise theosophical terminology and demonstrates what is known in the Persian rhetorical tradition as the quality of 'miraculous uniqueness' or "inimitability *(i'jāz)*" in his choice of words and the verve of his doctrinal expression.[53] This quality of inimitability was something to which Persian critics drew attention at an early stage of the discovery of the poem. Thus, Ibn Karbalā'ī, celebrating Shabistarī's spiritual rank in the middle of the sixteenth century, reveals the close affinity between mastery in the fields of mysticism and literary achievement, an affinity often assumed but rarely acknowledged in Persian literary history and criticism, as follows:

> One may verify from the *Garden* itself the spiritual perfection *(kamāl)* of the author of this book [the *Garden of Mystery]*. No man could have been the author of such a composition had he not himself realized the summit of perfection. As a testament to the inimitability *(bībadalī)* of this book, the Shaykh composed a few verses which he placed at the conclusion, stating:

Alas, sometimes my nature casts me in a pit;
sometimes her visage lifts me up to roses, gardens
wherefrom I've brought back this bouquet,
and made the *Garden of Mystery* its sobriquet.
In it secret buds of the heart burst apart;
its petals tell you truths none else reveal.[54]

All the poetic work of Shabistarī shows a peerless flair for metaphysical penetration combined with an aphoristic skill in synthesizing intricate dilemmas of Islamic theological and theosophical thought, unrivalled by any other mediæval Persian Sufi poet in brevity of output and profundity of content. Like Ibn 'Arabī's *Tarjumān al-ashwāq* or 'Irāqī's *Lama'āt,* the *Gulshan-i rāz* was composed in a series of semi-abstract aphoristic flashes of inspiration, the harmony of which is often only intuitively apprehended. Its couplets have the rare quality of *multum in parvo,* expressing 'much in little' as the old Latin phrase has it, each of which, as Coleridge's definition of the epigram goes, makes up a "dwarfish whole: its body brevity, and wit its soul." In Sufi circles where brevity of exposition and the weighty complexity of technical terminology was often viewed as an asset, Shabistarī's success at maintaining 'conciseness' has given the *Garden of Mystery* tremendous popularity. This conciseness was probably drawn somewhat from the poet's immersion in Ibn 'Arabī's *Futūḥāt,* a work characterized by a similar style of expression.[55]

Whereas traditional commentators such as Lāhījī have normally approached the *Garden of Mystery* as exegetes of its theosophy, and modern scholars, Oriental and Occidental alike, have been usually contented to admire it from afar, daunted by its dazzling and difficult metaphysical depth, few have investigated the literary roots and scholarly sources of the *Gulshan-i rāz.* A notable exception to this rule is the indefatigable Persian scholar 'Abd al-Ḥusayn Zarrīnkūb who, from the standpoint of modern comparative literature, has successfully applied his vast knowledge of the Persian literary tradition to analyse some of the hidden literary influences upon Shabistarī, detecting the submerged voices of Rūmī, Abū Ḥāmid al-Ghazālī and 'Aṭṭār in his thought.[56]

Shabistarī was also a legatee of what Annemarie Schimmel described as the "Rose and Nightingale" tradition of Persian Sufi poetry.[57] Rūmī (d. 672/1273), whose works, especially the *Mathnawī,* were known all over the Persian-speaking world, and whose fame reached the eastern fringes of the Muslim lands shortly after his death,[58] played an important role in the literary diffusion of this tradition. Although Shabistarī never directly mentioned Rūmī by name in either his poetry or prose, nonetheless Ẓarrīnkūb is right to note:

> Although the *Garden of Mystery* outwardly demonstrates the influence of Ibn 'Arabī and certain of his followers and commentators, if one considers the author's interest in 'Aṭṭār's literary style, it is also quite close to the fountainhead of Jalāl al-Dīn Rūmī's spirituality. This truth becomes more evident when we consider the fact that a number of commentators on the work occasionally cite Rūmī's *Mathnawī* to illustrate his ideas and points, which only goes to show that correct understanding of the contents of the *Garden of Mystery* is impossible without recourse to the *Mathnawī*. This same thread of inspiration which one finds woven into the work of a number of other Sufis—such as Awḥadī, Shāh Dā'ī and Pīr Jamālī Ardistānī—also reveals the presence and continuity of Rūmī's legacy in a major part of Sufi didactic poetry.[59]

Zarrīnkūb's comments about the importance of the *Mathnawī* as an hermeneutic tool for exegesis of Shabistarī is certainly borne out by Lāhījī, who in his commentary on the *Garden of Mystery*, features Rūmī as the most frequently cited poet. However, there is no distinctly visible influence of Rūmī's *Mathnawī* or *Dīwān-i Shams* in Shabistarī's own *oeuvre*, of the type that is found in many Timurid-period Persian poets, (as, for instance, in the works of Jamāl al-Dīn Ardistānī, d. 879/1474, who had been informed by the Prophet in a dream that "after the Koran and the *ḥadīth*, there is no better book than the *Mathnawī* of the venerable Master of the Gnostics, Mawlānā Jalāl al-Dīn Rūmī"[60]). And if, indeed, there was such an influence, Shabistarī himself never mentioned, much less acknowledged his debt to Rūmī. In this respect, Shabistarī's attitude to Rūmī is similar to his contemporary 'Alā al-Dawla Simnānī, who only mentions Rūmī occasionally and indifferently.

Although he lived in the 'Age of Rūmī', the era in which Persian lyrical poetry became "the monumental art of Persia"[61] and 'Sufi gnostic poetry' reached its apex[62]—Shabistarī's attitude towards the art of poetry was particularly negative. For him, poetry was subordinate to religious practice, and aesthetics served the cause of metaphysics.

> Were not these verses for me de rigueur
> would I have set pen to them?—oh, never!
> But the folk of this age love song and verse
> and so we scholars write poetry, of course.[63]

—He wrote in the *Sa'ādat-nāma*. In ranking religious scholarship above poetry he echoed a typically Sufi—and partially Islamic—aesthetic perspective. Had not Rūmī before him declared that poetry was but "tripe" of indifferent value to himself personally although fit for the appetite of guests whose inferior taste preferred verse to prose?[64] And had not 'Aṭṭār, who was set up by Shabistarī as a kind of literary ideal, pronounced the work of the poet to be no better than idolatry, considering his own verse to be but a veil obscuring the divine visage?[65] Such denigration of poetry by Sufis and religious scholars who, as Shahrokh Meskoob has observed, "always considered the profession of poetry beneath them . . . and belittled poets and regarded versifying with suspicion,"[66] should not be taken at face-value, as many modern Iranian intellectuals (Meskoob included) in their discussions of the poetic classics of the Mongol period in Persia, tend to do. While the idea of 'Art for art's sake' never had any place in Persian Sufi aesthetics,[67] an esoteric *double entendre* is never far away in any discussion of poetry among Sufis, as J.-C. Bürgel, describing the element of 'mightiness' of Sufi poetic aesthetics, has indeed pointed out:[68] poetry being, in Niẓāmī's words, "a shadow cast down from the becurtained court of Prophecy."[69] The subordination of Poetry to Prophecy, of Art to Love, is, indeed, the central fact in Sufi aesthetics.[70] Thus, Dawlatshāh Samarqandī (writing circa 892/1487), who always pandered to the palate of the mediæval Persian poetic taste by being highly sympathetic to both poetry and Sufism, does not hesitate to downgrade the rank of poetry in favour of Sufi spirituality. Of the Sufi poet Kamāl Khujandī (d. 803/1400),[71] for instance, he comments:

> Since his noble nature embarked upon the career of becoming a poet, we have included him among the Poets' Company, despite the fact that this master had realized the degree of saintship *(wilāyat)* and spiritual mastership, and being a poet

was his lowest degree. As the great master himself has declared:

> Of my own verse and rhyme I have no shame
> There is but one 'Aṭṭār in each millenium.[72]

In fact—a very significant one for our subject—the verse cited here by Dawlatshāh is *not* from Khujandī's pen. The "great master" and author of the above couplet is none other than Shabistarī! Indeed, the verse was gleaned from the prologue to the *Garden of Mystery!* Not that the views of Shabistarī and Kamāl Khujandī in regard to the respective merits of poetry and Sufism really differed significantly; nonetheless, Dawlatshāh's slip of pen is indicative of the exalted place Shabistarī's verse and transcendental aesthetics still held in the mind of the foremost literary historian of the Timurid period. Likewise, Jāmī's conviction in the *Nafaḥāt al-uns* that Kamāl Khujandī's "engagement in writing poetry and exertions in this art were but a disguise and cover-up so that his personality would not become overwhelmed by his inner spiritual being *(bāṭin),*"[73] could, without stretching the point too far, justifiably be applied to Shabistarī.[74]

Following the verse cited above from the *Garden of Mystery*—delightfully misquoted by Dawlatshāh—Shabistarī reflects upon the inspiration underlying the composition of his poetry and stresses the divine nature of his inspiration. His poetry is at the service of the expression of the 'archetypal meanings' *(ma'ānī)* of the Sufi gnostics, he claims, and since "archetypal sense won't fit in a cup" (that is to say, metaphysical 'Truth' cannot be quantified—"prosody and rhyme" being inadequate vehicles of expression for the higher senses of poetic inspiration), he begs the reader's apology for having recourse to such inadequate methods, and for discarding the quickening Spirit for the sake of the barren Letter. He excuses himself, saying:

> 56 Of my own verse and rhyme I have no shame
> There is but one 'Aṭṭār each millenium.
> 57 Could the mysteries of a myriad universes
> by such an idiom and mode of expression
> be put to verse, it's still but scraps and detritus
> from the store of 'Aṭṭār.
> 58 My verse is made by hazard and nondesign;
> I'm not a demon who's tapped an angel's line.[75]

Ṣamad Muwaḥḥid points out that in certain places Shabistarī incorporated ʻAṭṭār's hemistiches verbatim into the *Garden of Mystery,* revealing the influence of the earlier poet upon him. He furnishes, in fact, a list of six distiches where Shabistarī seems to have imitated ʻAṭṭār's *Asrār-nāma.*[76] ʻAṭṭār's influence is also underlined by Zarrīnkūb.[77] However, comprehension of the *inspiration* of the poet transcends the analysis of such purely literary issues, at least according to his exegete Lāhījī, who, when rising to the task of explaining what superficially appears to have been a direct literary influence, to which even the poet himself had seemingly confessed, wisely argues that

> When the poet says that whatever I have said in this book *"The Garden . . ."* is but scraps and gleanings from the store of ʻAṭṭār, no one should imagine that he has versified these ideas by way of *appropriating* them from ʻAṭṭār's writings or from anybody else! Quite the contrary! His discourse is all inspired by a special visionary unveiling and ecstatic consciousness *(mukāshafāt wa wijdān).* For this reason, he has stated:
>
> My verse is made by hazard and nondesign;
> I'm not a demon who's tapped an angel's line.[78]

Although many examples of the form and style of the *Garden of Mystery* are featured in translation in the ensuing chapters of this book, it will be useful here to comment briefly on the actual *mise en scène* of the poem's composition.

As explained in the introduction,[79] sometime in late December 1317/early January 1318, Mīr Ḥusayn Harawī (d. 16 Shawwal, 718 A.H./=December 1, 1318), a renowned Sufi author of Khurāsān,[80] addressed a short versified letter containing seventeen questions about mystical theosophy, Sufism, and wayfaring the spiritual Path *(sulūk)* to, as Shabistarī alleges: "the masters of spiritual *sense (arbāb-i maʻnī),"* that is to say, to the Sufi literati of Tabriz. In accordance with a literary custom quite popular among the learned classes and Sufis of this period, the primary purpose of this epistle was to break the ice of Iranian provincialism and make the acquaintance of some of the local Sufi Shaykhs of Northwest Persia.[81]

That master of the Sufi wayfarers, Sayyid Ḥusaynī, wrote a letter on the subject of archetypal meanings *(ma'nā)* addressed to adepts in symbolic meanings, mentioning therein a few problems in the technical sense of mystical expressions, dilemmas which confront all adepts in esoteric symbolism. Each question was couched in verse, each of which was a universe of significance summarized in a few phonemes. When the courier read aloud the letter's contents, the news was spread about among the crowd. In that assembly where such dear friends had gathered, all faces turned to this wretched dervish. Among those present was one man quite adept, who had a hundred times heard me analyse these issues. He insisted:

"Make reply, he said to me:
in one moment's breath, do it,
and from this, the entire world shall benefit."[82]

So at the urging of the "one man quite adept" in the congregation (who, as noted above, p. 6, was probably his spiritual master) Shabistarī took up the challenge to answer the seventeen questions. During his composition of the first response to the Harawī's queries, the poet was to all appearances seated in a large Sufi gathering. — "Among a throng of men all free of ties *(miyān-i jam' aḥrār),"* he calls this assembly a few verses on—the term *aḥrār* referring to the "free, noble-minded men"[83] among the Sufis. The fact that everyone in this assembly turned towards him for a reply to this epistle informs us of two matters about the poet's character. First of all, the poet's considerable fame[84] as an expert in Sufi theosophy prior to the poem's composition can be gleaned from this vignette. Second, the fact that the versified reply to Harawī's letter, which later became the *Garden of Mystery,* was composed "in one moment's space *(laḥẓa)*"—that is to say, within the 'eternal now' of 'metaphysical time'[85]—points to the divine inspiration of the poem. This phenomenon of transtemporal poetic inspiration has been well described by William Blake:

Every Time Less than a pulsation of the artery
Is equal in its period & value to Six Thousand Years,
For in this Period the Poet's Work is Done, and all the
Great

Events of Time start forth & are conceiv'd in such a
Period,
Within a Moment, a Pulsation of the Artery.[86]

In the following passage the divine nature of the poem's inspiration is reaffirmed:

46 So after all their ernest pleas
that I compose a reply in verse
I started out with this response.
With words exact I knit quite terse,
concise a text. I wrote
47 these words in just a moment's space
among a throng of men all free of ties,
—I took no pause to think, without
reflection or any repetition, it all flowed out . . .[87]

In his interpretation of the phrase "without reflection or any repetition" from the above verse, Lāhījī also emphasizes the "divine inspiration" of the poem, observing that "whenever interior purity of soul, natural grace of character, and realization of the archetypal sense of ideas *(taḥqīq-i ma'ānī)* as well as self-control in these affairs, is combined with divine inspiration *(ilhām-i ilahī),* for certain then, neither 'reflection or any repetition' will be necessary."[88]

Even so, Shabistarī's succinct reply, consisting of only one or two couplets[89] composed per verse in response to each versified question, did not fully resolve all the intricacies of the issues posed by Harawī's poetic epistle. Hence, Shabistarī's perspicacious friend, the "one man quite adept" who had first encouraged him to take up the challenge, urged him to compose a more detailed reply to the questions.

65 According to the word of he
who founded the Faith,[90]
I did not rebuff the query
of one who seeks for faith.
66 The parrot of my speech, to make this mystery
more manifest, did then burst forth
in this discourse . . .[91]

"The simile of the rational soul's power of speech*(nāṭiqā)* to a parrot," explains Lāhījī of the last-cited verse by Shabistarī, "was struck by the poet with the meaning that just as the parrot in his speech only imitates the trainer who instructs him, so this perfect being [i.e. Shabistarī] only wrote in his book whatever the divine Inspirer of Justice inspired and vouchsafed to him. [As Ḥāfiẓ sung in] verse:

> Behind the mirror I have been made to be like the parrot:
> I repeat what the Lord of pre-eternity has ordered me to say.[92]

### *The Book of Felicity (Sa'adat-nāma)*

Shabistarī's *Sa'ādat-nāma* (Book of Felicity) is a poetic masterpiece, albeit not as well known as the *Gulshan-i rāz,* comprising many verses which exhibit that same penetrating aphoristic genius and stunning power of paradox, driven by the same poetic ethos (placing, in the science of Sufi aesthetics, Beauty, the Queen, side by side with the Truth, as King, on the Throne of Speech) which one encounters in nearly every verse of the *Garden of Mystery.* Written in the same *khafīf* metre as Sanā'ī's *Ḥadīqat al-ḥaqīqat,* at 1571 verses, the *Sa'ādat-nāma* is some 567 couplets longer than the *Garden of Mystery,* and although shorter than Awḥadī's 4560-verse *Jām-i jam,* which was composed in the same metre, it rivals Awḥadī's masterpiece (composed in the same quarter century) in literary importance in mediæval Persian Sufi poetry. However, since the poem was published in Tehran for the first time in a critical edition in 1986 by Ṣamad Muwaḥḥid, and only was extant in manuscript before that, modern literary historians and critics have overlooked its significance.

The date of composition of the *Sa'ādat-nāma* is unknown, but bearing in mind that in the introduction to the *Gulshan-i rāz* Shabistarī states that he had never written a *mathnawī* poem before,[93] we may be certain that the *Sa'ādat-nāma,* which also belongs to the *mathnawī* genre, was composed *after* the former poem, that is, sometime between 717/1317 and the poet's death circa 740/1340. Thus, it can be safely assumed that it was written in the last twenty-three years of Shabistarī's life and that—if temporal longevity bear any correlation to wisdom—it is his most mature poetic work.

The *Sa'adāt-nāma* is largely devoted to the deliberate poeticization of subjects which properly belong to the science of *Kalām,* scholastic theology.[94] Both the literary structure of the poem and the discussion of these theological issues is cast in the mould of the threefold division of faith common in Sufi speculative metaphysics: the Lore of Certainty *('ilmu 'l-yaqīn),* the Eye of Certainty *('aynu 'l-yaqīn)* and the Truth of Certainty *(ḥaqqu 'l-yaqīn).* The difference between these three degrees, as Martin Lings has pointed out

> is illustrated by taking the element fire to represent the Divine Truth. The lowest degree, that of the Lore of Certainty, belongs to one whose knowledge of fire comes merely from hearing it described, like those who received from Moses no more than "tidings" of the Burning Bush. The second degree, that of the Eye of Certainty, belongs to one whose knowledge of fire comes from seeing the light of its flames, like those who were shown a firebrand. The highest degree, that of the Truth of Certainty, belongs to one whose knowledge of fire comes from being burnt in it.[95]

Primarily nomocentric in intent, the poet struggles in the *Sa'ādat-nāma* to isolate the orthodox Lore of Certainty from erroneous and blasphemous beliefs. Thus, his lemmas act as rhetorical counterpoints, with rubrics such as *ḥaqq al-yaqīn* set in contrast to, and rhyming with, subtitles such as "Blatant Error" *(al-ḍalāl al-mubīn)* in the main text, and various other items—illustration *(tamthīl)* and exemplum *(ḥikāyat)* —padding out the bulk of the poem. (This theological format of the poem does not, however, completely distract from its Sufi colouring, as will be seen below in our discussion in chapter four of the various Tabrizi Sufi masters whom Shabistarī cites in the poem in support of his views).

The same deeply 'scholastic' and inherently 'non-poetic' nature of Shabistarī's personality which pervaded the *Garden of Mystery* is also evident in the *Sa'ādat-nāma.* In the prologue, the poet states that "this science [of Theology] I propose to versify for the sake of furthering the work of religion."[96] Later on, he claims that his labours in the art of poetry have only one aim: to defend the good name of the *scientia sacra* of the Muslim faith *('ilm-i dīn)*[97]—thus effectively identifying himself with the theological project of Abū Ḥāmid al-Ghazālī (d. 505/1111), who in the composition of the

*Iḥyā' 'ulūm al-dīn* presumed like motives. Disdaining to besmirch his lofty spirit with the epithet 'poet', and fearing to demean his theological rank through association with such a dubious profession, in the following verses he both vaunts and blames himself for this taste and lust for verse:

> None has ever put these three in verse together:
> Proofs of Reason, verses of the Koran, with the taste of
> Vision,[98]
> nor yet collected the three in prose. These verses here
> harbor
> no bombastic cryptic rhetoric,
> nor jargon of ecstatic mystics.
> Though none before pursued this vein of speech
> it hardly lends lustre to my state and rank.
> My academic lore and learning I know
> sunk low when I clipped close
> the necklace of this verse.
> When I can split the hairs of prose
> why should I braid the hair of verse?
> Were not these verses for me de rigueur
> would I have set pen to them?—oh, never!
> But the folk of this age love song and verse
> and so we scholars write poetry, of course.[99]

The same scornful attitude towards poetry is reiterated later on in the poem. The following verses belong to the third chapter "on the divine attributes," where Shabistarī lashes out at philosophers and poets he felt were heretically deviant. Here, one such poet: the Ismā'īlī poet-philosopher Nāṣir-i Khusraw (394/1003-4 – 462/1069-70), bears all the brunt of his ire. The "group (of followers of philosophy)" mentioned in the first line below are the Peripatetic philosophers such as the Neo-platonic Ishrāqī philosopher Suhrawardī Maqtūl (d. 587/1191), as well as Avicenna (d. 428/1037), whom the poet had also assailed in the preceding section.

> Among this group (of followers of philosophy)
> Nāṣir-i Khusraw I see –
> a man who's turned an ancient creed
> of aberrancy into modern novelty.
> Although philosopher by genesis

he was—in blood and flesh—an utter heretic;
So blind of faith he followed precedent:
what a heretic he was—in every whit—
devoid of knowledge, lore, sagesse
and every sense of Unity!
The 'wisdom of his ignorance', that's what
these academic experts learn by heart . . .
yet all the world knows too well
his faithlessness and blasphemy.
Devoid of every virtue, art or lore,
what else had he except for *poesie?*

And what is poetry, that one should vaunt
or prate of it and boast magniloquent?
All poetry, they say, is only child's play
within the realm of men, among the real champions.
For me – it's plain to see – this poetry
is just an alibi, a kind of stratagem
which made me fall and brought me down
to this base earth from my own heaven.
My birth, alas, was contretemps – or ill-omened –
look on what an evil hour I have fallen!
What could be worse, that I should work
with such pretense and care on rhyme
and verse, and all for what—? To make renown
the *scientia sacra* of the Faith.

And so, to sum it up, the wickedness
and error of Nāṣir has spread abroad
and worldwide is now notorious.
Denial and darkness, disbelief and night
he bound in one and called it a 'Book of Light'.[100]
His artifice was quite complete: the soul
itself became his counterfeit, the spirit fake;
the Magians' words pure Koranic speech.
Most all his words are just like this:
extempore and rash, "half-truths whose ornament
obscures the show of evil,"[101] which is why he took
to rhetoric and spun his speech—just so the ignorant
would take the bait. His words are all like gall
that's stained like wine: a poison pill

with sugar coating. Since the creed of right belief
he never gained, he made a faith from gibberish.

Though Avicenna be the one who speaks
there is no fallacy which thus becomes the 'truth',
nor if it's Aristotle who holds forth—
there is, again, no truth which thus is fallacy;
for truth is truth although it's Avicenna saying it,
and false is false although a holy saint be preaching it.[102]

Although his indignation is obviously genuine, Shabistarī's poor judgment of Nāṣir-i Khusraw's character and poetry conveys to us the narrow-minded and biased side of his personality, hardly in keeping with the ecumenical humanistic spirit of the author of the *Garden of Mystery*. His judgement certainly does not match the prevalent views of later literary historians about this poet who was cited with approval by Dawlatshāh as "a sage of great erudition and of ascetic disposition . . . whose *Dīwān* is a compendium of wise *dicta,* preaching, wholesome sayings and pious exhortations."[103] Furthermore, Shabistarī's view of Nāṣir-i Khusraw as a poetaster who knew nothing else besides poetry is both uninformed and unfair, insofar as Khusraw shared the same views on the low place of poetry in the spiritual life, himself criticizing professional court panegryrists in many verses,[104] being, as 'Abd al-Raḥmān Jāmī underlines, "skilled in the poetic art and perfectly accomplished in philosophical mysticism *(ḥikmat).*"[105]

Nāṣir-ir Khusraw, of course, had gained notoriety by referring to the Sunni Caliph Ma'mūn as an "accursed demon *(dīv-i la'īn),*[106] and by advocating the Mu'tazilite doctrine of 'freewill' which was opposed to the doctrine of determinism *(jabr),* an essential tenet in Shabistarī's Sunni Ash'arite *madhhab.* Aside from these obvious theological differences between Khusraw's Shi'ite Ismā'īlism and Shabistarī's Sunni Sufism, another cause of the poet's animosity towards Nāṣir-i Khusraw may have derived from the popular belief harbored by most Sunni theologians during this period that the Ismā'īlī sect were to blame for the initial incursions of the Mongols into Khurāsān, and that it was at the instigation of the Shi'ite-Ismā'īlī philosopher Naṣīr al-Dīn Ṭūsī that Hülegü had killed the last Abbasid Caliph. This claim was made, for instance, by Ibn Taymiyya (d. 728/1327) in one in his diatribes against the Nuṣayrīs and other *bāṭinī* sects.[107] The Ismā'īlīs also conducted commando raids of salaried *fidāwī* agents who were sent from Egypt by the Mamlūk Sultan al-Malik al-Nāṣir against various Mongol notables, as Ibn Baṭṭūṭā noted.[108] So it is against this background of persecution and fear, combined with prejudice and rancour against these 'enemies of Islam' under the late Mongols that Shabistarī's attack on Nāṣir-i Khusraw's 'aberrancy' should probably be seen. Rather than viewing it as a violent personal polemic of one poet against another, his words might be better compared to the attacks on Marxism and Russian Communism by American poets (E.E. Cummings, for example, in the mid-twentieth century, against Soviet totalitarianism).

Whereas in the *Garden of Mystery* Shabistarī embraces without reservation the teachings of Ibn 'Arabī,[109] in the *Sa'ādat-nāma* he is more cautious and raises certain objections to him, relying mainly on the 'politically correct' Ghazālī. Thus, the latter poem exhibits a far greater interest in the theological framework of Sufism, a tendency which reflects the epoch in which it was composed: the reign of Sultan Abū Sa'īd (1317-1335). We know that at the instigation of the *fuqahā*, who were supported by the all-powerful Amīr Chūpān, all the wine and wine-jugs in Tabriz, Sulṭāniyya and Mosul were deliberately destroyed in Sha'bān 720/September 1320. Abū Sa'īd also commanded that all brothels and taverns be destroyed and that the churches in and around Tabrīz be demolished and mosques constructed in their place.[110] Shabistarī's emphasis on the exoteric *(ẓāhīr)* aspects of Islam in this work, in contrast to the overwhelming esotericism of the *Garden of Mystery*, goes hand in hand with Amīr Chūpān's (whose role under Abū Sa'īd can be compared to that of Nawrūz under Ghāzān[111]) ostentatious display of "piety and good works" which "may have been largely for foreign consumption," as Charles Melville comments.[112] The personal ideology of Chūpān, "the real master of the Mongol empire," as Claude Cahen called him[113] was rigidly attentive to the formalities of legalistic Islam and dominated Mongol Persia from 1317 (the year of the composition of the *Garden of Mystery)* until Shabistarī's death (circa 1339). Chūpān's rivalry with the Mamlūk Sultan al-Nāṣir Muḥammad, with whom he vied during the 1320's in sending richly laden pilgrimage caravans to the Hejaz, as well as his refurbishing of wells in Mecca[114] and conspicuously purchasing dead lands in Egypt in order to bring them back into cultivation and donate their proceedings as a charitable endowment to the haram in Mecca, are all aspects of the new revival of orthodox Islam under

Abū Sa'īd's reign – the same phenomenon of Islamic revival which is also visible in the *Sa'ādat-nāma*. The ground lost under the earlier tolerant 'infidel' Īl-Khāns was to be regained with an intolerant vengeance.

Even Shabistarī's change in attitude and opinion about the importance of Ibn 'Arabī—from one of admiration and acceptance of his teachings in the *Garden of Mystery,* composed during the reign of Ghāzān, to a critical stance and almost unfriendly attitude in the *Sa'ādat-nāma* towards the excessive interest in the Shaykh's writings among his contemporaries—was probably instilled by the criticism of Ibn 'Arabī's writings advanced by many of the legal authorities during the reign of Abū Sa'īd. Violent debates had been taking place for nearly a decade concerning the orthodoxy of Ibn 'Arabī's writings in Anatolia and Greater Persia during the same decade as the *Sa'ādat-nāma* was probably composed (that is, during the 1330's),[115] and this controversy inevitably led to mass book-burnings of the *Fuṣūṣ* and the *Futūḥāt al-Makkiyya.*[116]

In one place in the *Sa'ādat-nāma* we find the poet particularly piqued by the fact that certain charlatan mystics have taken to (mis)interpreting Ibn 'Arabī, which seems to be a direct echo, or, at the very least, a reflection of the same sense of juridical wariness and caution about the influence of the Shaykh al-Akbar's teachings upon the common folk. This passage is preceded by a barrage of quotations from Ghazālī, known by his traditional title, the 'Proof of Islam' *(Ḥujjat al-Islām),* concerning the evils of these pseudo-savants who avail themselves of the *dicta* of Bāyazīd and Ḥallāj to construct philosophical views based on heretical tenets—"killing one of these [heretical] people," he quotes Ghazālī approvingly, "is better than bringing back to life ten people."[117] For they "do not content themselves with learning 'philosophical mysticism'," Shabistarī moralizes, "but also latch on to 'Divine Unity' *(tawḥīd)* out of bewilderment and contentiousness, abandoning both the scriptural word *(kalām)* and divine texts *(nuṣūṣ)* so that they may understand the *Fuṣūṣ* at least once in their lives."[118] Although the last statement is an obvious jab at the fadish, but ignorant, popularity enjoyed by Ibn 'Arabī's *Fuṣūṣ al-ḥikam* during this period, at the same time the poet is engaged in a struggle against the so-called 'innovations' *(bidā',* sing. *bid'a)* in religious doctrine and practice which was waged by many Muslim theologians who wished to 'protect' the outer dimension of Islam from the encroachment of antinominianism under the cloak of Sufism. Such charlatan mystics "flee from the folk of the Sunna like demons, and mix with the demons of common people," he concludes – almost overlooking the fact that Ibn 'Arabī himself is said to have prohibited the study of his writings by 'commoners' who may be 'poisoned' by their raving insights.[119]

Yet his 'demonizing' of Ibn 'Arabī's *Fusūs al-ḥikam* in this passage—or the popular conception/reception of this work—also indicates that Shabistarī, in his later life, had considerably distanced himself from his earlier enthusiastic adoption of Akbarian terminology and theosophy in the *Garden of Mystery.* I believe that the motive for this radical change in spiritual direction, from esoteric theosophy to exoteric dogmatic theology, which can be found abundantly in the contents of Shabistarī's most mature composition, can perhaps be partially explained by the fact that, as the purported *ḥadīth* puts it: "People follow the religion of their rulers."[120] This is not to say that his poems are to be viewed as merely occasional compositions, but only that they did not remain aloof from the political atmosphere and theological spirit of his times. Whereas the *Garden of Mystery* can be seen to mirror the Sufi tolerance of Rashīd al-Dīn and Ghāzān Khān, the *Book of Felicity* should be recognized as a product of the theological intractability of Amīr Chūbān and Abū Sa'īd. Just as Abū Sa'īd had ordered the destruction of all the churches in Tabriz in 1320, so our poet seemingly followed this socio-political course, attacking the worship of idols *(but parastī)* with particular vehemence, if not intolerance, in the *Sa'ādatnāma,*[121] in a way quite contrary to that of the *Garden of Mystery.* (In fact the entire first half of the *Sa'ādatnāma* is devoted to the refutation of various so-called "heretical" sects, religions, and deviant philosophers, reviled by Shabistarī in very strong language).[122]

However, such intolerance is relative and certainly should *not* be mistaken for bigotry or fanaticism in the vein of a modern-day Wahhabist *faqīh* or a Hezbollah ayatollah.[123] In fact, just the opposite is true: his Sufi 'message' is presented in order to liberate men from the delimiting imagination of the dogmatic faith professed by the exoteric clergy.

Following Ibn 'Arabī's lead, Shabistarī exhibits extreme disdain for the exoteric clergy; and just as the Greatest Master remarked that "the exoteric scholars *('ulamā' al-rasūm)* in relation to the Folk of Allah [the Sufis] are like the pharoahs in relation to God's messengers. God created no one more onerous and troublesome for the Folk of Allah than these exoteric scholars" —so Shabistarī in the *Sa'ādat-nāma* virulently derides the Iranian mullahs:

> Although the mullah takes sixty kilograms of water to make his ablutions to pray, his head seems hollower than a calabash during Koranic recitation. Like the Devil performing the act of ritual prayer, he reveals to you worlds of scruples and irresolution. The mullah's flesh and bones is nourished off morsels gleaned from the kitchen of the local *amīr:* Look, he wipes his arse with his own sweat. They are all enslaved by property and possessions—don't call them 'jurisprudents' because they are lords . . . Through them the world has become an idiot's kingdom, through them [the mullahs] 'ass-head' has become a proper epithet for the jurisprudent. By them all artists are discomposed, for they all wears scowls on their faces."[124]

It is important to remember that long passages of similar criticism of the *'ulamā'* establishment forms the dénouement of both of Shabistarī's major poems, thus underlining the essentially anticlerical nature of Shabistarī's spiritual outlook. The *Sa'ādat-nāma* concludes, in fact, with an *envoi* on the evils of the mediæval mullahs,[125] (only the milder comments were translated in the above passage). Behind Shabistarī's animosity towards the Iranian mullahs lay the gloomy political reality of the decline and corruption of the Islamic judiciary system in Īl-Khānid Persia. Neither Ghāzān Khān nor his successors had been successful in changing, despite numerous edicts and ordinances, this unfortunate situation. One need only peruse the following comments by Howorth in his *History of the Mongols*—summarizing Rashīd al-Dīn's opinions—to sense the full extent of the decline in the judicial class and *shar'ī* jurisdiction in Iran:

> In Persia the Mongols only recognised those who followed the profession of the law by their turbans and costume, and they had no knowledge of jurisprudence or equity. It was natural, therefore, that ignorant men should usurp the distinctive insignia of the magistrature, and by presents, & c., secure the patronage of some Mongol grandee, and thus obtain juridical office, which led to the greater part of the more worthy magistrates resigning their posts, as they could not bear to have these men their equals. Presently, the evil deeds and injustices of these parvenus brought the whole profession of the law into contempt, and with it the Muhammedan faith

> also suffered. The Mongol commanders became the patrons of these judges, and in some cases received money from them.[126]

Like Ibn'Arabī,[127] Shabistarī was also highly skilled in the science of jurisprudence and his critique of the legal system reflects an educated experience. Thus, expressing his erudition in the science of *fiqh,* he states: "I am well-versed in jurisprudence, having read and composed many books on this science which are acclaimed far and wide, and require no commendation, so I do not say these negative things about the jurisprudents out of ignorance."[128] His vision is thus the very opposite of dogmatism—rather it is drawn from the very tradition of the exoteric sciences he later transcended and disdained. Such an aversion to the dogmatism of the Muslim clergy was not exclusive to Shabistarī, but characteristic of all the Sufi poets of this period, particularly all those who composed ghazals in the *qalandariyyāt* genre.[129]

Another important aspect of the *Sa'ādat-nāma*'s overall significance in Persian literature is the insight it provides into Shabistarī's own theological orientation and mystical persuasion. In one place in the poem, we find a direct declaration of his support for the pure Sufi doctrine of Habīb 'Ajamī (d. 119/737),[130] invoking God's blessings upon the wayfarers on the Sufi Path,[131] and demonstrating his orthodox Sunnism by singling out Abu'l-Ḥasan al-Ash'arī (873-935) for special mention as the thinker "who laid firm the foundation of devotion to God, establishing the Sunni faith and supporting the catholic community of Islam *(jamā'at).*"[132] Of course, Sunnism was also typical of the townsfolk of Tabriz during Shabistarī's lifetime as noted by Mustawfī in the *Nuzhat al-qulūb,*[133] as well as of the Shaykhs of the Kubrawī *silsila* in general,[134] among whom Shabistarī himself should probably be counted.

Shabistarī's admiration and citation of Abū Ḥāmid al-Ghazālī as a defendant of the orthodox Sunni cause has been noted above. Ghazālī, who has been described as "certainly the most important known 'precursor' of the explicitly metaphysical aspect of Ibn 'Arabī's writings,"[135] had a major influence upon the development of Shabistarī's theological views. From its inception, interpretation, study of, and commentary on Shabistarī's thought has been associated with the works of Ghazālī.[136] The attribution of a Persian translation of Ghazālī's *Minhāj al-'ābidīn*[137] to Shabistarī also underlines the theological importance of this influence, an influence which is most apparent in the *Sa'ādat-nāma* where the poet mentions him with deep veneration several times. In fact, a 'Ghazālī presence' seems to permeate the entire poem.

In the opening section of the poem, devoted to the Sufi theme of the "Gnosis of the Transcendent Being," following his prologue on "the cause for composition of this poem," Shabistarī employs Ghazālī's name as a kind of theological buttress for his own scholastic reasoning, and again introduces him by his celebrated sobriquet *Ḥujjat al-Islām* (the Proof of Islam):

> O God, each atom in truth attests
> to your Existence, gives proof in fact:
> For all which comes from the Non-apparent
> into Present Appearance
> flows through your grace into Existence.
> All things, vocal in their eloquence,
> hymn the praise of you, their Architect.
> What else is this but proof without stint
> made to the Maker by the artifact?
>
> What has more compulsion for Reason than Prophetic
> tradition
> and yet, read it again from the Koran:
> "Verily, all which is, does hymn his praise."[138]
> This praise makes of no atom an exception:
> whether they're free of blemish in sheer perfection,
> or weak and not quite right:
> before him it's all one and the same—
> whether the faith of the men of piety,
> or heretics in their heresy.
>
> From God's own word was not that verse
> enough to give you proof and lead to this?
> What host of proofs, a thousandfold or more,
> which in his works the 'Proof of Islam'
> amassed from the Scripture. So gaze within
> the arcanum of the Koran:
> you'll find the gist of my speech.[139]

As Zarrīnkūb points out, such verses recall Ghazālī's doctrine enunciated in his *Risāla al-amlā' fī ishkālāt al-Iḥyā'* (many centuries before Liebnitz) that this is the 'best of all possible worlds'.[140] Of course, these lines also constitute a rephrasing of the idea of the 'unity of devotional intention'—part of the poet's doctrine of the 'trancendental Unity of Religions' enunciated earlier in the *Garden of Mystery*—where the same verse from the Koran was cited (without reference to Ghazālī, however).[141]

Shabistarī also follows Ghazālī's ill-opinion of most Peripatetic philosophy almost word for word in the *Sa'ādat-nāma*. Ghazālī's views on the science of Logic expressed in the *Deliverance from Error (al-Munqidh min al-ḍalāl),* where the great theologian had pronounced that "nothing in logic is relevant to religion by way of denial or affirmation,"[142] and where he had asserted that in the sciences of Theology or Metaphysics "here occur most of the errors of the philosophers,"[143] is, as Zarrīnkūb notes, paraphrased in verse by Shabistarī. In the following passage, Shabistarī criticizes the entire Peripatetic school *(mashā'iyān)* from Aristotle to Avicenna.

> Rasṭālīs (=Aristotle) wrote, indeed, a good treatise on Logic, but it was in Theology where he went awry. He invented a tool but when it came to using it, through his fallacious imagination he fell into error. He thought up the equations of Logic in order to become a knower of God—alas, what a delusion! Because he was entrusted with his [purely human] implement, it became a cause of his error. Since by paralogic conjecture he went astray, according to the Sunnis he is to be considered excommunicated from the faith. No one can savour the taste of faith *(dhawq-i īmānī)* by speculation based on Grecian reason *('aql-i yūnānī)*. What was *his* reason, that it could realize divine Purity through use of logic and supposition?
>
> If someone could become a saint by use of logic, then Avicenna would surely be the Pontiff of the Sunni faith."[144]

This statement was probably inspired by Ghazālī's pronouncement in *Al-Munqidh* that students of logic "draw up a list of conditions to be fufilled by demonstration, which are known without fail to produce certainty. When, however, they come at length to treat of religious questions, not only are they unable to satisfy these conditions, but they admit an extreme degree of relaxation (of their standards of proof)." Thus, "the student who admires logic and sees its clarity, imagines that the infidel doctrines attributed to the philosophers are supported by similar demonstrations, and hastens into unbelief before reaching the theological (or metaphysical) sciences."[145]

Perhaps the most interesting example of Shabistarī's endorsement of Ghazālī's views on religious orthodoxy occurs in that scathing passage of the *Sa'ādat-nāma* referred to briefly above, but which I cite here in full:

> I have it heard it related from the 'Proof of Islam' *(Ḥujjat al-islām)* that he said: "There has appeared in this period an evil group of presumptuous folk who know neither the science of the principles nor the derivatives of faith. They hold discussions in every place concerning the awesome Qualities of the divine Essence, and then introduce the words of Ḥallāj and Bāyazīd without any conclusion or preface, tail or face. They cling to these sayings, yet like demons flee from honest farming. Killing one of these people is better, according to my religion, than bringing ten [dead] people back to life."
>
> After this, Imām Ghazālī cried out, in grief over the weakness in the religious life and the evil condition [of men in his time], saying: "Beware, look after your religion! Hasten to preserve it before such sayings become widespread and nothing be left of Islam! Root out this useless group or else your cherished religion will fall into disrepute."
>
> That which has come down to us from that eminent scholar [Ghazālī] has come to pass in this day and age. One sees how a foolish ignoramus has memorized two sections of some text in order to ensnare and deceive others. Studying treatises on philosophical mysticism *(ḥikmat)* he has learned a few of the incidental secondary topics of discussion in this science, and making a great show of exertion, has transformed himself into a 'sage' *(ḥakīm),* bending over backwards in the path of blasphemy and belief. His place belongs among the "hypocrites who waver;" the verse "they belong neither to these nor to those" [Koran IV: 143] was occasioned by the likes of him.[146]

In this passage, Shabistarī rails at the pseudo-mystics and false claimants to Sufism which had appeared in Persia during this period (see chapter IV below). His distress echoes the lament of that other great systematizer of Kubrawī Sufism, Najm al-Dīn Rāzī (d. 654/1256), who, a generation earlier in his *Mirṣād al-'ibād,* had complained how "many foolish claimants have now appeared among the people of the Path . . . [who] imagine, on the strength of a few rotten words snatched from someone's mouth, that they have attained the goal and purpose of this path in its perfection."[147]

The theological background of the poet's views also derives from his discerning awareness of the central role played by the true Sufis in the hierarchical social structure of mediæval Persian society. Shabistarī's social orientation draws upon Ghazālī's religious "hierarchism"—as Marshall Hodgson put it—according to which men are to be graded into three classes: blind believers, rationalist theologians and visionaries (i.e. Sufis): a distinction "not merely of knowledge but implicitly of moral function. For each class could teach those below it and might serve as an example to them."[148] From this hierarchical point of view, it necessarily follows that the worst of these three orthodox groups are those Sufis who are unfaithful to, or inadequate in fufilling, their teaching mission. In these lines, Shabistarī discharges his function as spiritual leader of the 'ignorant commonality' *('awwām)* in early fourteenth-century Tabriz by furnishing fresh support for Ghazālī's project of revivifing—through the principles of Sufi piety—Islamic culture.

As can be seen from the foregoing, Shabistarī's outlook on Peripatetic philosophy was hardly less negative than his attitude towards poetry. As a major systematizer of mediæval Persian Sufi thought of the Akbarian school, in his three major works (the *Garden of Mystery*, *Book of Felicity*, and the *Truth of Certainty*) Shabistarī consistently appeals to the certitude of mystical illumination *(kashf)* as the essential source of knowledge. The doctrine of *kashf* constituted the fulcrum of Shabistarian epistemology, and, as will be shown in chapter seven, logic played a very minor role in his thought. With this kept in mind, contrary to what some scholars have asserted, disregarding the unity of Shabistarī's total *oeuvre* and basing themselves solely on a study of his *Garden of Mystery*,[149] it is evident that there was not—in fact, that there could not have been—any Ishrāqī influence on his thought. He was vehemently opposed to all shades and hues of Neoplatonic Ishrāqī philosophy. This is stated unmistakably in the *Sa'ādat-nāma:*

> The science of 'philosophical mysticism' or 'wisdom' *(ḥikmat)* has arisen from the Prophets *(anbiyā);* not the wisdom which is crooked but that which is straight and true. God inspired Seth, and made all his words inspired prophetic utterances

> *(ḥadīth)*. After him, to Idris inspiration was sent, so that he might be seated in the chair of professor. From him all people received edification in the lore of religion and the planetary constellations. By oral transmission this wisdom went to Greece where it was passed to the base and vulgar crowd from its founding fathers. The Idrisian wisdom, which was like limpid water, became polluted by ignorance, heresy and error; his words were altered, transposed out of context so that the store and worth of his teachings turned to loss. The Ishrāqī Platonists compounded their opinions from diverse types of blasphemous notions, until at last the author of "Ishrāq"[150] put a silver coating *(talwīḥ)*[151] on the counterfeit coin of Stoic philosophy.[152]

It would seem then that "Ishrāqī tendencies" are non-existent in Shabistarī's thought. His disapproval of Avicenna immediately follows this passage (translated above, p. 35) in the *Sa'ādat-nāma* and although somewhat more politely expressed, and, as we have shown above, in line with Ghazālī's views, it is hardly less strident in its condemnation of the entire enterprise of Peripatetic philosophy.

In essence, Shabistarī's opposition to philosophy is more akin to that of Khāqānī,[153] than Ghazālī (who, after all, had appropriated much of Avicenna's thought for his own theology[154]). Shabistarī's outlook and position with regard to philosophy in many ways also dogs the steps of his intellectual mentor, Ibn 'Arabī, to whom "the only true philosopher who deserves the name of 'sage' *(ḥakīm* here becomes synonym for *'ārif,* gnostic), is he who endeavours to perfect his knowledge by means of contemplation and spiritual experience."[155]

However, since dogmatism, in whatever form, and Sufism are incompatible, although the Peripatetic project may be fundamentally mistaken, it is not entirely in vain, insofar as truth is not the exclusive property of any one sect or faith—

> For truth is truth although it's Avicenna saying it,
> and false is false although a holy saint be preaching it.[156]

### *The Truth of Certainty about the Knowledge of the Lord of the Worlds (Ḥaqq al-yaqīn fī ma'rifat rabb al-'ālamīn)*

After the two works discussed above, this small treatise, the *Ḥaqq al-yaqīn,* his only extant prose work, ranks third in importance in Shabistarī's *oeuvre.* It is divided into eight chapters *(abwāb:* 'Gates', corresponding to the eight Gates of Paradise), each of which is between two to five pages in length. These "Gates," in turn, are subdivided into discrete paragraphs with a separate lemma heading the text. Some of the lemmata typically featured include: A Reality *(ḥaqīqat)* – An Illustration *(tamthīl)* – *Nota Bene (tabṣira)* – Corollary *(far')* – Inference *(natīja)* – A Subtle Mystery *(sirr-i nāzurk)* – Natural Consequence *(lāzima)* – Beneficial Proposition *(fāyida)* – Subtlety *(daqīqa).* The book is thus subdivided into small passages, some of which are only a short paragraph in size, expounding a philosophical point or metaphysical truth, followed by a citation from the Koran. Sometimes such scriptural references are adduced as logical proofs to cinch the poet's argument; alternatively, these 'truths' serve to illustrate or elaborate Koranic *dicta.* Many selections from this treatise are translated in chapter seven.

The *Ḥaqq al-yaqīn* probably precedes in composition the *Garden of Mystery.* In the latter poem, when his interlocutor addresses Shabistarī and requests a versified response to his queries, the poet initially objects, "To what purpose? I have already presented these issues time and time again in treatises *(rasā'il).*"[157] Although, of course, Shabistarī later gives in and decides to versify his answers to Mīr Harawī's questions, this initial avowal does establish the priority in the poet's career of his prose over his poetic compositions. Furthermore, as is shown below (VII), the subject-matter of the *Ḥaqq al-yaqīn* is often identical, both in content, vocabulary and expression, to that of the *Garden of Mystery,* a fact to which Lāhījī, through frequent references to this treatise throughout his commentary, often draws our attention. From this fact, it is evident that the Shabistarian 'system' of Sufi philosophy was already quite developed, if not completely crystallized, before the composition of the *Gulshan-i rāz.*

A.J. Arberry's comparison of this treatise with the *Lamā'at* of 'Irāqī, which he claims it resembles somewhat, "in its style and contents . . . though at a lower poetical level,"[158] is not quite accurate. The *Ḥaqq al-yaqīn* is, in fact, composed completely in prose;

there is not one single verse in its entire text, so its "poetical level" cannot be comparable with 'Irāqī's masterpiece, which has been well described by S.H. Nasr as being "at once a metaphysical treatise and a work of art."[159] Nevertheless, Prof. Arberry's comparison is valid insofar as Shabistarī's treatise belongs to the same literary genre as 'Irāqī's work, and the two tracts discuss the principles of Ibn 'Arabī's theosophy in similarly highly stylized, erudite, often arcane language, whose beauty derives from sudden flashes of insight and bursts of paradox.

Like the *Lamā'at,* the treatise is also very much under the spell of Ibn 'Arabī's lexicon, expression and personality. Just as Ibn 'Arabī claimed that the literary expression of his doctrine was the result of visionary knowledge and grace inaccessible to scholarship—"I have not written one single letter of this book," he says of the *Futūḥāt,* "save by divine dictation *(imlā' īlāhī)* and dominical vouchsafing *(ilqā' rabbānī).*"[160]—so Shabistarī alleges that "this book *(Ḥaqq al-yaqīn)* was miraculously given by the Almighty to this helpless wretch from the bursary of the Supersensory Realm."[161]

Shabistarī's *Ḥaqq al-yaqīn* might be compared with greater fruitfulness to the *Sawānih* of Aḥmad al-Ghazālī. Javad Nurbakhsh, who has published critical editions in Persian of all three treatises mentioned above ('Irāqī's *Lamā'at,* Ghazālī's *Sawāniḥ* and Shabistarī's *Ḥaqq al-yaqīn,* and is therefore in a far better position than A.J. Arberry to adjudicate on the issue) points out in his introduction to the *Ḥaqq al-yaqīn:*

> At least in the Persian language, the *Ḥaqq al-yaqīn* is without a rival in its own genre. If we can consider Aḥmad al-Ghazālī's *Sawāniḥ* as one of the masterpieces of philosophical love-mysticism *('irfān-i 'ashiqāna)* in Persian, we should also count, in this respect, the *Ḥaqq al-yaqīn* to be one of the most important and principal texts in the field of speculative mysticism *('irfān-i naẓarī).*[162]

In this treatise Shabistarī undoubtedly follows the general tendency of the Kubrawī Shaykhs to interpret religion *(madhhab)* as being composed of various inner 'levels' of belief, as, for instance, espoused by Nasafī in the introduction to the *Kashf al-ḥaqā'iq.*[163] The intellectual context of Shabistarī's religious orientation (as well as the outlook of some of his contemporary Kubrawī masters—Nūr al-Dīn Isfarāyinī, Simnānī, and Maghribī,

d. 810/1408, in particular)—can be found in a philosophical tradition followed by Sufis, theologians and philosophers alike. This tradition emphasizes that knowledge can be attained by one or a combination of three means: (1) revelation *(waḥy)*, (2) reason *('aql)*, and (3) *kashf* (unveiling)—corresponding to the methods pursued respectively by the theologians, philosophers and Sufis. These apparently divergent perspectives held by members of the three schools, were, as W.C. Chittick has revealed, "much more complementary than exclusive."[164] Even if Shabistarī's own approach (as explained above, and later, below, VI), is entirely visionary, utilizing the Sufis' *kashf* and *dhawq* (heart-savour/creative intuition and sapiential 'taste'), and *taḥqīq* (direct experiental verification and realization), the theological background of his method, as it appears in the context of previous Islamic philosophy, is based on this unique tripartite structure.

Shabistarī illustrates the *scientia sacra* underlying his inspiration in the introduction to the *Ḥaqq al-yaqīn*, explaining the triadic structure of his theosophical doctrine with particular lucidity:

> To masters of the spiritual heart who are adept in interior vision, it is hardly concealed that the source of all the difficulty and error in matters of speculative thought and the ground of the differences which exist between **unitarians** *(muwaḥḥid)*, **scholastic theologians** *(mutakallim)* and **philosophers** *(ḥakīm)* have been summarized in this study, which, by the grace of God, has attained to the farthest reaches of certitude, being based on the Triology of: **Transmitted Science** *(naql)*, **Reason** or intellectual discussion *('aql)*, and **Heart-savour** *(dhawq)*. In order to verify any spiritual truth *(ḥaqīqatī)* or prove any argument in this composition, two just proofs based on Transmitted Science and Reason are adduced: that is, a clearly convincing proof and a citation from the Koran are submitted to the reader's consideration. After completion of the study of the rational and the transmitted sciences *('ulūm-i 'aqlī wa naqlī)*, the method to be followed by the reader is to seek the spiritual capacity *(isti'dād)* to understand this science through ecstatic consciousness borne of heart-savour *(dhawqiyyāt)*.[165]

From this statement it follows that Shabistarī conceived his writings as an elaboration and synthesis of the three main intellectual traditions in the Islamic world: that of, respectively, the scholastic theologians, the theomonist Sufis (= "unitaritians") and the philosophers. Although his message is addressed to all three groups and combines methodologies and terminology from them all—even preserving the study of the rational sciences[166] as an integral element of doctrinal knowledge—the actual realization of "this science," according to Shabistarī's system of thought, depends ultimately and uniquely on the spiritual capacity and the 'heart-savour' *(dhawq)* of the reader. This higher level of perception and consciousness is discussed in detail in the last three chapters of this book.

The *Garden of Mystery* was also based on a similar threefold structure of knowledge. Underlining his tripartite vision and integrating them into a fourth and supreme degree, Shabistarī concludes the *Garden of Mystery* with this *envoi* to the reader:

998 Its lily tongue is eloquent in recitation;[167]
its eyes are all narcissus-like in vision.
999 Consider every petal well with heartseen
contemplation,
till all this caviling doubt depart your vision.
1000 Perceive the whole—from truths revealed by
intuition,
to what's conceived by reason, to lore of tradition
all clarified within the Science of Minute
Particulars.[168]

The degrees of theosophy contained in these verses may be summarized as follows:

1. **revelation** as passed down in Scripture and Prophetic tradition *(manqūl)*.
2. **reason, intelligence** *(ma'qūl)*.
3. (the visionary disclosure of) **spiritual realities** *(ḥaqā'iq)*.

These three elements of knowledge are in turn subsumed within a higher, fourth degree, which Shabistarī in couplet 1000 terms as

4. **the science of spiritual subtleties or Minute Particulars** *('ilm-i daqā'iq),* which is perhaps verbosely, though more exactly, translated as "the science of the exact observation of the minute particulars of existence along with all their secret implications."

In this regard, I cannot help noting the extraordinary intellectual fraternity which exists between Shabistarī's conception of *'ilm-i daqā'iq* and the English visionary poet William Blake's view of the 'Minute Particulars' of phenomena. According to Blake's aesthetic theory and mystical theology, "All Sublimity is founded on Minute Discrimination,"[169] for

> he who wishes to see a Vision, a perfect Whole,
> Must see it in its Minute Particulars, Organized."[170]
> Labour well the Minute Particulars, attend to the Little-ones
> . . .
> For Art & Science cannot exist but in minutely organized Particulars
> And not in generalizing Demonstrations of the Rational Power.
> The Infinite alone resides in Definite & Determinate Identity.[171]

Commenting on the term *'ilm-i daqā'iq* in Sufism, the eighteenth-century Sufi encyclopædist Al-Tahānawī explains that the understanding of the science of Minute Particulars "is reserved for those who have transcended rational proofs and demonstrations, and having attained to the degree of divine 'unveiling' *(kashf),* witness directly that the reality of every thing is the Absolute Truth and that no other being beside the One Absolute Being exists."[172] Although Lāhījī does not offer his own interpretation of *'ilm-i daqā'iq,* in his commentary on line 1000 above, he informs us that:

> The term "transmitted science" *(manqūl)* refers to the study of the principles of belief according to Islamic law; the "intelligible sciences" *(ma'qūl)* relate to philosophical problems *(masā'il-i ḥakīmiyya).* "Spiritual realities" *(ḥaqā'iq),* on the other hand, is a technical term belonging to the lexicon of the unitarian Sufis. So the poet intends to say that: "I have strained off the excess superfluity, bombastic rhetoric and sophistry from all of the above [types of knowledge] through the science of spiritual subtleties and by careful scrutiny of delicate points, thereby, through this refining process, bringing it all to a point of perfection."[173]

On the basis of Al-Tahānawī's explanation and Lāhījī's interpretation of the science of Minute Particulars, it is evident that *visionary* knowledge forms the basis of Shabistarī epistemology. This point is discussed in more detail in chapter six.

Also significant for our understanding of the mystical theology of the *Ḥaqq al-yaqīn* is the following demand made on the reader of this treatise:

> . . . Another condition incumbent upon [any reader of this treatise] is that he or she should seek inner freedom from matters of pretension, liberation from the bonds of blind imitation *(taqlīd),* to refrain from doubts "as those who dispute concerning God without knowledge," [Koran XXII: 3] and relinquish the fanaticism *(ta'aṣṣub)* [of those whom] "God has led astray on purpose [knowing that his mind is closed to all guidance]"[174] [Koran XLV: 23][175]

This last "condition" reveals the liberal dimension of Shabistarī's religious thought, providing us with a welcome antidote to the superficial dogmatism which characterizes both mediaeval and modern Muslim fundamentalism. The reader of the *Ḥaqq al-yaqīn* is also enjoined in this same passage to "carefully deliberate and ponder upon each subject of discussion," the author recognizing that he has "chosen to adopt a very condensed style, using extreme brevity in my choice of expressions. In some cases, the veiling and hiding of certain ideas in this book is even intentional." The warning issued in this statement applies to all the readers and students of Shabistarī's other works, such as the *Garden of Mystery* (in fact, 'concise complexity' may be said to be the fundamental characteristic of Shabistarī's literary style).

### *The Treasure-Trove of Spiritual Realities (Kanz al-ḥaqā'iq)*

The Persian text of this poem was published some time ago in Tehran and attributed to Shabistarī[176] but as various literary historians have pointed out recently,[177] it is probably in fact the work of his contemporary, Pahlawān Maḥmūd Khwārazmī (d. 722/1322).

### *Stages of the Gnostics (Marātib al-'ārifīn)*

This treatise ascribed to Shabistarī has been published as part of his *Collected Works.*[178] But, as Ṣamad Muwaḥḥid pointed out, Shabistarī's authorship of this work is put into doubt by the Shi'ite terminology employed therein.[179]

### *The Mirror of Adepts (Mirāt al-muḥaqiqqīn)*

This short prose treatise[180] is divided into seven chapters: i. An exposition of the faculties of the natural soul, vegetative soul, animal soul, human soul and their functions. ii. On the emanation of living beings. iii. An exposition of the Necessary Being, possible being and impossible being. iv. An exposition of the wisdom of creation. v. On the origin and entelechy of existence. vi. On the correspondence between the outer world and the world of the soul, that is, between the human body and the world. vii. On the comparative relation between the world and the soul.

Although the treatise has been published among Shabistarī's *Collected Works,* attributed to him on the basis of several MSS. considered authentic by their editor Ṣamad Muwaḥḥid,[181] it does not bear the imprint of his 'concisely complex' literary style or show any trace of his genius for aphoristic paradox. Nor does it resemble in literary style, lexical expression or theosophical doctrine any of Shabistarī's other major works (i.e. the *Gulshan-i rāz, Sa'ādat-nāma* or *Ḥaqq al-yaqīn,* discussed above). The ontology and psychology of the work expouses doctrines of the Peripatetic school,[182] as well as those of its Ishrāqī sister-school; perhaps for this reason in some manuscripts *The Mirror of Adepts* has been attributed variously to Avicenna, Nāṣir-i Khusraw and Naṣīr al-Dīn Ṭūsī (d. 672/1274).[183] The author's citation of verses by Sanā'ī and 'Aṭṭār in the treatise precludes its attribution to either Ibn Sīnā or Nāṣir-i Khusraw.[184] It could very well be the work of a thirteenth century *Ḥakīm.* I have disregarded its attribution to Shabistarī by Muwaḥḥid and certain scholars[185] simply because, as shown above, Shabistarī is highly critical of the philosophies of both Ibn Sīnā and Suhrawardī Maqtūl in those key works which expound his true doctrine, namely, the *Gulshan-i rāz* and the *Sa'ādat-nāma.*

Furthermore, not only would it have been out of character for him to have composed such a work, but the very singularity of Shabistarī's literary style precludes the possibility of such attribution. Unlike his contemporary, Quṭb al-Dīn Shīrāzī (d. 710/1311), who was content to adapt certain aspects of the Peripatetic system of thought into his own work as independent units devoid of any overall unity,[186] Shabistarī's work exhibits remarkable intellectual integrity. His literary 'signature' is as distinct as Rūmī's or Ibn 'Arabī's. This makes it possible to judge the authenticity of the works ascribed to him on the basis of style alone.

## Notes

39 A metre popular among the Sufi poets. See Finn Theisen's *A Manual of Classical Persian Prosody* (Wiesbaden: Otto Harrassowitz 1982), p. 125.

40 Concerning Harawī's biography, see Muḥammad Lāhījī, *Mafātīḥ al-i'jāz fī sharḥ-i Gulshan-i rāz,* edited by K. Samī'ī (Tehran 1337 A.Hsh./1958), introduction, pp. 75-7; Jāmī, *Nafaḥāt al-uns,* edited by M. Tawḥīdīpūr (Tehran 1964), pp. 605-606.

41 Also, cf. the analysis by Zarrīnkūb, *Justujū,* p. 313.

42 *Voyages,* ed. Langlés, (Paris 1811), IV, p. 453.

43 Berlin 1825.

44 *Rosenflor des Geheimnisses* (Leipzig 1838).

45 E.H. Whinfield, *Gulshan-i Raz, The Mystic Rose Garden,* the Persian Text, with an English Translation and Notes, chiefly from the Commentary of Muhammad bin Yahya Lahiji (Lahore: Islamic Book Foundation 1978, reprint of the 1880 London edition), p. iv. For a summary of Western studies on the *Garden of Mystery,* see J.T.P. de Bruijn's article s.v. "Maḥmūd Shabistarī," in EI$^2$.

46 *Gulshan-i rāz,* edited by Dr. Javad Nurbakhsh (Tehran: Intishārāt-i Khāniqāh-i Ni'matullāhī 1976).

47 See chap. 1, note 2 above.

48 For summaries of these commentaries, see (in French) Henry Corbin, *Trilogie Ismaelienne* (Tehran/Paris 1961), pp. 21-23; and (in Persian) 'Azīz Dawlatābādī (ed.), *Sukhanwarān-i Ādharbāyjān* (Tabriz: Intishārāt-i Mu'asasa-yi Tārīkh wa Farhang-i Īrān 1355 A.Hsh./1976), I, pp. 162-73, who cites 49 different commentaries. See also Aḥmad Gulchīn Ma'ānī, *"Gulhan-i rāz* wa shurūḥ-i mukhtalif-i ān," *Nuskhahā-yi khaṭṭī,* daftar 4 (Tehran: Dānishgāh, no. 1039; 1344 A.Hsh./1965), pp. 53-124.

49 Cited by M.M. Shīrāzī, *Ṭarā'iq al-ḥaqā'iq,* edited by M.J. Maḥjūb (Tehran 1339 A.Hsh./1960), III, p. 130.

50 These two currents are explored in chapter 6 below.

51 On Lāhījī, see M. Glünz, "Sufism, Shi'ism and Poetry in Fifteenth-Century Iran: The Ghazals of Asiri-Lahiji," in Lis Golombek and Maria Subtelny (eds.), *Timurid Art and Culture: Iran and Central Asia in the Fifteenth Century* (Leiden: E.J. Brill 1992), pp. 195-200; B. Zanjānī (ed.), *Dīwān-i ash'ār wa rasā'il-i Asīrī Lāhījī* (Tehran: McGill

University's Institute of Islamic Studies, Tehran Branch 1978), N. Anṣārī's introduction.

[52] Kathleen Raine, *Defending Ancient Springs* (Suffolk: Golgonoonza Press 1985), p. 23 (referring to Vernon Watkins). Bausani's judgement *(Storia della Letteratura Persiana,* p. 740) that the poem's only value was in its content, and in terms of poetic expression, it is of mediocre quality, is quite uncharacteristic of its appreciative reception in Persia proper.

[53] Cf. Zarrīnkūb's comments, *Justujū,* p. 324.

[54] *Rawḍāt al-jinān,* II, pp. 88-9; MAS, *Gulshan-i rāz,* p. 108, vv. 995-7 (only vv. 996-7 are cited by Ibn Karbalā'ī).

[55] As Claude Addas observes: "Concise and to the point [Ibn 'Arabī's] prose in the *Futūḥāt* is generally speaking more easily accessible than in some of his earlier writings such as *'Anqā' mughrib,* or the superb *Kitāb al-'isrā'* with its cadences and symbolic expression which defy any attempt at translation." *Quest for the Red Sulphur* [translated by Peter Kingsley; Cambridge, U.K.: ITS 1994], p. 204.

[56] See his brillant essay: "Sayrī dar *Gulshan-i rāz,*" in his *Naqshī bar āb* (Tehran: Intishārāt-i Mu'īn 1368 A.Hsh./1989), pp. 256-94.

[57] See her *Mystical Dimensions of Islam* (Chapel Hill: University of North Carolina 1975), chap. 7.

[58] *Ibid.,* pp. 326-7.

[59] Zarrīnkūb, *Justujū,* p. 313.

[60] Jamāl al-Dīn Ardistānī, *Mirāt al-afrād,* ed. Ḥusayn Anīsīpūr (Tehran: Zawwār 1371 A.Hsh./1992), p. 22.

[61] To use Ehsan Yarshater's felicitious terms: "Some Common Characteristics of Persian Poetry and Art," *Studia Islamica* XVI (1962), p. 61.

[62] See Sīrūs Shamisā, *Sayr-i ghazal dar shi'r-i fārsī,* (Tehran 1983), chap. 4.

[63] MAS, *Sa'ādat-nāma,* p. 152, vv. 61-62.

[64] "One of my traits is that I do not like to distress anyone . . . I am so concerned to please others that when thee friends come to visit me, I dread the thought that they might become bored. So I recite poetry to keep them busy. Otherwise, what have I to do with poetry? By God, I detest poetry. In my eyes there is nothing worse." From his *Discourses (Fīhī mā fīhī),* trans. W.C. Chittick, *The Sufi Path of Love: the Spiritual Teachings of Rumi* (Albany: SUNY 1983), p. 270.

[65] *Ilahī-nāma,* ed. Hellmut Ritter (Istanbul 1940, reprinted Tehran: Tūs 1359 A.Hsh./1980), p. 369 (10), 370 (12-14).

[66] *Iranian Nationality and the Persian Language (900-1900): The Roles of Court, Religion, and Sufism in Persian Prose Writing,* trans. M. Hillmann (Washington, D.C.: Mage 1992), p. 52.

[67] See A.K. Coomaraswamy, "Notes on the Philosophy of Persian Art," in Roger Lipsey (ed.), *Coomaraswamy: Selected Papers on Traditional Art and Symbolism* (Princeton: Princeton University Press 1986; Bollingen Series 89), vol. I, pp. 260-5. Vicente Cantarino, describing the relation between Arabic poetry and religion, thus notes that Islam has been "the direct cause of the almost sacred interest in the language and of an aesthetic and linguistic awareness that borders on the reli-

gious." *Arabic Poetics in the Golden Age* (Leiden: E.J. Brill 1975), p. 17. According to many Oriental doctrines, poetry is the result of the imposition of the Spiritual and Intellectual Principle upon the matter or substance of the language, as S.H. Nasr has pointed out: "Poetry is not the expression of the subjective experiences of the separated ego of the poet, but the fruit of a vision of a reality which transcends the being of the poet and for which the poet must become the expositor and guide." "Metaphysics, Poetry and Logic in Oriental Traditions," *Sophia Perennis,* III/2 (1977), p. 124.

68 J.C. Bürgel, *The Feather of Simurgh: The "Licit Magic" of the Arts in Medieval Islam* (New York: N.Y. University Press 1988).

69 *Makhzan al-asrār,* (part of his complete works), ed. Waḥīd Dastgirdī (Tehran: Ibn Sīnā 1334 A.Hsh./1956), p. 41.

70 See Leonard Lewisohn, "The Life and Poetry of Mashreqi Tabrizi," *Iranian Studies,* vol. 22, nos. 2-3 (1989), pp. 119-20, for a discussion of this. Also cf. Bürgel, *The Feather of Simurgh*, III: 2, pp. 57ff.

71 On Khujandī, see Leonard Lewisohn, "The Life and Times of Kamāl Khujandī," in Maria Eva Subtelny (ed.), *Annemarie Schimmel Festschrift* in *Journal of Turkish Studies,* XVIII (Cambridge: Harvard University 1994), pp. 163-77.

72 *Tadhkirat al-shu'arā,* ed. Muḥammad 'Abbāsī (Tehran: Kitābfurūshī Bārānī, 1337 A.H.sh./1958), p. 363.

73 *Nafaḥāt al-uns,* ed. M. Tawḥīdīpūr (Tehran: Intishārāt-i Kitābfurūshī Maḥmūdī 1336 A.Hsh./1957), p. 611.

74 Weighing the worth of poetry and Sufism in Kamāl's personality, Kazārgāhī in the *Majālis al-'ushshāq* reaches a similar conclusion, commenting that "folk of the world are of two parties concerning him. Some say he belongs to the number of the saints *(awliyā')* and others say he belongs to the company of poets. Outwardly speaking, it would appear that he is an interface *(barsakh)* between the two groups, with the saintly aspect predominant in his personality, an idea which appears in some his verse." Bodleian Library MS. Add. 24, folio 101v.

75 MAS, p. 69, *Gulshan-i rāz,* vv. 56-58.

76 MAS, p. 11, introduction.

77 Zarrīnkūb, "Sayrī dar *Gulshan-i rāz*," p. 266.

78 *Mafātīḥ al-i'jāz,* ed. Khāliqī & Karbāsī, p. 38.

79 MAS, *Gulshan-i rāz,* pp. 69, vv. 32-69.

80 He was author of many books on Sufism including *Zād al-musāfirīn, Kanz al-rumūz* (in verse) and *Nuzhat al-arwāḥ, Rūh al-arwāḥ,* and *Ṣirāṭ al-mustaqīm* (in prose). See Najīb Māyil Harawī's introduction to his edition of Mīr Harawī's *Nuzhat al-arwāḥ,* (Mashhad: Zawwār 1392 A.H./1972).

81 As Zarrīnkūb, *Justujū,* p. 327, points out.

82 MAS, *Gulshan-i rāz,* p. 68, vv. 36-43.

83 C.E. Bosworth in his treatment of this term in *Encyclopedia Iranica,* I, p. 667, (s.v. *aḥrār* ) ignores its Sufi connotation, which refers, as Nicholson notes, to the "true mystics." In the words of Nūrī, "Sufism is liberty, so that a man is freed from the bonds of desire; and generosity and abandonment of useless trouble and munificence *(Al-taṣawwuf huwa*

*'l-ḥurriyyat wa 'l-futuwwat wa- 'l-tark al-taklīf wa- 'l-sakhā wa-badhl al-dunyā)* See 'Alī al-Hujwīrī, trans. R.A. Nicholson, *Kashf al-maḥjūb: The Oldest Persian Treatise on Sufism* (London: Luzac & Co. 1976), p. 43.

84 As he himself confesses elsewhere in the poem; see MAS, *Gulshan-i rāz,* p. 105, vv. 919-21.

85 On the meaning of this technical term in Sufism see Dr. Javad Nurbakhsh, *Spiritual Poverty in Sufism,* trans. Leonard Lewisohn (London: KNP 1984), "Metaphysical Time," pp. 134-39.

86 *Blake: Complete Writings,* ed. G. Keynes (London: OUP 1972), "Milton," 28: 62; 29: 1-3, p. 516.

87 MAS, *Gulshan-i rāz,* p. 69, vv. 45-47.

88 *Mafātīḥ al-i'jāz,* ed. Khāliqī & Karbāsī, p. 35.

89 That was the original form of the poem according to Lāhījī: *Mafātīḥ al-i'jāz,* ed. Khāliqī & Karbāsī, p. 39.

90 A reference to the Koranic injunction (XCIII: 10) not to drive beggars away.

91 MAS, *Gulshan-i rāz,* p. 69, vv. 65-66.

92 *Mafātīḥ al-i'jāz,* ed. Khāliqī & Karbāsī, p. 42.

93 MAS, *Gulshan-i rāz,* p. 69, v. 51.

94 See MAS, *Sa'ādat-nāma,* p. 152, v. 77.

95 *The Book of Certainty: The Sufi Doctrines of Faith, Vision and Gnosis* (New York: Weiser 1970), p. 12. This doctrine is derived from the Koranic verse (XXVII: 7): "Moses said to his household: Verily beyond all doubt I have seen a fire. I will bring you tidings of it or I will bring you a flaming brand that ye may warm yourselves."

96 MAS, *Sa'ādat-nāma,* p. 152, v. 76.

97 MAS, *Sa'ādat-nāma,* p. 186, v. 703, translated below.

98 *Kashf u burhān u āyat-i Qur'ān:* i.e. visionary revelation, logical demonstration and verses from the Koran, This corresponds to the traditional triadic Ghazālian scheme of the knowledge of *tawḥīd,* that is to say: *īmān* (faith through belief in Prophetic revelation, *'ilm* (=the science of Theology, Kalām), and *dhawq* (direct mystical experience, 'taste').

99 MAS, p. 152, *Sa'ādat-nāma,* vv. 55-63.

100 A reference to the *Rawshanā'ī-nāma,* a 550-verse poem composed in the *hazaj* metre. Although the veracity of its attribution to Nāṣir has since been questioned (see M. Mīnuwī, *"Rawshanā'ī-nāma*-yi Nāṣir-i Khusraw wa *Rawshanā'ī-nāma*-yi Manẓūm-i mansūb ba ū," in *Yād-nāma-yi Nāṣir-i Khusraw (*Mashhad: 1976), pp. 574-80, Francois de Blois counterargues that "no convincing arguments have been advanced against Nāṣir's authorship." *Persian Literature: A Bio-Bibliographical Survey, Poetry to ca. A.D. 1100,* V/1 (London: Royal Asiatic Society 1992), p. 209.

101 Koran VI: 112. Literally "embellished speech" or "varnished falsehood" (Lane III, 1223) "by way of delusion." For further commentary on this, see Muhammad Asad, who translates this phrase as "glittering half-truths meant to delude the mind" in his *The Message of the Qur'ān,* (Gibraltar: Dar al-Andalus 1980), p. 189, no. 98.

102 MAS, *Sa'ādat-nāma,* pp. 186-7; vv. 694-713.

[103] *Tadhkirat al-shu'arā*, ed. M. 'Abbāsī (Tehran: 1337 A.Hsh./1958), pp. 69, 73.

[104] For instance, these lines:

> If you take poetry as a profession
> Someone has also taken minstrelsy.
> You are standing there where the minstrel sits;
> It is fitting you cut out your impudent tongue.
>
> Cited by S. Meskoob, *Iranian Nationality,* p. 54.

Peter L. Wilson also comments that "one refreshing aspect of Nāṣir's poetry is the total absence of praise of rulers and the powerful." *Nāṣir-i Khusraw: Forty Poems from the Divan*, trans. P.L. Wilson, G.R. Aavani (Tehran, 1977), introduction, p. 14. As A. Schimmel points out, Nāṣir-i Khusraw also claimed to be exclusively inspired by religious motives in his poetry: *Make a Shield from Wisdom: Selected Verses from Nāṣir-i Khusraw's Dīvān* (London: KPI 1993), p. 22, introduction.

[105] Jāmī, *Bahāristān,* ed. Ismā'īl Ḥakīmī (Tehran: Intishārāt-i Iṭilā'āt 1367 A.Hsh./1988), p. 95.

[106] *Dīwān-i ash'ār-i Ḥakīm-i Nāṣir-i Khusraw,* ed. M. Minovi & Mehdi Mohaghegh, (Tehran: Institute of Islamic Studies 1978), p. 145. v. 23. I am indebted to Dr. Mohaghegh for this reference.

[107] Ibn Taymiyya, *Majmū' al-rasā'il,* (Cairo 1905), p. 97

[108] *The Travels of Ibn Baṭṭūṭah,* trans. H.A.R. Gibb (London: Hakluyt society 1962), I, p. 106. See also Michel M. Mazzaoui, *The Origins of the Ṣafawids, The Origins of the Ṣafawids: Šī'ism, Ṣūfism, and the Ğulāt* (Wiesbaden: Franz Steiner 1972), p. 39.

[109] See below, chap. 5.

[110] Charles Melville, "The Year of the Elephant" Mamluk-Mongol Rivalry in the Hejaz in the Reign of Abū Sa'īd (1317-1335)," *Studia Iranica,* XXII/2 (1992), p. 205, citing al-Maqrīzī, *Kitāb al-sulūk li-ma'rifat duwal al-mulūk,* ed, M.M. Ziadeh, (Cairo 1956ff), II, p. 211. See also my discussion below of the reign of Abū Sa'īd, chap. 3.

[111] Charles Melville, "The Year of the Elephant," p. 210.

[112] Charles Melville, "Cobān" in *Encyclopedia Iranica,* V, pp. 877-8.

[113] Claude Cahen, *Pre-Ottoman Turkey: A general survey of the material and spiritual culture and history c. 1071-1330,* trans. from French by J. Jones-Williams (London: Sidgwick & Jackson 1972), p. 301.

[114] Charles Melville, "The Year of the Elephant," pp. 205-6, citing al-Maqrīzī, *Kitāb al-sulūk,* II, p. 230.

[115] Alexander Kynsh notes that during this period "Ibn 'Arabī developed into an important cultural symbol, which was widely used by rival religious and political parties and groups, as well as family clans struggling for influence and domination in the society. . . . The debates that took place over his heritage took especially violent forms in Egypt, Syria and Yemen, where *practically all intellectuals were engaged in the pro or con polemic.*" "Ibn 'Arabī in the Later Islamic Tradition," in S. Hirtenstein & M. Tiernan (eds.) *Muhyiddin Ibn 'Arabī: A Commemorative Volume* (Dorset, U.K.: Element Bks. 1993); p. 314. Italics mine.

116 See Alexander Knysh, *ibid.*, p. 315. Also see below, chap. 5.

117 MAS, *Sa'ādat-nāma,* p. 180, vv. 602-604.

118 MAS, *Sa'ādat-nāma,* p. 180, vv. 616-18.

119 As Alexander Knysh, "Ibn 'Arabī in the Later Islamic Tradition," p. 312, points out.

120 *An-nasu 'alā dīni mulūkihim.* See Furūzanfar, *Aḥadīth-i Mathnawī,* (Tehran: Intishārāt-i Dānishgāh Tihrān 1956), no. 28.

121 As, for instance, Shabistarī's disparaging reference in the *Sa'ādat-nāma* to the Sabeans as polytheists, describing their doctrine as infidelity *(kufr)* and misguidance *(ḍulāl),* and their religion *(madhhab)* as filth (*Sa'ādat-nāma* vv. 381-93). In this section, it is important to note that while Shabistarī credits Abraham with the honor being the first iconoclast in human history, rejecting the Sabean astro-worship as a form of dualism and irreligion, he concludes his discussion on a more tolerant note, commenting: "The planets' worth in the eyes of God is by no means insignificant, as the verse 'By the Star' (Koran LIII, 1) bears witness. The darkness of the Sabean doctrine, however, derives from ascribing partners *(shirkat)* to (the oneness of) the Divine essence, not from the intellectual perception of (Divine) light in the Divine Signs (of the created world)."

122 These sects and thinkers reviled by Shabistarī in the *Sa'ādat-nāma* include: 1) the Sabeans (vv. 381-93); 2) the Nazarene, Nestorian, Jacobite, and Melchite Christian sects (vv. 394-97); 3) the Christian philosopher Nasṭūr al-Ḥakīm who flourished during the reign (813-833) of the Caliph Mā'mūn (vv. 397-405); 4) Zoroastrianism and Zoroaster (vv. 415-32); 5) Muḥammad Ibn Karrām, founder of the Karrāmiyya sect of anthropomorphists (vv. 560-65); 6) The *mutakallim* or scholastic theologians (vv. 567-80); 7) Pseudo-Sufis who ignore *Kalām* and study only the *Fuṣūṣ* of Ibn 'Arabī (vv. 599-625); 8) Peripatetic philosophers (Avicenna in particular) who is reproached with negating God's Attributes and denial of the corporeal resurrection (vv. 642, 649-63, 674-84); 9) The Ishrāqī Platonic philosophers *(ishrāqiyyān aflāṭūn),* Suhrawardī Maqtūl in particular (vv. 670-73); 10) The metaphysical Ismā'īlī poet Nāṣir-i Khusraw (cited above, pp. 26-9) whom Shabistarī execrates and curses abusively (vv. 694-710); 11) The Islamic rationalists (Mu'tazila) (vv. 714-720, 727-46); 12) Abū al-Ḥasan Maḥmūd 'Umar Zamakhsharī (467-538 A.H., author of *al-Kashshāf,* vv. 735-41).

123 See below, chap. 8.

124 MAS, *Sa'ādat-nāma,* pp. 240-1, v. 1535-38, 1542, 1559-60.

125 MAS, *Sa'ādat-nāma,* vv. 1531-48; 1552-60.

126 Howorth, *History of the Mongols,* (London: 1876-1927), III, p. 521. Also cf. A.K.S. Lambton, "The Law and its Administration," *Continuity and Change in Medieval Persia* (London: Tauris 1988), pp. 82-96.

127 On which, see Eric Winkel, "Ibn 'Arabī's *Fiqh:* Three Cases from the *Futūḥāt,*" *Journal of the Muhyiddin Ibn 'Arabi Society,* XII/1993, pp. 54-74.

128 MAS, *Sa'ādat-nāma,* p. 240, vv. 1547-48.

129 For further discussion of the Sufi-*'ulamā'* dichotomy, see Leonard

Lewisohn, "Overview: Iranian Islam and Persianate Sufism," in L. Lewisohn (ed.) *The Legacy of Mediæval Persian Sufism,* (London: KNP 1993), pp. 19-24. Cf. J.T.P. De Bruijn, "The *Qalandariyyāt* in Persian Mystical Poetry, from Sanā'ī Onwards," in *ibid.,* pp. 75-86.

130 MAS, *Sa'ādat-nāma,* p. 185, vv. 683-4.

131 MAS, *Sa'ādat-nāma,* p. 150,. v. 29.

132 MAS, *Sa'ādat-nāma,* p. 150, vv. 27-8.

133 Ḥamdu'llāh Mustawfi, in describing the townsfolk of Tabriz in 1340, relates that "Most of them are Sunnis of the Shāfi'ī *madhhab.*" Cited by Dr. R. 'Aivaḍī (ed.) *Dīvān-i Humām Tabrīzī,* (Tabriz: 1970) introduction, p. 40.

134 H. Algar, "Some Observations on Religion in Safavid Persia," *Iranian Studies* (1974), p. 288.

135 J.W. Morris, "Ibn 'Arabī and his Interpreters. Part II: Influences and Intrepretations," *J.A.O.S.,* 106/4 (1986), p. 738.

136 Zarrīnkūb, "Sayrī dar *Gulshan-i rāz,*" p. 260.

137 MAS, introduction, p. 11. This attribution has been shown to be false. See Aḥmad Sharī'at's edition of the Persian translation of this treatise by 'Umar ibn 'Abd al-Jabbār Sa'dī Sāwī (Tehran: 1980), p. xvii.

138 Koran XVII: 44.

139 MAS, *Sa'ādat-nāma,* p. 157; vv. XVII: 93-102.

140 Zarrīnkūb, "Sayrī dar *Gulshan-i rāz,*" p. 260 and *idem, Farār az madrasa: dar-bāra-yi zindigī wa andīsha-yi Abū Ḥāmid Ghazālī* (Tehran: 1369 A.Hsh./1990), p. 172ff. See also Eric L. Ormsby, *Theodicy in Islamic Thought: The Dispute over al-Ghazālī's "Best of All Possible Worlds"* (Princeton: University Press 1984).

141 MAS, p. 103, vv. 874-75. For a detailed analysis of these verses, see Leonard Lewisohn, "The Transcendental Unity of Polytheism and Monotheism in the Sufism of Shabistarī," *Legacy,* p. 389ff.

142 *Al-Munqidh min al-ḍalāl,* ed. Farid Jabre (Beyrouth: Libraire Orientale 1969), p. 22. Cf. the translation of this treatise by W. Montgomery Watt, *The Faith and Practice of al-Ghazālī,* (London 1953), p. 35 (93).

143 Adding that "They are unable to satisfy the conditions of proof they lay down in logic . . .", *ibid.,* W. Montgomery Watt, p. 37 (96).

144 MAS, p. 185, vv. 675-82. Cf. Zarrīnkūb, "Sayrī dar *Gulshan-i rāz,*" p. 260.

145 Watt, *The Faith and Practice of al-Ghazālī,* p. 36 (95).

146 MAS, p. 180, vv. 599-613.

147 *Mirṣād al-'ibād,* trans. H. Algar, *The Path of God's Bondsmen from Origin to Return* (New York: Caravan 1982), p. 310.

148 *The Venture of Islam,* II, p. 190.

149 Zarrīnkūb, *Justujū,* p. 320, thus mistakenly describes Shabistarī's imagery in *Gulshan-i rāz* as having an "Ishrāqī veneer."

150 Here Shabistarī refers directly to Shihāb al-Dīn Yaḥyā Suhrawardī "Maqtūl, (d. 5871191):" the author of *Ḥikmat al-Ishrāq* or *Theosophy of Oriental Illumination.*

151 An allusion to Suhrawardī's *Kitāb al-talwīḥāt al-lawḥiyya wa'l-'arshiyya,* which is a compendium of theological and philosophical sciences divided up into three section: Logic, Physics and Metaphysics.

Edited by H. Corbin in *Suhrawardī, Oeuvres Philosophiques et Mystiques* (Tehran/Paris: 1976), vol. 1.

152 MAS, p. 185, *Sa'ādat-nāma,* vv. 664-672.

153 See Aḥmad 'Alī Rajā'ī Bukhārā'ī, *Farhang-i ash'ār-i Ḥāfiẓ,* (Tehran, 1985, 2nd ed.), p. 453-4.

154 As Richard Frank, "Al-Ghazālī's Use of Avicenna's Philosophy," *Revue des Etudes Islamiques,* LV-LVII/1 (1987-89), pp. 271-85, demonstrates.

155 Claude Addas, *Quest for the Red Sulphur*, p. 105.

156 MAS, *Sa'ādat-nāma,* p. 187; v. 713

157 MAS, *Gulshan-i rāz,* p. 68, v. 44.

158 *Classical Persian Literature* (London: Curzon Press 1994, reprint of the 1958 edition), p. 303.

159 From S.H. Nasr's Preface to W.C. Chittick and P.L. Wilson, *Fakhruddin 'Iraqi: Divine Flashes* (London: SPCK 1982), p. xiv.

160 Cited by M. Chodkiewicz, *Seal of the Saints: Prophethood and Sainthood in the Doctrine of Ibn 'Arabī.* Translated from the French by Liadain Sherrard. (Cambridge: Islamic Texts Society, 1993), p. 18.

161 *Ḥaqq al-yaqīn,* ed. J. Nurbakhsh, (Tehran: Intishārāt-i Khānaqāh-i Ni'matu'llāhī 1354 A.Hsh./1975), p. 2.

162 *Ḥaqq al-yaqīn,* ed. J. Nurbakhsh, p. 8

163 Edited by Dr. Aḥmad Mahdawī-Dāmaghānī (Tehran 1965), pp. 7-8.

164 W.C. Chittick, "Mysticism Versus Philosophy in Earlier Islamic History: The Al-Ṭūsī, Al-Qūnawī Correspondance," *Religious Studies,* 17 (1981), p. 94.

165 MAS, p. 286; *Ḥaqq al-yaqīn,* ed. J. Nurbakhsh, p. 2. (My translation incorporates versions from both editions).

166 Definitions differ among Islamic speculative thinkers as to what exactly constitutes "rational science." According Ja'far Sajjādī's *Lexicon of Speculative Sciences* (*Farhang-i 'ulūm-i 'aqlī),* (Tehran: 1982), p. 416, "*'ilm-i 'aqlī* is knowledge of any matter which is not percieved by the senses."

167 That is to say, comments Lāhījī, "the tongue of spiritual feeling *(lisān-i ḥāl)* of the lily in this *Garden (of Mystery)* is vocal in acknowledging the fact that she has not been touched by any stranger, having remained virgin and unviolated." *Mafātīḥ al-i'jāz,* ed. Khāliqī & Karbāsī, p. 600.

168 MAS, *Gulshan-i rāz* p. 108, vv. 998-1000.

169 "Annotation to Reynolds," *Blake: Complete Writings,* ed. G. Keynes, p. 453. Also cf. his comment that "General Knowledge is Remote Knowledge; it is in Particulars that Wisdom consists & Happiness too. Both in Art & in Life, General Masses are as Much Art as a Pasteboard Man is Human. Every Man has Eyes, Noses & Mouth; this Every Idiot knows, but he who enters into & discriminates most Minutely the Manners & Intentions, the Characters in all their branches, is alone the Wise or Sensible Man & on this discrimination All Art is founded." *Ibid.,* p. 611.

170 *Ibid.,* p. 738, Jerusalem 91: 21.

171 *Ibid.,* p. 687, Jerusalem 55: 51, 62-4.

172 Al-Tahānawī, *Kashāf iṣṭilāḥāt al-funūn,* ed. M. Wajih, Abd al-Haqq and Gholam Kadir, with W. Nassau Lees (Calcutta 1862), I, p. 482.

173 *Mafātīḥ al-i'jāz,* ed. Khāliqī & Karbāsī, p. 601.

174 MAS, *Ḥaqq al-yaqīn,* p. 286; and *Ḥaqq al-yaqīn,* ed. J. Nurbakhsh, p. 3. My translation is based on the Nurbakhsh edition here.

175 Following the translation and interpretation of Muhammad Asad, *The Message of the Qur'ān,* p. 768, n. 24.

176 Ed. Sayyid Muḥammad 'Alī Ṣafīr (Tehran: 1346 A.Hsh./1967).

177 This is the opinion of Zarrīnkūb, *Justujū,* p. 353 and 'A.A. Dihkhudā, *Lughāt-nāma,* s.v. "Pahlawān;" but Angelo Pietmonese, "La Leggenda del Santo-Lottatore Pahlavān Maḥmūd Xᵛārezmī 'Puryā-ye Valī'," *Annali dell'Istituto Universitario Orientale di Napoli,* Nuova Serie, XV (1965), p. 206, leaves the question of its authorship open.

178 MAS, pp. 387-401. Based on MS. 3260, in the Library of the Islamic Council in Tehran, Iran.

179 MAS, introduction, p. 12.

180 MAS, pp. 347-77.

181 Dr. Muwaḥḥid's principal MS. is Ayā Ṣawfiyā 2062, dated 895 A.H.

182 Chapter one of the *Mirāt al-muḥaqiqqīn,* for instance, follows Avicenna's description of the faculties of the soul almost word for word; on which, see G. Cameron Gruner, *A Treatise on the the Canon of Medicine of Avicenna* (New York: Augustus Kelley 1970), pp. 135-42.

183 Munzawī, *Fihrist-i nuskhahā-yi khaṭṭī-yi Fārsī* (Tehran 1970), II, p. 842.

184 As Ṣamad Muwaḥḥid in his introduction to the MAS, p. 9, points out.

185 Such as Zarrīnkūb, *Justujū,* p. 323.

186 See John Walbridge, "A Sufi Scientist of the Thirteenth Century: the Mystical Ideas and Practices of Quṭb al-Dīn Shīrāzī," in L. Lewisohn (ed.), *The Legacy of Mediæval Persian Sufism,* pp. 339-40.

# III

# THE POLITICAL MILIEU OF MONGOL PERSIA

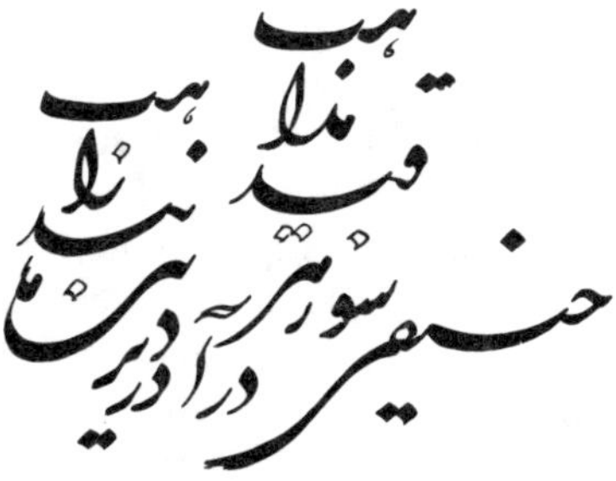

*Detach yourself, be* ḥanīfī
*And from all faiths' fetters free;*
*So come, like the monk, step up*
*into religion's abbey.*

If political consciousness can be defined in the first degree as sympathy with the social woes of one's fellow man, all poetry, even the most seemingly metaphysical, is also unavoidably political. As Shabistarī's contemporary, the great humanist Sufi Sa'dī (d. 690/1291) affirms,

The sons of men are members in a body whole related
For of a single essence are they each and all created.
When Fortune persecutes with pain one member surely
The other members of the body cannot stand securely.
O you who from another's troubles turn aside your view
It is not fitting they bestow the name of 'Man' on you.[187]

Many of Shabistarī's pronouncements in his two major poems, the *Gulshan-i rāz* and *Sa'ādat-nāma,* reflect, albeit indirectly, the political turmoil of his period. The poet's view of Christianity, his outlook on idolatry, and ill-opinion of the legalists and jurists of his epoch, for instance, are directly linked to contemporary events. They can be read as reflecting the political and social milieu of Mongol Persia, as well as poetic statements concerning purely 'humane principles'. The conquests of Genghis Khān, the tales of the Assassins of Alamut, and the legacy of the Mongol Īl-Khāns are the stuff of mythology and imagination as well as empirical realities of mediæval world history. Let us then briefly survey the events of this important epoch.[188]

'Nightmarish' is too light an adjective to use to characterize the horrific political history of Persia during Shabistarī's age: military invasions, massacres and religious pogroms in every corner of the land touched by the Mongol hordes. The Mongol invasion was, as Browne justly put it, "one of the most dreadful calamities which ever befell the human race."[189] The naked horror and utter terror of the Mongol conquests brought with them genocide and a scorched earth policy: recent scholars have confirmed the possibility of a ninety-percent extermination rate among the Persian populace of Khurāsān.[190] The "grandiose scale of mass-extermination" astounded the imagination of contemporary historians.[191] Genghis Khān's catastrophic invasion of northern Iran, for instance, was accompanied by the systematic extermination of the civilian population of all its major towns (Balkh, Marv, Nishāpūr, Herat, Ṭūs, Ray, Qazwin, Hamadhān, Ardabīl, etc.).[192] These ravages by Mongol and later, Timurid, tyrants, whose capricious wills wreaked havoc with the sedentary economy of mediaeval Iran, transforming it into a slave economy,[193] were dreadful. A constant state of insecurity, violence, internal warfare, banditry on the highways and the pillaging of private property by state officials, was the general order of the day in the thirteenth and fourteenth centuries.[194] The Mongol tax collectors produced unprecedented economic distress. Previously peasants—now serfs and slaves—were forced to maintain their dwellings in deliberate dilapidation lest they risk a visit from a Mongol dignitary whose very presence entailed a duty-tax *(nuzūl)*.[195]

Many scholars have argued that the only consolation for the ordinary man faced with such barbarity lay in the cultivation of Sufism[196] and that it was "the wide vogue of mysticism, far more than formal theology, that enabled Islam to survive this appalling catastrophe."[197] As 'Alī Rajā'ī Bukhārā'ī observes:

> The Persian writer of the twelfth and especially the thirteenth century has witnessed his house burned down, his city destroyed, his beloved relatives murdered, his independence

> eradicated. Foreigners control his possessions, his property, his very being. In such circumstances, how can one sing songs of joy or compose rhapsodies? How should the world be thought a happy abode, or life seem sweet? Thus the poetry of this period and the following century (eighth Muslim/fourteenth Christian century)—composed as it was by writers subjected to savage marauding Mongols and plundering Turks—is little more than an attempt to offer condolences to the reader. Yet, in the midst of this pessimism, anxiety, despair, apathy, political corruption and psychological terror, Sufism seemed to be the sole force capable of saving the soul of the Iranian populace, casting a ray of hope and courage into the traumatized hearts of the inhabitants of mediaeval Persia. For the Sufi masters promised the people—in the safety of Sufism—liberation from aggravation by their corrupt contemporaries, offering as companions individuals of refined and sensitive feelings, instead of blackguards and tyrants. They allowed their followers to pass their days without trouble in their *khānaqāh*s, engaged in musical concerts and dance, states of rapture and spiritual feelings.[198]

The Sufis—those of the Kubrāwiyya Order in particular—generally considered the Mongol invasion of Khwārazm in the years 615/1218–620/1223, resulting in ninety years of rule by non-Muslim 'infidels', as due in part to the misconduct towards the 'Friends of God' by their own 'Muslim' rulers. In line with the Sufis' conception of the sovereignty *(dawlat)* of the worldly ruler as being subject to the spiritual authority *(walāyat)* of the saints,[199] Nūr al-Dīn Isfarāyinī (639/1242–717/1317) held, for instance, that the execution of Majd al-Dīn Baghdādī (d. 616/1219) at the hands of Muḥammad ibn Tikish, the Shāh of Khwārazm, to be the true cause of the Mongol holocaust. He interpreted the destruction of the kingdom of Khwārazm, as a "summons issued from the court of Divine Grandeur to the *Sīmurgh* of Kingship *(salṭānat)* to fly from the blessed branch of Islam and to alight on the cursed tree of Infidelity *(kufr)*."[200] Likewise, Najm al-Dīn Rāzī (573/1177 – 654/1256), after escaping from the Mongol sack of Ray in 618/1221, where his family was massacred, observed a year later in his *Mirṣād al-'ibād:*

> In this age only a few God-fearing leaders have survived to care for religion and respectfully call the attention of kings to

> the damage caused by unbelief, so that they might undertake its repair. It is therefore to be feared as a matter of course that the empty chatter concerning religion which is still heard from some mouths will disappear, and the whole world will be submerged in the chatter of unbelief . . . It is on account of these inauspicious circumstances that God Almighty has sent His wrath in the shape of the unbelieving Tartars, so that *the reality of Islam having disappeared, He may also overturn the meaningless forms that remain.*[201]

Only the length of time since these events happened and the nonexistence of balanced historical records with which to confront the speculative and romancing texts of the Īl-khānid court apologists whose works alone have survived, make this reign of terror appear less dreadful than, for instance, the Nazi invasion of Poland. Shahrokh Meskoob comments, apropos of the personal motives in Mongol historiography, that:

> When a vizier such as Bal'ami or Rashidoddin Fazlollāh (1247?-1318) or 'Atāmalek Jovayni (1226-1283), who were in the center of the political and governmental life of their age, takes up history-writing, it is obvious that he also has more practical and tangible personal and social aims than heeding warnings and finding the straight path to heaven. These other aims relate to their social position and their relationship with the court and the government etablishment. Historians were usually either members of the court and government or dependent on them, directly or indirectly, which even a cursory look at some famous Il-khānid and Timurid historians will show. ... In the invasion of the Mongols, many people said that Muslims were facing divine wrath, because they were unable to account for that terrifying and 'illogical' event in any other way. In any case, only the rare historian in such periods was bound by ethical aims and theoretical issues.[202]

These viziers, however noble their intentions might have been, were at the mercy of the Mongol ruling classes and their position was little better than that of French officials of the Vichy government during the German occupation of France.[203]

Entering Transoxiana first in 652/1254 Hülegü Khān announced his intention to extirpate the Ismā'īlī strongholds in Khurāsān. By November 1257, thanks in part to a suggestion by his chief advisor, the Shi'ite philosopher Naṣīr al-Dīn Ṭūsī, Hülegü succeeded in luring the Ismā'īlī Grand Master Rukn al-Dīn down from his castle stronghold in Maymūn-Diz. Following the destruction of this fortress and many of his other castles in the region, the Ismā'īlī leader was put to the sword and his followers wherever they were found were exterminated.[204] This virtual obliteration of the Ismā'īlī sect by Hülegü, in the words of the great Mongol historian J.A. Boyle, "rendered a great, if unintentional, service to orthodox Islam."[205] In the same year Hülegü entered the central lands of Persia and sacked the town of Kirmānshāh, massacring its inhabitants.

The Mongol potentate now turned his attention towards the south-west, his military aim being to eradicate the caliphate and overthrow the Abbasid rule in Baghdad. By January 1258 he had reached the outskirts of the city. After a short siege, the city surrendered. He subjected the populace to the usual Mongol hospitable treatment: a sack of Baghdad which began on 13 February, and then the normal process of killing, looting and burning which continued for seven days. Only the houses of the Christians were spared.[206] The Caliph, after being forced to disclose the whereabouts of his treasures, was executed on 20 February 1258. So that his blood might not be spilt, the Caliph was rolled up in a felt carpet, then trampled to death by horses. The inhabitants of Baghdad, which, according to Ḥamdu'llāh Qazwīnī, totalled some 800,000, were then put to the sword.[207] "No European description of the People of Hell," commented Janet L. Abu-Lughod on the fall of Baghdad, "rivaled this tale of horror."[208] The Persian historian Vaṣṣāf described how the Mongols "with the broom of looting... swept out the treasures from the harems of Baghdad ... Beds and cushions made of gold and encrusted with jewels were cut to pieces with knives and torn to shreds; those hidden behind the veils of the great harem ... were dragged like the hair of idols through the streets and alleys; each of them became a plaything in the hands of a Tartar monster."[209] Subsequently, the city was reduced to a provincial capital, ruled from Tabriz.[210]

In the summer of 1258, around the time Shabistarī was born, Hülegü Khān paused in Tabriz, the third imperial province, where he left his eldest son Abāqā in charge before returning to the west. He set up his headquarters south of Tabrīz in the city of Marāgha, and ordered an observatory be built there from the plans of Naṣīr al-Dīn Ṭūsī.[211] By 1260 his hordes had conquered most of Syria, having first put to the sword many of the inhabitants of Aleppo. Here, his ally, the Armenian Christian King Het'um was granted permission to set fire to the Great Mosque. But the Mongol westward push received its first setback when Mamlūk forces led by Sultan Qutuz inflicted a crushing defeat on the Mongol forces on the 3rd of September, 1260 at 'Ayn Jalut. Hülegü passed the next five years of his life consolidating his gains in Persia, warring with rebellious Iranian vassals, campaigning against the commander of the Golden Horde Berke Khān (1257-1266) in the northwest, while defending his armies in the West from harassment by the Egyptian Mamlūks.[212] He died in 1265, to be succeeded by his eldest son Abāqā.

With Abāqā, the Īl-Khānid rule of Persia assumes a *de facto* significance. The Mongols, feeling themselves strangers in Islamic Persia, naturally allied themselves with the Christian princes of Georgia and Greater and Lesser Armenia, and although Abāqā was himself a practicing Buddhist, he had very close relations with the Christians, carrying on an earnest correspondence with the Pope in Rome.[213] Both Hülegü and Abāqā had Christian mothers and wives.[214] One of Abāqā's wives was a Christian princess, Maria, an illegitimate daughter of the Byzantine Emperor Michael Palaeologus, who, as Howorth observes, no doubt "used her influence to draw the Christians of the West and the Mongols near together."[215]

> This very friendliness and patronage of the Christians was no doubt a great cause of offence to his Muhammedan subjects and employés, who doubtless looked with much more favourable eyes upon his rival, the Sultan of Egypt, and made it easy to suspect that his end was hastened by some sinister act on the part of those who treated him as a heretic.[216]

Not only is Abāqā's friendliness with the Christians important to take into account when considering the development of Shabistarī's views of non-Islamic religions (see below, VIII), but also the fact that he made Tabriz the official political capital of Īlkhānid Persia,[217] the veritable "seat of government *(dar al-mulk)* during the Mongol period," (as Ḥamd-Allāh Mustawfī described it in his *Nuzhat al-qulūb),*[218] gives an important turn to his political status, turning our poet from a provincial sage, pontificating from a quiet country retreat, into a spokesman echoing the main religious currents circulating in the urban hub of the largest empire in the mediæval world. Although for some two decades Tabrix had been a major commercial centre, it was during his reign that "Tabriz developed as a major centre of international trade," as Charles Melville notes, "and despite its temporary eclipse as capital by Sulṭāniyya, it remained the most important city in the northwest of the country and the chief seat of the Mongol and Turkoman successor dynasties. Most of the historical monuments in Tabriz date from this [Mongol] period, which is marked by a steady increase in the number of visitors to the city."[219]

Given his Christian bias, we may safely assume that in the later 1260's and throughout the entire decade of the 1270's the construction of churches in Tabriz was a common occurrence,[220] a phenomenon Shabistarī would have witnessed. Shabistarī himself mentions certain Jewish and Christian "writings which have made the principles of true religion corrupted," as well as the "trinitarian errors" of the Nazarene, Nestorian, Jacobite, and Melchite Christian sects in the *Sa'ādat-nāma*.[221] Although Christians and Buddhists probably constituted a minority of the population, Christianity and Buddhism would have been the talk of the town. With the reigning monarch an ally of Christian Armenia, the jurisprudents and the Sufi masters would have all realized the academico-political necessity, if solely for polemical purposes, of being versed in the Torah and Gospels[222] (and probably the Pali Scriptures as well—although we have no record of Persian translations of these, it was not unlikely the Buddhist bonzes vigorously propagated the oral wisdom tradition of their faith). Islamic scholars would have encountered and conversed with both Buddhist and Christian monks and ministers. And yet, as A. Bausani notes:

> The real nature of Buddhism in Īl-khānid Iran and its influence on the Muslims of that country is an unsolved, and perhaps insoluble, problem, chiefly because of the lack of reliable sources. Iran must have been full of Buddhist temples – we hear of them only when they were destroyed in 1295-96 – and in these temples must have been numerous priests. Buddhism was particularly strong under Arghun [1284-1291], who even caused Buddhist priests to be brought from India.[223]

Abāqā also had the foresight to reinstate in his former position as governor of Baghdad 'Alā al-Dīn 'Aṭā' Malik Juwaynī, "one of the finest historians Persia has ever produced,"[224] and whose *Tārikh-i jahāngushā* was "the most important and most comprehensive Mongol history written during this period."[225] The dominant political figures until the mid-1280's were these two brothers: the historian 'Aṭā Malik and his brother the *ṣāḥib-dīwān* Shams al-Dīn.[226] The latter's (Juwaynī) role as Grand Vizier under the Īl-Khāns has been justly compared by one historian to that of Niẓām al-Mulk under the Seljuks.[227] In the beginning of this history, Juwaynī informs us that Genghis Khān followed no one religion or faith, disliked preferring one faith over another and abstained from religious bias and prejudice.[228] This disposition, it seems, was also shared by Abāqā. It was also during the reign of Abāqā Khān that Rashīd al-Dīn Faḍlu'llāh (d. 1318) came to enjoy "considerable influence and honour"[229] in his post of court physician. Born in Hamadān circa 1247, this great historian of the Mongols was described by E.G. Browne in 1930 in the third volume of his *Literary History of Persia* as "equally eminent as a physician, a statesman, and a public benefactor,"[230] and later praised by J.A. Boyle as "the first world historian,"[231] to whom belongs "the credit of producing, 600 years before Wells' *Outline of History,* the first World History in the true sense ever written in any language."[232]

Abāqā's rule rivalled that of Hülegü in its disastrous effect on the peasant economy of Iran. The first five years of his reign he was occupied in warring with Baraq, the ruler (from 1266-1271) of the Chaghatay Khanate.[233] Abāqā sacked and burnt Bukhārā in the course of a campaign in 1272-73;[234] however, he suffered a setback later in 1277 when the armies of Mamlūk Sultan Baybars (Malik al-Ẓāhir) invaded Seljuk territory from Egypt and inflicted a crushing defeat on the Mongol army at Abulustān.[235] Apparently, the Ismā'īlīs had in the meantime succeeded in recapturing Alamut in coalition with a descendent of the Khwārazmshāhs; this fortress they managed to retain for a year before Abāqā's armies dislodged them in 674/1275-6.[236] However, when the Īlkhānid Emperor heard of his army's defeat at the hands of the Egyptians in Syria in 1281, he was greatly distressed. He died in a state of *delirium tremens* on April 1, 1282 after a bout of heavy drinking.[237]

Abāqā's brother Tegüder ("perfect" in Mongol) Khān, the eldest surviving son of Hülegü Khān, succeeded him. Tegüder was a recently converted Muslim and upon ascending the throne, he adopted the Islamic name Aḥmad. His reign (1282-1284), however, was too brief to significantly alter political or religious policy in the Mongol Empire. In any case, his adoption of Islam did not cause any decline in the esteemed position held by Christianity among the Mongols, and Bar Hebraeus stresses his exceptional liberality towards the Christian churches.[238] Supported by senior members of the Mongol Buddhist aristocracy,[239] he was soon supplanted by Abāqā's son, Arghūn Khān (1284-1291), a convinced Buddhist.

The penetration of Buddhism into the heart of Iran during Arghūn's reign, the inter-faith fluidity and religious openness of the Mongol rulers is vividly illustrated by the following vignette drawn from the autobiography of the great Kubrāwī Shaykh 'Alā al-Dawla Simnānī, the chronology of whose life (659/1261–736/1336) and spiritual genealogy parallels that of Shabistarī almost exactly. Simnānī's father was an official at the court of Arghūn (and later Ghāzān), and was subsequently (in 694/1288) promoted to the post of *Ṣaḥib-i Dīvān* (minister of finance and civil administration) of Irāq.[240] After completing his studies in Simnān, young Simnānī, at age 14,[241] following in his father's footsteps, was sent to the Mongol court to be inculcated with *courtesie*. Ten years later at age 24, in the year 683/1284, while fighting on horseback loyally defending the cause of Arghūn in his struggle against the perceived pretender to the throne Aḥmad Tegüder in Qazwīn, 'Alā' al-Dawla experienced a vision which turned his heart from the present life to the hereafter. Shortly thereafter he found the spiritual consolation he sought in the form of the Kubrāwī Sufi Shaykh Akhī Sharaf al-Dīn Sa'dallāh b. Hannūya—a disciple of Nūr al-Dīn Isfarāyinī—under whose direction he entered the Path.[242] In 686/1282, robed in a motley dervish mantle, he set out, without the consent of Arghūn, to visit his supreme master, Shaykh Isfarāyinī in Baghdad. However, midway, in Hamadān, he was arrested. Simnānī recounted:

> Now the Sultan of the age, who was Arghūn, knew that I was going to Baghdad, and so sent out a group of men after me. They detained and brought me back to the city. Then they took me to another place, the camping-ground used by the royal entourage during the summer, where he was busy in the construction of the city of Sulṭāniyya which his father, Sultan Ūljāytū,[243] had founded. There, he had assembled the Buddhist bonzes from India, Kashmir, Tibet, and Īghur, along with the ascetics and the religious leaders of the idolators around him, to engage in disputation with me. So I discussed and disputed

> with them. But God Almighty lent me strength, and I was able to refute all of them by means of [arguments drawn from principles taken from] their own faith, and to disgrace and humiliate them. Then the Sultan, despite my 'heresy' praised and applauded me, pulled me over to his side, and begged me to stay with him while keeping my own dervish garb. "Your words please me," he admitted, "I feel a thrill within me when hearing your discourse, and I realize that these words do not proceed from you, for you were at my service for some ten years, yet I never heard you speak in such a fashion."[244]

Despite entreaties and kindnesses the Īl-Khān was never able to persuade his former protégé Simnānī, now absorbed in an affair of the spiritual heart, to return to his former life as a courtier, and the Mongols thus lost a potential future statesman and instead acquired one of the most "unusually original"[245]—in Bausani's words—Sufi saints of the period.

The reign of Arghūn was not only very favourable to the spread of Buddhism[246] but also to Christianity,[247] and under him the Georgian Christian ruler Dimitri was allowed to dominate all of Armenia.[248] Both Abāqā and Arghūn had minted coins with the Christian emblem of "the Father, Son and Holy Ghost—the One" upon them.[249] As a ruler, however, Arghūn was inefficient. He made a point of excluding Muslims from his bureaucracy, in this respect "departing from the practice of his father and grandfather in terms of his pronounced distrust of the Muslim population."[250] Where Abāqā and Aḥmad had patronized the Juwaynī family, Arghūn found them guilty of corresponding with the Mamlūks. Resolving to extirpate the entire clan, on 16 October 1284, the former *Ṣāḥib-i Dīwān* Shams al-Dīn Juwaynī was executed with four of his sons.[251] After setting up his own son Ghāzān as the governor of the provinces of Khurāsān, Māzandarān, Ray and Qūmis, Arghūn appointed a Jewish physician Sa'd al-Dawla of Abhar, "a man of pleasing address conversant with both the Turkish and the Mongol languages,"[252] to the post of Grand Vizier. Although an efficient administrator according to many Muslim historians, such as Vaṣṣāf, who described him as "a man of great quality and profound sagacity,"[253] and a "financial genius,"[254] this minister nonetheless "was detested by all Muslims, who ascribed to him the most sinister designs against Islam,"[255] an aversion no doubt due as much to his religious pedigree as to his unscrupulous and nepotistic behaviour.

The Syrian historian Bar Hebraeus was of the opinion that the reason why Arghūn appointed Sa'd al-Dawla to the post of Grand Vizier was his disgust with the perpetual intrigues of the so-called 'Muslim' administrators,[256] but Howorth's somewhat anti-Semitic gibe: "The elevation of a Jew to such a high position as vizier, in which he controlled the lives and fortunes of so many believers, was indeed a proof of the terrible degradation of Islam during the Mongol supremacy"[257] —is true only if one believes that any such abstract concept as 'Islam' is capable of 'elevation', be it to a political or cultural 'high', when the majority of Muslims indulge in intolerant sectarian wrangling with each other.[258] In any case, as Manūchihr Murtaḍawī rightly states, in Persian history of the Islamic era it can be asserted that during the reign of Arghūn Khān and his Jewish vizier Sa'd al-Dawla, Islam plunged to the nadir of its strength and influence.[259]

When Arghūn died in 1291 savage pogroms against the Jews were carried out in Tabriz and Baghdad.[260] He was succeeded by his brother Gaykhatu (1291-95), better known for his riotous lifestyle than for any *noblesse oblige,* and whose disastrous experiment with the introduction of paper money *(chao)* into the country's finances—modelled after the Chinese—on 12 September 1294 in the capital city Tabriz, precipitated a riot.

> It was accompanied by an edict declaring that whoever refused to accept it, whoever bought or sold for other money than chao, and whoever did not take his coin to the mint to be exchanged for paper money, was to be punished by death. The fear of punishment caused the order to be obeyed for eight days, but afterwards the shops and markets were deserted. Nothing was to be bought in the city, and people began to leave. . . . The Mussulmans met in their mosque on the Friday, and broke out into lamentations. Presently open murmurs were heard, and imprecations were flung . . . and attempts were made on the lives of the vizier and his people . . . The Vizier presently saw the ill-effects of his experiment. An ordinance permitting the use of coin in buying provisions was issued, and coin appeared again in other commercial affairs. For two months commercial dealings had virtually ceased, the shops were empty, the roads were deserted by traders, while wits and poets emulated each other in constructing lampoons and gibes at the expense of the paper money and its authors.[261]

Both as a consequence of this ruinous financial policy and his own debauchery young Gaykhatu (aged 24) was deposed and his rival Baydū, a cousin of Arghūn, gained control of the Mongol state for some seven months (April-October 1295), before he too was seized and executed by Ghāzān on 4 October 1295.[262] Baydū's reign, short as it was, was favourable to the Christians, to whose faith he was a convert.[263]

Historians concur that with the accession of Ghāzān Khān to the throne a new era in the history of the Īl-khānid rule of Persia was ushered in; the young king's conversion to Islam marked "a transition from the blatant exploitation of Iran by Chinggisid and Ilkhānid conquest states, to a more responsible attitude to government within the pre-existing Islamic ethos."[264] "The Īl-khānate," as A.K.S. Lambton correctly judges, "from then on became a Persian dynasty, no longer seeking sanction from outside."[265] Indeed, Ghāzān Khān's political policy of unrelenting animosity towards the Egyptian Mamlūks has also been viewed as that of a "Persian Islam" in opposition to an "Arab Islam."[266]

The accession of Ghāzān meant the triumph of one of two political trends which had, until then, dominated the political life of Īl-khānid Persia. The first trend, which Ghāzān pursued with success, was that of "a centralizing feudal state together with a ramifying bureaucratic apparatus," which "aimed at the creation of a strong central authority in the person of the Īlkhān, the adoption by the Mongol conquerors of the old Iranian state traditions of a centralized feudal form of government, and in connexion with this the curbing of the centrifugal proclivities of the nomad tribal aristocracy;" but it rang the death knell for the second tendency, which was that of "feudal disintegration together with a system of military fiefs."[267] I.P. Petrushevsky's summary of these developments is revealing:

> From the eighties to the nineties of the thirteenth century the Īlkhānid state experienced a colossal economic crisis, caused by the devastating results of the Mongol conquest and the taxation policy of the conquerors. . . . Search for a way out of the crisis prompted Ghāzān-khān (1295-1304) to get on good terms with the Muslim (on the whole Iranian) civil bureaucratic and ecclesiastical aristocracy, to adopt Islam and to make it again the official religion as well as to carry out a taxation reform and some other kinds of reforms. It was in connection with this that Rashīd al-Dīn was appointed to the

> office of deputy vizier under Ghāzān-khān and in fact became the chief minister and the man who carried out the reforms of this Īlkhān . . . Rashīd al-Dīn was the most notable representative and ideologist of this policy.[268]

Rashīd al-Dīn Faḍlu'llāh, as noted above, had been Abāqā's court physician, but when Ghāzān ascended the throne in 1295 he was promoted to succeed the dismissed and executed prime minister Ṣadr al-Dīn Zanjānī, a post which he held together with a co-vizier Sa'd al-Dīn.

During the reign of Ghāzān Khān (674/1295–704/1304-5), Tabriz "attained its greatest splendour," being "the real centre of the empire which stretched from the Oxus to Egypt."[269]

> As a result of the downfall of the Abbasid Caliphate, Iran's commercial activities had found a new focus: it is true that Baghdad continued to be an economically important city, but in the 8th/14th century Tabriz, the seat of the Il-Khāns, had taken precedence over all other cities in Iran. The ravages of the Mongol invasion, which had set other cities far back from their former stage of development, had long since been repaired in Tabriz.[270]

The city continued to be the capital of Persia under Ghāzān's reign, when, in fact, it experienced remarkable architectual growth. We should note, however, that the capital of the Īl-Khān's kingdom was essentially itinerant in nature; it was a "peripatetic monarchy" as Charles Melville called it,[271] which was on the road most of the year, migrating between summer and winter quarters—not a palace-centered monarchy, but a nomadic kingdom of which the *ordu* was its wandering capital. Vladmir Minorsky's article on Tabriz in the *Encyclopedia of Islam* illuminates the unique position of the city during this period.

> In 699 [1299] on his return from the Syrian campaign, Ghāzān began a whole series of buildings. He intended Shām [a village west of Tabriz] as the site of his eternal rest. A building was erected there higher than the *gunbad* of the Sultan Sanjar at Marw, which was then considered the highest building in the Muslim world. Beside this mausoleum, which was crowned by a dome, there was a mosque, two madrasas (one Shāfi'ī

> and the other Ḥanafī), a hostel for Saiyids *(dār al-siyādat),* a hospital, an observatory like that at Marāgha, a library, archives, a building for the affairs of these establishments . . .
>
> In the town of Tabriz great improvements were also made. Ghāzān gave it a new wall of 25,000 gām ("paces") in length (4 &1/2 farsakhs). All the gardens and the Kūh-i Waliyān and the Sandjarān quarters were incorporated in the town. Within the wall on the slopes of the Kūh-i Waliyān (now Kūh-i surkhāb or 'Ainali-Zainalī) a series of fine buildings was erected by the famous vizier Rashīd al-Dīn and the quarter was therefore known as the Rab'-i Rashīdī . . . As if to emphasize the fact that Tabriz was the real centre of the empire which stretched from the Oxus to Egypt, the gold and silver coins and the measures were standardized according to the standards of Tabriz.[272]

However, upon the head of Ghāzān's new found faith there soon sprouted the inevitable horns of religious extremism and fanaticism, common to many new converts to alien faiths. On 4 October 1295, he delivered his first religious edict following his conversion to Islam: to destroy all the pagodas, churches, synagogues, and fire temples. Howorth describes these events as follows:

> The idols were broken and tied to pieces of wood, and promenaded through the streets of Tebriz. Nuruz had already, before this, when pursuing Baidu, given orders to destroy these buildings, to kill the buddhist priests, to treat the clergy with contumely (sic.), and to insist on their paying taxes like other people. Christians were not to appear in public without having a zonar, or peculiar girdle, about their waist, nor Jews unless they wore a special head-dress. The people of Tebriz detroyed all the churches in that town, and it is impossible to enumerate the indignities the Christians had to endure, especially in Baghdad, where none of them dared appear in the streets. The women used, in consequence, to do all the buying and selling, as they could not be distinguished from the Muhammedan women, but if they were recognised they were insulted and beaten. . . . The same persecution extended to the Jews and to idolatrous priests, and it was particularly hard for the latter, who had been so tenderly treated by the Mongol sovereigns,

> who used to spend immense sums in making gold and silver idols. Many of these priests now became, at least outwardly, Mussulmans, though secretly favouring the old faith.[273]

In the following year this same edict (which was apparently prompted or given by Amīr Nawrūz, not by Ghāzān himself[274]) was revoked, Ghāzān placing the blame for the destruction of the churches on Nawrūz's lack of foresight. As J.A. Boyle has observed, this decree to destroy all the churches and pagodas in Tabriz was primarily

> due to the fanaticism of men like Nawrūz who had brought Ghāzān to power and whose policies, for a time at least, he was obliged to follow. Once established on the throne he reverted, as far as was consistent with his Muḥammadanism, to the religious tolerance of his predecessors, and we are told by Rashīd al-Dīn that when two years later, on 21 July 1298, the Tabriz mob proceeded to wreck such churches as were left still standing, the Īl-khān was angry and saw to it that the ringleaders were punished.[275]

Nonetheless, Ghāzān's reign was not greatly marked by Islamic radicalism, and if indeed, unlike his predecessors, Ghāzān did not permit the construction of churches, Buddhist temples or fire-altars nor the open practice of non-Islamic faiths, neither did he prevent the members of other religions from inhabiting the country, presenting them rather with the alternative of departing abroad or practising in private.[276] "Once upon the throne, Ghāzān decreed that all Mongols and Uighurs must adopt Islam, and all the Mongols in Iran became, officially, Muslim."[277] Although he no longer accorded the Christians the privileges and rights they had enjoyed under Abāqā and Arghūn, they were allowed to exist as legal religious minorities in Persia.[278] As a new convert to Islam and one who was also thoroughly versed in Mongol wisdom-lore and Buddhist tradition, Ghāzān (given the conservative Islamic values of his Muslim subjects), in fact, exhibited extreme religious tolerance, and as Marshall Hodgson puts it, he not only "patronized Islamic learning, but also retained the old breadth of vision."[279]

It is significant that between Shabistarī's views on the spiritual meaning of polytheism (expressed in the *Garden of Mystery*, composed in 1317, some twelve years after the death of Ghāzān) and Ghāzān's own outlook on idolatry are to be found many similarities. The following passage exemplifies the ruler's views as recorded by his apologist, Rashīd al-Dīn:

> There are sins which God never forgives. The greatest of these is the worship of idols. I have been gulity of this myself through ignorance, but God has enlightened me. *Those who first made an idol only wished to commemorate the memory of some man more perfect than the rest.* Full of confidence in his merits, they accepted him as their intercessor, and supplicated him to secure their prayers being answered, forgetting that this man when alive had never asked for such deference, nor would he in fact have permitted that anyone should prostrate himself at his feet. Living in humility, he would have thrust down into the nether regions those flatterers who give birth to pride in the heart. They address their prayers to him, but how can he tolerate men who adore the image of his body? It will not hear them. *The body is nothing without the soul which animates it; one is the image of hell, the other of paradise. An idol is only fit to be used as a threshold upon which travellers may tread.* The soul will be delighted to see the image of the body in that position of humility by which it attained its perfection when they were united. Men would thereupon say, 'Since the body belonging to a soul so perfect is reduced to dust, and its very image to a doorstep, what should our body be to us, who are so far from perfection?' Such reflection will cause them to neglect their perishable bodies. They will think only of the soul—of life eternal, and where the blessed dwell. It is thus they may improve the present life, for man was only made to pass from this land of shadows to the land of light.[280]

In the following lines from the *Garden of Mystery* Shabistarī expresses in a slightly more radical fashion (given the poet's theomonist Akbarian views) the same conception of idol as icon, which, if beheld properly, may become, in Ghāzān's words, "a threshold upon which travellers may tread."

> If Muslims knew what idols were, they'd cry
> that faith itself is in idolatry.
> And if polytheists could just become aware

of what the idols are, they'd have no cause to err
in their beliefs. The graven image they
have seen is but external handiwork and form,
and so by Holy Writ their name is 'infidel'.
No one will call you 'Muslim' thus, by the word of Law
if you cannot perceive the Truth concealed therein,
see the God within an idol hid.[281]

In chapter four further comments will be made on Rashīd al-Dīn's patronage of the Sufis and indeed, Ghāzān Khān's own endowments of Sufi *Khānaqāhs* in mediæval Persia. Here, I should only point out that the relationship between Ghāzān and organized Sufism was from the inception quite intimate. In common with the Mongol Khān of the Golden Horde, Berke (reg. 1257-67), who had embraced Islam under the guiding influence and presence of the Kubrāwī Shaykh Sayf al-Dīn Bākharzī (586/1190–659/1261) in his *Khānaqāh* in Fatḥ-Ābād in Bukhārā,[282] the conversion of Ghāzān to Islam in 1295 was presided over by another Kubrāwī Shaykh, Ṣadr al-Dīn Ibrāhīm Ḥamūya. A recent study of the conversion ceremony demonstrates that Ghāzān not only embraced Islam but was also initiated into Sufism on this occasion, demonstrating the "clear preference among the Mongols for Sufism rather than the more formal orthodox *madhhabs*, due in part to various areas of similarity between Shamanist and Sufi rituals and ideas."[283] Another particular incident in Ghāzān's biography underlines his predilection for Sufism. In 1303 he put himself through the discipline of the Sufis' 'Forty-day Retreat' *(chilla)* under the supervision of a Sufi master *(pīr),* "during which he took little food, gave himself up to meditation, and was waited upon by the dervishes."[284] In the *Ḥabīb al-siyar,* Khwānd-amīr relates that when Ghāzān Khān decided to construct a town-complex which was to surround his mausoleum in the village of Shanb-Ghāzān outside of Tabriz, he ordered that "during matins and vespers in the Khānaqāh there the poor folk and beggars should be given soup on a daily basis and twice a month the Sufis and the singers should hold a public singing session and concert *(khwānandagī wa samā' kunand),* and on those days, food and sweetmeats should be prepared for them."[285]

As a ruler, however, Ghāzān Khān was stern and unforgiving, executing some five Mongol princes during the first five months of his reign, which as Browne remarks, "was marked by a terrible toll of executions . . . there is hardly a page of Rashīd al-Dīn at this time without a notice of the execution of some public functionary."[286] Thus, one reads how Ghāzān put to death his former regent and subsequent rival Amīr Nawrūz, husband of his paternal aunt and the man who had first agitated for his conversion to Islam,[287] executed Jamāl al-Dīn Dastajirdānī, Baydū's former premier on 27 October 1296, and condemned his *Ṣāḥib-i Dīwān,* Ṣadr al-Dīn Zanjānī to death on 30 April, 1298.[288]

Ghāzān was initially successful in his Syrian campaigns, his armies conquering Damascus on 26 December 1299 where, the following January, the *khuṭba* was read in his name. However, in 1303 his armies suffered defeat at the hands of the Mamlūk Sultan of Egypt. On 11 May 1304 the "greatest of the Īl-Khāns, a remarkably gifted man by the standards of any age of history," died and was laid to rest in his self-designed mausoleum, the Gunbad-i A'lā in Tabriz.[289]

Ghāzān's brother Khudā-banda Ūljāytū, another converted Muslim, succeeded him. The transition to power was quite smooth. He immediately confirmed in their posts the previous joint Chancellors of the Exchequer Sa'd al-Dīn Sāvajī and Rashīd al-Dīn.[290] He also confirmed his adherence to Islamic Law and all the recent Mongol *Yāsā*s which his brother Ghāzān had laid down.[291] During Ūljāyjū's reign Rashīd al-Dīn established a mini-city in the suburb of Tabriz known as the Rab'-i Rashīdiyya.[292] Describing the virtues of Rashīd al-Dīn and his son Ghiyāth al-Dīn, the Sufi chronicler Ibn Karbalā'ī commented:

> These two high-ranking notables were both endowed with virtuous qualities such as equity, justice, compassion, generosity, and always directed their will towards improving the welfare of religion and state and proper maintainence of all national and govermental affairs of which they were in charge. The sayyids, theologians *('ulamā'),* and Shaykhs were all revived and gained new life through the beneficience and boons of these two lords, towards whom they were continually beholden and thankful. The savants *(fuḍalā)* during the reign of these two notable ministers found themselves rescued from the tenebrity of material need and their thirst quenched at the wellspring of leisure and security.[293]

Under Ūljāytū, the Mongols suffered defeat at the hands of the Mamlūks in Syria in late 1313 in a battle which was to be last conflict between the two dynasties.[294] In 1312, Ūljāytū had Sa'd al-Dīn Sāvajī executed,[295] and replaced him with Tāj al-Dīn 'Alī-Shāh as co-Chancellor of the Exchequer with Rashīd al-Dīn (the rivalry between these two viziers under Abū Sa'īd ultimately resulted in the latter's demise). Even if he did not lose any previously conquered territory during his military campaigns, Ūljāytū was generally more successful in holding Iranian territory in northern Iran than in the West. He conducted an inconclusive campaign in the Caspian province of Gīlān in 1307, and in the following year, one of his generals conquered the city of Herat (in modern-day Afghanistan).[296]

Ūljāytū had been baptised a Christian and then had converted to Buddhism. Finally, he adopted Sunni Islam at the same time as his brother Ghāzān.[297] However, soon becoming disgusted with the incessant rivalry between the the Ḥanafī and Shāfi'ī schools during his reign, Ūljāytū converted to Shi'ism in 1307-8. In the same year he ordered that all the "musicians and prostitutes" throughout the land publically repent of their ways. "All women were forbidden to leave their homes," declares Vaṣṣāf, "not even to attend religious preaching assemblies." He also closed down all the taverns and wineshops, "cutting off the revenue and contributions which had been alloted to them out of the state funds."[298] These measures, however, did not extend to the Mongol court itself, in which music, the free mixing of the sexes, and dancing girls were the order of the day.[299]

Many of the Persian historians, such as Ḥamdu'llāh Mustawfī (who considered his reign the zenith of Mongol rule[300]) and Vaṣṣāf (who composed a long *qāṣīda* in his honour on the occasion of the founding of the observatory in Sulṭāniyya in 710/1311[301]), "refer to his clemency and justice and to the good order of the kingdom, which were the main criteria for judging such things."[302] When Ūljāytū died in 1316 his son Abū Sa'īd, who had previously been designated as his heir—although he was only 12 at the time—succeeded him.

Crowned in his thirteenth year in 1317, the young prince initially maintained in their positions the various tutors who had previously run state affairs for him.[303] However, court intrigues soon ruptured the relations between the various ministers, as a result of which the great Īl-khānid historian, Rashīd al-Dīn Faḍlu'llāh fell from grace, and succumbing to internal rivalries, was executed on 17 July 1318 at age 73. "His property was confiscated, his relatives were persecuted and despoiled, his pious foundations were robbed of their endowments, and the Rab'-i Rashīdī, the suburb which he had founded, was given over to rapine."[304] Howorth provides a more detailed description of his death, based on Quatremère's introduction to his *Histoire des Mongols de la Perse:*

> The quarter of Tebriz built by Rashid, named Raba Rashidi, including his house, was given up to pillage, and his family were seized as slaves by the first comers. All his lands and goods, and those of his sons, were confiscated, even those he had devoted to pious uses. His head was taken to Tebriz, and carried about the town for several days amidst cries of "This is the head of the Jew who has dishonoured the word of God; may God's curse be upon him." One account says that he was dismembered, and that his limbs were exposed in various places, while his body was burnt; but it would seems that he was buried at Tebriz, near the mosque which he had built there.[305]

During this period both Rashīd al-Dīn and his son Ghiyāth al-Dīn (Grand Vizier of Sultan Abū Sa'īd from 727/1327 to 15 Ramaḍān 736/29 April 1336, when he too, encountered the same fate as his father)[306] were great patrons of the Tabrizi Sufis, who in turn, lent them the expected legitimatizing respect. Ibn Bazzāz in the *Ṣafwat al-ṣafā,* a hagiographical account of Ṣafī al-Dīn Isḥaq Ardabīlī (d. 735/1334-5), claims that Vizier Ghiyāth al-Dīn was initiated into Sufism by Shaykh Ṣafī al-Dīn Ardabīlī, and furthermore that "he had complete faith and steadfastfastness in the *ṭarīqa* as long as the Shaykh remained in the world."[307] He also cites Ghiyāth al-Dīn's own claim to have "known the science of Sufism very well."[308] Awḥādi Marāghī (b. ca. 673/1274-5–d. 738/1337-8), a major Persian Sufi poet contemporary with Shabistarī, wrote numerous poems in praise of Sultan Abū Sa'īd and his vizier Ghiyāth al-Dīn Faḍu'llāh. Awḥādi composed his 4571 couplet-long poetic masterpiece *The Cup of Jamshid (Jām-i jam)* in Tabriz[309] between Ramaḍān 732/June 1332 and Ramaḍān 733/May-June 1333 and dedicated it to Rashīd al-Dīn Faḍu'llāh's son, Ghiyāth al-Dīn. The poet gilds the vizier's character in pious Sufi imagery and in the introductory section of his *Jām-i jam* depicts the Sufi virtues of this prime minister:

> From end to end all your works
> are charismata wrought by the saints.

Your essence is a mystic wayfarer
traversing Stations of the Path.[310]

Given Ghiyāth al-Dīn's own claim to have known the science of Sufism very well and his close relations to the Tabrīzī Sufis mentioned above, I doubt that this is purely and simply the typical hyperbole found among many poets of the age. Rather such verses seem reflective to a large degree of the minister's true mystic persona and descriptive of his actual piety, not merely a convenient personification of princely benevolence suitable to the needs of Awḥādī's personal *mamdūḥ*.

Ibn Karbalā'ī evokes the relationship between the Persian Sufis and Vizier Ghiyāth al-Dīn with great pride, stating that "the venerable lord was always the object of the alchemically transformative attentions of Shaykh 'Alā' al-Dawla Simnānī, Shaykh Ṣafī al-Dīn Isḥaq Ardabīlī, Shaykh 'Abd al-Razzāq Kāshī and Shaykh Ṣadr al-Dīn Ibrahīm Ḥamūya and other of the scholars and masters"[311] One of the main edifices in the Rab'-i Rashīdī was a *khānaqāh* annexed to a large congregational mosque. Thus, in the *Ṣafwat al-ṣafā* the frequent visits of this Sufi master "to the *Khānaqāh-i Rashīdiyya,*" where it is recorded that "the Shaykh—may God sanctify his spirit—stayed at the invitation of the Vizier Ghiyāth al-Dīn,"[312] feature as constant *mirabiles dicta* throughout Ibn Bazzāz's narration of his beloved Shaykh's tale.

The architectual achievements of the Rab'-i Rashīdī were made into particular objects of celebration by Awḥādī in his *Cup of Jamshid.* In particular, its *khānaqāh* and *madrasa* are described in grandiloquent terms, where the "innovative creators of 'Be! and it is!' have transported its four corners beyond the six spatial directions;" for its "ground is made of musk, and its stone of marble; its breeze a scent from Paradise and its waters from Kawthār."[313] This suburb, he states, bestows "the golden light of divine Fortune upon Tabriz." He concludes his eulogy with a strange hyperbole whose cosmological imagery glorifies the culinary delights within the Rab'-i Rashīdī:

To attest the largesse of your mealcloth
and to cover the spread of its baskets of bread
The heavens are filled with stars,
while all the millers stand before the waters of
Bilānkūh.[314]

In the introduction to the *Jām-i jam,* Awḥadī also wrote an eulogy of forty-six couplets (10419-65) on the Mongol Sultan Abū Sa'īd and another one hundred and ninety-five couplets (10465-10660) in praise of his vizier Ghiyāth al-Dīn. In lines which glorify the spiritual disposition of Sultan Abū Sa'īd, Awḥadī's muse again waxes hyperbolic:

Such a Shāh who seeks felicity in spirit
and purity of flesh; his art is that of a Sufi
his words bespeak true profundity!
Such a Shāh whose nights in prayer
and vigils pass to seek serenity
and peace, who makes retreats with purity!
Such a Shāh whose words are few and temper pure,
Silence, insomniac invigilance,
solitude from society, and stoic frugality!
These, his virtues, are the groundwork of his sainthood, victory.
Whoever has such qualities, God-given from eternity,
by these miracles, becomes the Prince of Saints.

... Why recall the tales of Junayd and his city?
Behold before you both Junayd and Baghdad!
His *ṭarīqat* is enough as a guide to the Faith;
His *ḥaqīqat* is enough as a revealer of the Truth.
If you ask of me the state of this king:
Here reclines Gabriel on a throne.[315]

The sincerity of Awḥadī's sentiments—the entirely non-panegyric dimension of his compliments—becomes more evident when we consider the fact that Awḥadī himself was not a panegryic poet either by profession or habit. In fact, he strongly condemns panegyrical poetry in the *Jām-i jam,*[316] the dominant theme of which is "the etiquette of the Sufi Path" *(ādāb-i ṭarīq),"*—that is to say, Sufism—as Dawlatshāh observes,[317] (rather than simply ethics as Zarrīnkūb suggests). Furthermore, Awḥadī strongly condemns Sufi Shaykhs who associate with princes:

What business does the saint *(walī)* have with the governor *(wālī)?*
Does the falcon ever make mosquito prey?

Look at the Shaykh who takes the Amir as patron:
and strike with your fist his puffy dough.
The dervish sabre is the sword of the Lord,
whereas the sultan's scimitar strikes by force of the police.
. . . Whoever has God's grace as his power of will
makes the king's knowledge his patron.[318]

Among the rulers in Persia during these decades Awḥadī only mentions Ghāzān Khān and Abū Sa'īd.[319] Whereas of the former he has nothing positive to say in his *Dīwān,* the spirituality—authentic, should we assume?—of Abū Sa'īd, as we have seen, evokes his praise.

It would also appear that Abū Sa'īd's vizier Ghiyāth al-Dīn had his own personal *khānaqāh* in Tabrīz, where he was an active participant in *Samā'* ceremonies.[320] This *khānaqāh,* according to Ibn Bazzāz, belonged to his wife, who was a great-granddaughter of Shaykh Shihāb al-Dīn 'Umar Suhrawardī (d. 632/1234).[321] An eminent modern Iranian historian has observed that the Vizier Ghiyāth al-Dīn had indeed "inherited the wisdom, learning and vision of his father and was a true patron of Sufism and its *ṭarīqat* institutions. He lavished much attention on those who lived in the *khānaqāhs*, and seconded his father in his participation in Sufi ceremonies and devotion to the masters of the Sufi Path."[322] Ḥamdu'llāh Qazwīnī also speaks highly of Ghiyāth al-Dīn as a "minister of angelic temperment" in his *Ta'rīkh-i Guzīda* which is dedicated to him.[323] As Awḥadī's verses cited above demonstrate, Sultan Abū Sa'īd was also a great patron of Sufism (as well as a poet himself passionately devoted to *belles lettres).* His veneration for 'Alā' al-Dawla Simnānī and entreaty for spiritual guidance from Shaykh Ṣafī al-Dīn Ardabīlī, mentioned in the *Ṣafwat al-Ṣafā,*[324] all highlight his deep devotion to the *ṭarīqat* and personal commitment to the doctrines of Sufism.[325]

Abū Sa'īd was known for his strict Sunni sympathies, although, according to some sources, he often maintained a tolerant attitude towards Christianity. This may have been merely for economic motives, "as when in his commercial treaty with Venice in 1320 he granted permission for *frari Latini* to build oratories in the cities of his empire."[326] However, due to conflicting accounts in diverse sources, his religious attitude is difficult to evaluate. According to Vaṣṣāf, in the same year in which the treaty with Venice was concluded, at the instigation of the *fuqahā',* who were supported by the all-powerful Amīr Chūpān, all the wine and wine-jugs in Tabrīz, Sulṭāniyya and Mosul were deliberately destroyed. Abū Sa'īd also commanded that all brothels and taverns be destroyed and that the churches in and around Tabrīz be destroyed and mosques constructed.[327]

Abū Sa'īd was soon obliged to fight two wars on the northern border of the Īl-Khānid empire, in Māzandarān and Darband. Thanks mainly to the help of Amīr Chubān, Ūljāytū's former commander-in-chief, they were successful in defending the Empire's boundaries in both battles. In 1324, following the death of his vizier 'Alī-Shāh, Abū Sa'īd appointed a protégé of Amīr Chubān named Rukn al-Dīn Ṣā'in to the vizierate.[328] Shortly thereafter Amīr Chubān fell from the Īl-Khān's graces, and Abū Sa'īd decided to eradicate his former commander-in-chief with his entire family.[329] Even the intercession of the venerable 'Alā' al-Dawla Simnānī was to no avail, and Amīr Chubān was eventually executed treacherously by the ruler of Herat in 1327.[330] In 1328 the vizierate was confided to Rashīd al-Dīn's son Ghiyāth al-Dīn. With Abū Sa'īd's death in 1335 "the House of Hülegü had virtually become extinct."[331]

So much, then, for the general characteristics of the political climate in which Shabistarī's *oeuvre* was composed, from the invasion of Khurāsān in 1254 by Hülegü Khān until Abū Sa'īd's death in 1335 and the poet's death in the late 1330's. We now turn to the role of the city of Tabriz during this period, to give us a taste of the urban setting outside the *Garden of Mystery,* before commenting on the influence of Mongol religious policies on Shabistarī's theosophy.

## Tabriz: the Urban Setting

It was noted above that during the reign of Ghāzān Khān (674/1295 – 704/1304-5), Tabriz had attained its greatest splendour—being the real centre of the empire which stretched from the Oxus to Egypt. In fact, by the early fourteenth century, shortly before Mīr Ḥusaynī Harawī's courier relayed his questions to Ādharbāyjān to be answered by Shabistarī in Tabriz, the city "had taken the place of Baghdad as the principal commercial centre in Western Asia."[332]

The city held this position for nearly fifty years, from the reign of Abāqā (664/1265–680/1281) until the death of Ūljāytū 'Khudābanda' (reg. 704/1304-5–716/1316), continuing to maintain it in many respects well down to Timurid times—as the great chronicle of Ibn Karbālā'ī (composed in 883/1478) attests. It was, in a way, both the literary, the cultural and the mystical capital of Persia.[333] In his study of Shabistarī, Zarrīnkūb underlines the importance of the influence of the social climate of Tabriz on the poet's works:

> At the birth of Shabistarī . . . Tabriz to all intents and purposes numbered as one of the main centres of Persian literary culture and mysticism. Like Marāgha and Sulṭāniyya, Tabriz was a monument to the rising power of the Mongols in that period. Of special interest is that the Mongol ascendancy created a kind of intellectual anarchy. There was an intense rivalry in the Īlkhānid court among the Islamic, Christian and Buddhist faiths, until finally, in 696 [/1297], when Shabistarī was but an infant, Ghāzān Khān was converted to Islam and in this manner quelled the dispute. The existence of 'Bābās' and Sufi *pīrs* during this era and the preceding epoch created an especially fervent and passionate ambience in Tabriz as well.[334]

Aside from the city's cultural and political significance, one also encounters a certain 'sacred vision' of fourteenth-century Tabriz as a mystical centre. This vision can be observed for instance, in the *Dīwān* of Kamāl Khujandī (d. 803/1400), who describes the metropolis as a kind of paradise on earth (recalling William Blake's visions of early 19th century London as a 'Heavenly Jerusalem') in the following verses:

> Go seek paradise, oh pietist!
> Kamāl prefers Tabriz
> and its Mount of Saints.[335]
>
> * * *
>
> From the kingdom of heaven
> in God's glory and excellence
> to the town of Tabriz
> is but half a league.[336]

Of course, Kamāl's preference for Tabriz's 'Mount of Saints' was not so much for the secular city as for its celestial counterpart, forever reflected on earth by "the power of the holy dead," depicted through that sacred "grid of shrines" of Sufi saints scattered throughout bricks and stones of the temporal polis. Their tombs "clearly indicated *loci* where Heaven and Earth met." Considered in this light, the 'holy' city of Tabriz was the *"locus sanctorum*, . . . a place where the normal laws of the grave were held to be suspended."[337]

As Michel Chodkiewicz has revealed, the nature and locus of one's terrestial abode was of the highest importance among the Sufis, and insofar as "L'espace terrestre n'est pas neutre: le passage d'un saint ou son séjour posthume y déterminent en quelque sorte un champ de forces bénéfiques,"[338] Particular cities, caves, rooms in mosques, etc., thus took on special significance. Kamāl Khujandī, like Ibn Karbalā'ī a century later, could thus adore Tabriz for its supernatural sanctity as much as for its mundane beauty. For the other Sufis resident there, as a cursory reading of the *Rawḍāt al-jinān* demonstrates, the graveyards of Tabriz, such as Valīyānkūh, Surkhāb and Charandāb, can well be described (as were the cities of Christian tombs in Europe during this period) as "privileged places, where the contrasted poles of Heaven and Earth met." These tombs were "centers of the ecclesiastical life of their region. This was because the saint in Heaven was believed to be 'present' at his tomb on earth."[339]

The physical beauty of the city was also often celebrated by poets contemporary with Shabistarī. Khwājū Kirmānī (679/1281 – 742/1342), one of the most important Persian Sufi poets of this period, as well as a renowned panegyrist of the Īlkhānid Sultans, whose style of speech Ḥāfiẓ in his ghazals professed to imitate, in the following verse written in memory of the patronage of the Vizier Ghiyāth al-Dīn (d. 1324) during his stay in Tabriz, celebrated the "land of Tabriz":

> In Baghdad beside the Tigris, O Khwājū,
> *there* lies paradise, but pleasanter still
> I tell you, is the land of Tabriz.[340]

Indeed, the vast hospitals, caravanserais, baths and madrasas constructed by Rashīd al-Dīn Faḍlu'llāh, the famous vizier of Ghāzān and Ūljātjū, historian statesman and patron of scholars and Sufis, excelled anything of its kind in mediæval Europe at this time.[341] The enduring glory of Tabriz—architecturally, economically and socio-culturally—is also apparent from many international travellers' descriptions of the city. Marco Polo, who visited Tabriz in the early 1270's, thus observes how "the city is so favorably situated that it is a market for merchandise from India and Baghdad, from Mosul and Hormuz . . . ; and many Latin merchants come here to buy merchandise imported from foreign lands. It is also a market for precious stones . . . [and] a city where good profits are made by travelling merchants."[342] The wide-ranging Moorish voyager Ibn Baṭṭūṭā (d. 780/1378) visited Tabriz in 1326 in the retinue of Sultan Abū Sa'īd, and enthusiastically described the sites of the city:

> I entered the town and we came to great bazaar, one of the finest bazaars I have seen the world over. Every trade is grouped separately in it. I passed through the jewellers' bazaar, and my eyes were dazzled by the varieties of precious stones that I beheld. They were displayed by beautiful slaves wearing rich garments with a waist-sash of silk, who stood in front of the merchants, exhibiting the jewels to the wives of the Turks, while the women were buying them in large quantities and trying to outdo one another. As a result of all of this I witnessed a riot—may God preserve us from such! We went on into the ambergris and musk market, and witnessed another riot like it or worse."[343]

A century later, in June 1404, Clavijo, the Spanish ambassador to Persia, special emissary of King Henry VII of Castille, arrived in Tabriz and was equally enthusiastic about its grandeur:

> On Wednesday the 11th of June at the hour of vespers we entered the great city of Tabriz, which lies in a plain between two high ranges of hills that are quite bare of trees. . . . Throughout the city there are fine roadways with open spaces well laid out: and round these are seen many great buildings and houses, each with its main doorway facing the square. Such are the caravanserais: and within are constructed separate apartments and shops with offices that are planned for various uses. Leaving these caravanserais you pass into the market streets where goods of all kinds are sold: such are silk stuffs and cotton cloths, crapes, taffetas, raw silk and jewelry: for in these shops wares of every kind may be found. There is indeed an immense concourse of merchants and merchandise here. Thus for instance in certain of the caravanserais

> those who sell cosmetics and perfumes for women are established and to be met with, the women coming here to these shops to buy the same, for they are wont to use many perfumes and unguents.
>
> Now the dress the women wear in the streets is that they go covered in a white sheet, and they wear over their faces a black mask of horse-hair, and thus they are concealed completely so that none may know them. Throughout Tabriz many fine buildings may be seen, the Mosques more especially these being most beautifully adorned with tiles in blue and gold; and here they have glass bowls [for the lamps] even as we had seen in Turkish lands. . . . Tabriz is indeed a very mighty city rich in goods and abounding in wealth, for commerce daily flourishes here. They say that in former times its population was even greater than it is now, but even at the present day there must be 200,000 householders within the city limits, or perhaps even more.[344]

Although the same cultural dynamism and cosmopolitan atmosphere of this metropolis which one finds in the descriptions of world travellers cited above is not explicitly reflected anywhere in Shabistarī's works, the final section of the next chapter, which is devoted to the Sufi masters of Tabriz mentioned in the *Sa'ādat-nāma,* does reveal the influence of the intellectual ambience of this capital city on his mystical vision.

## Shabistarī and the Mongols' Legacy of Religious Tolerance

It is difficult to assess the effect of the Mongols on Persian society, particularly in the religious sphere. While in Iran proper, Buddhists and Christians often gained an upper hand in the Mongol administration, as, for instance, under Abāqā (for Christianity) and Arghūn (for Buddhism), the majority of the population clearly remained Muslim. Claude Cahen points out that all through this period "Asia Minor remained a Muslim country," and "that the reduction of Islam to the rank of one religion along with others, a situation which to some extent had characterized the early period of Mongol domination in Iran and Mesopotamia *(waqf*s in those countries being more or less integrated into the general economy and used for the benefit of the different creeds without distinction) occurred hardly at all under the protectorate of Asia

Minor."[345] He also stresses the total domination of Anatolian society by the Muslim majority during the entire Mongol reign.[346] The same is also partially true in the Eastern Iranian Mongol kingdom "under Infidel Government"—as David Morgan calls the pre-Ghāzān Īl-Khānid era (663/1265–694/1295)[347]—where Islam certainly remained the most dominant current in the religious life of Persia. Nonetheless, as Trimingham notes, the most immediate consequence of the Mongol conquest was displacement of Islam as the state religion throughout the region, and this meant that "Islam now had to prove itself and accommodate itself to non-Muslim rulers, Shamanist, Buddhist, or crypto-Christian."[348] This epoch, being "un inextricable mélange des religions," as Jean-Paul Roux represents it,[349] contained a new spiritual dynamic which was, to use Trimingham's simile: "pregnant with possibilities."[350] At the same time, the Mongols' peripheralization of Islam had serious consequences.

> One important aspect of the Mongol conquest is that for the first time Persia and other large areas of the Muslim world found themselves governed, at least from 1221 to 1295, that is to say for three generations, by non-Muslim rulers, pagan shamanists or Buddhists who ignored differences of religious belief among their subjects, who used Christian auxiliaries, and who employed Jewish ministers alongside administrators from the Far East. This humiliation for the Muslim world is paralleled only by the colonial system of government of modern times. However, it has been remarked by some scholars that, despite the terrible devastation that it brought with it, Mongol rule did provide certain virtues, such as the reunification of large areas, safety of travel, the establishment of new trade routes, etc.[351]

However, the most significant change which did occur during the Mongol period was *the establishment of Islam on a Sufi foundation.* The Mongol invasion in fact, indirectly prompted a great period of flowering of Sufism in Persia, as is demonstrated later by the phenomenal rise of the Kubrāwiyya, Nūrbakhshiyya, Naqshbandiyya and Ni'matu'llāhiyya Orders,[352] probably due to the economic advantages given to the *'ulamā'* and Sufi *fuqarā'* alike (exemptions from taxes, liberal endowments to their mosques and *khānaqāh*s, offers of *tarkhān* and grants of *soyūrghāl*s, etc.).[353] The predilection of Mongol princes like Ghāzān Khān for Sufism (commented upon above, p. 71), rather than for purely exoteric and legalistic religiosity, has been underlined by H. Landolt's monograph on the thirteenth-century Kubrāvī master Nūr al-Dīn Isfarāyinī.[354] The Sufi affiliations of the Mongol ruler Ūljāytū Khān (reg. 1304-1316) are evident by his reconstruction of the tomb of Bāyazīd Basṭāmī and his naming of three sons after this Sufi saint: Basṭām, Bāyazīd, and Ṭayfur.[355]

One may also see how deeply the Persian culture of the period was steeped in Sufi mysticism by recalling the tale related by Sayyid 'Alī Hamadānī about 'Alā' al-Dawla Simnānī presiding over a convocation of four hundred scholars assembled by Khudā-banda Ūljāytū.[356] Here and elsewhere in his biography, Simnānī appears in Īl-Khānid history as a scholar who 'held the King's ear', the Sufi master most heeded by the Mongol state. According to the *Ḥabīb al-siyar,* Ūljāytū's successor to the Mongol throne, Sultan Abu Sa'id, on visiting Simnānī, "after rising to pay his respects, sat the Shaykh beside him, and then knelt respectfully before him."[357] Although some scholars have commented on the Mongols' "indifference to the various divisions of Islam,"[358] it is fair to say that they did exhibit a marked preference for Sufistic Islam.[359]

*Religious tolerance,* most scholars concur, was also a—if not *the*—central feature of Persian piety under the Mongols.[360] The Mongols' amorphous Shamanistic faith was from the start far from exclusive; they were rather "known for their tolerance – even their indifference to – all religions."[361] As Michel M. Mazzaoui points out:

> The Mongol period was marked with tremendous religious controversies; but at the same time it was a period of co-existence of various Muslim religious views. This co-existence amounted almost to a freedom of religious beliefs and reciprocal toleration. . . . The Mongol *sulṭāns*, by and large, seem to have been playing the part of innocent bystanders . . . they showed interest in and appreciation of the lively controversies. But they remained essentially foreign to what was going on along the religious level.[362]

Insofar as the Mongols espoused a shamanistic brand of Buddhism and made it the creed of the ruling family in the lands they ruled (at least from 1221-1295), Muslims were forced to tolerate differences of religious belief, leading among other factors, to the rise in the popularity of Sufism, for which tolerance is second-nature.[363] There was also an openness to Christian evangelism of various denominations, demonstrated, among other things, by the presence of an estimated fourteen Franciscan convents in the Īl-Khānid Persian state.[364] Although in England, it was not until 1526 that the Bible was translated from Latin into English—and even then its translator, William Tyndale, was persecuted and burned at the stake as a heretic, and as late as 1600, only 30 of the 6,000 volumes in the Oxford University Library were in English—as early as the late thirteenth century, during the Īl-Khānid reign in Persia, the first Persian translation of the Gospels had already appeared. Indeed, after a succession of strictly 'Islamic' dynasties ruling the land, it was only during the Mongol rule that the political climate of Persia was favourable enough for the translation of such a text.[365]

In his study of "La Tolérance Religieuse dans les Empires Turco-Mongols,"[366] Jean-Paul Roux has demonstrated that there were five basic qualities which characterized the religious policy of all the Turkish and Mongol peoples, exemplifying their basically tolerant attitude towards divergent faiths:

i) The freedom to worship, offer religious instruction and apostleship;
ii) Emphasis on the mutual cohabitation of religions and belief in their equal value;
iii) a liking for the organization of religious colloquies;
iv) veneration of the religious leaders of all faiths and belief in the efficacy of their prayers on behalf of the ruling sovereign;
v) belief in the placeless, immanent ubiquity of God over reverence for particular places of worship.

Thus, it was tolerance, summarizes Roux, "qui demeure l'attitude la plus évidente et la plus constante dans les Empires turco-mongols."[367]

In Shabistarī's theosophy, the transcendental unity of all religions and the emphasis on the placeless ubiquity of the divine presence were also of fundamental importance—concepts which correspond to items one and five in Jean-Paul Roux's enumeration of the 'elements of tolerance' in Turco-Mongol religious policy. Although it is impossible to prove the existence of any direct historical 'influence' of Mongol religious policy upon Shabistarī's poetry, the many correspondences between the political milieu of tolerance towards non-Islamic faiths described above and the ambience of poetic freedom which permeates the *Garden of Mystery*, I believe, make the inference of such an influence entirely reasonable.

Both Awḥadī Marāghī, whose relationship to Sultan Abū Sa'īd was noted above, and Shabistarī shared a common interest in Christianity and Christian symbolism. The former's introduction of the name of Jesus into the *Jām-i Jam* more than any other Persian poet of the period,[368] and the latter's consecration of last two sections of the *Garden of Mystery* (vv. 927-1004) to esoteric ('Sufi') Christianity together represent one of the first serious excursions into comparative mysticism in the history of Persian poetry. In two sections of *Jām-i jam* (13621-38 & 14329), Awḥadī describes the meaning of 'Jesus' in the Sufi lexicon. In the first and longest section: an "Inquiry into the Meaning of the Heart and Soul According to the Religion of the Mystic Wayfarers," Awḥadī spends some seventeen lines expounding the meaning of the "Jesus of the Heart." In the second section he allegorizes the crucifixion with the image of "the ass of Jesus," which "lies in a trough of dust," while "his spirit, devoid of mount, flies toward heaven."

Shabistarī also shares this esoteric Christology, discussing the "Jesus of the Heart" who "becomes heavenly" in the beginning of the *Garden of Mystery*.[369] No doubt the use of Christian imagery and symbolism by both poets owed much to the large Christian presence and numerous churchs in Tabriz in the early thirteenth century, as Marco Polo in his visit to Tabriz in 1295, had noted.[370] Awḥadī's hometown Marāgha was also an important centre of Christianity in Persia under the Mongols. Arghūn had his son baptised there in 1289, and the celebrated Christian philosopher Mār Bar Hebraeus (d. 1286) had lectured on Greek philosophy in the "new monastary" there.[371] As noted above, for a period of nearly forty-five years – from 1250 to the accession of Ghāzān Khān in 1295 to the Īl-Khānid throne – the presence and influence of Christianity was greater than that of Islam in the Mongol courts, with Christians being given special benefits and privleges.[372] The political freedom accorded to Christianity and Buddhism during these years, undoubtedly was a factor in Shabistarī's tolerant outlook on non-Islamic faiths in the *Garden of Mystery*.

Below, I will summarize the poet's universalistic attitude which is found in his doctrine of the "theophanic unity of all religions based on the transcendental unity of religions" and the "cosmo-ontological source of religious diversity."[373] The doctrine of the theophanic unity of all religions is set out in the following verses from Shabistarī's *Garden of Mystery:*

> All infidelity has Faith inside;
> within each idol's heart a soul resides
> and every heresy has hymns and litanies
> and daily, infidelity recites the rosary—
> "Verily, all which is, does hymn his praise."
> So, where's your enmity?
> In what I say—have I digressed or missed the Way?
> Say "'God!'—and leave these fools in vanity and play."
> Who else but God could gild its face
> or give an idol such finesse and grace?
> Unless it be his will, who'd be an idol's votary?
> The Doer, Orator and Agent-actor too—
> all these were him. He acted not amiss, he spoke
> aright, and was in fact, both well and good.
> 'See One, say One, know One:' this axiom
> sums up the root and branches of *Imān.*
> The Koran's word attests to this, not I alone
> confess to it: "No fault exists," the Scripture says,
> "in the creation of the All-Beneficent."[374]

Lāhījī's commentary on some of these verses is as follows:

> If the Muslim who professes Divine Unity *(tawhīd)* and disavows the idol, were to become aware and conscious of what the idol is in reality, and of Whom it is a manifestation of, and of what Person it is who appears in the idol's form – he would certainly comprehend that the religion of the Truth *(Ḥaqq)* is in idolatry. Since the idol is a theophany *(maẓhar)* of the Absolute Being Who is God *(Ḥaqq),* in respect to its essential reality, the idol is God. Now, given that the religion of Muslims is Truth-worship *(Ḥaqq-parastī)* and [as has been explained above] idolatry and Truth-worship are one and the same, true religion lies in idolatry.
>
> . . . Likewise if the polytheists *(mushrik)* who adore idols were to become aware of the idol and its reality, and were to understand that the idol is actually a theophany of God, and

> that God manifests Himself through its form, so that he actually prostrates, adores and is devoted to the One Supreme Being – how then in his religion and faith could he have gone astray, and have fallen into error? . . . If you, who make claims to adhere to Islam and orthodoxy, perceive naught but the idol's visible form and do not envision God hidden behind the veils of the its determined form—and it is this particular form which is a corporeal receptacle for God's theophany—you properly and legally *(dar sharḥ)* also cannot be called a Muslim. In fact, you are an infidel *(kāfar)* because you have veiled God's theophany appearing in the idol.[375]

What should be underscored in the above verses and Lāhījī's commentary upon them is that, in Shabistarī's thought, the basic tenets of the Sufi science of comparative religion more or less parallel the Īl-Khānid rulers' advocation of religious equality of all faiths (cf. Roux's point 2 above). Of course, the intention of these doctrines is quite different. Whereas Shabistarī's doctrine aims to achieve a mystical realization of the theophany of God everywhere and in every form, the Mongol advocation of religious equality was based on the pragmatic principle which considered different religious communities as constituting distinct political 'cells', each of which needed to be nurtured in order to maintain the healthy organization of the body-politic of the realm.[376]

Shabistarī's recognition of symbolic value, and hence, religious truth within non-Islamic faiths is especially conspicuous in his treatment of Christianity. His understanding of the *communio sanctorum* of the Sufi notion of saintship *(walāya),* conceived of in the Akbarian tradition as "an all-inclusive and universal function that never comes to an end,"[377] dogs Ibn 'Arabī's belief in the authentic spirituality, which, the latter believed, could still be found in certain 'Christ-like saints'. This conception lead the Shaykh al-Akbar "to depict *walāya* in a way which is far more inclusive than the definitions which confine it within the framework of a sociological Islam."[378] Shabistarī's attitude towards Christianity clearly reflected this liberal Akbarian perspective.

In the *Garden of Mystery,* one encounters an ideal inscape and interiorized topography of what might be termed 'esoteric Christianity'. His hermeneutical description of Christianity *(tarsā'ī)* as symbolic of the state of detachment *(tajrīd)* both from the world and the hereafter as well as from any desire for compensation and reward, involving single-minded concentration in acts of devotion, was also, I believe, highly indebted to the climate of religious tolerance in early fourteenth-century Īl-Khānid Tabriz.

In this context, after presenting a Sufi gloss on the Christian faith with this verse:

> Non-attachment and detachment—
> Freedom from the fetters of imitation,
> are the pith and whole design
> I see in Christianity.

he goes on to combine Christian imagery (taken from both social institutions and dogmatic theology), Persian popular mythology (the "Simurgh"), Ptolemaic astronomy, and Sufi psychological theories into a uniquely interiorized view of the role of Jesus in the spiritual life:

> Within the inner court of sacred Unity
> lies the soul's monastery,
> perch of the Simurgh of subsistent Eternity,
> From the Spirit of Allah such labor sprang,
> brought forth by the Holy Spirit.
> A trace of sanctity lies manifest
> in the God-bestowed soul before you.
> If you acquit yourself of this passionbound
> soul of humanity, then step within
> the inner court of sacred Divinity.
> Whoever, like an angel, becomes detached,
> liberated from matter's trappings,
> ascends to the fourth heaven
> like the Spirit of God.[379]

In Islam, all prophets are, by the very nature of their Prophethood, saints as well, and thus, Jesus is regarded as a saint as well as a prophet. The famous passage in the Gospel of John (XVI: 16), where Jesus states "I go to the Father," is therefore taken by the Sufis to imply that the saints are spiritual children of God. Shabistarī ventures to give a Sufi gloss on this verse from St. John in the following passage in the *Garden of Mystery:*

First the suckling infant,
bound to a cradle, is sustained on milk.
Then, when mature, becomes a wayfarer,
and if a man, he travels with his father.

The elements of nature for you
resemble an earthborn mother.
You are a son whose father
is a patriarch from on high.

So Jesus proclaimed upon ascension:
"I go to my Father above."
You too, O favourite of your father,
Set forth for your Father!

Your fellow-travelers went on; you too pass on!
If you wish to be a bird in flight,
Leave the world's carcass to vultures.[380]

In another verse, he portrays the 'Christian monk' *(rāhib)* as the true Sufi who seeks the interior reality within various religions and overlooks illusory formal differences while regarding their unifying spirit.

Detach thyself, be *ḥanīfī*
And from all faiths' fetters free;
So come, like the monk, step up
into religion's abbey.[381]

As a follower of Ibn 'Arabī, Shabistarī was no doubt aware of the Shaykh al-Akbar's doctrine that living 'executors' *(awṣiyā)* of past prophets who are also numbered among the Sufi *awliyā'*[382] always exist (and that is one reason why the Prophet forbade the killing of monks *(ruhbān)*, ordering that they should be left alone to pursue their devotions).[383] In this fashion, while Western Europe was undergoing an orgy of religious intolerance during the heat of the Inquisition, the Sufis of Persia such as Shabistarī were portraying 'Christianity' as the symbolic model of their transcendent Islamic faith, and the 'Christian monk' as an exemplar of religious unity! Lāhījī's commentary on the above line is most illuminating and reveals the profundity of Shabistarī's attitude to religious freedom:

> Be detached and free and pure from contamination by the restrictions of religion, imitative devotion, customs and habit. Be like the true monk and "step up into religion's abbey," which means to come into mosques and other places of worship, girding yourself with the cincture of service, acting as the monk whose very vocation is detachment, being liberated and disengaged from all formal and spiritual interests or obstructions.
>
> Do not be inhibited by the fetters of 'infidelity' *(kufr)* and Islam, for whatever is in essence good, and is a cause of human perfection, is, of course, praiseworthy.
>
> Leave every religion and people to their own rites and observances, since to be bound by mere words and expressions generally employed in other religions—such as "Idol" *(but)*, "Cincture" *(zunnār )*, "Monestary" *(dayr)*, "Christian" and "Ḥanīfa"—is itself just another type of infidelity *(kufr)*. Endorsing such conceptual restrictions is contrary to the way and method of the Sufi gnostics.[384]

It is obvious that if we were to consider Lāhījī's above explanation of Shabistarī's verse as a manifesto of a socio-political doctrine, rather than as merely a tenet of Islamic comparative mysticism, it would constitute an excellent *apologia* for the Mongols' vision of a ubiquitous divine presence above and beyond the verbal definition (church, synagogue, mosque, etc.) attached to the material edifice which constitutes a certain place of worship (cf. Roux's point 5 above). As Roux has demonstrated, Mongol religious polity was founded on the perspective which saw that "l'espace spirituel l'emporte sur l'espace géographique."[385]

Shabistarī's tolerant outlook on other religions is most apparent in his doctrine of the 'Law of Contraries', which espouses the relativity of heresy and true faith and dictates the necessity for the existence of other faiths.[386] Faith is only sincere when performed in the spirit; the mere rite or form, the letter or the ritual act are themselves valueless. In fact, states Shabistarī, they constitute a type of secret idolatry insofar as "any type of devotion which is performed out of habit and by rote is merely food for passion. The only remedy [from hypocrisy] for a person of religious sensibility is to be found in the form of contraries *(ṣūrat-i aḍdād)*. That is to say, it is more virtuous for you to frequent a Christian cloister *(dayr)* than to attend a mosque while imagining yourself superior to others."[387] Such a doctrine, although obviously aimed at stimulating the moral purification of the soul, also has clear echoes of the Mongol's disdain of geographically-focused worship and temple-centred piety, perhaps best illustrated by Genghis Khān's view that "the universe is the temple of God," and, in Islamic terms, his celebrated mockery of the pilgrimmage to Mecca.[388]

* * *

Although the Mongol irruption should be primarily viewed as a negative phenomenon,[389] a disaster for Persian culture, nonetheless, their domination of Persia did have some positive aspects. First of all, the unification of Central Asia, Persia and China by the Mongols meant that for the first time in a thousand years China and Europe enjoyed direct contact.[390] In Turco-Persia the Mongols tended to patronize the construction of wondrously decorated mosques and imposing palaces; their 'military patronage state' "from the first acted in a spirit of monumental achievement: they destroyed in the grand manner, they built in the grand manner too."[391] Historiographically speaking, the Mongol period represents the most glorious period of history writing in Persian history. The immense bulk of works which were left (most of which were composed in Persian rather than Arabic), by authors enjoying a wide range of interests and liberality of views, is unequalled in any other epoch of Persian history.[392]

There was also "an intensification in the production of works of art;"[393] Persian miniature painting flourished in the ateliers of Shiraz, Baghdad, and Tabriz almost without any break of style,[394] while in Iraq and Ādharbāyjan under the patronage of the Jalā'irid Mongol princes (1336-1410) Persian miniature painting entered its formative period. In calligraphy, the *ta'liq* style which had been developed by the Tabrizi master Mīr 'Alī (d. 1420), in the fourteenth century was transformed into the *nasta'līq* script under later Timurid patronage in Herat,[395] while Persian Sufi poetry, in particular in the *mathnawī* and *ghazal* forms, realized its greatest perfection in the poetry of Sa'dī and Ḥāfiẓ.[396] Shabistarī's *Garden of Mystery,* insofar as it encased the entire Persian mystico-philosophical tradition in a little over a thousand couplets, was, of course, a major stepping stone in this literary process in general, and in the evolution of post-Ibn 'Arabī Sufi poetry in particular, the intensely metaphysical bent of his poetry preparing the way for the development of the 'gnostic lyric' *(ghazal-i 'ārifāna),* the genre of poetry most utilized by post-Mongol and Timurid period Sufi poets.

## Notes

187 Translation by T.C. Young, "The National and International Relations of Iran," in T.C. Young (ed.), *Near Eastern Culture and Society* (Princeton: Princeton University Press 1951), p. 204.

188 The conclusions reached in the following study are based on a careful analysis of findings in recent secondary sources and studies on the Īl-Khānid period, as well as some reference to the Persian primary historical sources. The period covered below embraces the years 1257-1335 (roughly following the chronology of the poet's lifetime). I would like to acknowledge my gratitude to Dr. Charles Melville for his patient reading and critique of several earlier drafts of this chapter.

189 *A Literary History of Persia,* III, p. 4.

190 See I. P. Petrushevsky's description of "The Consequences of the Mongol Invasion," in his chapter on "The Socio-Economic Conditions of Iran under the Īl-Khāns" in *The Cambridge History of Iran,* V, (Cambridge University Press, 1968), pp. 484-88, where he discusses the Mongol massacres in Ṭabaristān (Māzandarān) and Khurāsān in great detail.

191 *Ibid.,* p. 486.

192 *Ibid.,* p. 484.

193 See A. Bausani, *The Persians: from the earliest days to the twentieth century,* trans. J. Donne (London 1971), p. 116. Similar observations are made by Qāsim Ghanī, *Baḥth dar āthār va afkār va aḥwāl-i Ḥāfiẓ: Tā'rīkh-i taṣawwuf dar islām az ṣadr-i islām tā 'aṣr-i Ḥāfiẓ* [Tehran, 1997, 3rd. ed.], II, pp. 497-99.

194 See Anjawī Shirāzī (ed.), *Diwān-i Shams al-Dīn Muḥammad Ḥāfiẓ* (Shiraz 1982), introduction, p. 85ff.

195 Bausani, *The Persians,* p. 115.

196 Cf. Manūchihr Murtaḍawī, *Masā'il-i 'aṣr-i Īlkhānān,* (Tehran: Intishārāt-i āgāh 1370 A.Hsh./1991), pp. 311-50.

197 A.J. Arberry, *Aspects of Islamic Civilization* (Ann Arbor: University of Michigan Press 1967), p. 16.

198 *Farhang-i ash'ār-i Ḥāfiẓ,* pp. 454-55.

199 According to Simon Digby ("The Sufi Shaykh and the Sultan: A Conflict of Claims to Authority in Medieval India" in *Iran: Journal of the British Institute of Persian Studies,* XXVIII [1990], pp. 71, 75) "The territorial *wilāyat* of the Sufi shaykh was considered as having a direct influence on the political events and material destiny of the realm over which it was exercised. ... The corollary of the belief that an offence against a Sufi shaykh will lead to the downfall of a ruler, is the belief that such shaykhs also have had the power to bestow kingship upon individuals whom they encountered, or to foresee the attainment of a throne by such men."

200 Cited by H. Landolt, *Nūruddīn Isfarāyinī,* French introduction, p. 34.

201 H. Algar (trans.), *The Path of God's Bondsmen,* pp. 382-3. Italics mine.

202 *Iranian Nationality and the Persian Language*, pp. 77-79.

203 As David Morgan notes, *(Medieval Persia,* [London: Longman, 1988],

p. 66): "The basic function of the Mongols' Persian ministers was a straightforward one: the extraction of as much revenue from the Persian taxpayers, for the benefit of the Mongol ruling classes. . . . The acceptability to the Mongols of a Persian *wazīr* would be measured before all else by the revenue receipts."

204 Farhad Daftary, *The Ismā'īlīs: their history and doctrines* (Cambridge University Press 1992), pp. 421-30. See also J.A. Boyle, "Dynastic and Political History of the Īl-Khāns" in J.A. Boyle (ed.), *The Cambridge History of Iran,* V, p. 345.

205 J.A. Boyle, *ibid.* Jūzjānī, for instance, who did not hesitate to condemn the atrocities committed by Genghis Khān, whom he calls 'the Accursed' *(mal'ūn)* in his *Ṭabaqāt-i Nāṣirī* (ed. 'A Ḥabībī, 2 vols., 2nd ed. Kabul 1342; II, p. 182), praised the Mongols' service to orthodox Islam in exterminating the Ismā'īlī sect. Juwaynī made similar comments as well: see J.A. Boyle (trans.), *The History of the World-Conqueror,* 2 vols. (Manchester 1958), II, p. 685.

206 *Ibid.,* p. 348. Dokuz Khātūn, the Christian wife of Hülegü, was apparently behind this. See Jean-Paul Roux, "La Tolérance Religieuse dans les Empires Turco-Mongols," *Revue de l'Histoire des religions,* CCIII-2/1986, p. 135.

207 Cited by Boyle, *History*, p. 485.

208 Janet L. Abu-Lughod, *Before European Hegemony: The World-System A.D. 1250-1350* (New York/Oxford: OUP 1989), p. 194.

209 Cited by B. Spuler, *History of the Mongols, Based on Eastern and Western Accounts of the Thirteenth and Fourteenth Centuries,* translated from German by Stuart & Helga Drummond (Berkeley: University of California Press 1972), p. 121.

210 Janet L. Abu-Lughod, *Before European Hegemony,* p. 195.

211 $EI^2$, "Marāgha," V, p. 502.

212 J.A. Boyle, *The Cambridge History of Iran*, V, p. 354.

213 "The Mongol Viceroys of Persia regarded the Christians as their natural allies against Egypt and Islam in the second half of the 13th century." Thomas Haining, "The Mongols and Religion," *Asian Affairs,* XVII/I (1986), p. 24.

214 Manūchihr Murtaḍawī, *Masā'il-i 'aṣr-i Īlkhānān,* p. 114. For a discussion of Abāqā's relations with Christianity, see pp. 119-21.

215 Henry Howorth, *History of the Mongols,* (London 1876-88), III, p. 278.

216 Henry Howorth, *History of the Mongols,* III, p. 283.

217 $EI^1$, s.v. "Tabrīz", p. 586.

218 *The Geographical Part of the* Nuzhat al-Qulūb *composed by Ḥamd-Allāh Mustawfī of Qazwīn in 740 (1340),* ed. G. Le Strange (London: Luzac 1915), Persian text, p. 76.

219 Charles Melville, "Historical Monuments and Earthquakes in Tabriz," *Iran,* XIX (1981), p. 163.

220 The Christian historian Bar Hebraeus (*Chronography,* trans. E.A. Wallis Budge, London 1932, p. 450) notes that on the night of Wednesday, 18 January 1273 there was a severe earthquake in Tabriz which destroyed many monuments. However, the Christian church in the city was completely unharmed, "protecting the Greeks, Armenians and Nestorians

who took refuge there." Cited by Charles Melville, "Historical Monuments and Earthquakes in Tabriz," p. 162; apropos of which Dr. Melville observes that "the religious bias of his account is interesting and serves to demonstrate the freedom of worship enjoyed by non-Muslims under the Īl-Khāns, as well as their presence in some number in the commercial capital of the country." *Ibid.*, p. 174n. 28. And, as Jean-Paul Roux points out, a bishopric was established in Tabriz by Abāqā's wife. "La Tolérance Religieuse dans les Empires Turco-Mongols," p. 137.

221 MAS, p. 239, v. 1517 & pp. 170-1, vv. 394-97.

222 The Gospels were translated into Persian during this period, as Qamar Āriyān, *Chihra-yi Masīḥ dar adabiyāt-i fārsī,* (Tehran: Intishārāt-i Mu'īn 1369 A.Hsh./1990), p. 87, points out.

223 "Religion under the Mongols," in J.A. Boyle (ed.), *The Cambridge History of Iran,* V, p. 541. Of Abāqā, B. Spuler also observes, "He is said to have built Buddhist temples in many towns of Persia, and even in some villages ... In spite of Abaqa's efforts, the position of Buddhism in the empire of the Il-Khans was so isolated that it could hardly be expected to gain acceptance among the whole population." *The Mongols in History,* trans. G. Wheeler (London: Pall Mall 1971), pp. 40-1. On the many Buddhist influences in Persian poetic imagery, see A.S. Melikian-Chirvani, "L'Évocation Littéraire du Bouddhisme dans L'Iran Musulman," in *Le Monde Iranien et l'Islam,* I (1971), pp. 1-72 and *idem.,* Bāztābhā-yi adābī āyīn-i Būdda dar Īrān Islāmī', *Iran Nameh,* VIII/2 (1990), pp. 273-90.

224 E.G. Browne, *A Literary History of Persia,* III, p. 20.

225 Sharukh Meskoob, *op. cit.,* p. 87. See also Juwaynī, J.A. Boyle (trans.), *The History of the World-Conqueror,* vols. 1-2.

226 D. Morgan, *Medieval Persia,* p. 66.

227 J.A. Boyle, *The Cambridge History of Iran,* V, p. 369.

228 See Ḥaqqwardī Nāṣirī's introduction to his edition of 'Azīz Nasafī's *Zubda al-ḥaqā'iq* (Tehran: Ṭahūrī 1363 A.Hsh./1985), p. 14.

229 *A Literary History of Persia,* III, p. 69.

230 *Ibid.*

231 "Rashīd al-Dīn: the First World Historian," in J.A. Boyle, *The Mongol World-Empire 1266-1370* (London 1977), XXIX, pp. 19-26.

232 "Rashīd al-Dīn: the First World Historian," p. 26. Also cf. K. Jahn, "Rashīd al-Dīn as a World Historian," in *Yādnāma-yi Jan Rypka* (Prague 1967).

233 J.A. Boyle, "Dynastic and Political History of the Īl-Khāns," *The Cambridge History of Iran,* V, pp. 356-60.

234 J.A. Boyle, "Dynastic and Political History of the Īl-Khāns," *The Cambridge History of Iran,* V, p. 361.

235 *A Literary History of Persia,* III, p. 19.

236 Farhad Daftary, *The Ismā'īlīs: their history and doctrines,* p. 445.

237 *The Cambridge History of Iran,* V, p. 364.

238 Peter Jackson, "Aḥmad Takūdār," *Encyclopedia Iranica,* I, p. 662.

239 Spuler, *The Mongols in History,* p. 45.

240 See J. Van Ess, "'Alā' al-Dawla Semnānī," in *Encyclopedia Iranica,* I, p. 774.

[241] See Simnānī's *Al-'Urwat li'l-ahl al-khalwat wa'l-jalwat,* ed. N.M. Harawī, p. 297.

[242] J. Van Ess, "'Alā' al-Dawla Semnānī," p. 775.

[243] Simnānī (or the editor of the MS.) has muddled accounts here—Arghūn was the father of Ūljāytū, not the other way round.

[244] Simnānī's *Al-'Urwat,* p. 320.

[245] Bausani, "Religion under the Mongols," *The Cambridge History of Iran,* V, p. 545.

[246] P. Jackson, "Arğūn Khan," *Encyclopedia Iranica,* II, p. 404; D. Morgan, *Medieval Persia,* p. 65.

[247] "La Tolérance Religieuse dans les Empires Turco-Mongols," p. 138.

[248] Howorth, *History of the Mongols,* III, p. 313; for a detailed discussion of Arghūn's attitude towards Buddhism, see Lambton, *Continuity and Change in Medieval Persia,* pp. 254ff.

[249] Qamar Āriyān, *Chihra-yi Masīḥ dar adabiyāt-i fārsī,* p. 86; J.G. Kolbas, "Mongol Money: The Role of Tabriz from Chingiz Khan to Uljaytu, 616 to 709 AH/1220 to 1309 AD," NYU Doctoral dissertation 1992 (Ann Arbor: University Microfilms International 1992), chapter 6-8.

[250] P. Jackson, "Arğūn Khan," *Encyclopedia Iranica,* II, p. 404.

[251] J.A. Boyle, "Dynastic and Political History of the Īl-Khāns," *The Cambridge History of Iran,* V, p. 369; *A Literary History of Persia,* III, pp. 27-8.

[252] J.A. Boyle, "Dynastic and Political History of the Īl-Khāns," *The Cambridge History of Iran,* V, p. 368.

[253] *Taḥrīr-i Tā'rīkh-i Vaṣṣāf;* ed. 'Abd al-Muḥammad Āyatī (Tehran: Mū'assisa-yi Muṭāla'āt wa Taḥqīqāt-i Farhangī 1372 A.Hsh./1993), p. 132. This book is an abridged version of Vaṣṣāf's own work *Tajziyat al-amṣār wa tazjiyat al-a'ṣār,* ed. M.M Iṣfahānī (Lith. Bombay 1269/1852).

[254] *Taḥrīr-i Tā'rīkh-i Vaṣṣāf,* p. 133.

[255] E.G. Browne, *A Literary History of Persia,* III, p. 31.

[256] Cited by Howorth, *History of the Mongols,* III, p. 332.

[257] Howorth, *History of the Mongols,* III, p. 331.

[258] Thus, the historian Juwaynī admitted that during his time, the Mongols, contrary to their former custom, regarded Muslims contemptuously, but he blames this attitude on the Muslims themselves who only intrigued with each other, instead of uniting against their mutual enemy. See W. Barthold, *Turkestan Down to the Mongol Invasion* (London: Luzac & Co., 3rd. ed. 1968), p. 481. Vaṣṣāf, speaking of the reign of Abū Sa'īd, sarcastically exclaimed: "How strange! The Mongols in order to honour their dead, impale a live horse upon the grave (they call it *qūyalghān)* so that the birds may prey upon it and become sated; yet, on the other hand, the followers of the faith of Muḥammad make every effort to destroy their good deeds and pious foundations, devoting all their energy to the unjust pursuit of pleasure and means of self-advancement and rank!" *Taḥrīr-i Tā'rīkh-i Vaṣṣāf;* pp. 344-5.

[259] Manūchihr Murtaḍawī, *Masā'il-i 'aṣr-i Īlkhānān,* p. 114.

[260] *The Cambridge History of Iran,* V, p. 372; *A Literary History of Persia,* III, pp. 33-6; P. Jackson, "Arğūn Khan," *Encyclopedia Iranica,* II, p. 402.

261 Howorth, *History of the Mongols,* III, p. 371.

262 *A Literary History of Persia,* III, pp. 39-40

263 Howorth *(History of the Mongols,* III, p. 387), citing Prince He'thum's History and Bar Hebraeus, states that "he was a good Christian, rebuilt the Christian churches and forbade the preaching of Muhammedanism among the Tartars."

264 C. Melville, *"Pādishāh-i Islām:* the Conversion of Sultan Maḥmūd Ghāzān Khān," in C. Melville (ed.), *Pembroke Papers I: Persian and Islamic Studies in honour of P.W. Avery,* (Cambridge: University of Cambridge 1990), p. 159.

265 *Continuity and Change,* p. 250.

266 Manūchihr Murtaḍawī, *Masā'il 'aṣr-i Īlkhānān,* p. 122.

267 I.P. Petrushevsky, "Rashīd al-Dīn's Conception of the State," *Central Asiatic Journal,* XIV (1970), pp. 148-9.

268 *Ibid.,* pp. 150-1.

269 Vladmir Minorsky, EI[1], s.v. "Tabrīz", p. 586.

270 Bert Fragner, "Social and Internal Economic Affairs," *Cambridge History of Iran,* vol. 6, p. 524.

271 Charles Melville, "The Itineraries of Sultan Öljeitū, 1304-16," *Iran: Journal of the British Institute of Persian Studies,* XXVIII (1990), p. 55.

272 EI[1], p. 586.

273 Howorth, *History of the Mongols,* III, p. 396.

274 C. Melville, *"Pādishāh-i Islām,"* p. 170.

275 J.A. Boyle, "Dynastic and Political History of the Īl-Khāns," *The Cambridge History of Iran,* V, p. 380.

276 Howorth, *History of the Mongols,* III, p. 398, 454.

277 C. Melville, *"Pādishāh-i Islām,"* p. 172.

278 Manūchihr Murtaḍawī, *Masā'il-i 'aṣr-i Īlkhānān,* p. 117-8. Also cf. D. Morgan, *Medieval Persia,* p. 72.

279 *The Venture of Islam,* II, p. 415.

280 Cited by Howorth, *History of the Mongols,* III, p. 397-8. Emphasis mine.

281 MAS, *Gulshan-i rāz,* p. 103, vv. 879-882.

282 See M.I. Waley, "A Kubrawī Manual of Sufism: the *Fuṣūṣ al-ādāb* of Yaḥyā Bākharzī," *The Legacy of Mediæval Persian Sufism,* p. 292; J. Richard, "La conversion de Berke et les debuts de l'islamisation de la Horde d'Or," *Revue des études islamiques,* 35 (1967), pp. 173-9.

283 C. Melville, *"Pādishāh-i Islām,* p. 168, who also notes that the young prince was obliged to wear wool *(ṣūf)* during his conversion ceremony and that his "apparently confirms the Sufi affiliations of Ṣadr al-Dīn and suggests that Ghāzān was himself initiated as a Sufi."

284 Howorth, *History of the Mongols,* III, p. 480.

285 *Ḥabīb al-siyar,* ed. Muḥammad Dabīr-siyāqī (Tehran: Khayyām 1362 A.Hsh./1983), III, p. 188.

286 *A Literary History of Persia,* III, p. 41.

287 C. Melville, *"Pādishāh-i Islām,* p. 162.

288 *A Literary History of Persia,* III, pp. 39-41; J.A. Boyle, "Dynastic and Political History of the Īl-Khāns," *The Cambridge History of Iran,* V, p. 385ff.

289 As J.A. Boyle represents Ghāzān, "Dynastic and Political History of the Īl-Khāns," *The Cambridge History of Iran,* V, p. 396.

290 *Taḥrīr-i Tā'rīkh-i Vaṣṣāf,* p. 253.

291 *Ibid.*

292 See EI[1], s.v. "Tabrīz."

293 Ḥāfiẓ Ḥusayn Ibn Karbalā'ī, *Rawḍāt al-jinān,* I, p. 511.

294 *A Literary History of Persia,* III, p. 57; *The Cambridge History of Iran,* V, p. 403.

295 *Taḥrīr-i Tā'rīkh-i Vaṣṣāf,* p. 278.

296 J.A. Boyle, "Dynastic and Political History of the Īl-Khāns," *The Cambridge History of Iran,* V, p. 401; D. Morgan, *Medieval Persia 1047-1797,* p. 77.

297 Spuler, *The Mongols in History,* p. 52; Qamar Āriyān, *Chihra-yi Masīḥ dar adabiyāt-i fārsī,* p. 86.

298 *Taḥrīr-i Tā'rīkh-i Vaṣṣāf,* p. 271.

299 Cf. the account of a royal party in Baghdād provided by Vaṣṣāf, *Taḥrīr-i Tā'rīkh-i Vaṣṣāf,* p. 272; also cf. pp. 273-4. Also see the observations by Charles Melville, "The Itineraries of Sultan Öljeitū, 1304-16," p. 63, on his preoccupation with drinking. The Sufi affiliations of Ūljāytū are discussed below.

300 Ḥamd-Allāh Mustawfī, *Tārīkh-i guzīda,* ed. 'A. Nawā'ī (Tehran: 1362 A.Hsh./1983), p. 606. Cited by Charles Melville, "The Itineraries of Sultan Öljeitū, 1304-16," p. 56.

301 See *Taḥrīr-i Tā'rīkh-i Vaṣṣāf,* pp. 280-87, for a full description of this panegyric and Ūljāytū's reception of it.

302 Charles Melville, "The Itineraries of Sultan Öljeitū, 1304-16," p. 56.

303 See Charles Melville, "Abū Sa'īd and the Revolt of the Amīrs in 1319," in D. Aigle (ed.) *L'Iran face à la Domination mongole* (Damascus/Paris: 1995). I would like to acknowledge my gratitude to Dr. Melville in furnishing me a typescript of this paper.

304 *A Literary History of Persia,* p. 71; see also *Rawḍāt al-jinān,* I, p. 514.

305 Howorth, *History of the Mongols,* III, p. 589

306 See Sa'īd Nafīsī (ed.) *Dīwān-i Awḥadī Maraghī* (Tehran: Amīr Kabīr 1340 A.Hsh./1961), introduction, p. 57.

307 *Ṣafwat al-Ṣafā,* pp. 242-3, cited by Manūchihr Murtaḍawī, *Masā'il 'aṣr-i Īlkhānān,* p. 364.

308 *Ibid.,* p. 365.

309 See Sa'īd Nafīsī (ed.) *Dīwān-i Awḥadī Maraghī,* introduction, p. 57.

310 *Dīwān-i Awḥādī Marāghī,* edited by Sa'īd Nafīsī, p. 495, v. 10491.

311 Ḥāfiẓ Ḥusayn Ibn Karbalā'ī, *Rawḍāt al-jinān,* I, p. 515.

312 Cited by M.J. Mashkūr, *Tārīkh-i Tabrīz,* p. 560.

313 *Dīwān-i Awḥādī Marāghī,* pp. 497-498, vv. 10551-2. On the construction of this *khānaqāh*, see Jean Aubin, "Le Patronage Culturel en Iran sous les Ilkhans: une Grande Famille de Yazd," *Le Monde Iranien et l'Islam,* III (1975), p. 114.

314 *Ibid.,* p. 561. Bilānkūh—also known as Walīyānkūh (Mount of Saints)—is located in Eastern Tabriz, and is the source of the waters which, flowing through its qanāt system, provided for the rest of Tabriz. *Ibid.,* p. 114.

[315] *Dīwān-i Awḥadī Maraghī*, pp. 492-3.
[316] *Dīwān-i Awḥadī Maraghī*, pp. 560-1.
[317] *Tadhkira al-shu'arā*, p. 236.
[318] *Dīwān-i Awḥadī Maraghī*, p. 614.
[319] *Dīwān-i Awḥadī Maraghī*, introduction, p. lviii.
[320] *Ṣafwat al-Ṣafā*, p. 298-9; *Masā'il 'aṣr-i Īlkhānān*, p. 366; 332-5.
[321] *Ṣafwat al-Ṣafā*, p. 298-9; *Masā'il 'aṣr-i Īlkhānān*, pp. 335-6
[322] *Masā'il 'asr-i Īlkhānān*, p. 363.
[323] See E.G. Browne, *A Literary History of Persia*, III, p. 56.
[324] *Ṣafwat al-Ṣafā*, p. 243.
[325] Manūchihr Murtaḍawī, *Masā'il 'aṣr-i Īlkhānān*, p. 349.
[326] P. Jackson, "Abū Sa'īd Bahādor Khān," in *Encyclopædia Iranica*, I, p. 376.
[327] Charles Melville, "The Year of the Elephant" Mamluk-Mongol Rivalry in the Hejaz in the Reign of Abū Sa'īd (1317-1335)," *Studia Iranica*, XXII/2 (1992), p. 205, citing al-Maqrīzī, *Kitāb al-sulūk li-ma'rifat duwal al-mulūk*, ed, M.M. Ziadeh, (Cairo 1956ff), II, p. 211.
[328] J.A. Boyle, "Dynastic and Political History of the Īl-Khāns," *The Cambridge History of Iran*, V, p. 409.
[329] For a good account of the extermination of the Chūbān clan, see P. Jackson, "Abū Sa'īd Bahādor Khān," in *Encyclopædia Iranica*, I, p. 375; Charles Melville, "Cobān" in *Encyclopædia Iranica*, V, pp. 875-78.
[330] J.A. Boyle, "Dynastic and Political History of the Īl-Khāns," *The Cambridge History of Iran*, V, p. 411. E.G. Browne, *A Literary History of Persia*, III, pp. 55-6.
[331] J.A. Boyle, "Dynastic and Political History of the Īl-Khāns," *The Cambridge History of Iran*, V, p. 413.
[332] H.A.R. Gibb (trans.) Ibn Battuta, *Travels in Asia and Africa* (London: Routledge & Sons 1929), p. 349, no. 27.
[333] See Ehsan Yarshater, *Shi'r-i fārsī dar 'ahd-i Shāh-rukh* (Tehran: Danishgāh 1334 A.Hsh./1955), p. 9.
[334] *Justujū*, p. 319.
[335] *Dīwān-i Kamāl al-Dīn Mas'ūd Khujandī*, ed. K. Shidfar (Moscow 1975), ghazal no. 571.
[336] *Dīwān-i Kamāl al-Dīn Khujandī*, ed. 'Azīz Dawlatābādī (Tehran 1958), introduction, p. 4.
[337] Peter Brown, *The Cult of the Saints: its Rise and Function in Latin Christianity* (University of Chicago Press 1981), pp. 10-11.
[338] *Le Sceau des saints: Prophétie et sainteté dans la doctrine d'Ibn Arabī* (Paris 1986), p. 18.
[339] Peter Brown, *The Cult of the Saints*, p. 3.
[340] *Dīwān-i Khwājū Kirmānī*, ed. Aḥmad Suhaylī Khwānsārī (Tehran 1336 A.Hsh./1957), p. 12 introduction. Elsewhere in his *Dīwān* (p. 588, for instance), however, Khwājū disparages Tabriz.
[341] See E.G. Browne, *A Literary History of Persia*, III, p. 86.
[342] Ronald Latham (trans.), *The Travels of Marco Polo* (London: The Folio Society 1958), p. 43.
[343] H.A.R. Gibb (trans.) Ibn Battuta, *Travels in Asia and Africa*, pp. 101-2.

[344] Ruy Gonzalez de Clavijo, *Embassy to Tamerlane 1403-06*, tr. Guy Le Strange (London: 1928), pp. 151-4.

[345] Claude Cahen, *Pre-Ottoman Turkey: A general survey of the material and spiritual culture and history c. 1071-1330,* trans. from French by J. Jones-Williams (London: Sidgwick & Jackson 1972), p. 348.

[346] "Christians had nowhere really regained the upper hand, the Muslims being so much in a majority and so dominant socially that, even at a time when they had not been converted, the Mongols could not but recruit the bulk of their administrative personnel, including the viziers, from among them. And this situation was only accentuated when the Mongols were converted to Islam. In its institutions Asia Minor had remained Muslim, the whole administrative personnel was Muslim, and the Muslim viziers of the Ilkhāns themselves were anxious to figure as Muslim patrons, sometimes even more than in their own country." *Ibid.*

[347] *Medieval Persia 1047-1797* (London: Longman 1988), chap. 7.

[348] J.S. Trimingham, *The Sufi Orders in Islam* (Oxford: OUP 1973), p. 90.

[349] Jean-Paul Roux, "La Tolérance Religieuse dans les Empires Turco-Mongols," p. 132.

[350] J.S. Trimingham, *op. cit.,* p. 90

[351] A. Bausani, *The Persians*, p. 117.

[352] Cf. S.H. Nasr, "Sufism and Spirituality in Persia," in S.H. Nasr (ed.), *Islamic Spirituality II* (New York: Crossroad 1991), p. 210.

[353] For a good discussion of which, see Jean-Paul Roux, "La Tolérance Religieuse dans les Empires Turco-Mongols," pp. 159-63; Manūchihr Murtaḍawī, *Masā'il-i 'aṣr-i Īlkhānān,* pp. 311-50; Jean Aubin, "Le Patronage Culturel en Iran sous les Ilkhans: une Grande Famille de Yazd," *Le Monde Iranien et l'Islam,* III (975), pp. 107-18; A.K.S. Lambton, "Mongol Fiscal Administration in Persia," *Studia Islamica* LXIV (1986), Part 1: p. 89; also some of Maria Eva Subtelny's observations in her "Socioeconomic Bases of Cultural Patronage under the Later Timurids," *IJMES* 20 (1988), pp. 480-82, are relevant to the Mongol period as well. Of course, such explanations ignore the movements of that spiritual *Zeitgeist,* which itself is both cause and effect. As Annemarie Schimmel put it: "Strangely enough this [Mongol] period of the most terrible political disaster was, at the same time, a period of highest religious and mystical activity. It seems as though the complete darkness on the worldly plane was counteracted by a hitherto unknown brightness on the spiritual plane." *The Triumphal Sun: A Study of the Works of Jalāloddin Rumi* (London: Fine Books 1978), p. 9.

[354] See "Le milieu baghdādien: politique et religion" in H. Landolt (ed.), *Nūruddin Isfarāyinī*, French introduction, pp. 31-36

[355] See. P. Soucek, "Iranian Architecture: The Evolution of a Tradition", in E. Yarshater & R. Ettinghausen, *Highlights of Persian Art* (Boulder: Westview Press, 1979), p. 148.

[356] As retold by M. Molé, "Les Kubrawiya entre Sunnisme et Shiisme aus Huitième et Neuvième Siècles de l'Hégire," in *Revue des études islamiques* [1961], p. 112-13.

357 See the introduction. by Dh. Ṣafā to ʻAbd al-Rafīʻ Ḥaqīqat (ed.) *Divān-i kāmil-i ashʻār-i fārsī u ʻarabī-yi ʻAlā' al-Dawla Simnānī* (Tehran 1985), p. 15.

358 Claude Cahen, *Pre-Ottoman Turkey*, p. 348.

359 As David Morgan notes: "Ṣūfī masters like Shaykh Ṣafī al-Dīn Ardabīlī, founder of the Ṣafawid order and ancestor of the Ṣafawid dynasty (died 735/1334) were often treated with respect and favour by the Īlkhāns. The usual explanation for this, which may have an element of truth in it, is that a charismatic, perhaps wonder-working religious figure would most appeal to a nomad whose principal previous contact with men of religion had been with the shamans." *Medieval Persia 1047-1797,* p. 73.

360 Noting that "there was a very considerable degree of tolerance within the Mongol Empire," Thomas Haining cites this article from Genghis Khan's Yāsa: "It is ordered that there is only one God, Creator of Heaven and Earth, Who alone gives life and death, riches and poverty as pleases Him, and Who has over everything an absolute power. . . . Leaders of a religion, preachers, monks, persons who are dedicated to religious practices, the criers of mosques, physicians and those who bathe the bodies of the dead are to be freed from all public charges." – "The Mongols and Religion," *Asian Affairs,* XVII/I (1986), p. 26. Also see Manūchihr Murtaḍawī's lengthy discussion of the Mongols' lack of religious prejudice: *Masā'il-i ʻaṣr-i Īlkhānān,* pp. 359-68.

361 D. Morgan, *Medieval Persia 1047-1797,* p. 53.

362 Michel M. Mazzaoui, *The Origins of the Ṣafawids,* p. 38.

363 See L. Lewisohn (ed.), *The Legacy of Mediæval Persian Sufism,* "Overview," pp. 38-40.

364 Jean-Paul Roux, "La Tolérance Religieuse dans les Empires Turco-Mongols," p. 137 and Qamar Āriyān, *Chihra-yi Masīḥ dar adabiyāt-i fārsī,* p. 87.

365 Qamar Āriyān, *Chihra-yi Masīḥ dar adabiyāt-i fārsī,* p. 87.

366 Jean-Paul Roux, "La Tolérance Religieuse dans les Empires Turco-Mongols," *Revue de l'Histoire des religions,* CCIII-2/1986, pp. 131-68.

367 Jean-Paul Roux, "La Tolérance Religieuse dans les Empires Turco-Mongols," p. 132.

368 At least, so claims his respected editor Saʻīd Nafīsī, *Dīwān-i Awḥadī Maraghī,* in his introduction, p. 57.

369 MAS, p. 80, v. 335.

370 Cf. Saʻīd Nafīsī (ed.) *Dīwān-i Awḥadī Maraghī,* introduction, p. 57.

371 EI², s.v. "Marāgha," V, p. 302.

372 Manūchihr Murtaḍawī, *Masā'il-i ʻaṣr-i Īlkhānān,* p. 111.

373 For a lengthier study of these and related doctrines, see Leonard Lewisohn, "The Transcendental Unity of Polytheism & Monotheism in the Sufism of Shabistarī," pp. 394-8.

374 MAS, *Gulshan-i rāz,* p. 103, vv. 874-80.

375 *Mafātīḥ al-iʻjāz*, ed. Khāliqī & Karbāsī, pp. 538-9.

376 Cf. Jean-Paul Roux, "La Tolérance Religieuse dans les Empires Turco-Mongols," p. 142.

[377] As Ibn 'Arabī in the chapter on Ezra in the *Fuṣūṣ al-ḥikam* explained; see R.J.W. Austin (trans.) *Ibn al-'Arabī: The Bezels of Wisdom* (New York: Paulist Press 1980), p. 168.

[378] Michel Chodkiewicz, *Seal of the Saints,* p. 79. On Ibn 'Arabī's tolerant outlook on non-Islamic faiths, see W.C. Chittick, *Imaginal Worlds: I bn 'Arabī and the Problem of Religious Diversity* (Albany: SUNY 1994).

[379] MAS, *Gulshan-i rāz,* p. 105, vv. 927-32.

[380] MAS, *Gulshan-i rāz,* pp. 105-6, vv. 932-38.

[381] MAS, *Gulshan-i rāz,* p. 106, v. 956.

[382] See Michel Chodkiewicz, *Seal of the Saints,* pp. 78-9.

[383] Bukhārī, *anbiyā',* 45; Muslim, *Tawba,* 46-7; *Zuhd,* 73.

[384] *Mafātīḥ al-i'jāz*, ed. Khāliqī & Karbāsī, p. 577.

[385] Jean-Paul Roux, "La Tolérance Religieuse dans les Empires Turco-Mongols," p. 143.

[386] On this doctrine, see Leonard Lewisohn, "The Transcendental Unity of Polytheism & Monotheism in the Sufism of Shabistarī," pp. 392-3, and chapter 8 below.

[387] MAS, *Sa'ādat-nāma,* p. 232, vv. 1384-86. A reference to the Koran, Surah XXXVIII: 76. "Iblis said: I am better than him. Thou created me of fire, whilst him Thou didst create of clay."

[388] Cf. Jean-Paul Roux, "La Tolérance Religieuse dans les Empires Turco-Mongols," pp. 158-9.

[389] As David Morgan (*Medieval Persia 1047-1797,* p. 82) puts it, summarizing his historical analysis of the Mongol period: "For Persia, the Mongol period was a disaster on a grand and unparalleled scale," while Hodgson judges that "one cannot overlook one of the most startling differences between the Mongols and the Arabs themselves: the Mongols brought nothing comparable to the Qur'ān and the Islamic spiritual impulse." *The Venture of Islam,* II, pp. 386-7.

[390] The unintended consequence of this, of course, was the spread of the spread of the Black Death pandemic from Mongolia to Europe in the mid-14th century, which later resulted in the outbreak of the Black Death in the second third of the fourteenth century. For a good analysis of this, see Abu-Lughod, *Before European Hegemony,* pp. 170-5.

[391] M. Hodgson, *The Venture of Islam,* II, p. 405.

[392] D.O. Morgan, "Persian Historians and the Mongols," in D.O. Morgan (ed.) *Medieval Historical Writings in the Christian and Islamic worlds* (London: SOAS Publications 1982), p. 110.

[393] Claude Cahen, *Pre-Ottoman Turkey,* p. 359.

[394] Bausani, *The Persians*, pp. 116-17. See also L. Binyon, J.V.S. Wilkinson & B. Gray, *Persian Miniature Painting* (New York, Dover Books reprt., 1971), p. 21. According to Sussan Babaie and M.L. Swietochowski *(Persian Drawings in the Metropolitan Museum of Art,* New York, 1989, p. 3), "The earliest substantial number of Persian drawings on paper that have survived date from the second half of the fourteenth century, the period associated with Muzaffarid and Jalayrid rule in Iran."

[395] A. Schimmel, "Poetry and Calligraphy: Some Thoughts about their

Interrelation in Persian Culture," in R. Ettinghausen & E. Yarshater (eds.), *Highlights of Persian Art* (Colorado: Westview Press, 1979), p. 196.

[396] J. Rypka, "Poets & Prose Writers of the Late Saljuq and Mongol Periods," *The Cambridge History of Iran,* V, p. 555.

# IV

# THE MYSTICAL MILIEU

## *Spiritual Masters and Sufi Institutions in Shabistarī's Poetry*

*To 'haunt the tavern regularly' means liberty*
*from self. Although it bear the look of piety,*
*Selfhood is pure infidelity.*

### The Thirteenth Century Revival of Sufism

As may be gleaned from the last chapter, the most important spiritual force to be reckoned with in studying the background of the Safavid era is undoubtably Sufism[397] which underwent a renaissance during the Mongol period.[398] Although for nearly a century and half, shortly before Shabistarī was born, Sufism had been described as the "institutionalized mass religion" of Persia, during his lifetime it entered its period of greatest bloom.[399] The great American Islamicist Marshall Hodgson characterized Sufism during this period as "the most important inward religious experience in the region from Nile to Oxus."[400] During the later part of what he describes as the Earlier Middle Period [945-1258], the most important period of activity in the development of Sufism occurred.

The *'ulamā'* scholars, who had been wary of the early Sufism of an elite, were mostly persuaded by the early twelfth century

> to accept the new Sufism of the masses, in conformity with populist principles, and to try to discipline it. Then with their acceptance, around the latter part of the twelfth century the reorganization of Sufism was completed with the establishment of formal Sufi brotherhoods or orders *(ṭarīqah)* . . . The distinctive marks of the new Sufism were two: its organization into these formal 'orders' and its concentration on a formal method of mystical worship, the *dhikr*.[401]

This spiritual revival was due in part to the two major literary figures in thirteenth-century Sufism, namely Ibn 'Arabī and Rūmī, whose works, like those of Abū Ḥamīd Ghazālī two centuries earlier, were to change forever the course of Islamic spirituality. Victor Danner thus pronounced the "Sufi literary and spiritual fruits of the thirteenth century as forming, in their ensemble, a veritable spiritual message that would govern the general outlook of Islamic civilization and affect all facets of society for centuries."

> The philosophical mysticism of Ibn al-'Arabī and poetical mysticism of Rūmī are but two of the different genres used by thirteenth-century Sufism to effect a spiritual reanimation of Islam that would be the literary counterparts to the eruption of Sufi orders all over the face of the Islamic world. All of these literary works and the new Sufi brotherhoods together constitute a spiritual revival much more analytical, much more discursive, much more openly esoteric and spiritual and philosophical or theosophical than we see in earlier times. . . . The Path was everywhere in evidence; the many Sufi orders had millions of adherants coming from all ranks of society.[402]

This high period of Persian Sufism was to last well down into Timurid times and beyond: when, after the Safavids effected the expulsion of institutional Sufism from Iran, its heartland, the Sufi poets and masters continued their mission of ecumenical tolerance and anti-sectarianism in India. By the late fifteenth century, the centrality of Sufism in the piety of Persian Islam was a phenomenon which could no longer be overlooked. As Ehsan Yarshater points out, by the 'Age of Shāh Rukh' it was "clearly evident" that "mystical concepts, Sufi theoretical constructs and the theosophical doctrine of dervishhood *(mashrab-i darvīshī)* had permeated the entire socio-cultural milieu, so that one rarely encounters a poet or scholar in the annals of the age who did not 'enjoy the taste' of Sufi theosophy or who had not traveled a few steps along the Sufi Path."[403]

The last half-century of the Mongol period (663/1265–737/1337) into which Shabistarī's lifetime falls also coincided with the greatest epoch in the history of Persian literature. E.G. Browne well represents the situation when, in his *Literary History of Persia,* he observes that "allowing for the terrible crisis through which Persia was passing, when heathen rulers dominated the land, and Christians and Jews lorded it over Muslims, the period of Mongol ascendancy, from the death of Hulugu Khan on February 8, 1265, until the death of last Mongol Il-khan, Musa, in 1337, was wonderfully rich in literary achievements.[404] As was shown in the last chapter, there was an incredible upsurge in interest in institutional Sufism during the Mongol period. Manūchihr Murtaḍawī observes that

> The practices and mannerisms *(ādāb)* of Sufism were the mode of the day. The great number of *Khānaqāh*s and Sufis and the patronage lavished by the Īlkhāns and their viziers upon them and the receptive welcome given to '*Khānaqāh*-Sufism' *(taṣawwuf-i khānaqāhī)* by people from every walk of society, as well as the existence of eminent mystics such as Shaykh Ṣafī al-Dīn Ardabīlī and Shaykh Maḥmūd Shabistarī, are central issues in any account of the history of Mongol Persia.[405]

## The *Khānaqāh* & *Kharābāt* Topos in Shabistari's Poetry

The Persian word for a 'Sufi meeting house'—*khānaqāh*—first occurs in texts dating from the third/ninth century, although the insitution itself did not probably crystallize until the following century.[406] We know that most of the important founders of Islamic mysticism hailed from north-eastern Persian Transoxiania (a region inclusive of Mawarannahr, Khwārazm and northern Khurāsān). There, in the late second/eighth or early third/ninth century, the first Sufi *khānaqāh*s or meeting-houses were established, and by the early fourth/tenth century, Islamic esotericism as the 'Sufi Path' or *ṭarīqa* (with its own institutions, rites and doctrines) had spread, in virtually a fully developed form, throughout the entire Islamic world. The political substructure and social fulcrum of the Sufi *ṭarīqas* lay in the establishment and diffusion of the *khānaqāhs*; thus, it is necessary to examine their traditional status in mediæval society[407] in order to grasp the historical reality of Persian poetry in the ambience of Sufism itself.

Although there is no direct historical source linking Shabistarī with a specific *Khānaqāh* as can be observed in the biographies of most of the Sufi poets during this period, he was certainly affiliated with institutional Sufism. The following observation made by Grace Martin Smith concerning the Turkish Sufi poet Yūnus Emre (d. 720/1321-2), who flourished during the same period, might be applied with equal justice to Shabistarī:

> I do agree with those who think that he was connected with a *tekke,* perhaps living there, breathing the *tekke*'s religious atmosphere, performing his dervish duties (including missionary duties), attending the sheikh (spiritual leader), and participating in the dervish rituals and fellowships, which would have been enhanced by his songs and poems. It seems to me that, unless Yūnus had been a dervish himself, he could never have written poems and songs so knowledgeable about and so sympathetic with *tekke* life and thought and so closely responsive to the emotional and religious needs of the *tekke* congregations that they have been sung in *tekke*s down to the present.[408]

Martin's opinion of the Yūnus Emre's probable affiliation to institutionalized Sufism is borne out by all the historical circumstances of the *Khānaqāh* institution in thirteenth-century Persia, which had become greatly diffused throughout all Islamic lands touched by Persianate culture, reaching the apex of its social and political influence.[409] In my opinion, there does not seem to have been a single Sufi poet who was *not* affiliated with, usually as a leader within, a *ṭarīqat* organization in association with its dominant institution, the *Khānaqāh,* during the reign of the Īl-khāns in Persia.[410] As Aḥmad Rajā'ī notes:

> The popularity and growth of the *khānaqāh* institution during this period [6th/12th and 7th/13th century] is of great significance. On the one hand, these *khānaqāhs*, with their highly developed organization and unique social situation, were

centres in which disciples could be trained, their problems solved, and novices instructed in the code of conduct governing travel, musical audition, and internal *khānaqāh* discipline. On the other hand, certain practical spiritual instructions could be given concerning the kinds of austerities to be practised, ranging from commemoration of God *(dhikr)* and seclusion to various types of superogatory prayer.

*Khānaqāhs* were not reserved exclusively for the Sufis but were also open to all travelers, functioning as hotels where room and board were provided. This social aspect of the *khānaqāh* greatly increased its appeal, especially since all classes of people were allowed to participate in the Sufi assemblies, listen to their sermons, public teachings and musical concerts. Naturally, the Sufis' simple life-style, shorn of corrupt worldliness and luxury, tended to convert both mystics and non-mystics to their teachings. In fact, so widespread did the social influence of the *khānaqāh* institutional during this period become, that the State authorities began to credit the institution officially—giving the director *(pīr)* of the *khānaqāh* the title of *Shaykh al-shiyukh,* (Master of masters) which became an official worldly position like the rank of *Qaḍī al-Quḍāt* (Attorney-general).[411]

Most Sufi poetry, in fact, from its very inception, was usually inspired by the ambience of the *khānaqāh* (Arabic: *zāwīya;* Turkish: *tekke),* the Sufi house of assembly. Shabistarī's verse in this respect is no different. Until this day, one can still hear Persian dervishes chant the *Gulshan-i rāz* in their mystical seances very movingly. Shabistarī's poetry is both melic and lyrical (derived from the Gr. *lyra* or musical instrument), and still enjoys considerable liturgical use in the social context of the *khānaqāh* institution. In fact, it is as difficult to imagine the existence of Sufi poetry without a *khānaqāh* for it to be sung in, as it is to read George Herbert's poems in *The Temple* without recalling the intimate connection of his verse to the life of a seventeenth-century parson in the Church of England.

In this regard, one can see how highly significant is the account provided by Dawlatshāh Samaqandī in his *Memoirs of the Poets* (written in 892/1487) of how many of the major Sufi poets of Shabistarī's day in 12th/13th-century Persia, such as Kamāl Khujandī, Humām-i Tabrizī (d. 714/1314), Fakhr al-Dīn 'Irāqī (610/

1213-688/1289) and 'Imād Faqīh Kirmānī (d. 773/1371), to give but a few examples, were all either proprietors or frequenters of *khānaqāhs*.

The Sufi poet, Humām-i Tabrīzī (d. 714/1314), usually considered the foremost follower of Sa'dī in the romantic ghazal genre *(ghazal-i 'ashiqāna)* in Persian poetry, and the equal of Sa'dī in respect to metrical fluency and grace of expression,[412] administered, for instance, a *Khānaqāh* in Tabriz which was supported financially by one of the sons of the Īlkhānid Vizier Shams al-Dīn Juwaynī (d. 683/1283) named Khwāja Hārūn (d. 685/1286), for whom he composed his *Mathnawī* poem *Ṣuḥbat-nāma*.[413] Humām was a disciple of the Tabrizi Sufi Shaykh Ḥasan Bulghārī.[414] He was also connected with the Kubrāwī Order, having written an eulogy *(madḥ)* of Sa'd al-Dīn Ḥamūya (d. 650/1252) and the latter's son, Shaykh Ṣadr al-Dīn Ibrāhīm Ḥamūya.[415]

Humām's Sufi centre in Tabriz was also favoured by the great Juwaynī himself, who, in a letter of support for the poet, formally beqeathed him money from the royal treasury towards his *Khānaqāh*'s upkeep, describing him as "a man unique in his age, the most perfect of men among the human species."[416]

> . . . For the maintenance of his *khānaqāh* he alloted him an annual allowance of one thousand dinars. When he went to Anatolia to supervise the affairs of the Mu'īn al-Dīn Parwāna, he appointed Humām to the position of boon-companion and attendent. His son, Khwāja Hārun, accepted the invitation of Humām and visited his *khānaqāh* in Tabriz.[417]

Humām-i Tabrizī reciprocated his royal patron's largesse by inviting Shams al-Din Juwaynī to his *khānaqāh* where he served him and his guests a meal prepared in four hundred Chinese platters. About to be executed (17 October 1284), the *Ṣāhib-i Dīwān* Juwaynī specifically mentions Humām's name in his farewell epistle to the *'ulamā'* of Tabriz.[418] Concluding his obituary of Humām, Dawlatshāh claims that in Tabriz "his *khānaqāh* is still functional,"[419] by which observation, one may deduce that his followers still gathered there to sing Sufi poetry on Thursday nights.

Dawlatshāh also recounts how three other Sufi poets of this period, Fakhr al-Dīn 'Irāqī, Awḥādī of Marāgha and Amīr Sayyid Ḥusaynī (d. 718/1318; the latter had asked Shabistarī the questions which inspired the *Gulshan-i rāz)*, once held a common spiritual retreat in "the *khānaqāh* of Shaykh Awḥad al-Dīn [Kirmānī (d. 635/1238)] in Kirmān." During this retreat," he claims, "they composed some of their finest mystical poetry."[420] Another renowned Sufi poet of the same period, 'Imād Faqīh Kirmānī, whose poetry by Dawlatshāh is highly vaunted, is also spoken of as "possessing a *khānaqāh* which is still operative unto this day"[421] (the late Timurid period, when Dawlatshāh was writing). Even if such stories be apocryphal—and so many of Dawlatshāh's tales are—they certainly underscore the centrality and importance of the *khānaqāh* institution in mediæval Persian literary history.

The *khānaqāh* institution during this period had both a private and a public aspect. The public, social dimension of the *khānaqāh* involved giving spiritual counsel to non-initiates, delivery of public homilies on various moral themes as well as general proselytization of Sufi teachings. The private, individual dimension addressed issues concerning various contemplative disciplines connected with fasting, meditation, prayer and retreat. The atomosphere of the *khānaqāh* was especially enlivened by the presence of *samā'* ceremonies, which tended to dissolve class differences and reduce prince and pauper to a common denominator.[422] Such a bold 'mixing of classes' was quite unlike any other institution in mediæval Europe of the same period. "Perhaps more than their peers in any other major cultural environment," observed Marshall Hodgson (describing Persian *ṭarīqa* Sufism), "the Sufis succeeded in combining a spiritual elitism with a social populism."[423]

The *khānaqāh*s were so extremely widespread that they could be found in every Muslim community which contained a mosque. Often, the *khānaqāh*s were financed by laymen and partially connected with an order whose primary affiliation was to a guild and so provided financing for its upkeep. They "had some of the same functions as a European monastery," being "basic centers of social integration" for both men and women. It was the mosque rather than the *khānaqāh* which was under the protection of the State:

> The worship at the mosque never ceased to be associated in some degree with political authority; it was a state function. The *khānaqāh*s were eminently private from the very beginning. Even when endowed by an amīr, they retained this air. When the *khānaqāh*s became the foci of the more private, personal side of worship, they reinforced the frag-

mentation of Muslim societies in apolitical social forms (and at the same time gave these forms legitimacy and spiritual support.[424]

The *khānaqāh* institution was thus relatively apolitical, emphasizing the individual's relation to God, rather than his condition as a social or political entity. However, a set of elaborate rules and manner *(adab)* of *Khānaqāh* life were broadly elaborated in textbook style by Shihāb al-Dīn Abū Ḥafṣ 'Umar Suhrawardī's (d. 632/1234) *Awārif al-ma'ārif,*[425] to be then reinstated a century later in Shabistarī's day by Shams al-Dīn Ibrāhīm Abarqūhī in his *Majma' al-baḥrayn,*[426] composed circa 711-714/1311-1315 and, lastly, elaborated and redefined in Abū'l-Mafākhir Yaḥyā Bākharzī's (d. 736/1335-6) celebrated manual of Sufism.[427]

The Mongol Sultans and Amirs also took the lead in patronizing this institutionalization of the spiritual life led by Sufi mystics. In the list of charitable endowments *(waqf-nāma)* left by Ghāzān Khān (reg. 1295-1304) a fascinating account of items with which a certain *khānaqāh* was furnished is given.[428] "Musical concerts *(samā')* must be held twice a month," the document declares (a more enlightened attitude to music than that which existed in the 'Islamic Republic' of Iran where, for an extensive period in the early 1980's, all music was banned![429]) Hermann Landolt in his monograph on Shabistarī's contemporary: Nūr al-Dīn Isfarāyinī, with whom Shabistarī may have been affiliated, records that Khudā-banda Ūljāytū endowed this Shaykh with various properties, including two boats (one on the Tigris and the other on the Euphrates), several villages and herds of sheep, as well as a *khānaqāh* in the Western quarter *(bāb-i garbī)* of Baghdad (circa 709/1309).[430] The son and *khalīfa* of Isfarāyinī who succeeded his father in 717/1317 as spiritual director of this *khānaqāh,* was later, in 1352 according to Jāmī, appointed to the post of the *Shaykh al-islām* of Baghdad.[431]

One of the founders of the Khalvatiyya Order, Dede 'Umar Rushānī (d. 892/1487) lived in Tabriz in a *khānaqāh* bequeathed him by the Āq Quyūnlū leader Uzun Ḥasan (reg. 1453-78); the latter's wife Seljuq Khatūn being one of disciples. His *khānaqāh* had been originally erected by Jahān Shāh Qarā Quyūnlū.[432] The life and poetry of the another Tabrizī Sufi poet, Qāsim-i Anwār (d. 837/1433-34), was primarily focused on proselyization of Sufism within the *khānaqāh* institution; in one place in a prose treatise Qāsim mentions that he resided in Herat with a Khalvatī master in "the new *khānaqāh*" there (which was, in fact, a centre for the diffusion of the teachings of the Safaviyya Order).[433]

We know that Kamāl Khujandi (d. 803/1400) dwelled, or was offered accomodation in, two *khānaqāhs* in Tabriz, one of which Sulṭān Ḥusayn Jalayir (reg. 776-84/1374-83) furnished for him between the years 1374-83, and the other was presented—but rejected—to him by Shaykh Ibrahīm Kujujī, sometime after 1396, following the poet's exile in Sarāi.[434] In his *Memoirs of the Poets* Dawlatshāh Samarqandī relates how Sulṭān Ḥusayn "built a house of great beauty for the Master (Khujandī) in the vicinity of Tabriz, giving numerous bequests to his almshouse *(langar)*. This 'house' was apparently a Sufi hospice or *khānaqāh* of sorts, insofar as the poet celebrated his acceptance of this royal boon in an occasional quatrain (actually a *dū-baytī)* which mentions the fact that musical concerts were held there night and day:

> If within this city's midst
> King Ḥusayn has built a niche
> for me, none should dispute it,
> for there the lovers hold concert
> and play sweet tunes and strains
> both vespers and matins
> in the scale of 'Ḥusayn'.[435]

This poet's historical connection and, in fact, residence in a state-supported *khānaqāh* is thus quite evident. In Ibn Karbalā'ī's biography of Kamāl Khujandī in the *Rawḍāt al-jinān*, as noted above, mention is made of another *khānaqāh* given to the poet by the chief religious authority (Shaykh al-Islām) in late 13th-century Tabriz, Shaykh Kujujī. According to the account related by Ibn Karbalā'ī, Kamāl declined to accept this present, and a study of his *Dīwān* revealed a *dū-baytī* recording his refusal.[436] Many other verses in his *Dīwān,* wherein Kamāl Khujandī mentions that his poetry was a popular spiritual staple for the Persian Sufis inclined to the practise of *samā'* in their *khānaqāhs*, establish his artistic affliliation with this institution.[437]

Ultimately, however, Kamāl Khujandī favors Ḥāfiẓ's opinion that the divine mysteries are not contained within the confines of the Sufi *khānaqāh,* deriding, like Rūmī before him,[438] this institution as hidebound to useless formalities:

Bring me a cup of wine which is the rite
in the church of the inward sense,
Since in the *khānaqāh* of outer form
no work of mine was ever done.[439]

The ubiquitious prevalence of Sufi institutions throughout all of mediæval Persia is perhaps best summed up in Ibn Battuta's description of the *khānaqāhs* he encountered during his 120 mile journey in the first half of the fourteenth century (his travels lasted from 1325-1349) through a remote corner of southwestern Persia Khuzistan: from Bandar-i Ma'shūr to Shūshtar in the early fourteenth-century.

> As we passed through Luristan, we found a *zāwīya* at each of the way-stations on the road which furnished bread, meat and khalwa for travelers . . . Each *zāwīya* had its own Shaykh, prayer-leader, and Muezzins with servants and chefs.[440]

In the last section of the *Garden of Mystery* Shabistarī devotes a long section to the interpretation of the symbolic meaning of the Christian child *(tarsā-bacha),* who is the personification of the spiritual master *(pīr)* in his lexicon of Sufi symbolism.[441] In this passage he also mentions the effect made by the presence of this master—apparently an ideal embodiment of Shabistarī's own teacher—on the Sufis who pass their lives in the *khānaqāh.* He describes his master's visage as having conveyed him into the sacred garden, from whence he plucked the bouquet which later became the *Garden of Mystery.*

The Christian child, that 'idol' is but a symbol
of light that's pure and manifest from the faces
of idols: iconic forms of his theophany.
All hearts he welds together, conjunct:
Sometimes, the lutanist, he sweeps the strings;
sometimes, the Saki, he purveys the wine.
What a bard—whose key of grace chimes
such measure, it sets aflame the coffers
of a hundred pietists, a myriad pharisees . . . !
And what a Saki—whose beaker's brew
bereaves of self and stirs to ecstasy
two hundred men of over seventy.

Drunken in a stupor, if he comes at dusk
to the *khānaqāh,* he shows the Sufi's piety
to be but cant—all spells and conjury.
If at dawn, for matins he goes
into a Mosque, no man therein he leaves
in sober sense, of self cognizant.
Like a drunk in masquerade, he goes in the Madrasa—
the judges and the jurists there, he leaves in dire straits.
Not just the judges does he befuddle,
the puritans, from love of him are shorn
of kith and kin, of house and home.
One man from him becomes an 'infidel',
Another – pure and 'faithful'. It's he who fills
the world with such mêlée and misery,
from him come all these woes and ills.
The Tavern of Ruin blooms
with life and health from his lips;
his visage beams light and lustre
upon the mosque. Thus, everything for me
by him seems now easy: because I see
through him the possibility of liberty
from this egocentric heresy: my soul-of-infidelity.[442]

Commenting on the verse "Drunken in a stupor, if he comes at dusk/to the *khānaqāh,* he shows the Sufi's piety/to be but cant—all spells and conjury," Lāhījī remarked:

> The Perfect Man's being in comparison with ordinary novices on the Path to God, is like an ocean before a drop of water. When such a mystic enters the *Khānaqāh,* which is the house of wayfarers traveling the Way of the *Ṭarīqat,* he enters as one drunk on the noctural wine of contemplation of the Absolute Divine Beauty, a beverage which is imbibed in the symposium of the Divine Selfhood held in the nonmanifest or supraformal realm. The reason why he said "at dusk" is that perception and intellectual discrimination cannot penetrate into the non-manifest side of the Divine Selfhood. So alas, he makes the 'mystical states' of the Sufis who pass their time in *Khānaqāh*s seem but idle flights of fancy, or as he says, "cant, spells and conjury." That is because the mystical states of the Sufis who are undergoing the station of the 'journey to

> God and with God' *(sayr ilā Allāh wa ma'a Allāh)* which is a station of flucuation wherein one is merely endowed with realization of the variegated divine illuminations, levels and theophanies of the God's Acts, in relation to the spiritual plentitude of the Perfect Man . . . are completely vainglorious. His entry [into the *khānaqāh*] reveals to them the worthless hallucinatory nature of their spiritual experiences.[443]

As Lāhījī emphasizes in this passage, to the Perfect Man who has attained to the sublime heights of Reality *(ḥaqīqat)*, the Path itself appears a chimera, its rites and regula mere flights of fancy suitable only for dull pedestrians. One recalls in this regard the famous tale told in the second book of the *Mathnawī* of the itinerant dervish who visited a *Khānaqāh* to partake of the Sufis' musical concert and victuals, giving fodder to his ass in their stable, only to find later that the Sufis had sold it while he was diverted by a greed for spiritual joy (having, in the meantime. become an enthralled participant in their *Samā')*. Realizing that this phony Sufi group in the *Khānaqāh* had duped him, he curses his own blind imitation *(taqlīd)* of the dervishes. Rumi moralizes: "Among a thousand mystics there are few true Sufis; the rest of them are all sustained by the spiritual empire and grace of that one saint"[444]—thus alluding, among other things, to the deteriorating condition of institutional Sufism in his day.

Shabistarī's own low opinion of the *Khānaqāh* institution to which he was more than likely affiliated, and his comparison of the piety of the Sufis inhabiting its edifice to "cant, spells and conjury," thus echos the general opprobrium expressed by most Sufi authors for the vulgar socialization of Sufism during the Mongol period. One might say that the evolution and crystallization of the spiritual ideals *(ma'ānī)* of Sufism into popularly exteriorized 'Orders' represented a collective socialization of Divine Love, a ritualization of the heart's original self-sacrificing service. The classical masters had always recognized that Sufism was ultimately, a matter of "making the One single" as Ḥallāj's last words went, and it was in this spirit that Abū Sa'īd ibn Abī'l-Khayr (d. 440/) remarked "Sufism was at first heartache *(alamān);* only later it became a subject to write about *(qalamān).*"[445] Needless to say, the same ladders by which you mount up become a heavy burden once you must carry them about. This negative attitude towards institutional Sufism is best reflected in the ghazals of Shabistarī's follower,

Maghribī, whose distaste for the political Sufism of the Timurid *khānaqāh*s and the institutions of exoteric Islamic scholastic theology is quite evident in these stanzas:

From oratory, monastery, and *khānaqāh;*
From shrine and convent have we fled,
From moments-in-meditation
Litanies, orations and recitations,
At last we've found respite.

Seminary and university we cast aside;
Its discourse, dictum and 'lectio',
Its issues and flaws, its 'quaestio'—
Its essays, doubts and subjects—transcended.

Beyond both pagoda and Ka'ba have we gone,
Beyond the Christian cincture and the cross,
And now we're free of bar and pub; the lane
That leads to the Tavern of Ruin, we need not walk.[446]

All the Sufi poets and writers from the sixth/twelfth century onward generally expressed their dislike for this malady of formalism, ritualization and the gradual 'watering down' of the high tradition of Sufism with its strict adherance to the ideals of spiritual poverty and abstraction from creation—which the external rites of the *khānaqāh* institution, to their mind, had come to represent. Instances of such ill-opinion of the institution are found in nearly all of Shabistarī's contemporaries. An outstanding example of this unconscious negative attitude is found in the symbolic interpretation of the term *khānaqāh* provided by Yaḥyā Bākharzī (d. 736/1335) in his Kubrawī manual of Sufism, the *Awrād al-aḥbāb wa fuṣūṣ al-ādāb,* in a passage devoted to elucidation of certain "Expressions of the Sufi Singers in *Samā',*" where he writes:

> The terms: *masjid, madrasa* and *khānaqāh* all allude to bondage and attachments and devotional works of both an inner and outer nature, such as common religious useages, habits, principles and commandments as well as [mystical states such as] grief, contraction, spiritual combat, asceticism, fear, hope and the known spiritual stations. Thus if a man sees

> one of these three places in a vision during retreat, the interpretation is the same: that his time of meditation *(waqt)* will be visited by contraction and restriction that day and his heart will experience less spiriutal expansion. If he beholds a congregational mosque, the interpretation is that his meditative time will be given greater concentration, although this interpretation is not absolute.[447]

It is obvious that if we accept Aristotle's view that "nothing exists in the imagination which did not first exist in the senses," *(De Anima* III. 3.429a) and assuming that an archetypal *khānaqāh* beyond the vicissitudes of socio-cultural change does *not* exist, one can only conclude that Bākharzī's theory of dream and vision interpretation—of the *khānaqāh* symbol at least—is based upon some obviously disagreeable sensory experiences he had had in the *khānaqāh*s of his own day. Another contemporary of Shabistarī, 'Izz al-Dīn Maḥmūd Kāshānī (d. 735/1334) in his Persian textbook and manual of Sufi theosophy and practise, the *Miṣbāḥ al-ḥidāya,* despite "his deep concern to to defend Sufism from its detractors and to demonstrate its roots in the Koran and Hadith,"[448] is honest enough to confess that the *khānaqāh*s of his day had experienced serious degeneration:

> Even if the establishment of the *khānaqāh* and its consecration as a place of congregation and residence for the Sufis is one of the more recent customs and virtuous traditions of the Sufis, this edifice has a direct connection and analogy with the *suffa,* which in the days of the Prophet served as the residence for the *fuqarā-yi ṣahāba.* . . . There is no doubt that the establishment of *khānaqāh*s, built in line with the original intent which this Islamic tradition represents, is one of the beautifying ornaments of the nation of Islam. Thus, the degeneration which has arisen in the present day [in the *khānaqāh* institution]—caused mainly by the deteriorating state of the sciences and disappearance of the traditions of the Sufis—should not be a reason for questioning and mocking the propriety of its original plan and Rule.[449]

Kāshānī's comments, illustrating the considerable decadence which had already occurred in the *khānaqāh* institution of his day, also convey the reason why the 'Rule' of the *khānaqāh*s had come to be regarded by many Persian Sufi poets as fetters to the free spirit of the 'inspired libertine' or 'pious rogue' *(rind)*. The *khānaqāh*'s rules and rituals were contrasted to a supra-institutional 'higher Sufism', represented by the symbolic term 'Tavern of Ruin' *(kharābāt),* the path to which, as 'Irāqī had sung, could be fared by "drunkards alone."[450] This latter symbol[451] was also highly celebrated by Shabistarī in the *Garden of Mysteries,* where it represented the spiritualized ideal which the temporal institution of the *khānaqāh,* immersed in the petty jealousy and fraternal discord to which all communal life is heir, could never hope to match. By means of the symbol of the 'Tavern', where intoxicated, one loses one's finite senses, leaving all physical direction behind, where personal profit and loss lose their significance, and where the self confronts its once and future ruination, the Persian Sufi poets recovered what the outward institution of Sufism, the *khānaqāh,* had denied them: a home that was not a house, an inner peace unconfined by time or space.

Making use of an exclusively Islamic symbolic lexicon the Persian Sufis found themselves unable to communicate the esoteric truths of this transcendental life of the spirit, so their mythopoeia expanded, like their inspiration itself, to embrace all climes and all faiths. As Bausani has pointed out, Zoroastrianism, the religion of Pre-Islamic Persia, became a particular object of celebration. Thus, the poetic topos of the 'Magian Tavern of Ruin' *(kharābāt-i Mughān)*—to ordinary Muslims a place of infidelity—became to the Persian Sufi poets, who styled themselves 'people of Reality' *(ahl-i ḥaqīqat),* a symbol of the Temple of Tolerance, lending a transcendental function to their vision which neither the corner Mosque nor the state-supported *khānaqāh* could provide. Ḥāfiẓ, refering to the Koranic verse XXIV 35: "God is the Light of the Heavens and the Earth" thus communicates the eternal 'placelessness' *(lā-makān)* of all true worship:

> It's Divine Light I see
> in the Magian Tavern of Ruin
> What a marvel! Just see,
> what light I behold
> & from where it comes!

Shabistarī's expression of this truth in the *Garden of Mystery* is as follows:

To 'haunt the tavern regularly' means liberty
from self. Although it bear the look of piety,
Selfhood is pure infidelity.

You have been given a sign of the Tavern of Ruin, that 'Unity is the abrogation of all but God'. The Tavern of Ruin belongs to the world without analogies; it is the station of careless lovers. The Tavern of Ruin is the nest of the bird of the soul; it is the threshold of 'placelessness'. The tavern haunter is ruin upon ruin, a realm in which the whole world appears as a mirage. The tavern haunter has neither compass nor termination; no one has ever seen his beginning nor end. Even if you raced a hundred years across the realm of ruination, neither any 'body' or nor 'self' would you find. One group there seems all footless and faceless, denuded of both toe and crown, neither faithful believers nor yet infidels. The wine of selflessness, having gone to their heads, has made them abandon both good and evil. They have imbibed a wine without either throat or lip, and found liberation from both shame and name. All the Sufis' pious clichés and words of ecstasy, the fantasia of solitude, mystical illuminations and miracles, they have cast away for one scent of the dregs, fallen over like drunkards, enamored of Nothingness: the toothpick, staff, prayer-mat and rosary, all pawned purely away for the dregs of the wine. Falling down and rising up through mud and water, their eyes are filled with blood instead of teardrops. Sometimes they are elated with joy in the realm of love like a royal footman, proud and exultant. Sometimes they turn their faces in shame to the wall; sometimes with radiant rosy complexions gladly ascend the gallows. Sometimes in the ecstatic mystic dance of the Beloved, they lose head and foot like the whirling heavens. Every strain which the minstrel plays conveys to them another ecstasy from the other world. They have shorn themselves of all color and odor and removed from their heads that ten-layer vesture. They have removed all hue, whether black, green or blue, being purged of all blemish with that unadulterated claret. They have quaffed one wine-cup of that clear wine, until like Sufis they have become refined from all qualities.[452]

One of the most enjoyable things about Sufi poetry to the modern reader is its expansive freedom from dogmatic and sectarian constrictions. The effect on the soul is one of ecstasy and liberation. In general, the mark of genuine Sufism (versus some modern forms of Islamic fundamentalism which decks itself out in Sufi terminology) and of Persian Sufism in particular, is this poetic freedom which bows to no authority but the God of the heart, and prays in no direction but from where the *viña divina* is poured. Expressing this boundless love of God, Ḥāfiẓ says:

> Every man longs for the Friend, the drunkard as much as
> the sober
> Every place is the House of Love, the Synagogue as much
> as the Mosque.[453]

Whereas Shabistarī's connection with the *Khānaqāh* institution is a matter of speculation, and his admiration of the *kharābāt* symbol in the *Garden of Mystery* reflects his transcendence of the social mores of popular Sufism, his relation to specific Sufi Shaykhs in his native Tabriz can be determined with a greater degree of historical accuracy, thanks in part to his own account, provided in the *Book of Felicity,* to which we now turn.

## Shabistarī and the Sufi Shaykhs of Tabriz in the *Sa'ādat-nāma*

One of the most interesting aspects about Shabistarī's *Sa'ādat-nāma,* a work which, although less celebrated than the *Garden of Mystery,* is equally valuable as a work of didactic poetry and unjustly judged by many critics to be of minor literary value, is the poet's incorporation for his own homiletic purposes of the sayings of many of the famous Sufis and savants of Tabriz who flourished either in the two centuries preceding him or were his contemporaries. As noted above, Shabistarī's work was deeply influenced by the many different mystico-religious currents circulating in Mongol Tabriz, steeped, as it was, in an intellectual milieu when the 'Bābās' and Sufi *pīrs* during this era and the preceding epoch, created an especially fervent and passionate spiritual ambience.[454]

Tabriz was only some forty miles southeast of the poet's birthplace, Shabistar, while only a few miles east of Shabistar lay the village of Sīs where the Kubrāwī Shaykh Ismā'īl Sīsī's (d. 785/1383 at age 118) *khānaqāh* was located.[455] Shabistarī composed his treatise on the *Human Exemplar of Divine Beauty (Shāhid-nāma,* a work no longer extant),[456] for a disciple of Sīsī named Shaykh Ibrāhīm according to the *Majālis al-'ushshāq* (written 908/1502), a work whose fictional and hagiographical nature has been frequently criticized.[457] Despite the fact that there is no mention of Shaykh Sīsī in Shabistarī's collected works and that this particular story is likely to be apocryphal, Shabistarī was probably well-acquainted with this eminent Kubrāwī master who counted among his protégés or disciples two of the greatest poets of the fourteenth century: Muḥammad 'Aṣṣār Tabrīzī (d. 792-3/1390-1)[458] and Qāsim-i Anwār. (One should also mention that Marāgha, birthplace of famous Sufi poet Awḥādī, was located only some seventy miles south of Tabriz. As noted in the last chapter, Awḥādī's *Jām-i Jam* was composed in Tabriz).

Some forty miles northwest of Tabriz, in the county of Marvand (the southern villages of which skirt the northern suburbs of Shabistar), lay the village of Ammand, birthplace of the celebrated Sufi poet Maghribī, who among the Persian Sufi poets of the next generation in Tabriz was, in many ways, as much Shabistarī's spiritual grandson, as his literary heir.[459] Two of Maghribī's foremost disciples, Aḥmad Farzand-i Musā Rashtī[460] and 'Abd al-Raḥīm Khalwatī, better known as Mashriqī Tabrīzī (d. 859/1454),[461] composed commentaries on the *Garden of Mystery.*

Aside from the various references by Ibn Karbalā'ī to Shabistarī's two spiritual masters (Amīn al-Dīn Tabrīzī, and Shaykh Bahā' al-Dīn), whose relation to the poet were discussed in chapter one, there are also many references in the *Sa'ādat-nāma* to the *dicta* and *exempla* of Sufi masters who resided or visited Tabriz in former times. These are discussed below in chronological order.

### Bābā Faraj Tabrīzī

Bābā Faraj bin Badal ibn Faraj Tabrīzī (d. 568/1172-3) was an eminent Tabrizi mystic, perhaps best known as one of the masters of the eponymous founder of the Kubrawiyya Order, Najm al-Dīn Kubrā.[462] He is mentioned twice in the *Sa'ādat-nāma.* Bābā Faraj's *zāwiya*-tomb complex in Tabriz during the Mongol period was highly venerated—"brighter in its glory than the sun," as it was described by Ibn Karbalā'ī.[463] Since Bābā Faraj had passed away on a Saturday, it was still the custom in the early Safavid period (Ibn Karbālā'ī's day) for people to regularly visit his tomb every Saturday, seeking its blessings.[464] However, Ibn Karbālā'ī seems to be relatively uninformed about Bābā Faraj, piecing his biography together from tidbits gleaned from both classical texts and local sources, citing his sources as being Jāmī's *Nafāḥāt al-uns,* a certain *Tadhkira* by Najm al-Dīn Zarkūb[465] and Ḥusayn Khwārazmī's *Sharḥ-i Mathnawī.*[466] Thus, commenting on Bābā Faraj's connection with institutional Sufism, he observed:

> "Najm al-Dīn Abū Bakr Zarkūb [d. 712/1312], who was one of the greatest masters, wrote that Shaykh 'Abd al-'Azīz al-Harawī—may God have mercy upon him—who was one of the perfect saints, spent seven years cleaning out the privies in the *Khānaqāh* of Bābā Faraj, from which statement may be deduced that Bābā Faraj occupied himself in the training of wayfarers *(sālikān,* i.e. on the Sufi Path)."[467]

According to a popular Sufi tradition recorded by Ibn Karbālā'ī, Rūmī's reference in the fifth book of his *Mathnawī* [468] to a certain Sufi who "rent his clothes in exasperation, and after being rent, he attained relief *(farajī).* Thus, his 'rent garment' was named 'Farajī" from this"—was inspired by the following famous account, which, in the version given by Jāmī, features the encounter of young Najm al-Dīn Kubrā with Bābā Faraj. As a young law student in Tabrīz, Najm al-Dīn took his teacher and fellow students to visit Bābā Faraj:

> We all entered and sat down before Bābā Faraj. After a moment our state was suddenly transformed. We witnessed an awesome majesty come over the face of Bābā Faraj. His countenance seemed to be burning as bright as the sun's disc. Suddenly, his clothes were rent apart. After an hour, he returned to his normal condition. He rose and attired me in these same clothes, saying, "It is not the proper time for you to be reading books. It is the time for you to make the head-lines in the book of the world." At that, I experienced a total change of inner state, and everything but God left my consciousness.
>
> When we left Bābā Faraj's house, my teacher enjoined me, "There is still some reading left to do if you are finish the

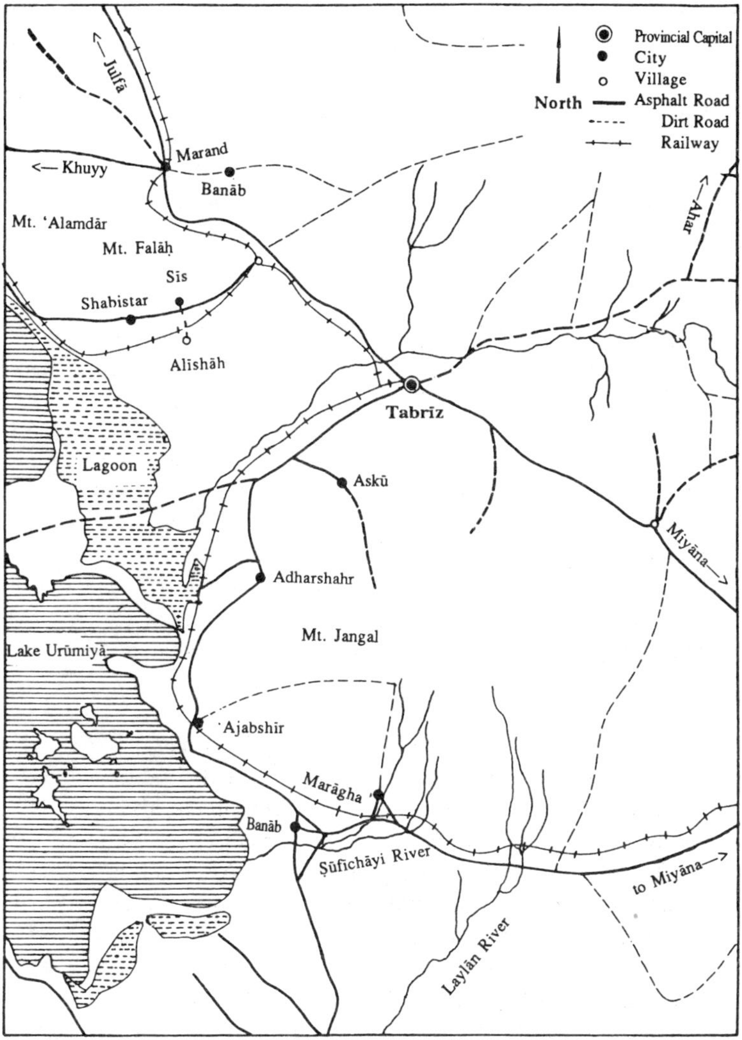


Map of Tabriz and its Environs. Courtesy of Muhammad Ali Pournurbakhsh.

*Commentary on Al-Sinat*.[469] Continue reading it for another two or three days; then go do as you will."

So I returned to my books. I saw Bābā Faraj enter my room. He said, "Yesterday, you experienced a thousand spiritual stations of the 'Knowledge of Certainty', yet today you have gone back to your books?"

Hearing this reproach, I abandoned my studies and busied myself with ascetic practices and retreats until arcane divine knowledge and the will to understand occult things appeared to me . . . ."[470]

This intimate relationship between Najm al-Dīn Kubrā and Bāba Faraj Tabrīzī, is, of course, one of the most important points made by the above tale. Shabistarī takes up this Kubrawī connection in the *Sa'ādat-nāma,* where he mentions Bābā Faraj in two places. In the first instance of a 'Bābā Faraj tale', he uses Bābā Faraj's adept riposte to a sceptic to illustrate his own doctrine of the 'relativity of evil'.[471]

—"Evil in itself,"
Bābā Faraj once said,
does not exist, and what
you see as 'bad' is not
an evil in itself."

An idiot who'd heard him speak
just then observed a cut-throat infidel.
He pressed the master, "Please tell
me what's the 'good' within that heathen fiend?"

Faraj replied, "Two secret virtues there are in him
that neither saint nor holy prophet have.
The first, whoever kills the fiend,
numbers among the fighters for the Faith.
Second, the man who's slain by him
becomes a chosen martyr whom all acclaim."

It's thus the eye that's chaste
and free of sin should see.
Unto the lovely all seems lovely.
The dervish sees all things like this;

that is the Sufi path of scrutiny.
Alas! I miss their company!
Suspecting ill of men is not a sign
of goodwill unto mankind. For you
to note and mark the faults and flaws
in fellow men and women
betrays the dervish way.[472]

Elsewhere in the *Sa'ādat-nāma,* another dictum of Bābā Faraj is used to illustrate a philosophical point about the createdness of the world. In this story, Bābā Faraj is interrogated by the famous Shāfi'ite jurisprudent and preacher Imām Abū Manṣūr Muḥammad Ḥafadat al-'Aṭṭārī al-Ṭūsī (d. 573/1177 or 571/1175), otherwise known as 'Khwāja Imām', who, like Najm al-Dīn Kubrā, was also a student of the Tabrizi jurisprudent Imām Muḥyī Sinat. Khwāja Imām was both Najm al-Dīn Kubrā's professor in *ḥadīth,* and a disciple in Sufism of Bābā Faraj.[473] Shabistarī states:

> Bābā Faraj gave a perfect reply when asked by Khwāja Imām, "Is the world of temporal origin *(muḥdath)* or eternal *(qadīm),* which view is maintained by those pure in heart?"
>
> Bābā replied—with a certainty borne of direct spiritual realization, making a point more precious than a pearl—"From the very first day that Faraj opened his eyes, the 'world' never entered the range of his vision. Why do you ask me for the description of something that neither the heart nor the eye has ever seen?"
>
> With this, Khwāja Imām recognized that here was a man of action *(mard-i kār)*[474] and so tossed his timber raft of (exoteric) knowledge back into the ocean.[475]

The heart enrapt with the light of Truth
for the space, the mass, the length and breadth
of the world has no regard. How long
with empty rhetoric, with greed
and graspingness, shall you go on?
Strive hard yourself to reach this stage.[476]

### Bābā Ḥasan

Another important Tabrizī Sufi Shaykh mentioned by Shabistarī was Bābā Ḥasan (d. 610/1213) who was born in the village of Nahand, part of the district of Rūdqāt in Tabriz.[477] He also directed a *khānaqāh* in Tabriz.[478] Ibn Karbālā'ī praises him very highly as

> the chief and leader of the Sufi Shaykhs of his day. This expression in respect to him is well known, that "'he is the Bābā of seventy Bābās', since it is said that in his day there were some seventy of the 'friends of God' *(awliyā')* who were all devotees of that sublime portal (and his *zāwiya* and *khāngāh* is in the same spot where his tomb is presently located).[479]

After providing the names of all these masters, among whom is included Khwāja Ṣā'īn al-Dīn Yaḥyā (d. 683/1284; discussed below, p. 134), Ibn Karbālā'ī goes on to comment that "many dear mystics have attained exalted degrees by means of his training *(tarbiyat)* and high-powered spiritual regard *(naẓar-i 'ālī himmat)*. Khwāja Muḥammad Kujujānī,[480] in particular, benefited from his spiritual regard."

Describing the Sufi doctrine of 'voluntary death', Shabistarī cites this tale of Bābā Ḥasan in the *Sa'ādat-nāma*:[481]

> Bābā Ḥasan saw a common man gripped by the throes of death. "Alas!" This is only the first time that he is losing his life; his distress arises from this. Go and give your soul unto the Oversoul, or else when it comes time to die, you will harrow your soul and fret to death. Whoever is an intimate confidant of the Beloved, with every breath he breathes, his soul takes a hundred 'last gasps'.[482]

### Sa'd al-Dīn b. Hamūya

Author of several works on Sufism, Shaykh Sa'd al-Dīn b. Ḥamūya (d. 658/1260) is perhaps best known as the spiritual master of 'Azīz Nasafī (d. between 1281-1300),[483] and the father of Shaykh Ṣadr al-Dīn Muḥammad ibn Ḥamūya, under whose direction Ghāzān Khān had embraced Islam. His name is featured at the head of the list of those Sufi masters who flourished in the Mongol period in

Ḥamdu'llāh Mawtawfī Qazwīnī's *Select History*.[484] He is also mentioned by the poet in the *Sa'ādat-nāma*.

According to Ibn Karbālā'ī, in 640/1242-3 Shaykh Sa'd al-Dīn visited Tabriz and stayed there for nine months.[485] During this period, he focused his spiritual regard *(naẓar)* on Najm al-Dīn Abū Bakr Zarkūb Tabrīzī (d. 712/1312; although the latter was but a child at the time) in the same manner that Bābā Faraj had endowed with spiritual insight *(naẓar)* Ḥamūya's own master—that is to say, Najm al-Dīn Kubrā—who had been a student in Tabriz some years earlier. This disciple, Najm al-Dīn Zarkūb, was a Sufi author contemporary with Shabistarī.[486] Shabistarī mentions Shaykh Ḥamūya in the *Sa'ādat-nāma* in order to expound his subtle exegesis of the phenomenon of the 'projection' of one's bad qualities on to others. Having explained that the moral philosophy of Sufism presupposes psychological self-awareness, and that all religious injunctions to do good *(amr bā'l-ma'rūf)* and prohibitions from doing ill depend upon purity of heart, Shabistarī relates:

> The venerable master, Shaykh Sa'd Dīn Ḥamūya was passing along a road with grace and dignity. A lake lay in the way of the master across which all had to pass. The master's steed approached the bank of the lake and jumped back when it saw its own reflection in the water.
>
> "Muddle and churn the water up so that his reflection will be concealed to him," said the Shaykh.
>
> At once the water became muddy and opaque, and the master's horse rode swiftly across the lake without trouble. The Shaykh then beckoned to his followers on every side:
>
> "This is the course for you to take," he indicated: "The horse of your lower soul *(nafs)* is like a restive unbroken colt. Take care that you do not become discomposed by it. As long as this horse flees from something, know that this derives from the reflection it has seen. When this steed is quieted down from the (frightening) vision of its 'self', you can of course mount it smoothly and ride it tamely."
>
> If by putting in practice a prophetic tradition *(sunnah)* it (the steed of your passions) views its (alarming) self, then go choose something which is religiously permissible *(mubāḥ)* instead of that.[487] Any act of devotion *('ibādat)* which is performed by you out of habit and by rote *('ādat),* only increases the strength of your lower soul *(nafs)*. Thus, the only

> remedy [from hypocrisy] for a person of religious sensibility is to act according to the form of contraries *(ṣūrat-i aḍdād)*. That is to say, it is more virtuous for you to frequent a Christian cloister *(dayr)* than to attend a mosque imagining yourself superior to others. All religious prescriptions in their essential core but prescribe (awareness of one's own) impotence; anyone with discrimination, understands this."[488]

As we can see from this passage, Shabistarī was deeply versed in the psychological lore which had been utilized for centuries by Muslim mystics to discipline the passions of the lower soul *(nafs)*. The worst sin is egocentricism, states the poet, and the highest form of knowledge is recognition of one's own impotence. Since all piety depends upon interior compunction, consequently, contrition is the source of all the virtues.

## 'Abd al-Raḥīm Tabrīzī

Another Sufi Shaykh of the same century mentioned in the *Sa'ādat-nāma* is Khwāja 'Abd al-Raḥīm Tabrīzī (d. 655/1257), whom Shabistarī praises for his extraordinary comprehension of Koranic hermeneutics and his comparison of the outer letter of the Koran with the human form, both of which conceal secret spiritual worlds.[489] Ibn Karbālā'ī also reiterates Shabistarī's praise and records 'Abd al-Raḥīm Tabrīzī's accomplishment in Arabic literary studies, describing him as a unique scholastic theologian *(mutakallim)* among the other Sufi Shaykhs and notables of his period—"for although outwardly illiterate *(ummī)* and having studied under no teacher, he had been vouchsafed the direct grace from the 'Mother of the Book' *(umm al-kitāb)*, so that whenever he parted his lips he spoke in a difficult and pleasantly abstruse Arabic diction, which could only be understood with great difficulty by learned scholars and savants."[490]

## Muḥammad Kujujī

The most celebrated local Sufi Shaykh to be mentioned by Shabistarī was Shaykh Muḥammad Kujujī, or "Kujūjānī" (d. Dhu-ḥihaj 677=April, 1279),[491] as Ḥamdu'llāh Mawtawfī Qazwīnī calls him,[492] a poet and master whose sons later occupied the post of "Shaykh al-Islam" in Tabriz under the early Jalāyirids and Timurids.[493] He was contemporary with Abāqā Khān (reg. 1265-82), the first successor of Hūlūgū Khān.

The virtues and spiritual attainments of Shaykh Kujujī were eulogized both by Shabistarī and Muḥammad 'Aṣṣār Tabrizī, and his *dicta* and *exempla* were made the subject of a separate hagiographical work in Arabic by Ḥasan al-Palāsī al-Shīrāzī. This treatise was later translated into Persian in 811/1408[494] by Najm al-Dīn Ṭāramī,[495] entitled *Tadhkira-yi Shaykh Muḥammad Ibn Sadīq al-Kujujī.*[496] Ibn Karbalā'ī's long account of Shaykh Kujujī[497] in his *Rawḍāt al-jinān wa jannāt al-janān* consists mainly of quotations from this *Tadhkira* by Ḥasan al-Palāsī. Unfortunately, aside from the *Tadhkira* by al-Pālāsī, no trace of the literary works of Shaykh Kujujī, whether in prose or verse, have been left to posterity. There is also very little known of his biography. However, his personality and spiritual presence did leave its mark among a few of his contemporaries in Tabriz—in particular, upon Maḥmūd Shabistarī and Muḥammad Aṣṣār Tabrīzī.

Shabistarī's notice of Shaykh Kujujī in the *Sa'ādat-nāma* is closely related to his exposition of Ibn 'Arabī's experiential understanding of *waḥdat,* divine Unity. His introduction of the "Tale" *(ḥikāyat)* of Muḥammad Kujujī into the *Sa'ādat-nāma* concludes, in fact, a prior demonstration of the verity of the inward experiential gnosis of the Sufis. The fifteen couplets of this "illustration" *(tamthīl),* nine of which are translated below, explain the poet's theory of mystical knowledge – outlining difference between *qadam* (foot) and *qalam* (pen): practical 'plodding' the Sufi Path vs. theoretical 'penmanship', *ḥāl* and *qāl,* that is to say: direct spiritual realization vs. discursive knowledge.[498] The couplets are used to introduce Kujujī's "Tale" *(ḥikāyat)* which immediately follows them.

Knowledge *('ilm),* states Shabistarī, can be compared to direct vision, ability *(qudrat)* to speech, and action *(af'āl)* to writing; each of these represent progressively inferior degrees; for this reason, he states:

> What spiritual vision *(naẓar)* senses
> in a breath of mystic consciousness
> no pen can write in the space of fifty years.
> Nor in a moment's span can anyone write
> What treading the way takes years to teach.

Tongue and pen are but envoys of the heart:
Ministers, consuls and attachés to the heart.
Attachés, yes, may mark the way
yet stages rise when attachés back away.
Gnostics have turned their eye into foot
and then have made of tongue a pen.
Thus Being and Nullity
to the Man of Divine Unity
in word and deed are one and the same.[499]

Immediately following these verses, Shabistarī launches into the "Kujujī Tale" mentioned above. This is clearly intended to demonstrate how this doctrine of mystical knowledge which is acquired by 'direct experience' had been put into practice by Shaykh Kujujī. The moral of the story teaches the same theosophical principle expressed by Rumi in the *Mathnawī:* that a rose's fragrance cannot be imbibed from the letters "R.O.S.E."—or to put it plainly: practical discipline and ethical application are the root of all speculative Sufism.

Before presenting this tale, it should be noted that Muḥammad Lāhījī in his famous commentary on the *Garden of Mystery* cites several lines from this same *ḥikāyat* to illustrate the doctrine of the threefold degrees of religious faith: the Lore of Certainty *('ilmu 'l-yaqīn),* the Eye of Certainty *('ainu 'l-yaqīn)* and the Truth of Certainty *(ḥaqqu 'l-yaqīn).*[500] Lāhījī's analysis of this doctrine, in the form of a gloss on two verses from Shabistarī's *Gulshan-i rāz,* of course, sheds considerable light on the mystical theology hidden within these lines. Thus a brief review of them will be helpful before studying the translation.

The two couplets in the *Gulshan-i rāz,* subject to Lāhījī's interpretation, relate to the story of Shaykh Kujujī. In them Shabistarī's informs us that the path of the Sufi wayfarer involves only two steps: 1. transcending the "S" of "Self-identity" *(hā-yi huwiyyat),* and 2. traversing the "plain of self-existence" *(ṣaḥrā-yi hastī).* Lāhījī interprets the first step (of the "S" of "Self-identity") as a reference to transcending the distorted vision which causes "essential determinations of the Absolute Being which create an (illusory) appearance of Multiplicity and make the One to appear as Many." One must overcome the delusion of the 'concretization' of existence with all its bewildering plurality, and "lift the veil of Multiplicity from the Face of divine Unity. Thus, the wayfarer witnesses Unity within Multiplicity, and sees God epiphanized in all things through the theophanies of His divine Names."[501] In this fashion, all of Nature is contemplated through the "Eye of Certainty." In short, upon taking the first step, "the aspirant percieves everything as Truth/Reality/God *(Ḥaqq)."*[502]

The second step involves an ascension to the station of the "Truth of Certainty." This journey is that of "the mystic wayfarer possessed by the power of divine attraction," who "traverses the vale of multiplicity through the process of mystico-moral development *(sulūk)* and interior self-purification *(tasfiya),* and so encompasses and passes beyond all the spiritual stations." Finally, he advances to the degree of 'the essential unitive state' *('ayn al-jam')* and 'Transcendent Unity' *(aḥadiyyat),*[503] at which point, "he beholds his being and all phenomena which stimulate the illusion of duality as eradicated and annihilated, thereby realizing 'subsistence-[in God]-after-annihilation [in God]. Whatever exists, he percieves and recognizes to be himself."[504]

In this same context, Lāhījī also discusses the phenomena of the spiritual stations *(maqāmāt)* of the Path, complaining that:

> The great masters of the *Ṭarīqat*—may God hallow their spirits—have determined that between the seeker and the Sought there are some one hundred stations, each of which includes another ten stations within it. "Verily between God and the devotee there are a thousand stations of light and darkness."[505] So long as the seeker has not completely traversed these stations by way of direct spiritual realization *(ḥāl),* he will never attain Union with the Reality, the Object of his Quest, by direct contemplative vision *(shuhūd).* Hence, it is plain to see that the company [of pseudo-Sufis] who — notwithstanding the fact that they contradict the principles of the *Sharī'a* in their behaviour and refuse to tread the path of the prophets and the saints—lay claim to realization of the truths of Reality *(ḥaqīqat)* and 'gnosis' *('irfān),*[506] are lost and in error, deprived of the [vision of the] beauty of the realities of Faith."[507]

And it is at this point that Lāhījī sees fit to introduce into his exegesis nine couplets from the Shabistarī's *Sa'ādat-nāma.* These verses are, in fact, from the following 'Tale of Shaykh Kujujī':[508]

A simpleton one day went to see the Master Muḥammad
Kujujī.[509]
"IT'S ME." he said, "Master, all that IS: I AM IT."
Take my word, I know I'm right."
The shaykh said, "Sunlight never once said:
" 'Let the press bring me proof that I've got light'
or asked for herald and printed dispatch to prove it shines.
The sun's brightness itself is proof enough
Listen well too: When did anyone ever commandeer a
bequest?
Who can seize a gift that's already his?"
How fine, how nuanced an answer he gave!
May God exalt that eminent man in grade!
His discourse all purveys such light,
as if the moonlight showered, or sunshine
strew down a rain of pearls,
his words thus flash and gleam. It seems
Each inch of earth in Kujujan is a mine
of such a living heart and mind.
The Man who percieves divine Unicity
in everything, never utters 'I' or 'me',
even if his light within outshine the sun.
No discourse is held, no word is spoke
by those who keep company with Unity
since all word and speech bear the taint
and mark of 'I' and 'mine' and 'me'.
'I' and 'mine' and 'thine' and 'thee'
are dieties framed by false duality.
What harmony remains between such clichés
and those who keep company with Unity?
Swarthy night and pure Light do not unite
The candle taper is snuffed out by raging gusts
The Path to Oneness is pure Experience:
it's a path to traverse, not to make converse;
On the floor of the sea, what place has alloquy?
Without CONTENTMENT, TRUST-IN-GOD & IMMATERIALITY
How can a man profess UNITY?
Of all the tales this crowd recites of Unity
What's left but ignominy?

This story reflects Shabistarī's awareness of the breach between speculative and practical Sufism *(taṣawwuf-i naẓarī wa taṣawwuf-i 'amalī)* and his perception that bridging the gap between these two perspectives ultimately depends upon transcending the 'S' of Selfhood. This tale, emphasizing the practical over the analytical and intellectual approach to Ibn 'Arabī's doctrine of the Unity of Being,[510] immediately follows Shabistarī's review of Ibn 'Arabī's philosophy and works (discussed below, V). His use of Shaykh Kujujī as a kind of poetic *deus ex machina* brought onto the poem's stage to defend the practical approach to this doctrine, underlines the poet's predilection for the mild and philosophical humour of this Tabrizī master. Kujujī did not directly deny his claimant's vision, but only gently and indirectly pointed out the simpleton's erroneous egocentric attitude. No clearer indication of Shabistarī's interest in the Sufi saints of Tabriz and the adoption of their *exempla* to the uses of his poetry than this passage can be found.

The tale also demonstrates how attuned the author of the *Sa'ādat-nāma* was to local mystical trends in Tabriz. Shaykh Kujujī was famed for his tolerance and mild temperment, as his biographer Ḥasan al-Palāsī recounts:

> Spite had no place in his breast, and in his chest lay deposited many of the Koran's secrets, esoteric interpretations and occult truths, all of which he expressed in the particular idiom and according to individual understanding of each sect who sought his guidance, in such a manner that nothing better can be imagined. . . . According to [the *ḥadīth]*, "Speak to people according to the mental capacity,"[511] he never spoke above anyone's level of understanding, and always gave his listeners their just due, both inwardly and outwardly. In word and deed he was devoid of hypocrisy and passion; his entire blessed being was an incarnation of beneficence and goodness towards the world and its inhabitants.[512]

Muḥammad 'Aṣṣār, another admirer of Shaykh Kujujī, in praise of this saintly master composed the following verses:

> Khwāja Muḥammad Shaykh Kujujī—how well he spoke to us:
> If you fare this path as a man, these words of his are enough:

He said: "Tread so well the way of the Law[513]
that none will raise their brows at your words;
and then, fare the Sufi Path[514] in such a way
you need not lay your hands on anyone else's words.[515]

The above quotations from Shabistarī and Muḥammad 'Aṣṣār, both Sufi poets from Tabriz who belonged to the generation succeeding Shaykh Kujujī, testify to the deep impression his saintly character, *dicta* and *exempla* had made upon the Persian mystics in this area of Ādharbāyjān. These sources depict both a man of action and contemplation, and a saintly personality renowned for uniting practice with preaching. His words, while steeped in a highly sophisticated erudite Islamic scholarship, yet bear all the marks of a Sufi saint's spontaneous creative freedom.

## Khwāja Ṣā'īn al-Dīn Yaḥyā

Last in chronological order among the Sufi Shaykhs of Tabriz mentioned by Shabistarī is Khwāja Ṣā'īn al-Dīn Yaḥyā (d. 683/1284), identified by Zarrīnkūb as merely "a famous preacher *(wā'iẓ)* and Shaykh."[516] However, Ibn Karbalā'ī portrays his character with more detail, noting that Khwāja Ṣā'īn al-Dīn directed a Sufi convent *(zāviya)* in Tabriz which at the end of the sixteenth century was still thriving famously:

> His convent was a centre of congregation for all the great saints, and particularly in his own day all the saints who resided in sweet land of Tabriz and its outlying districts, and even devotees from faraway countries used to take up residence there, considering service to Khwāja as the greatest honour of their lives. The reverend Khwāja himself held it his bounden duty to serve these people with his heart and soul.[517]

This highly venerated mystic, according to Ibn Karbalā'ī, was "one of the poles of the age . . . endowed with knowledge in the exoteric sciences *('ulūm-i ẓāhir)* and a renowned exotericist *(ahl-i bāṭin)* as well . . . contemporary with Shaykh Muḥammad Kujujānī . . . he died on 10 Rajab 684 [=Sept. 23, 1284], six years following the death of Shaykh Muḥammad Kujujānī . . . Shaykh Sa'd al-Dīn Maḥmūd Shabistarī . . . in the *Sa'ādat-nāma* quotes the dicta of

Khwāja [Ṣā'īn al-Dīn] concerning the difference between the Divine Command *(amr)* and Divine Will *(irādat),* in these lines:

> Have you heard that Khwāja Ṣā'īn Dīn said that the true guide in religion is one who himself follows the path of the Divine Command while regarding humankind from the standpoint of the Divine Will. How well and clear he spoke! —May God sanctify his pure spirit. May God Almighty grant us both the dual benefits of knowledge and justice to both you and I.[518]

As Zarrīnkūb points out, these reflections on Ṣā'īn al-Dīn in the *Sa'ādat-nāma* "bear witness to the influence of the spiritual atmosphere of Tabriz on the poet."[519]

* * *

The above brief study of six native—with the exception of Shaykh Sa'd al-Dīn b. Ḥamūya—Tabrizi mystics illustrate the intense passion for direct mystical realization and immediate experience which animated the intellectual life of this city. While each anecdote adduces some precise moral within the context of the didactic structure of the entire poem, and so, from a literary point of view makes the *Sa'ādat-nāma* comparable to the late didactic *mathnawiyyāt* of Sanā'ī or the *Būstān* of Sa'dī, each also gives us a unique glimpse into the cultural background of the poet's personality.

We have also observed above how the ambience of organized *Khānaqāh* Sufism pervades mediæval Persian literary history, insofar as most of the Sufi poets of the Mongol period were directly connected with, usually as leaders within, a *ṭarīqat* structure and Order centred around the *Khānaqāh* edifice. It is, in fact, this explicitly institutional nature of the lives of the Sufi poets in Mongol Persia which is the cultural foundation of their inspiration, and forms the social framework for most of their imagery and symbolism.

## Notes

397 This is also underlined by S.H. Nasr, "Spiritual Movements, Philosophy and Theology in the Safavid Period," *The Cambridge History of Iran,* VI, p. 658.

398 See my overview to *The Legacy of Mediæval Persian Sufism,* pp. 33-6 for a lengthier study of this revival.

399 Hodgson, *The Venture of Islam,* II, p. 211.

400 *The Venture of Islam,* II, p. 211.

401 *Ibid.*

402 Victor Danner, *The Islamic Tradition,* (New York: Amity House 1988), pp. 99-100.

403 *Shi'r-i fārsī dar 'ahd-i Shāh Rukh,* p. 19.

404 *A Literary History of Persia,* III, p. 17.

405 Manūchihr Murtaḍawī, *Masā'il 'asr-i Īlkhānān,* p. 322. On the Mongol's patronage of Sufism, see also Aḥmad Rajā'ī's lengthy discussion in his *Farhang-i ash'ār-i Ḥāfiẓ,* pp. 465-68, where he notes that "the strongest patrons of the eighth [fourteenth]-century Sufis were the Il-Khānid Mongols." -p. 465.

406 "The appearance of *khawānik* in Islam took place in the fourth century after Hegira. These buildings were founded by the Sufis exclusively dedicated to the worship of God Almighty." Thus wrote the Arab historiographer Maqrīzī (d. 865/1461). *Al-Khiṭaṭ al-Maqrīziyya* (Lebanon: Dār Iḥyā' al-'ulūm, n.d.) vol. 4, p. 271, cited in Aḥmad 'Alī Rajā'ī Bukhārā'ī, *Farhang-i ash'ār-i Ḥāfiẓ,* p. 161. *Khawānik* (the plural of Khānkāh) is a word of Persian origin meaning both 'house' and 'the place where a dinner-cloth is spread', that is to say, a restaurant. The word probably represents a combination of either of two terms: *khāna+gāh* or *khwān+gāh: khāna* meaning house' and *khwān* meaning 'foodcloth'. For an extended discussion of the philology of the term, see Kiyānī, *Tārīkh-i khānaqāh dar Irān,* (Tehran: Kitābkhāna Ṭahūrī, 1369 A.H.sh./1990), pp. 55-64. On the early history of the institution in Khurāsān, see Jacqueline Chabbi, "Remarques sur le développement historique des mouvements ascétiques et mystiques au Khurasan," *Studia Islamica* 46 (1977), pp. 5-72 and Margaret Malamud, "Sufi Organizations and Structures of Authority in Medieval Nishapur," *International Journal of Middle Eastern Studies,* 26/3 (1994), pp. 427-42.

407 For further discussion on which, see Hodgson, *The Venture of Islam,* II, p. 213ff.

408 Grace Martin Smith, *The Poetry of Yūnus Emre, a Turkish Sufi Poet* (University of California Press 1993), p. 5.

409 In the seventh/thirteenth century the Bākhārzī family, to give but one example out of a myriad, constructed and endowed the most impressive *khānaqāh* in (Fatḥābād, a suburb of) Bukharā which contained a madrasa attached to it. Abū'l-Mafākhar Bākhārzī (d. 736/1336) constructed a hospice for travellers, stables and a public bath in the 8th/14th century annexed onto the original edifice there. See Muhammad Isa Waley, "A Kubrawi Manual of Sufism: the *Fuṣūṣ al-ādāb* of Yaḥyā Bākharzī," in L. Lewisohn (ed.) *The Legacy of Mediæval Persian Sufism,* pp. 289-310; Muḥsin Kiyānī, *Tārīkh-i khānaqāh dar Irān,* pp. 192-95. Throughout the rest of Persia intensive activity in the construction of *khānaqāhs* continued as well during this period. In the seventh/twelfth and eighth/thirteenth centuries in the province of Yazd (southern Persia) according to the mediæval histories (such as the *Ṭarīkh-i Yazd* and the *Ṭarīkh-i jadīd-i Yazd)* some forty-five *khānaqāhs* are recorded as having been constructed and charitably endowed. (On which, see Īrāj Afshār,

"Khānaqāh-hā-yi Yazd," *Sufi, Faṣl-nāma-yi Khānaqāh-i Ni'matu'llāhī,* no. 8, Fall 1369 A.H.sh./1990, p. 11).

410 Walter Feldman has demonstrated that a similar situation existed *vis-à-vis* the creators of Ottoman Sufi poetry after the 15th century; see his "Mysticism, Didacticism and Authority in the Liturigical Poetry of the Halvetî Dervishes of Istanbul," *Edibeyat,* IV/2/NS (1993), p. 247.

411 *Farhang-i ash'ār-i Ḥāfiẓ,* p. 456; these reflections are also echoed by Q. Ghanī', *op. cit.,* p. 500.

412 *Dīwān-i Humām-i Tabrīzī,* ed. Rashīd 'Aywaḍī (Tabriz: 1351 A.Hsh./1972), introduction, p. 62.

413 *Dīwān-i Humān-i Tabrīzī,* p. 267.

414 *Rawḍāt al-jinān,* I, p. 106.

415 *Dīwān-i Humān-i Tabrīzī,* pp. 51, 14-5.

416 *Dīwān-i Humān-i Tabrīzī,* introduction, p. 47-48.

417 *Dīwān-i Humān-i Tabrīzī,* introduction, p. 73.

418 E.G. Browne, *A Literary History of Persia,* III, pp. 27-8.

419 Dawlatshāh's *Tadhkirat al-shu'arā,* ed. M. 'Abbāsī, pp. 241-42.

420 *Tadhkira al-shu'arā,* ed. Muḥammad 'Abbasī, pp. 246-47.

421 *Tadhkira al-shu'arā,* ed. Muḥammad 'Abbasī, p. 284.

422 Q. Ghanī, *op. cit.,* p. 501.

423 Hodgson, *The Venture of Islam,* II, pp. 217-18.

424 *The Venture of Islam,* II, pp. 213-14.

425 Beirut: Dār al-Kitāb al-'Arabī 1983.

426 *Majma' al-baḥrayn,* ed. Majīb Māyil Harawī, (Tehran 1364 A.Hsh./1985), pp. 292-303.

427 See chapters 28-30 of his *Awrād al-aḥbāb wa fuṣūṣ al-ādāb,* 2nd vol., ed. Īrāj Afshār (Tehran 1345 A.Hsh./1966), one of which has been translated and discussed by Muhammad Isa Waley, "Yaḥyā Bākharzī on Service in the *Khānaqāh,*" *Sufi: A Journal of Sufism,* issue 20 (1993), pp. 12-14.

428 *Farhang-i ash'ār-i Ḥāfiẓ,* p. 466.

429 For a chronicle of censorship in this regard, see Middle East Watch's publication: *Guardians of Thought: Limits on Freedom of Expression in Iran* (Washington, D.C./New York 1993).

430 H. Landolt, *Nūruddīn Isfarāyinī,* French introduction, p. 28.

431 *Ibid.,* p. 15.

432 Muḥammad Javād Mashkūr, *Tarīkh-i Tabrīz,* p. 801.

433 *Kullīyāt-i Qāsim-i Anwār,* ed. S. Nafīsī (Tehran: Kitāb-khāna Sanā'ī 1337 A.H.sh./1958), p. 402 (cf. pp. 83-85 of the editor's introduction).

434 See Leonard Lewisohn, "The Life and Times of Kamāl Khujandī," in Maria Eva Subtelny (ed.), *Annemarie Schimmel Festschrift,* pp. 163-77.

435 *Dīwān,* ed. Shidfar, # 1069

436 *Dīwān,* ed. Shidfar, # 1022

437 *Dīwān,* ed. Shidfar, #'s 133 (maqṭa'); 322 (maqṭa'); 412, v. 4; 452, v. 7; 633, v. 5.

438 For the chief derogatory references to the *Khānaqāh* institution, see *Mathnawī,* Book I: 156; II: 514; VI: 3856-60.

439 *Dīwān,* ed. Shidfar, # 706.

440 *Safar-nāma Ibn Baṭuṭṭa,* translated into Persian by Muḥammad Muwaḥḥid (Tehran, BTNK, 1337 A.H. sh.), p. 181. Cf. Kiyānī, *Tārīkh-i khānaqāh dar Irān,* p. 236.

441 See Javad Nurbakhsh, "A Glossary of Sufi Terms Relating to Christianity," in his *Jesus in the Eyes of the Sufis,* trans. Leonard Lewisohn, Terry Graham (London: KNP 1983), p. 421, for further discussion of this image.

442 MAS, *Gulshan-i rāz,* vv. 969-79.

443 Lāhījī, *Mafātīḥ al-i'jāz,* ed. Khāliqī & 'Iffat Karbāsī, p. 590.

444 *Mathnawī,* ed. R.A. Nicholson, 8 vols. (London: 1925-40), II: 534.

445 From the *Asrār al-ṭawḥīd;* cited by Javad Nurbakhsh, *Ma'ārif Ṣūfiyya* (London 1362 A.Hsh./1983), p. 26.

446 See Leonard Lewisohn (ed.) *Dīwān-i Muḥammad Shīrīn Maghribī* (Tehran: Tehran University Press; London: SOAS Publications 1993), p. 253, ghazal 122.

447 *Awrād al-aḥbāb wa fuṣūṣ al-ādāb,* ed. Īrāj Afshār, p. 248.

448 W.C. Chittick, s.v. "*'Awāref al-Ma'āref*" in *Encyclopedia Iranica,* II, p. 115.

449 'Izz al-Dīn Maḥmūd Kāshānī, *Meṣbāḥ al-ḥidāya,* edited by J. Humā'ī (Tehran 1946), p. 151.

450 In the same ghazal he also comments:

> None but the drunkard knows the tavern's secrets—
> how could the sober unveil the mysteries of that street?

—*Fakhruddin 'Iraqi: Divine Flashes,* trans. W.C. Chittick/P.L. Wilson, p. 41. "The term *kharābāt* symbolizes placelessness *(lā-makān),* wrote Muḥammad ibn Dārābī in his lexicon of Ḥāfiẓ's Sufi symbolism, the *Laṭīfa-yi ghaybī:* "The term *dayr-i kharābāt* 'convent of the Tavern of Ruin stands for the realm of archetypal meanings *('ālam-i ma'nā)* and the inner being of the perfect gnostic." 'Irāqī also describes the *kharābāt* as designating the runination of the attributes of humanity, and in a ghazal *(Dīwān-i Fakhr al-Dīn 'Irāqī,* ed. Sa'īd Nafasī, Tehran: n.d., p. 141) delineating the visionary topography of this transcendent Temple he says:

> This is no mosque, for us always to open the door for you, for you to dash in and run up to the front aisle. This is the Magian temple of ruin. Inside are living hearts, the place of the 'witness' and candle, the wine and ghazal, the lute and the song. Money and wit carry no weight beneath these arches. Its tenants's profit is all loss, land their loss, all profit.

451 The word (from whence "Cabaret"?) means both Tavern, Casino and Brothel. It first appeared in Persian literature in the poetry of Manūchihrī Dāmghānī (d. 432/1041), who used the term to mean a casino, a place where backgammon *(nard)* is played. In the poetry of Mas'ūd Sa'd Salmān (d. 515/1121) and Mu'azzī (d. 542/1147) it denoted a tavern, the same meaning which one finds in the poetry of 'Aṭṭār, in Hujwīrī's *Kashf al-maḥjūb* and in Ibn Munawwar's *Asrār al-tawḥīd.* The first recorded mystical useage of the term is in the poetry of Sanā'ī

(d. 535/1141). For good discussions of the etymology and evolution of the meaning of this term in Persian literature, see Aḥmad Rajā'ī, *Farhang-i ash'ār-i Ḥāfiẓ*, pp. 187-97 and Bahā' al-Dīn Khuramshāhī, *Ḥāfiẓ-nāma* (Tehran: Intishārāt-i 'Ilmī 1372 A.Hsh./1993, 2nd edit.), I, pp. 151-55.

452 MAS, *Gulshan-i rāz*, vv. 836-857.

453 *Dīwān-i Ḥāfiẓ*, ed. Parwīz Nātil Khanlarī (Tehran: Sahāmī 'ām 1362 A.Hsh./1983; 2nd ed.), ghazal 78: 3; p. 172.

454 Zarrīnkūb, *Justujū*, p. 319.

455 See Leonard Lewisohn, "A Critical Edition of the Divan of Maghribī (with an Introduction into his Life, Literary School and Mystical Poetry)," University of London, SOAS Ph.D. thesis 1988, pp. 198-208.

456 Zarrīnkūb, *Justujū*, p. 319.

457 E.G. Browne, *A Literary History of Persia*, pp. 339-40; Zarrīnkūb, *Justujū*, p. 319.

458 See Ḥasan Sādāt Naṣīrī (ed.), *Atashkada* of Loṭf 'Alī Bigdilī (Tehran: Amīr Kabīr 1957), p. 131n; Ibn Karbalā'ī, *Rawḍāt al-jinān*, I, p. 363.

459 Maghribī's relationship to Shabistarī is outlined by Ibn Karbalā'ī, *Rawḍāt al-jinān*, II, pp. 85-95; also cf. Zarrīnkūb, *Justujū*, p. 319.

460 *Sharḥ-i Aḥmad bin Musā*, written 844 A.H.; an MS. of this commentary exists in the Kitābkhāna Malik (no. 2257), dated 984 A.H. and another copy of the same is in the Kitābkhāna Majlis, dated 1048 A.H. See 'Aziz Dawlatābādī, *Sukhanvarān-i Ādharbāyjān*, p. 163.

461 His *Sharḥ-i bar baḍī az abyāt-i mushkila-yi Gulshan-i rāz* is cited by Ibn Karbalā'ī, *op. cit.*, I, p. 86. On Mashriqī, see Leonard Lewisohn, "The Life and Poetry of Mashreqi Tabrizi," pp. 99- 127.

462 A fact which lends him, in Ibn Karbālā'ī's eyes at least, an exalted spiritual rank: "The spiritual degree of the Reverend Bābā may be deduced from the fact that the likes of Najm al-Dīn, the 'Fashioner of Saints' *(walī-tarāshī)*, who was unequalled in the training of novices, and the like of whom has never appeared before, obtained spiritual insight *(naẓar)* from Bābā Faraj." *Rawḍāt al-jinān*, I, p. 377. Of Bābā Faraj's initiatic lineage, Ibn Karbālā'ī relates: "He was a disciple of Shaykh Aḥmad Marshaṭī; the latter was a disciple of Shaykh Muḥammad Sālim and the latter was a disciple of 'the leader of the Sufis' *(shaykh al-ṭā'ifa)* Junayd Baghdādī." *Ibid.*

463 He also records how a decade after Shabistarī's death the whole edifice was renovated (in 755/1353). *Rawḍāt al-jinān*, I, p. 376

464 He relates that that his own master would encourage people to visit his tomb and ask Bābā Faraj's spirit to solve their problems, "He would say, 'Go and stand across from the tomb of the venerable Bābā and present your problems to him in the same manner that men address their problems to living folk." *Ibid.*

465 Unknown, but certainly not the *Futuwwat-nāma* published in the collection edited by M. Ṣarrāf: *Rasā'īl-i Jawānmardān* (Tehran 1370).

466 That is to say, Kamāl al-Dīn Ḥusayn Khwārazmī's (d. 839/1436) *Jawāhir al-asrār wa zawāhir al-anwār.*

467 *Rawḍāt al-jinān*, I, p. 377.

468 *Mathnawī*, ed. R.A. Nicholson, V: 354-55.

469 A work on jurisprudence composed by Imām Muḥyī Sinat.

470 *Rawḍāt al-jinān,* I, p. 378.

471 On this doctrine, see L. Lewisohn, "The Transcendental Unity . . .", pp. 391-2.

472 MAS, pp. 198-99, *Sa'ādat-nāma,* vv. 925-31.

473 *Rawḍāt al-jinān,* I, pp. 286-7.

474 That is to say, a mystic whose principles matched his application of them; a man of spiritual practice rather than mere theory.

475 Exoteric knowledge *('ilm)* is compared to a flimsy potoon unable to fare the stormy seas of Certainty. Cf. Shakespheare *(Troilus & Cressida):*

On smooth Seas
How many Bawble Boats dare set their sails,
And make an equal way with firmer vessels:
But let the Tempest once enrage the Sea,
And then behold the string ribb'd Argosie
Bounding between the Ocean & the Air,
Like Perseus mounted on his Pegasus;
Then where are those weak Rivals of the Main?
Or to avoid the Tempest fled to port,
Or made a prey to Neptune. Even thus
Do empty shew & true priz'd Worth divide
In storms of Fortune . . .

476 MAS, p. 224, *Sa'ādat-nāma,* vv. 1232-9.

477 M.J. Mashkūr, *Tārīkh-i Tabrīz tā payān-i qarn-i nuhum-i hejrī,* p. 770.

478 "He was a disciple of "Pīr-i Hama"('Everybody's Master'), who in turn was a disciple of Shaykh Ṣadīq, who was a disciple of Bābā Aḥmad Shādābādī, who was a disciple of Muḥammad Khūshnām, who was a disciple of Akhī Faraj Zanjānī (d. 457/1065)." According to Ibn Karbālā'ī, the proper name of Pīr-i Hama is Pīr-i Mammad. —*Rawḍāt al-jinān,* II, p. 10.

479 *Rawḍāt al-jinān,* I, p. 49.

480 On Muḥammad Kujujānī or Kujujī, see *Rawḍāt al-jinān,* II, p. 10ff. and below, p. 128 ff.

481 This story is also cited by Ibn Karbālā'ī, *Rawḍāt al-jinān,* I, p. 53.

482 MAS, p. 176; *Sa'ādat-nāma,* vv. 504-507.

483 On their relationship, see Lloyd Ridgeon, "The Life and Times of 'Azīz Nasafī," *Sufi,* issue 22 (1994), pp. 31-35.

484 *Tā'rīkh-i guzīda,* ed. 'Abd al-Ḥusayn Nawā'ī (Tehran: Amīr Kabīr 1364 A.Hsh./1985), p. 670.

485 However, a visit to Tabriz at this date is not mentioned by Najīb Māyil Hirawī in his illuminating biographical study introducing his edition of Ḥamūya's *Al-Miṣbāḥ fī'l-taṣawwuf* (Tehran 1362 A.Hsh./1983), p. 13. Hirawī states, in fact that, Ḥamūya encountered his master, Najm al-Dīn Kubrā in 641 and was living in the city of Naṣībīn in 640 and thus could not have been in Tabriz.

486 *Rawḍāt al-jinān,* I, p. 418.

487 In Islamic theology, the *exempla* and *dicta* of the Prophet, and all that

which has made his life an example to Muslims, are called *sunnah* ('religiously obligatory'), whereas *mubāḥ* refers to that which the Prophet judged to be merely lawfully permissible or licit.

[488] MAS, pp. 231-2, *Sa'ādat-nāma,* vv. 1374-86. The last hemistich literally reads " . . . than to attend a mosque imagining 'I am better'," which is a reference to the Koran, XXXVIII: 76. "Iblis said: I am better than him. Thou created me of fire, whilst him Thou didst create of clay."

[489] MAS, p. 204, *Sa'ādat-nāma,* v. 1017.

[490] *Rawḍāt al-jinān,* I, pp. 117-18.

[491] This date is that which is found on his tombstone, which is still standing, according to Ja'far Sulṭān al-Qurrā'ī (ed.), Ibn Karbalā'ī Tabrīzī, *Rawḍāt al-jinān,* II, p. 532.

[492] *Tā'rīkh-i gūzīda*, p. 672. According to Qazwīnī he died in 670/1272-3.

[493] *Tadhkirat al-shu'arā (The Memoirs of the Poets),* ed. E.G. Browne, (London: 1901), p. 310; Javād Mashkūr, *Tarīkh-i Tabrīz,* pp. 846-7.

[494] *Rawḍāt al-jinān,* II, p. 533.

[495] A brief account of Najm al-Dīn Ṭāramī is given by Ibn Karbālā'ī who describes him as a "learned man" and praises the beauty of his translation of this *Tadhkira. (Rawḍāt al-jinān,* II, p. 223). Kamāl Khujandī wrote a *dūbaytī* in his honour, speaking of him hyperbolically, by way of a pun upon his name, as a "Star in Heaven" rivalling the Creator of the Firmament in his brillance.

[496] *Tadhkira-yi Shaykh Muḥammad Ibn Ṣadīq al-Kujujī* (Tehran: Chupkhāna Packitchi 1947).

[497] *Rawḍāt al-jinān,* II 9-38. Also cf. *Tārīkh-i Tabrīz tā payān-i qarn-i nuhum-i hijrī,* pp. 846-7

[498] On these two categories, see S.H. Nasr, "Persian Sufi Literature: its Spiritual and Cultural Significance" in L. Lewisohn (ed.) *The Legacy of Mediæval Persian Sufism*, p. 3

[499] MAS 169; *Sa'ādat-nāma,* vv. 352-60.

[500] See above, p. 25 ff.

[501] Lāhījī, *Mafātīḥ al-i'jāz,* ed. Khāliqī & 'Iffat Karbāsī, p. 201, vv. 6-10.

[502] *Ibid.,* p. 200, v. 3.

[503] *Aḥadiyyat* is the transcendent Oneness which excludes all multiplicity, which is distinct from divine Unity *(waḥidiyat)* which include multiplicity as well as the archetypal essences of things. On this distinction, see Toshiko Izutsu, *A Comparative Study of the Key Philosophical Concepts in Sufism and Taoism–Ibn 'Arabī and Lao-Tzu* (Tokyo 1966), pp. 48-9, 54-6. A.J. Arberry in his commentary on Niffarī's *Mawaqif and Mukhatabat* (London 1978; pp. 339-40), cites Sarrāj's definition of in the *Kitāb al-Luma'* that *"Jam'* is a general term referring to God without creation and the phenomenal world."

[504] Lāhījī, *Mafātīḥ,* p. 201, vv. 15-18

[505] A similar version of this *ḥadīth* is recorded by Muslim, Ibn Māja and Ibn Hanbal.

[506] J. Cooper notes that in Lāhījī's period (the early Safavid epoch) "the term *'irfān*, 'gnosis' gains currency in a more specific sense as the expression of inward illumination in a philosophic or quasi-philosophic language. Moreover, this inward illumination is now increasingly

attained through a spiritual affiliation to the Shi'ite *Imams*, most importantly to the Twelfth al-Mahdī. Sufism or *taṣawwuf,* for the gnostics *'(urafā'),* thus occasionally takes on a pejorative sense of charlatanry, while *'irfān*, for the Sufis, sometimes takes on a correspondingly pejorative sense of intellectual pretension. These two terms take on their various colourings from the political and religious contexts in which they are used." "Rūmī and *Ḥikmat:* Towards a reading of Sabziwārī's Commentary on the *Mathnawī,*" in L. Lewisohn, (ed.) *Classical Persian Sufism: from its Origins to Rumi,* (London: KNP 1994), p. 417. *'Irfan,* according to Lāhījī may be acquired by two methods: "The first method is particular to the theologians *('ulamā')* and is by way of logical demonstration, and involves going from effect to cause, or from [divine] Act to [divine] Quality and from Quality to the divine Essence. The second method is particular to the Prophets, Saints and Gnostics *(anbiyā, awliyā', wa 'urafā)* and is by way to purification of the inner being *(taṣfiya-yi bāṭin),* emptying of the transconscious *(takhliya-i sirr),* and the illumination of the spirit *(tajliya-yi rūḥ),* and this is the way of gnosis *(ma'rifat),* which is obtained by means of visionary disclosure and contemplation *(kashfī wa shuhūdī),* and is not known to anyone except for the absolutely enraptured mystic *(majdhūb-i muṭlaq)." Mafātīḥ,* p. 7. On the terms *taṣfiya, takhliya, tajliya,* see Javad Nurbakhsh, trans. Terry Graham, *Sufi Symbolism VII,* (London: KNP 1993), pp. 68-77

507 *Mafātīḥ,* p. 200, vv. 6-11.

508 From MAS, p. 170, vv. 377-79.

509 Shabistarī actually writes "Kujūjān."

510 Cf. Javad Nurbakhsh, "Two Approaches to the Principles of the Unity of Being," in L. Lewisohn (ed.), *The Legacy of Mediæval Persian Sufism,* pp. ix-xiii.

511 A *ḥadīth* often used by the Sufis. See Rūmī, *Mathnawī,* IV: 2577-84.

512 *Tadhkira-yi Shaykh . . . al-Kujujī,* p. 9.

513 *Sharī'a.*

514 *Ṭarīqa.*

515 Cited by Ja'far Sulṭān al-Qurrā'ī, *Rawḍāt al-jinān,* II, p. 533.

516 Zarrīnkūb, *Justujū,* p. 318.

517 *Rawḍāt al-jinān,* I 297

518 *Rawḍāt al-jinān,* I 296-7; MAS, p. 201, vv. 971-74. The difference between the Divine Command and Will refers to a problem in the scholastic theology (Kalām), which discusses how it is that God can command Obedience and exhort unto Good, yet at the same time also *will* Disobedience and Evil.

519 *Justujū,* p. 318.

# V

# SHABISTARĪ AND IBN ARABĪ

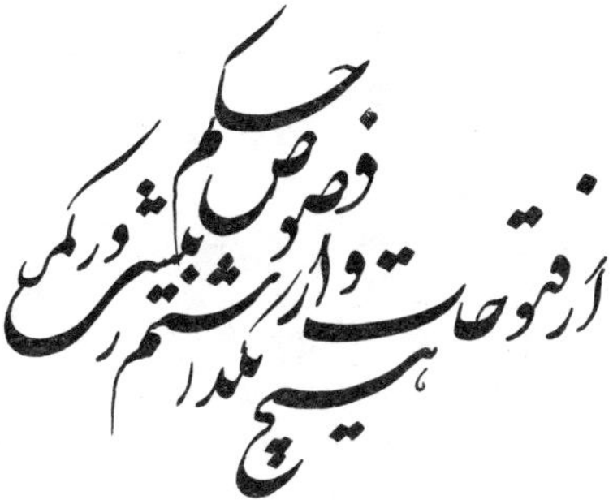

*I took pains in the study of the* Futūḥāt al-Makkiya *and the* Fuṣūṣ al-ḥikam, *neglecting no minute detail in either book.*

## The Akbarian Tradition of the *Garden of Mystery*

Among the Persian writers of the late thirteenth and early fourteenth centuries, Shabistarī was, with the possible exception of 'Irāqī, the foremost author to introduce Muḥyī al-Dīn Ibn 'Arabī's ideas and terminology into Persian poetry. One of the main reasons that his *Garden of Mystery* ranks as one of the greatest masterpieces of Persian literature is that it encapsulates, despite its brevity, the main philosophical doctrines of post-Ibn 'Arabīan Persian Sufism. Shabistarī's terse, pithy, epigramatically penetrating style in this poem had a lasting impact on subsequent Sufi devotees of Ibn 'Arabī's views.[520] The effect of Ibn 'Arabī's theosophy upon the works of Shabistarī is stressed by almost all modern scholars of his work; one hardly ever finds any mention of the *Garden of Mystery* in Persian literary studies which is not usually prefaced by certain explanatory comments locating his poem in the philosophical context of the Akbarian School. Thus, the *Gulshan-i rāz* has been described by three eminent Islamicists of the twentieth century, namely S.H. Nasr, Annemarie Schimmel and Henry Corbin, as, respectively, "the synopsis of all Sufi doctrine as expounded by Muḥyī al-Dīn, expressed in verses of celestial beauty that have become the common heritage of all Persian-speaking people"[521] – "the handiest introduction to the thought of post-Ibn 'Arabī Sufism,"[522] and "une sorte de vade-mecum des soufis iraniens."[523] Slightly less precise, another scholar pronounces it to be "like the works of Nasafī, an interesting example of the early, popular Sufi assimilation of many of Ibn 'Arabī's ideas (e.g. concerning the *insān kāmil)* in form not yet heavily influenced by the more systematic philosophic and theological language of the school of Qūnawī."[524] The fact that Shabistarī introduces the name of the Ibn 'Arabī in the first 350 couplets of his *Sa'ādat-nāma* (see below), and the deliberate tone of his statements concerning the pains he took in the study of the *Futūḥāt* and *Fuṣūs al-ḥikam*, also underlines the focal importance of Ibn 'Arabī not only in his own private education but also in the academic curricula of his epoch.

The teachings of Ibn 'Arabī had a momentous impact on the literary expression of Persian Sufism. Intellectual discourse, both in prose and verse, became subject to the influence of his literary style and imbued with his highly sophisticated metaphysical terminology. "His influence is so penetrating," a modern-day commentator on the Shaykh has maintained, "that it is impossible to understand the history of Islamic thought after the thirteenth century without a good understanding of Ibn 'Arabī. Especially in the Sunni world, where rational theology *(kalām)* suffered gradual ossification and 'Hellenistic' philosophy *(falsafa)* disappeared, it is not an exaggeration to say that *Ibn 'Arabī's thought became the only theology and philosophy*."[525]

The study of his teachings in Persia generated an extended family of Sufis with little physical geographical proximity and even less spiritual geneological affinity to each other, yet all of whom, in the words of Michel Chodkiewicz, shared by way of "the often unconscious phenomenon of impregnation" the technical vocabulary and *lingua franca* of Ibn 'Arabī.[526] Some of the most eminent Sufi scholars and poets of the Mongol and Timurid period are included among his followers, most of whom expressed their alliance with, and often, reliance upon, the Shaykh's teachings. Again, as Michel Chodkiewicz contends:

> His [Ibn 'Arabī's] work, in distinction to all that preceded it – including in my opinion that of Ghazālī – has a distinguishing feature . . . it has an answer for everything. Ontology, cosmology, prophetology, exegesis, ritual, it encompasses without exception all the domains on which the *ahl al-tasawwuf* need a trusted guide.[527]

Living in an intellectual milieu totally steeped in the philosophy of the Shaykh, in the age when a number of important commentators on Ibn 'Arabī's works flourished, it can hardly be considered a breach of philosophical practice that Shabistarī should have come under his influence. Some of the greatest names in Persian Sufism were counted as disciples or interpreters of his doctrines, including the likes of Awḥād al-Dīn Kirmānī (d. 635/1238), Ṣadr al-Dīn Qūnawī (d. 673/1274),[528] Fakhr al-Dīn 'Irāqī (d. 688/1289),[529] Sa'īd al-Dīn al-Farghānī (d. 699/1299),[530] 'Azīz al-Dīn Nasafī (d. circa 699-700/1300),[531] Mu'ayyid al-Dīn Jandī (d. 700/1301), 'Abd al-Razzāq al-Kāshānī (d. 740/1339 or 736/1335-6), 'Alā al-Dawla Simnānī,[532] Dāwūd Qayṣārī (d. 751/1350), and Rukn al-Dīn (Bābā Ruknā) Mas'ūd Shīrāzī (d. 768/1367),[533] not to mention those of the generation succeeding Shabistarī, such as "Ibn 'Arabī's faithful interpreter"[534] Maghribī, and Khwāja Muḥammad Pārsā (d. 822/1419).[535]

The transmission of Ibn 'Arabī's teachings to the Persian Sufis of later generations was carried out by rite of initiation, through transmission of the Akbarian *khirqa,* as well as by study of the commentaries composed on his works by Ibn 'Arabī's learned followers and the Shaykh's own books under scholars authorized to teach them. Considering the central role played by the Persian Sufis in the diffusion of the teachings and concepts of Ibn 'Arabī,[536] the following examples merit our consideration.

Awḥād al-Dīn Kirmānī, the well-known Persian poet and adherent of the school of Aḥmad Ghazzālī, met Ibn 'Arabī in 602/1205 and was later given the responsibility of being the guardian of Ibn 'Arabī's young stepson who was to become his foremost exponent: Ṣadr al-Dīn Qūnawī (d. 673/1274). Ibn 'Arabī praises Kirmānī highly in the *Futūḥāt.*[537]

Ibn 'Arabī's teachings also infiltrated, at an early stage, one of the most visionary Sufi Orders in Persia, the Kubrawiyya, founded by Najm al-Dīn Kubrā (d. 618/1221).[538] Two of Najm al-Dīn

Kubrā's students: Sa'd al-Dīn ibn Ḥamūya and Najm al-Dīn Rāzī (d. 654/1256) were in close contact with Ṣadr al-Dīn Qūnawī. Ḥamūya had spent time with Qūnawī in Aleppo and Qūnawī met Rāzī in Konya.[539] In the *Sa'ādat-nāma* (as noted in the last chapter, pp. 127-8), Shabistarī mentions Ḥamūya in relation to his subtle exegesis of the phenomenon of the projection of one's lower qualities onto others.[540]

The early eighth Muslim/late fourteenth Christian century was thus a very rich mystical milieu and the teachings and students of Ibn 'Arabī were everywhere to be found.

## Shabistari's Shadow in the Mirror of Ibn 'Arabi

As explained in chapter two, the influence of Ibn 'Arabī's theosophy on Shabistarī's prose and poetry is visible throughout all works. By his own admission Shabistarī spent a long time absorbed in deciphering his thought.[541] The most explicit evidence of the poet's absorption in Ibn 'Arabī's theosophy is found in the *Sa'ādat-nāma* (vv. 346-51). Here, in the one and only reference made concerning his mystical pedigree and *ṭarīqa* allegiance, he states that his "master and teacher" (*Shaykh wa istād-i man),* Amīn al-Dīn, could really give you good answers." That is to say, Amīn al-Dīn was both academically qualified to interpret the works of Ibn 'Arabī, as well as his spiritual guide on the *ṭarīqat*—the term *shaykh* here being indicative of his initiatory function and the epithet *ustād* ('master') an allusion to his academic professorship.

It is also highly relevant to note that Shabistarī's main literary heir in the succeeding generation of Akbarian poets in Tabriz, Muḥammad Shīrīn Maghribī, in the introduction to his own *Dīwān,* informs the reader that "the composer of this type of poetry, along with true visionaries and visionary men of the Truth, has said the same thing which the author of the *Tarjumān al-ashwāq* (=Ibn 'Arabī) has said . . . "[542] Maghribī then cites a long Arabic poem by Ibn 'Arabī and paraphrases it in Persian verse of his own. According to Ibn Karbālā'ī, Maghribī traced two lines of his spiritual pedigree to a *khirqa akbariyya,* that is, to initiatic descent from Ibn 'Arabī, both through his "spirituality" (by 'transcorporeal' initiation) and through his living disciples.[543] This initiatic and poetic kinship also explains why Maghribī is – after Rūmī – the poet most frequently cited by Shabistarī's exegete Muḥammad Lāhījī to illustrate the subtleties of the *Garden of Mystery.*

Although Shabistarī, like Maghribī, acknowledges his profound debt to the *Shaykh al-Akbar*, unlike him, he falls short of pledging total allegiance to his theosophy. In one passage in the *Sa'ādat-nāma*, as was noted in chapter two, he is highly critical of what appears to have been almost an 'Ibn 'Arabī fad' current among his contemporaries.[544] Elsewhere, in the beginning of the *Sa'ādat-nāma*, while voicing his erudite appreciation of Ibn 'Arabī, he admits to having certain reservations about the 'scandalous' nature of the Andalusian master's doctrine:

> [334-37] I spent a long part of my life studying the science of divine Unity, traveling through Egypt, Turkey, and Arabia, day after day, night after night. Year in and year out, for months on end, like time itself, I trekked through town and country, sometimes burning the midnight oil, sometimes making the moon my bedside lamp.
>
> [338-43] How vast were the climes I covered and many the scholars of the Sufic art I met—whose wondrous sayings I loved to collect to make the subject of my own esoteric compositions. In particular, I took pains in the study of the *Futūḥāt al-Makkiyya* and the *Fūṣūṣ al-ḥikam*, neglecting no minute detail in either book. Despite these exertions in scholarship, my heart still felt restless. I was puzzling over this disquiet and anxiety, when a hidden voice seemed to cry out within me, saying: "These words are written in the language of the heart; seek their meaning from your heart. Do not follow every quest and call; knock not upon every door."
>
> [344-46] Although the writings of Ibn 'Arabī revived both state and religion, they could not provide my heart any comfort. Although I saw the truth in all those good words, yet there was still something disturbing *(nū'-ī az āshūb)* about them. When I asked my Master to explain this mystery of this condition which had overcome me, he replied:
>
> > [347-49] "Ibn 'Arabī's whole intent and effort was to expound in words the mystical vision which he beheld *(naẓar)*. However, because his pen *(qalam)* lagged behind his footsteps *(qadam)* in exposition, certain slips of the pen occurred.[545] It wasn't that the riot *(fitna)* and spite *(kīnih)* came from Ibn 'Arabī himself; it was only an ugly negro[546] reflected in a mirror."

> [350-51] My Shaykh and Master, Amīn al-Dīn, could really give you good answers. Bless his pure soul. I have never seen another master of his calibre.[547]

Shabistarī's perplexity and discomposure expressed above (lines 344-46) in face of Ibn 'Arabī's writings, was, in fact, quite a normal reaction among the *'ulamā'* of this period. A modern commentator on his theosophy has even hypothesized that

> The image of Ibn 'Arabi provided by the subsequent Islamic tradition is often so ambiguous and contradictory that the reader's final impression is that of bewilderment and perplexity, i.e. exactly the state that Ibn 'Arabī always sought to induce by his difficult and dialectical writings. In his opinion, this state of mind and spirit helps transcend the established mental categories and judgements, and reach the highest possible understanding of the Reality.[548]

Shabistarī was no doubt also aware of the violent debates prompted by Ibn 'Arabī's writings in Egypt during the same period in which the *Sa'ādat-nāma* was composed. Shams al-Dīn al-Dhahabī (d. 751/1350) recorded how

> In 738 AH [i.e. 1337] the learned men of Egypt reached an agreement ordering them [Ibn 'Arabī's works] to be forsaken and prohibiting their study. The *qādī* Badr al-din al-Malikī says that [at present] the books by Ibn 'Arabī are non-existent in both Cairo and Alexandria, and no one dare even to show them in public. If they are found [in somebody's house] they are confiscated and burnt. As for the owner, he is tortured, and if he turns out to be an adept of [the ideas expressed in the writings] he is executed. Once the *Fuṣūṣ* was discovered in the book market. It was [immediately] confiscated, tied up with rope and dragged along the street to the chief *qādī,* where it was burnt, for the common good.[549]

No doubt such ritual book-burnings of Ibn 'Arabī's works and the inquisition of his followers by the mediæval Egyptian mullahs also lay heavy on Shabistarī's mind when he reflected that there was "something disturbing" about the books of al-Shaykh al-Akbar. On the other hand, his reservations about Ibn 'Arabī were fashioned most likely for the consumption of non-specialist readers; they were directed at the 'vulgar masses' or 'common folk' (*'amm)* rather than Sufi adepts. Michel Chodkiewicz, noting that "there are frequent instances of *mashāyikh* who have expressed reservations about Ibn 'Arabī, criticized his attitudes or forbidden their disciples to read his works," thus comments astutely that "these warnings or prohibitions are prompted by a concern to avoid the circulation of ideas which, although intrinsically true, would be ill understood by disciples whose spiritual qualifications are insufficient, and would put the orthodoxy of their faith in danger."[550]

Another passage (lines 344-51) in the selection from the *Sa'ādat-nāma* cited above communicates significant information about the poet's relationship with Ibn 'Arabī. Here, the lexicon of analytical psychology, provides us, I believe, with an important aid in understanding Shabistarī's disquieted reaction to Ibn 'Arabī. Shaykh Amīn al-Dīn diagnosed the poet's reaction to Ibn 'Arabī's writings as the type of the phenomenon which has since been described by C.G. Jung in modern psychological terms as the "projection of the shadow."[551]

Shabistarī's reaction was subjective. It hardly represented a proper assessment of Ibn 'Arabī's writings. As Amīn al-Dīn was careful to point out to him, the works of the *Magister Maximus*, in fact, did not harbor in themselves any *fitnah* (=riot, disturbance, i.e. cause of offence) or *kīnih* (="spite," but here referring to the 'rancour' generated by the reading scandalous material): rather, it was the dark half of the psyche, the "black face," – or, 'shadow', in psychological terms – which was shown to the poet through reading these works. The image of the 'black demon' – or "ugly negro reflected in a mirror," as the simile of Shabistarī's Shaykh depicted it – is an archetypal motif common to the folklore in diverse cultures throughout the world. As Marie-Louis von Franz, in her study of the phenomenon of projection in Jung's psychology, reveals:

> In many places mirrors are used as a defense against the evil eye of both human beings and of spirits, because it was thought that mirrors throw the harmful 'rays' back upon their source. In Spain, in Tripoli, and generally in China, mirrors are used for this purpose. A similar purpose is served by 'fear masks', that is, revoltingly evil-looking distorted faces that show the demon his own image, from which he flees in terror.[552]

The genius of Shabistarī's spiritual guide was to show him the inner demon within his own psyche—which was manifested and beheld in the mirror of Ibn 'Arabī's writing. "The demons are archetypal formations that appear in the field of human projections," as von Franz explains.[553] The unconscious psyche possesses a "mirroring" surface:

> For primordial man the phenomenon of mirrors and mirroring had the quality of a miracle; for him the mirrored image was a reality in its own right. *Spiegel,* the German word for "mirror," is cognate with the Latin word *speculum* and goes back to the Old High German *scukar,* "shadow-holder," from *skuwo,* "shadow," and *kar,* "vessel." . . . The mirrored image was regarded as shadow or as Doppelgänger, that is, as an image of the soul, and mirror therefore possessed great magical significance; *it was an instrument for becoming objectively conscious of one's soul by means of reflection,* in the literal sense of the word.[554]

The poetic image of the shadow-self, the Dr. Jekyll-like "face of the negro in a mirror" *(zisht zangī buwad bih ā'yīnih),* was thus successfully utilized by Shaykh Amīn al-Dīn to identify (to use our modern jargon) the phenomenon of "projection of the shadow" on the part of his disciple Shabistarī. The poet was thus made conscious, by means of reflection, in the mirror of his own soul, of his demonization of Ibn 'Arabī.

Interestingly enough, the poetic image of the "face of the negro in a mirror" used by Shabistarī here—or rather by Amīn al-Dīn to rebuke Shabistarī—seems to have been adopted by the poet from the third book of the *Mathnawī* (vv. 3439-44), where Rūmī, using the same image while reflecting on the fear caused by remembrance of death, exclaims:

> The tint and color of 'death' of every man
> belongs, my friend, to him alone.
> Death's a friend to the friend,
> and a foe to the foe.
> Before the Turk the looking-glass appears to shine.
> A mirror before the Negro's black like him.
> O you, who live in fear of death
> in flight from it

—your own 'self' it is you fear—oh soul, take note!
Your own face it is
that's hideous,
not the visage of Death.
Your soul is like a tree,
and Death: the fruit.
Your every unconscious thought and wish,
fair and foul, the pretty and the ugly,
has all been sown and spawned
by *you.*[555]

In these lines Rūmī propounds the same moral lesson which Shabistarī's mentor, Amīn al-Dīn, had meant to teach his student about Ibn 'Arabī's doctrine. The poetic topoi in both the poets cited above is certainly the same. Where Rūmī says "Your own face it is that's hideous," *(rū-yi zisht-i tū'ast)* and "A mirror before the Negro's black like him *(pīsh-i zangī āyina ham zankī'ast),"* Shabistarī's Shaykh (paraphrasing Mawlānā) sets forth the same image and idea. The spiritual teaching administered in both cases is also the same. "What man dreads so much [from death]," R.A Nicholson commented on these lines, "is really something conceived and produced by himself."[556] Just as the hideous visage of death is nothing but the frightening consciousness of one's own spiritual malady, Shabistarī's appalled reaction to Ibn 'Arabī, that nausea provoked by his reading the *Fuṣūṣ,* Amīn al-Dīn informs the poet, was nothing but the frightening vision of his own ignorance.[557]

Before we take leave of our psychoanalytical examination of this important passage in the *Sa'ādat-nāma,* one point remains to be considered. It took the insight of his erudite Sufi Shaykh to show our poet his 'ugly face': to display to him how misplaced were his views of Ibn 'Arabī. But can we not still see in him the presence of a hyper-critical tendency, a certain insecurity and immature intolerance of any views divergent from his own? The answer to this, as we examine his work, will be, I think, both yea and nay. Although Shabistarī severely criticized whatever he considered to be blasphemous, scandalous and contrary to the Ash'arite *madhhab, by his own standards,* that is, according to the Sufi tenets he held sacred and worthy of intellectual defence, he was not however an intolerant man. He certainly discerned deeply the value of tolerance, and in the same poem clearly recognized—in fact, describes in depth and detail—the phenomenon of the 'projection of the shadow', handing his own Shaykh's admonition back to us, the reader:

> The 'evil' thing you consider
> to hail from another,
> in truth it's just your ego: 'you'
> your 'self'—if you only knew.[558]

## Ibn 'Arabi's Presence in Shabistari's *Garden of Mystery*

As Lāhījī's commentary demonstrates, each verse of the *Garden of Mystery*, condensed in its crystalline conciseness, actually encapsulates entire chapters of the Shaykh's theosophy. One could just as well say that the *Mafātīḥ al-i'jāz* amounts to a monograph on Shabistarī's poem written in Akbarian technical terminology. Considering that the new critical edition of this commentary edited by Muḥammad Riḍā Barzgār Khāliqī and 'Iffat Karbāsī, when combined with its formidable number of useful indices, runs to some 818 pages of small print, no exhaustive analysis of Ibn 'Arabī's influence on the poet will be possible within the scope of a single chapter. I can only hope to outline a few of these influences in order to illustrate the vast inner world of the *Mundus imaginalis* represented by Ibn 'Arabī's teachings[559] as they are expressed in Lāhījī's commentary. Although Ibn 'Arabī's doctrines in the *Mafātīḥ al-i'jāz* crop up on almost every page and references to his commentators and followers, such as Maghribī, 'Irāqī, and Qayṣārī, abound, there are only a handful of direct references to Ibn 'Arabī himself. These include one citation from his *Dīwān*,[560] one reference to the *Futūḥāt al-Makkiyya*,[561] and six direct quotations from the *Fuṣūṣ al-ḥikam*.[562]

By way of illustration of how the Shaykh's teachings were integrated into mediæval Persian Sufism in general,[563] and into Shabistarī's lexicon in particular, some of these references will be reviewed below. In general, the best introduction to the subject of Ibn 'Arabī's impact on the inspiration of the *Gulshan-i rāz* are the following remarks by Prof. Zarrīnkūb:

> The influence of Muḥyī al-Dīn Ibn 'Arabī [on Shabistarī] is visible in most places in the *Gulshan-i rāz* and is especially apparent in the poet's treatment of subjects such as Being

*(wujūd),* [Existential] Manifestation *(ẓuhūr),* Non-being *('adam),* and the Effusion of Existence *(fayḍ).* It is also not merely perfunctory that in the *Sa'ādat-nāma* he remarks on his previous deep erudition in the *Futūḥāt* and the *Fuṣūṣ al-ḥikam.*

Particularly noteworthy among all such references is his statement that the world is like a body within which Man is the Spirit – recalling Shaykh Muḥyī al-Dīn's statement in the first chapter (on "The Wisdom of Divinity in the Word of Adam") of the *Fuṣūṣ al-ḥikam*[564] where Shaykh al-Akbar comments that the world was at first at "undifferentiated thing . . . without anything of the Spirit in it," and that Adam was its "Spirit."[565] The statement [by Shabistarī] that the world is a reflected image *('aks)* of God *(Ḥaqq*=the divine Truth or Reality) and that man is the eye within that reflected image, also recalls the concept enunciated by Ibn 'Arabī that man is the "Pupil of the divine Eye" *(ḥadaqat-i 'ayn-i Allāh).*[566]

Likewise, Shabistarī's reference [GR 263] to the Koranic description of man as "a tyrant and a fool" [Surah XXXIII: 72], where he incorporates the idea that these two descriptive attributes are "contrary to light," is most likely taken from the Shaykh al-Akbar's allusion in his chapter on Noah in the *Fuṣūṣ al-ḥikam,*[567] where he states that the term "the oppressors *(al-ẓālimīn)*" [in the verse, Koran LXXI: 28] "and increase not the oppressors in aught save ruin," is etymologically derived from the idea of 'darkness' *(ẓulmāt),* which is, of course, 'contrary to light', 'foolishness' also being, like 'darkness' in respect to man, the effect of his alienation from light.

The point raised by the poet in answer to the questioner's query concerning the apparent separation between the Eternal *(qadīm)* and created Being *(muḥdith):* that the Eternal Being is in fact not separate from created Being,[568] and that whatever one considers 'created' has no existence apart from the Eternal Being, is based on the idea that Creation *(ḥudūth)* and Eternity *(qidam)* are both qualities which belong to the 'determined forms' of Being *(a'yān-i mujūdāt)* and these forms are, in Ibn 'Arabī's doctrine, nothing but divine Words *(kalimāt Allāh).*[569] Now, to attribute 'temporal createdness' to these Words pertains only to their manifested condition *(ẓuhūr),* whereas from the standpoint of their 'immutablity' *(thubūt),* they are, in fact, Eternal. Hence, Shabistarī's assertion that the created and the Eternal are not, in fact, separate from each other, is derived from the statement of Ibn 'Arabī in the chapter on Moses of the *Fuṣūṣ al-ḥikam* where he expounds this idea in detail.[570]

The influence of the compositions of Ibn 'Arabī on the inspiration of the *Gulshan-i rāz* is found throughout this poem, and this is the reason why this small poem was considered as a *Summa theologica* by most of the reputable thinkers of the Safavid period, although, of course, Shabistarī was also deeply versed in the other sciences of his day, as is evident from his powerful theological talents and mastery.[571]

With these remarks of Zarrinkūb's on the formative role of Ibn 'Arabī's teachings in the creation of Shabistarī's poem in mind, we may now turn to an examination of specific verses in the *Gulshan-i rāz* relevant to this influence and their exegesis by Muḥammad Lāhījī according to the technical terminology of Ibn 'Arabī. My discussion below will be confined to three key themes in Shabistarī's thought: i.) Mystical Union; ii.) the Microcosm and the Perfect Man; and iii.) Prophecy and Sainthood.

## Mystical Union

The eleventh question which Shabistarī was challenged to versify in the *Garden of Mystery* concerns how man, who is, theologically speaking, a temporally 'created' being *(makhlūq),* fabricated by God, subject to all the limitations of the flesh, with his thought in constant flux, dazed by the constantly alternating psychological scenery of phantasy – can be said to realize 'Union' with the Divine, the Eternal Being Whose Existence is not subject to the limitations of this 'human, all too human' condition. To this question:

465 How can they say that man: a 'creature' frail, begotten
became "One" in "union" with the Divine?
How can man attain to the spirit's voyage and soul-
progression?

—the poet retorts:

466 It is divorce from created artifice,
which becomes fusion with the One divine.

It's enough to cast off 'self', your 'I' and 'mine':
to find Intimacy and Cognizance.
467 When possibility wipes free its dusty contingency
What's there to see—but Necessary Being, the Self-mandatory?
468 Both worlds are just like a fantasy,
eclipsing themselves each instant of their permanency.[572]

As posed, it seems that the question merits no reply except through paradox, for it posits an irreconcilable duality between humanity and Divinity, assuming the existence of an insurmountable metaphysical rupture between *animus* and *Spiritus*. In his reply, Shabistarī claims that this duality is only a mental construct and a psychological delusion. And, Lāhījī adds, one must not think that awareness, in a theoretical sense, of the world's 'illusion' or the self's 'delusion', will be, in itself, enough to induce gnosis or realization. Rather, the methodology of Sufism must be applied:

> Through the process of spiritual inquiry *(taḥqīq)* and [through the realization of] certainty *(yaqīn)* one must understand that what the Shaykh in these verses, and in the verses below and above them states—that one must become disengaged from [the human condition of] 'createdness' and distance oneself from imaginary appearances—refers to the pursuit of the course of 'ethical conduct' *(ṭarīq-i sulūk,* or 'soul-progession) and the spiritual method of the masters of the Spiritual Path *(rawish-i arbāb-i ṭarīqat)* under the guidance of a Perfect Man so that one may reach the stage of Annihilation-in-God *(fanā' fī 'llāh)* and Subsistence-in-God *(baqā' bi'llāh)* and finally, 'Union-with-God' is realized. It is not enough that one simply imagines that 'I do not exist' or merely reflect on the whence and whither of his self-identity and being. Such an attitude will merely lead to one's fall, and result in serious errors in one's thought. As long as one has not tasted honey, its relish is unknown; the mere mention of the word 'honey' never makes the mouth sweet.[573]

Interpreting the last line (468) cited above, while drawing upon the *Fuṣūṣ al-ḥikam,* Lāhījī notes that there is a direct link between the deceptive nature of fantasy and the illusory nature of the world.

The world is a theophanic appearance, a shadow of the Necessary Being, yet, by itself

> the existence of the world is an illusion, no more substantial or real than an image flitting through one's imagination. Shaykh Muḥyī al-Dīn 'Arabī—may God sanctify his spirit—in his chapter on Joseph (peace be upon him)[574] declares: "know that you are an imagination, as is all that you regard as other than yourself an imagination. All [relative] existence is an imagination within an imagination, the only Reality being God."[575]

Lāhījī concludes his exegesis of these lines by explaining that the world, having no existence apart from or independent of the Necessary Being, is in fact never divorced from its actual state of 'non-existence', its eternal contingency *vis-à-vis* God. Here, he has taken a cue from Shabistarī's *Sa'ādat-nāma,* where the same principle had also been elucidated.[576]

Some forty lines later on in the *Garden of Mystery,* we find Shabistarī still engaged in responding to the same query about the possiblity of 'mystical union' between creature and Creator. At this juncture in his exegesis, Lāhījī also finds occasion to introduce another reference to Ibn 'Arabī's *Fuṣūṣ al-ḥikam,* or rather—to the *Sharḥ-i Fuṣūṣ* by Dāwūd Qayṣārī. The verses he comments upon are the following:

500 Intellectus, animus, the total cosmos,
primum mobile and the globes of heaven
know – are all from outset
to end just one droplet.
501 When Death's Angel rings the knell
the existence of planets and firmaments
sinks into nothingness.
502 Surf surges and one wave cascades:
the cosmos, look, is effaced.
Beyond all doubt you'll know that verse:

"The earth in all its ornament . . . Our Order comes
We make it stubble, some mowed-down corn
as though yesterday it flourished not."[577]

503 Imagination all at once is swept aside
till in this House of Life just God abides.
504 You realize in that instant Proximity to God
beyond the 'you' and 'me' and 'thee' of self-identity
you are united then with the Friend.[578]

Lāhījī's rather lengthy commentary on these lines reveals that the manifestion of the fullness of divine Perfection entails both creation and destruction, insofar as the divine Essence and Names demand both manifestation and concealment. Basing himself on the verse of the Koran (Surah LV: 26-27) which states:

> All that dwells upon the earth is perishing, yet still
> abides the Face of thy Lord, majestic, splendid . . .

Lāhījī explains that as long as all appearances of creation are not utterly obliterated and annihilated, the divine Essence will remain concealed behind the veil of the Names and Attributes, occluding the absolute divine Unity. Just as the process of creation takes place by means of the epiphany of various divine Names (viz. the "Originator," *al-Mubdi'*, "the Creator," *al-Khāliq*, etc.), likewise

> the concealment and dissipation of the essential determinations of being is accomplished by medium of the theophany of the divine Names of the Essence, such as 'the One' *(aḥad)*, 'the Unique' *(fard)*, 'the Dominator' (*qahhār*), 'the Restorer' *(Mu'īd)*, 'the Slayer' *(Mumīt)*, 'the Obliterator' *(Māḥī)*, and 'the Rich' *(Ghanī)*. As long as both of these contrary significances remain unmanifested, universal knowledge, which is the basic purpose of creation, remains unmanifested."[579]

He goes on to explain that true understanding of these contrary attributes is only realized by the *'ārif* who is 'the Perfect Man'. Perfect Men can be found in every period; they are the 'Poles' *(aqṭāb)* and 'the Solitary Ones' *(afrād)*, who bear witness to the 'Greater Resurrection' occurring during their own lifetimes, "who, in this sensible condition of being, contemplate the ideal form of the resurrection; they behold their resurrection occurring here and now" before it occurs at the end of time. It is by virtue of their presence, their spiritual attainment and gnosis, that the world continues to subsist. But not until one has reached the degree of 'voluntary death' *(marg-i ikhtiyārī)* which rends the shrouds of gloom and the veils of light, "can this mystical state *(ḥāl),* which is the zenith of perfection of the contemplative vision of divine Unity, be realized."[580]

Apropos of the final couplet cited above (504), commenting on realizing "Proximity to God," Lāhījī sees fit to furnish the reader with a personal account, in the form of a vision, of the purport of these verses. Excusing himself for sidestepping into his own mystical 'trip', he remarks with adept Persian *courtesie* that his vision "was due to a grace which was constantly being renewed from a propitious locus in the Invisible Realm, and is only mentioned here for the sake of the divine grace to which it bears witness." Not only is Lāhījī's account a rare and important document in Islamic spirituality, and a testimony to the depth of his own visionary experience, personal engagement and degree of realization in the contemplative disciplines of Sufism, it also demonstrates the definitive status and sway which Qayṣārī's commentary on Ibn 'Arabī's *Fuṣūṣ* held in the mind of this eminent mystic exegete.[581] It is also significant that after this "dreadfully illuminative" mystic incident befell him, he should have turned to this text to illustrate the verse from the *Garden of Mystery* upon which he was engaged in exposition:

> During a period which I had spent in retirement, I had made an intention to undergo a forty-day retreat *(arba'īn).* Now, just when the composition of the commentary on the *Garden of Mystery* had come to this precise place in the text, one morning, after finishing the recitation of my dawn litanies and the spiritual duties entailed by these times *(waẓīfa-yi awqāt),* I had engaged in meditation. In the midst of my contemplation *(murāqaba)* a state of 'absence' *(ghaybat)*[582] presented itself, and I saw during a 'mystic incident' *(wāqi'a)* that a person had come to the door of my cell and said *Bismi'llāh.* I opened the door. I saw a person of dreadful luminosity enter, embrace me and then fly off up into space, carrying me up with him. Up in space, the entire world appeared to be full of light and luminosity. And then suddenly, he disappeared. At once, I saw that whatever pertained to this *faqīr* of personal essence *(ta'ayyun)* or self-existence *(hastī),* and whatever belonged to the world, was obliterated and nullified. I beheld the whole world as one single Light. And I saw that I was

> that Light, and that I was absolutely detached and devoid of all essential determinations and ties *(ta'ayyunāt wa qiyūd),* and besides myself nothing else existed. And after that, I emerged from that state . . .
>
> Hence, Shaykh Dawūd Qayṣārī—may God sanctify his spirit—in the eleventh chapter of his introduction to the *Sharḥ-i Fuṣūṣ* pronounced: "The denial of whoever has not tasted of this visionary site is considered by gnostics as a sign that his knowledge is inferior to those who have realized Union. His state, they say, indicates a sort of impotent perverseness, resulting from the weakness of his faith in the Prophets—peace be upon them. May God cure him of this and brighten his eyes with the light of faith, and illumine his heart with the sun of vision, so that he discover that essential properties *(a'yān)* of the world in a state of perpetual mutation and his own essential determination obliterated and overthrown, as the Almighty declares: "Yet they are in doubt about the new creation." [Koran L: 11][583]

Not only does the presence of Ibn 'Arabī permeate Lāhījī's hermeneutics, as can be seen from the allusion to the *Fuṣūṣ al-ḥikam* in his interpretation of the lines cited above (500-4) on mystical union, but the Shaykh al-Akbar also appears in the above recital as the supreme *magister ceremoniarum* in Lāhījī's own realm of visionary experience. It would seem that this pervasive presence of Ibn 'Arabī is, indeed, one of the more important "keys to the eloquence" *(mafātīḥ al-i'jāz),* in Lāhījī's words, to the *Garden of Mystery.*

## The Microcosm and the Perfect Man

Another theme which draws the attention of Lāhījī is the idea of the 'Human Form Divine', of Man as Microcosm as it appears in the *Garden of Mystery.* His discussion is laced with a mediæval love of minute detail, and by interweaving the technical terminology of Ibn 'Arabī into his exegesis, he cracks open the shell of Shabistarī's words, presenting the pith of the poet's doctrine from an erudite Akbarian perspective. Lāhījī's commentary presents the metaphysical microcosm within Shabistarī's concise and brief aphoristic verses, providing, as can be seen from the following evocative passage, a profoundly sapiential complement to the poem. The verse he is commenting on is:

649 A likeness exists exactly in the soul and body
of man of all that is—from the peaks to the depths
650 of the cosmos. Like you the cosmos is a creature,
a person, individual, distinct of feature.
The world's soul is you: its *anima mundi,*
and it, your body.[584]

—upon which Lāhījī gives this lengthy exposition:

The cosmos or world in sum is just like man;[585] it is one particular individual. Just as man has a body and a spirit, and his life and perfect physical development all derive from the spirit, in the same manner, the body without the spirit resembles an inanimate object. The cosmos or world is just like the body is in relation to man – man being its Spirit therein. As Shaykh Muḥyī al-Dīn Muḥammad 'Arabī—may God sanctify his spirit—states: "The Reality gave existence to the whole Cosmos [at first] as an undifferentiated thing without anything of the spirit in it, so that it was like an unpolished mirror . . . Thus the [divine] Command required [by its very nature] the reflective characteristic of the mirror of the Cosmos, and Adam was the very principle of reflection for that mirror and the spirit of that form . . . "[586]

The underlying cause of this phenomenon is that the cosmos had reached the full extent of its completion which was the purpose of creation, having attained its total realization in the human form. Although every particular object amid all the various parts of the cosmos is a theophanic receptacle manifesting *(maẓhar)* one of the divine Names, man alone manifests the totality of these Names, for man is a theophanic receptacle of the Name *Allāh,* the Name which is a comprehensive epitome of all the other divine Names. No other being so comprehensively manifests the totality of the divine Attributes as man. For this reason, he [Ibn 'Arabī] compared the world prior to man's existence—who totally integrated it into his microcosmic being—to a spiritless form.

. . . Without man the Face of God *(wajh-i Allāh)*[587] would not be shown forth to the world; rather, only certain aspects of other Names would be revealed. Now, since the spirit and reality of all the divine Names is the Comprehensive Name *Allāh,* likewise the spirit and reality of the world is the Perfect

> Man *(insān-i kāmil)* who is a theophanic receptacle of the Name *Allāh.* Because of the inseparable unity which exists between the object of theophany *(maẓhar)* and its formal exteriorization *(ẓāhir)* in existence, it should be understood that just as the divine Ipseity is diffused throughout everything, the Perfect Man likewise permeates the entire cosmos, the spirit and reality of the cosmos being, in actuality, the Perfect Man. That is why the poet said: "Like you the cosmos is a creature, a person, individual, distinct of feature" – meaning that the world, considered in its totality, is just like man, being one particular individual, called the 'Great Man' *(insān-i kabīr)* because of the appearance in it of the human reality.
>
> Just as each particular man has his own unique spirit and body, so all the various hierarchial degrees of the cosmos can also be likened to a body – with man as their spirit. This is why the poet stated: "The world's soul is you: its *anima mundi,* and it, your body." That is to say: 'you, man, are as the soul of the world, and the world in relation to you is as a body. Just as the accomplishments and knowledge which the body possesses all are due to the mediation of the spirit, likewise the gnosis, knowledge and true perfection of the world is generated by man—for no other being besides man is capable of attaining true gnosis'.[588]

The doctrine of the 'Perfect Man' referred to throughout the above passage, who is both the *homo imago Dei* and the *anima mundi* permeating all creation, can be found both in the *Futūḥāt* and the *Fuṣūṣ al-ḥikam* of Ibn 'Arabī. Although space does not permit a comprehensive examination of the idea here, a short summary will be given below based upon the monograph by Masataka Takeshita on *Ibn 'Arabī's Theory of the Perfect Man and its Place in the History of Islamic Thought.*[589] Combining the *homo imago Dei* theme with the *mundus imago hominus* motif in his theory of the Perfect Man, "because both man and the universe are created in His image,"[590] in his *'Uqlat al-mustawfiz,* Ibn 'Arabī states:

> God knew Himself, then knew the universe. Therefore the universe came out in the image, and God created man as a noble compendium, in which he united the concepts *(ma'ānī)* of the greater world, and He made man a copy *(nuskha)* which unites both what lies in the greater world and the Divine

> Names which are in the Divine Presence. Concerning this, the Prophet said, "God created Adam in His image."[591]

The idea of the ubiquity of the Perfect Man throughout all creation is based both upon Ibn 'Arabī's epistemology and ontology. According to his epistemological theory, "the universe exists in the image of man, and man in the image of the universe . . . because of this correspondence, man's self-knowledge amounts to his knowledge of the universe."[592] As expressed in Ibn 'Arabī's ontological theory, the ubiquity of the Perfect Man throughout creation described above by Lāhījī derives from the 'Unity of Being' according to which God's Existence is beheld as immanent in all things equally.[593] To Ibn 'Arabī, the Perfect Man is "the heart to the body of the universe,"[594] insofar as

> There is no one among existents who can contain God except the Perfect Man. He does not contain Him except through receiving [His] image. He [the Perfect Man] is the locus of God's self-manifestation.[595]

Thus, in essence, the divine *imago* which man displays is nothing other than the Divine Presence, which is the domain of the divine Names,[596] as Ibn 'Arabī notes in the *Futūḥāt:*

> All the Divine Names are bound to him [man=Adam] without one single exception. Thus, Adam came out in the image of the Name *Allāh,* because this name comprises all the Divine Names.[597]

From the above summary of the concept of the 'Perfect Man' it is obvious how Lāhījī's belief that "Without man, the Face of God would not be shown forth to the world; rather, only certain aspects of other Names would be revealed" – is directly derived from Ibn 'Arabī's anthropocentric theory that, in the words of Takeshita, "the Divine Names need man in order to be fully differentiated in the universe, because man's knowledge of the universe is essential to the differentiation of the universe. Ibn 'Arabī's seems to think that, if man were not in the universe, a tree would not even be a tree, and a mountain not a mountain."[598] The eminent Persian poet Jāmī, a contemporary of Lāhījī and a follower of the School of Ibn 'Arabī, thus explains the metaphysical reason why the God 'needed' man to manifest Himself:

> The One Essence willed to manifest Itself in the universal locus of manifestation, which is the all-embracing generated being *(al-kawn al-jāmi')* which also encompasses the divine Reality. This is the Perfect Man, for he is a locus of manifestation for both the Absolute Essence and the Names, Attributes and Acts, because of the all-comprehensiveness and equilibrium of his universal mode of existence and because of the scope and perfection of his state of being a locus. Moreover he unites the realities of the Necessary Being and the relations pertaining to the Divine Names with the realities of the possible beings and the attributes of creatures. So he brings together the level of all-comprehensive unity with that of particularization and embraces all that there is from the beginning to the end of the chain of being.[599]

In summary, it is evident from the foregoing study that each image, metaphor and idea employed by Shabistarī in couplets 649-50 cited above was deeply infused with an 'Ibn 'Arabī presence'.

## Prophecy and Sainthood

Shabistarī follows Ibn 'Arabī's doctrine in respect to Sainthood and Prophecy fairly closely, as can be seen from the discussion given by Lāhījī on our poet's couplet:

338 The Prophet is like the Sun
  and the Saint just like the moon.
Yet both combine to stand side by side
  within "I have a time with God."[600]

Although Lāhījī develops his commentary with considerable originality and visionary rigour, his explanation of the various degrees and kinds of prophecy is heavily influenced by Dāwūd Qayṣārī's *Sharḥ-i Fuṣūṣ*.[601] Indeed, as a leader of the Kubrāwī Order, Lāhījī was also affected by the doctrine of such Kubrāwī authors as Sa'd al-Dīn Ḥamūya and 'Azīz al-Dīn Nasafī, according to whom *walāya* is the interior dimension *(bāṭin)* of *nubuwwa,* and *nubuwwa* is the exterior dimension *(ẓāhir)* of the *walāya.*[602] Before considering the influences generated by Ibn 'Arabī upon Lāhījī's exegesis of this couplet, it is worth reviewing his own thought on this issue, which exhibits considerable originality. First, he elucidates the thorny dilemma of the so-called 'heretical' Sufi theory of the superiority of the saint to the prophet, and citing a "saying of one of the mystic notables"—here probably referring to the highly critical coverage given by 'Alā' al-Dawla Simnānī in his *Chil majlis* of Sa'd al-Dīn Hamūya's (d. 650/1253) and Ibn 'Arabī's views of this doctrine[603] —that "Saintship is superior to Prophecy and Saintship is higher than Prophecy," he comments that this can only have one meaning: that the saintly nature or *walāya* of a Prophet, which he enjoys by virtue of his nearness to God, is superior and higher to his own prophetic nature, that is, his *nubuwwa*. "This is because *walāya* represents an eternal, timeless and divinely Real dimension *(jahat-i ḥaqqānī abadī)* which has no temporal conclusion, whereas *nubuwwa* belongs to that dimension which exists in relation to creation, and is subject to termination." The poet's comparison of the Prophet to a sun and the Saint to a moon stems from the fact that

> The Prophet receives the light of prophecy and spiritual perfection from the sun of his own *walāya,* for being bathed in perfect illumination, he has no need of another person, nor does he follow anyone else. Thus, he is like a sun which is luminous by its very nature and has an enlightening influence upon others. However, the Saint—that is, *the Saint who is not also a Prophet*—is comparable to a moon because, howeversomuch the saint may be illumined and enlightened by the light of *walāya* and perfection, his light is still derived from the sun of the Prophet's Prophecy, since if the Saint does not follow the Prophet, he will not be able to attain to the most complete rank of Saintship.[604]

Lāhījī spends several pages on the analysis of the above-cited verse (338), noting, first of all, that the Prophet Muḥammad's mystical state to which Shabistarī referred, wherein (according to the famous *ḥadīth)* the Prophet claimed to enjoy "a time with God known to no previous Prophet nor any of the archangels," is something realized also by the Saint, being a grace vouchsafed from "the spiritual station of unification *(ittiḥād)* which both of them experience." He explains:

> Prophecy *(nabuwwat)* is an intermediary and ithmus *(barzakh)* between Saintship *(walāyat)* and Apostleship *(risālat),* insofar as Prophecy consists of information *(akhbār)*

concerning the divine realities *(ḥaqā'iq-i ilahiyya)* – that is to say, knowledge *(ma'rifat)* of the divine Essence, Qualities and Commands. This information is of two kinds:

The first type concerns knowledge of the divine Essence, Qualities and Commands and is particular to Saintship, whether or not this information is manifested through the medium of a Saint or a Prophet.

The second type of information pertains to that which involves the propagation of decrees of the religious law *(aḥkām-i shar'iyya)*, moral teachings, instruction in practical wisdom and applied political science. Such information is particular to apostleship, and is also termed 'Legislative Prophecy' *(nubuwwa-yi tashrī'ī)*, in contradistinction to the first (type of information described above) which is called 'General Prophecy' *(nubuwwa-yi ta'rīfī)*. Although 'Legislative Prophecy' came to end with the Prophet (Muḥammad), 'General Prophecy', which also entails Saintship *(walāyat)*, still remains active.

Now, Saintship is a property common to both Prophecy and Apostleship, and Prophecy *(nubuwwa)* generally includes both Apostleship and—more especially—Saintship. This is because every Apostle *(rasūl)* is, as a matter of course, a Prophet *(nabī)*, and every Prophet is a Saint *(walī)*, without it thereby being necessary that every Saint be a Prophet or every Prophet be an Apostle.

An exposition of this concept is provided by Shaykh Muḥyī al-Dīn Muḥammad 'Arabī—may God sanctify his spirit—in his chapter on Ezra [in the *Fuṣūṣ al-ḥikam]* where he states: "Know that Saintship is an all-inclusive and univeral sphere that never comes to an end, dedicated as it is to the universal communication [of divine truth]. As for the legislative function of Prophecy and Apostleship, it came to an end in Muḥammad. After him there will no longer be any law-bringing prophet or community to receive such, nor any apostle bringing divine law."[605]

After this direct citation from Ibn 'Arabī, Lāhījī continues his commentary on couplet 338 with a summary in Persian of some paragraphs of Ibn 'Arabī's exposition in the *Fuṣūṣ al-ḥikam* on the meaning of *walāya* and *nubuwwa*. Thus, where Ibn 'Arabī had pronounced:

> The special name of 'Friend' *(walī)* [of God] is not widely used of the servant in that he does not presume to share a name with his Lord, Who is God. God Himself is not called by the names 'prophet' or 'apostle', but He does call Himself "the Friend," and is so described. He says, *God is the Friend of those who believe,*[606] and, *He is the Friend, the Praiseworthy.*[607] The name is also often applied to God's servants, both alive and dead. With the termination of Prophecy and Apostleship, however, the servant no longer has another name not applicable also to the Reality.[608]

Lāhījī essentially paraphrases, without directly quoting, this text from the *Fuṣūṣ,* stating:

> Now, whereas the names Prophet and Apostle are not ascribed to God *(Ḥaqq),* since, of course, Prophecy and Apostleship have come to an end, the name 'the Friend' *(walī)* is ascribed to God, insofar as [God says]: *God is the Friend of those who believe,* and, *He is the Friend, the Praiseworthy,* and hence, this name will be subsistent forever. In the same manner, God, speaking through the mouth of Joseph, states: *You are my Friend in the world and the Hereafter.*[609] In this way the name *Walī* ('Saint') became prevalent as a term of reference used for the elect servants of God, due to their assumption of the character traits of God *(takhalluq-i īshān bih akhlāq-i illahī),*[610] their realization of annihilation in the divine Essence and Attributes, and subsistence in God following their annihilation and sobriety after [self-] obliteration *(baqā' ba'd al-fanā' wa ṣaḥw ba'd al-maḥw).*[611]

Thus, Shabistarī's vision of the respective roles of Prophecy and Saintship, as Lāhījī's commentary demonstrates, is completely grounded in Ibn 'Arabī's terminology and thought. While the poet's vision represents, indeed, his own personal experience and expression, it is also completely integrated into the Akbarian tradition of his contemporaries Qayṣārī and Kāshānī.

* * *

Among poets, as Northrop Frye pointed out long ago, the phenomenon of such a direct influence of philosophical ideas upon poetic imagery or doctrine—as has been demonstrated above in regard to

Shabistarī and Ibn 'Arabī—is not uncommon. In this respect, one may recall the all-pervading influence of Swedenborg's mysticism upon William Blake's early epic poetry, the overwhelming effect which reading Frazer's *Golden Bough* had on the early writings of Ezra Pound,[612] and the prevalence of the Indian imagery in the poetry of W.B. Yeats during the period in which he was engaged in the study of Vedanta philosophy.[613] While such modern poets are certainly 'original' in style and expression, their aesthetic taste and imagery was influenced by the philosophies they prized.[614]

## Notes

520 See Ṣamad Muwaḥḥid, MAS, introduction, p. 10; Zarrīnkūb, *Justujū,* p. 313.

521 S.H. Nasr, *Sufi Essays,* (London: George Allen & Unwin 1982), p. 99

522 Annemarie Schimmel, *Mystical Dimensions of Islam,* (Chapel Hill: University of N. Carolina 1975), p. 280.

523 Henry Corbin, *Histoire de la philosophie islamique,* (Paris: Editions Gallimard 1986), p. 420.

524 J.W. Morris, "Ibn 'Arabī and his Interpreters. Part II (Conclusion): Influences and Interpretations," *J.A.O.S.,* 107/1 (1987), p. 111.

525 Masataka Takeshita, *Ibn 'Arabī's Theory of the Perfect Man and its Place in the History of Islamic Thought* (Tokyo 1987), p. 1. Italics mine. Of this penetrating influence, James Morris observes: "Paraphrasing Whitehead's famous remark about Plato—and with something of the same degree of exaggeration—one could say that the history of Islamic thought subsequent to Ibn 'Arabī (at least down to the 18th century and the radically new encounter with the modern West) might largely be construed as a series of footnotes to his works."– J.W. Morris, "Ibn 'Arabī and his Interpreters. Part II: Influences and Intrepretations," *J.A.O.S.,* 106/4 (1986), p. 733.

526 Chodkiewicz, "The Diffusion of Ibn 'Arabī's Doctrine," *JMIAS,* IX (1991), p. 42.

527 *Ibid.,* p. 51.

528 On Qūnawī and Ibn 'Arabī, see W.C. Chittick, "Ibn 'Arabī and His School," in S.H. Nasr (ed.) *Islamic Spirituality II* (New York: Crossroad 1991), pp. 54-56.

529 See W.C. Chittick and P.L. Wilson (trans.), *Fakhruddin 'Iraqi: Divine Flashes.*

530 See Jalāl al-Dīn Āshtiyānī's introduction to his edition of Farghānī's *Mashāriq al-darārī* (Tehran 1979).

531 See Fritz Meier, "The Problem of Nature in the Esoteric Monism of Islam," in Joseph Campbell (ed.), *Spirit and Nature: Papers from the Eranos Yearbook,* (New York: 1954), vol. 1, pp. 149-203.

532 See H. Landolt, "Simnānī on *Waḥdat al-Wujūd,*" in M. Mohaghegh and

H. Landolt (eds.) *Collected Papers on Islamic Philosophy and Mysticism* (Tehran: 1971), pp. 91-110.

533 Author of the *Nuṣūṣ al-khuṣūṣ fī tarjumat al-Fuṣūṣ,* cited above, no. 32.

534 Annemarie Schimmel, *Mystical Dimensions of Islam*, p. 167.On Maghribī and Ibn 'Arabī, see L. Lewisohn (ed.) *Dīwān-i Muḥammad Shīrīn Maghribī,* Persian introduction, pp. 9-15.

535 On Muḥammad Pārsā and Ibn 'Arabī, see Hamid Algar, "Reflections of Ibn 'Arabī in the Early Naqshbandī Tradition," *JMIAS,* X (1991), pp. 47-48

536 Some of these influences are recorded by Claude Addas, *Quest for the Red Sulphur: The Life of Ibn 'Arabī* , pp. 229-33 and S.H. Nasr, "Seventh-century Sufism and the School of Ibn 'Arabī," in his *Sufi Essays,* pp. 97-103.

537 *Futūḥāt,* I, p. 127. See Claude Addas, *op. cit.,* p. 230.

538 See Muhammad Isa Waley, "Najm al-Dīn Kubrā and the Central Asian School of Sufism," in S.H. Nasr (ed.) *Islamic Spirituality II*, pp. 80-104.

539 *Nafaḥāt al-uns,* ed. M. Tawḥīdīpūr, pp. 429; 435. Cited by Claude Addas, *Quest for the Red Sulphur,* p. 231. For the Timurid-period historian Ḥamdu'llāh Mawtawfī Qazwīnī, Shaykh Hammūya heads the list of the important Sufi masters who flourished in the Mongol period. *Tā'rīkh-i guzīda,* p. 670.

540 MAS, pp. 231-2, vv. 1374-84.

541 MAS, *Sa'adatnāma,* p. 168, vv. 334-43.

542 *Dīwān-i Maghribī,* ed. L. Lewisohn, p. 4.

543 *Rawḍāt al-jinān,* I: 67-9. For a translation and discussion of this pedigree, see L. Lewisohn, "A Critical Edition of the Dīwān of Maghribī (with an Introduction into his Life, Literary School, and Mystical Poetry)," I, pp. 68ff.

544 MAS, p. 180, *Sa'ādat-nāma,* v. 618.

545 *Pā'yi taḥrīr az ān sabab larzīd.* Literally: "the foot of his writing stumbled."

546 The term 'ugly negro' *(zishtī-yi zangī)* here has no racist overtones; the reference is moreover to the 'black-faced' – that is to say, 'disgraced' person as a topos which belongs to the general stock of classical Persian imagery, and implies no prejudice against any particular race or color on the poet's part. Just as the Hindu is described as a base slave, so the negro is often described as 'ugly' in Persian poetry, as Annemarie Schimmel points out: "Turk and Hindu: A Poetical Image and its Application to Historical Fact," in S. Vryonis Jr. (ed.), *Islam and Cultural Change in the Middle Ages,* (Wiesbaden: Harrosowitz 1975), pp. 107-26.

547 Shabistarī, *Sa'ādatnāma,* in MAS, p. 168. Concerning Amīn al-Dīn, see chapter 1.

548 Alexander Knysh, "Ibn 'Arabī in the Later Islamic Tradition," in S. Hirtenstein & M. Tiernan (eds.) *Muhyiddin Ibn 'Arabī: A Commemorative Volume*, p. 314.

549 From the *Mukhtasar* of Ibn al-Ahdal, cited by Alexander Knysh, "Ibn 'Arabī in the Later Islamic Tradition," p. 315

550 "The Diffusion of Ibn 'Arabī's Doctrine," p. 39.

551 For a good study of Jung's theory, see Marie-Louis von Franz, *Projection and Re-Collection in Jungian Psychology,* translated from the German by W.H. Kennedy (London: Open court 1980).

552 *Projection and Re-Collection*, p. 183.

553 See her chapter "The Evil Demons" in *Projection and Re-Collection*, p. 117.

554 *Ibid.*, pp. 182-3. Italic mine. Also cf. Robert Bly, *A Little Book of the Human Shadow,* ed. William Booth (San Francisco 1988), pp. 29-43.

555 *Mathnawī,* ed. R.A. Nicholson, III, vv. 3439-43

556 Nicholson, *ibid.*, commentary on book 3 of the *Mathnawī,* p. 87.

557 A modern student of Ibn 'Arabī, noting the prevalence of popular misapprehension of his thought, has thus remarked: "Stressing the contrast between the 'real' Ibn 'Arabī, and his image shaped by the subsequent Islamic tradition and polemic, one should not overlook the common feature of both: their controversial character, which makes them an ideal starting-point for all kinds of debates. The Shaykh's image invested with either positive or negative qualities may be treated as a sort of illustration of his famous thesis concerning 'the God created in belief'. See R.J.W. Austin (trans.) *Ibn al-'Arabī: The Bezels of Wisdom,* pp. 282-3. Paraphrasing his words: He is what people think Him to be, however far is their notion from the reality. If we further extend this daring (or maybe far-fetched) comparison, we can assume that Ibn 'Arabī is understood by any man in accordance with his eternal 'predisposition' *(isti'dād),* and ability to grasp the subtleties of the Shaykh's personality and thought. In this regard, he seems to have shared the fate of almost all great men, who usually lose their true identity to popularity and end up as ideological symbols and political slogans. . . . In any case, being a symbol presupposes justified as well as unjustified attributions and suppositions, which contribute to the further shaping of an image." –Alexander Knysh, "Ibn 'Arabī in the Later Islamic Tradition," p. 320.

558 MAS, *Sa'ādat-nāma,* v. 1356. Also cf. vv. 1167-0; 1175-80 and especially the fascinating analysis of the phenomenon of projection in lines 1374-83, where the poet remarks: "As long as you find in your lower soul something which causes you dread and offence, realize that is but an image cast from the vision of itself reflected in that thing." Cf. also the study of Sa'd al-Dīn Ḥammuya in chapter 4 above.

559 Cf. Ibn 'Arabī's remark in the *Futūḥāt:* "What we deposit in every chapter, in relation to what we have, is but a drop in the ocean." –Cited by W.C. Chittick, *The Sufi Path of Knowledge: Ibn al-'Arabī's Metaphysics of Imagination* (Albany: SUNY 1989), p. xii.

560 Lāhījī, *Mafātīḥ al-i'jāz,* ed. Khāliqī and Karbāsī, pp. 102,

561 *Ibid.*, p. 117. There is also a citation from the *Futūḥāt* on p. 350, without mentioning it as a source.

562 *Ibid.*, pp. 117, 170, 232, 329, 424, 434.

563 For further comments on this, see my essay on "The Transcendental Unity of Polytheism and Monotheism in the Sufism of Shabistarī," in *The Legacy of Mediæval Persian Sufism,* pp. 379-81.

564 See Lāhījī, *Mafātīḥ al-i'jāz,* ed. Khāliqī and Karbāsī, p. 474.

565 For the full text of this statement with a study, see below: p. 159 ff. The original quotation (given by Lāhījī, *ibid.)* from Ibn 'Arabī referred to here is as follows: "The Reality gave existence to the whole Cosmos [at first] as an undifferentiated thing without anything of the spirit in it, so that it was like an unpolished mirror. ... Thus the [divine] Command required [by its very nature] the reflective characteristic of the mirror of the Cosmos, and Adam was the very principle of reflection for that mirror and the spirit of that form ... " –R.J.W. Austin (trans.) *Ibn al-'Arabī: The Bezels of Wisdom,* pp. 50-51.

566 See MAS, p. 72, v. 140, and Lāhījī, *Mafātīḥ al-i'jāz,* ed. Khāliqī/Karbāsī, p. 96.

567 See R.J.W. Austin (trans.) *Ibn al-'Arabī: The Bezels of Wisdom,* p. 81, referring to Koran LXXI: 28. Lāhījī in fact refers to this chapter in the *Fuṣūṣ,* and to Ibn 'Arabī by name, when interpreting this verse; see his *Mafātīḥ al-i'jāz,* ed. Khāliqī & Karbāsī, p. 170. Lāhījī seems to have been following Qayṣarī's *Sharḥ-i Fuṣūṣ* here, which was reproduced in Persian (circa 835-838/ 1431-38) with a great deal of additions by Tāj al-Dīn ibn Ḥasan Khwārazmī in his own commentary also entitled *Sharḥ-i Fuṣūṣ al-ḥikam,* ed. Najīb Māyil Harawī (Tehran: 1368 A.Hsh./1989, 2nd ed.), p. 205. For an interesting and original exposé of Ibn'Arabī's ideas along these lines, quite different from the commentaries of Qayṣarī/Khwārazmī, see also Rukn al-Dīn Mas'ūd Shīrāzī, *Nuṣūṣ al-khuṣūṣ fī tarjumat al-Fuṣūṣ,* ed. Rajab'alī Maẓlūmī (Tehran: 1359), pp. 334-35.

568 MAS, p. 96, v. 702ff and Lāhījī, *Mafātīḥ al-i'jāz,* ed. Khāliqī & Karbāsī, pp. 455-6.

569 As the Shaykh himself states in the *Fuṣūṣ,* ed. Abū al-'Alā 'Afīfī (Beirut: Dār al-kitāb al-'Arabī, n.d.), I, p. 211. For a good discussion of this idea in Ibn 'Arabī's works, see Su'ād al-Ḥakīm, *Al-Mu'jam al-ṣūfī,* (Beirut 1981), p. 976ff.

570 For a good exposition of Ibn 'Arabī's view of this in the *Fuṣūṣ,* see Khwārazmī, *Sharḥ-i Fuṣūṣ al-ḥikam,* p. 764-65.

571 Zarrīnkūb, "Sayrī dar *Gulshan-i rāz,*" p. 261.

572 MAS 465-68; Lāhījī, *Mafātīḥ al-i'jāz,* ed. Khāliqī & Karbāsī, p. 328-9.

573 Lāhījī, *Mafātīḥ al-i'jāz,* ed. Khāliqī & Karbāsī, p. 329.

574 See *Fuṣūṣ al-ḥikam,* ed. Abū al-'Alā' 'Afīfī (Beriut: Dār al-Kitāb al-Arabī 1946), p. 104, v. 10ff. Also see R.J.W. Austin (trans.) *Ibn al-'Arabī: The Bezels of Wisdom,* p. 125.

575 Lāhījī, *Mafātīḥ al-i'jāz,* ed. Khāliqī & Karbāsī, pp. 329-30.

576 See MAS, p. 167, vv. 318-19.

577 Koran X: 24.

578 MAS, p. 88, vv. 500-04; GR, p. 34.

579 Lāhījī, *Mafātīḥ al-i'jāz,* ed. Khāliqī & Karbāsī, p. 342

580 *Ibid.*

581 W.C. Chittick notes that the commentaries on the *Fuṣūṣ* by Qayṣārī and Kāshānī (who was Qayṣārī's master), "have been studied perhaps more than any other by serious seekers of knowledge up to modern times." "The Five Divine Presences: from al-Qūnawī to al-Qayṣārī," *The Muslim World,* LXXII/2 (1988), p. 107.

582 'Izz al-Dīn Maḥmūd Kāshānī (d. 735/1334) in his *Miṣbāḥ al-hidāya* (ed. Jalāl al-Dīn Humā'ī, Tehran 1946; p. 171) notes that "those who engage in the practice of spiritual retreat *(khalwat)* while being immersed in the practice of *dhikr,* sometimes experience certain mystical states in which they become 'absent' *(ghāyib)* from sensible things, such that certain realities concerning the affairs of the invisible world are revealed to them, in the same way that a sleeper experiences dreams. The Sufis call these experiences 'mystical incident' *(wāqi'a).*" On these terms see also Javad Nurbakhsh, (trans. Terry Graham *et al*), *Sufi Symbolism VII: Contemplative Disciplines, Visions and Theophanies, Family Relationships, Servants of God, Names of Sufi Orders* (London: KNP 1994), pp. 121ff.

583 Lāhījī, *Mafātīḥ al-i'jāz,* ed. Khāliqī & Karbāsī, p. 343-4.

584 Lāhījī, *Mafātīḥ al-i'jāz,* ed. Khāliqī & Karbāsī, p. 424; MAS, p. 94, vv. 649-50.

585 The Perso-Arabic term here is, of course, *insān,* which means simply "human." The term "man" used in the translation here transcends all gender distinctions; its scope of connotation encompassing both the female and male.

586 *Fuṣūṣ al-ḥikam,* ed. Abū al-'Alā' 'Afīfī, p. 49; and R.J.W. Austin (trans.) *Ibn al-'Arabī: The Bezels of Wisdom,* pp. 50-51.

587 *Wajh* is the plural of the Arabic noun: *wujūh,* meaning 'face', 'countenance,' 'front', which is the root-form substantive of *WJH,* meaning 'to be a man of distinction'. The Anandarāj and Dihkhudā dictionaries list six basic meanings of *wajh* in Persian: 1) face, visage *(rū'i, chihra),* 2) essence, 3) state of being, mode *(ḥāl),* 4) the origin of time, 5) quality, sense, 6) aspect, viewpoint. Our translation here takes these various connotations into account. 'Alī ibn Muḥammad Jurjānī in his *Al-ta'rifāt* (ed. G. Fluegel; Lipsiq 1845, p. 169), in his interpretation of its sister-term *Wajh al-ḥaqq,* notes that "this expression indicates that everything is Reality *(ḥaqq)* with regard to this *wajh,* since there is no other reality besides God, as God's word implies: "Wherever you turn, there is the Face of God." [Koran II: 18] Hence, in truth, the subsistence of everything depends upon the Face of the Real Thus, the one who contemplates the presence of God in everything, can be said to perceive the Face of the Real in all things."

588 Lāhījī, *Mafātīḥ al-i'jāz,* ed. Khāliqī & Karbāsī, pp. 424-5.

589 Tokyo 1987.

590 Takeshita, *op. cit.,* p. 58.

591 Cited by Takeshita, *op. cit.,* p. 59.

592 Takeshita, *op. cit.,* p. 65.

593 Ibn 'Arabī states in the *Fuṣūṣ,* p. 55: "Were it not for the permeation *(saryān)* of God, by means of His form *(sūra)* in all existents, the universe would have no existence." – Takeshita, *op. cit.,* p. 116.

594 *Futūḥāt:* III, p. 295, cited by Takeshita, *op. cit.,* p. 114.

595 *Futūḥāt:* II, p. 464, cited by Takeshita, *op. cit.,* p. 115.

596 Takeshita, *op. cit.,* p. 66.

597 *Futūḥāt:* II, p. 124, cited by Takeshita, *op. cit.,* p. 67.

598 Takeshita, *op. cit.,* p. 72. Of course, this is an absurd deduction on

Takeshita's part. Commenting on the opening statement of the first chapter of the *Fuṣūṣ al-ḥikam,* (from the 'Wisdom of Divinity in the Word of Adam', that "The Reality wanted to see the essences of His Most Beautiful Names or, to put it another way, to see His own Essence . . . "), Rukn al-Dīn Shīrāzī writes: "If someone objects that this statement implies that God Almighty can only realize perfection through the medium of another *(ghayr),* our answer is as follows: Although a mirror [i.e. Adam=Man=*homo imago Dei* ] is a locus of theophany and a divine 'illustration', it is not absolutely 'other' *(ghayr)* [than God] either—in the sense that it could require some 'other' entity for its complete realization.

The mirror, in fact, has two dimensions. On the one hand, there is the dimension of the mirror's individual essence, i.e. its un-Real *(lā-ḥaqq)* dimension and the aspect of its 'otherness' *(ghayriyyat).*

On the other hand, there is the mirror's ontological dimension *(jahat-i wujūdī),* insofar as all existent beings subsist by virtue of Existence, which is identical with God's Existence. In support of the truth of this answer, he [i.e Ibn 'Arabī] said: *"as it were* in a mirror" because the mirror, in itself, has no actual being. On the contrary, the principle of all the determined forms *(ta'ayyunāt)* is the Absolute Undelimited Being — whose dignity transcends all temporal created being." *Nuṣūṣ al-khuṣūṣ fī tarjumat al-Fuṣūṣ,* p. 54.

599 Jāmī, *Naqd al-nuṣūṣ,* edited by W.C. Chittick (Tehran 1977), pp. 60-1. Cited by W.C. Chittick, "The Perfect Man as the Prototype of the Self in the Sufism of Jāmī," *Studia Islamica,* XLIX (1979), p. 151.

600 MAS, *Gulshan-i rāz,* p. 80, v. 338; Lāhījī, *Mafātīḥ al-i'jāz,* p. 232. This refers to the Prophet's *ḥadīth:* "I have a time with God" which the Sufis use to describe their experience of the 'Eternal Moment' outside of serial time. For the chain of transmission on this *ḥadīth,* see Furūzanfar, *Aḥadīth-i Mathnawī,* no. 100.

601 Cf. Khwārazmī, *Sharḥ-i Fuṣūṣ al-ḥikam,* p. 480 infra.

602 See Marijan Molé, "Les Kubrawiya Entre Sunnisme et Shiisme Aux Huitieme et Neuvieme Siecles de l'Hegire," *Revue des études islamiques,* 1961, p. 75, no. 52. Also cf. Michel Chodkiewicz, *Seal of the Saints,* pp. 47-59; Nasafī, *Bayān al-tanzīl,* Indian Office Library, M.S. no. 1806, fol. 53a.

603 See Najīb Māyil Harawī (ed.), Simnānī, *Chil majlis yā Risāla-yi Iqbāliyya* (Tehran 1366 A.Hsh./1987), pp. 172-75. For Ḥamūya's only explanation based on letter symbolism, see his *Al-Miṣbāḥ fī al-ṭasawwuf,* edited by Najīb Māyil Harawī,, p. 81 where he explains *walāya* and *nubuwwa* as being two similar "powers," the first in *actu* and the second in *potentia.*

604 Lāhījī, *Mafātīḥ al-i'jāz,* ed. Khāliqī & Karbāsī, p. 234.

605 Lāhījī, *Mafātīḥ al-i'jāz,* ed. Khāliqī & Karbāsī, p. 232. The above translation from the *Fuṣūṣ* with minor changes follows that by R.J.W. Austin: *Ibn al-'Arabī: The Bezels of Wisdom,* p. 168.

606 Koran, II: 257.

607 Koran, XLII: 28.

608 R.J.W. Austin (trans.) *Ibn al-'Arabī: The Bezels of Wisdom,* p. 168.

609 Koran, XII: 101.

610 A reference to the saying, often attributed to the Prophet, "Assume the character traits of God" *(takhallaqū bi saklāq Allāh).* For an interesting discussion of Ibn 'Arabī's views on this saying, see W.C. Chittick, *The Sufi Path of Knowledge,* pp. 283-86.

611 Lāhījī, *Mafātīḥ al-i'jāz,* ed. Khāliqī & Karbāsī, p. 233.

612 See T.S. Eliot (ed.), *Literary Essays of Ezra Pound* (London: Faber & Faber 1985), p. 343; John B. Vickery, *The Literary Impact of The Golden Bough,* (New Jersey: Princeton University Press 1973), p. 107 ff.

613 See Kathleen Raine, *Yeats the Initiate: Essays on certain themes in the writings of W.B. Yeats* (London: Dolmen Press 1986), chap. 6 and *idem,* "Yeats and Kabir," in *Temenos: A Review Devoted to the Arts of the Imagination,* 5 (1984), pp. 7-28.

614 "Any serious study of literature shows that the real difference between the original and the imitative poet is simply that the former is more profoundly imitative." N. Frye, *Anatomy of Criticism,* (Princeton University Press 1957), p. 97. For a profound and extensive discussion of the influence of tradition on creative originality, see *ibid.,* pp. 96-103.

# VI

# SHABISTARI'S AESTHETICS AND HERMENEUTICS[615]

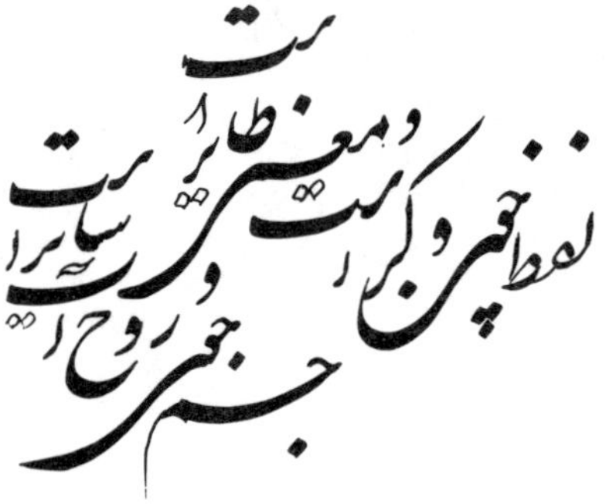

*Words are only nests. Meanings winged creatures*
*aflight. Bodies are rivers,*
*the Spirit their steady current.*[616]

## The Symbolist Tradition in Classical Persian Sufi Poetry

There are basically two schools of thought in the field of classical Persian literary criticism of Sufi poetry:

(i) Scholars such as A. J. Arberry, and more recently, Michael Hillmann, and Annemarie Schimmel,[617] who treat the Persian Sufi poetry from primarily an aesthetic and literary standpoint, usually interpret the Sufi motifs in the ghazal as—to use a term devised by Rosemund Tuve—an "imposed allegory."[618] The truly allegorical quality in Sufi poetry is seen as a disguise for eroticism, and the metaphysical, archetypal nature of the poem is considered as a whitewash over a profane romanticism. They speak of tensions to resolve the dichotomy of erotic and metaphysical love,[619] hence using concepts which unconsciously reflect, as Henry Corbin observed, the situation of a *conscience malheureuse*,[620] mainly derived from the study of Westem pietistic poets such as Donne or Marvell.[621]

(ii) Those who approach Sufi poetry as a statement of archetypal logopoeia,[622] that is to say, as a communication derived from the imaginal world *('ālam-i mithāl)* or the realm of archetypal meanings *('ālam-i ma'nā),* understanding it as an expression of precise symbolic meanings working systematically at a supraconscious associative level. Although scholars such as Toshihiko Izutsu, S. H. Nasr, and Henry Corbin[623] have examined Persian philosophical doctrines from this point of view, no one has examined Persian metaphysical poetry from this standpoint, even though this is the mode of classical literary criticism employed by the Sufis themselves.[624] Considering the importance of symbolic structure and meaning as the main criterion of assessing a poem's ultimate meaning among the Sufis,[625] it seems worthwhile to investigate the underlying philosophical assumptions of this poetic symbolism, the study of which has been neglected by Iranologists East and West alike.[626]

For this purpose, in this chapter I will discuss Shabistarī's *Garden of Mystery* as well as Lāhījī's commentary upon it, both works having a direct bearing on the interpretation of Sufi symbolism, expounding the Sufi theory of archetypal meanings: *ma'ānī,* with unusual clarity. Although Shabistarī's verses in the *Garden of Mystery* might appear to the uninitiated sensibility as a series of abstract and often unrelated flashes of mystical ideas, Lāhījī, in his commentary, like a translator of a forgotten language, fluently evokes the spiritual necessity animating each verse. It is also significant that Lāhījī, in the course of his commentary, constantly cites the poetry of both Maghribī, a Tabrīzī Sufi symbolist poet who was highly influenced by Shabistarī[627] as well as that of Jalāl al-Dīn Rūmī, in order to illustrate the hidden meanings in Shabistarī's work. This fact alone informs us of the existence of a homogeneous symbolist tradition in Persian mystical poetry, which aims at expressing and recapitulating ever more articulately fundamental theosophical doctrines, based on precise symbolic terminology.

## The Aesthetic Theory of Shabistarī

The following 24 verses from Shabistarī's *Garden of Mystery* are a key document in the Sufi aesthetic theory, constituting a pivotal point for analysis of all subsequent Sufi poets in 15th and 16th century Iran.[628] Lāhījī's ensuing commentary on these lines (examined below, pp. 186ff.) encapsulates, in one sense, the entire theosophy of poetic inspiration and creative intuition *(dhawq)* of all the major Sufi poets in the Timurid period in Tabriz: Kamāl Khujandī, Qasim-i Anwār, Muḥammad 'Aṣṣār, 'Abd al-Rahim Khalwatī ('Mashriqī'), and Muhammad Maghribī—as well as those deeply influenced by this genre of symbolic poetry, such as Jāmī. Poetic inspiration arises from creative intuition or *dhawq,* a term that literally means 'tasting', but which refers in Sufism to a faculty of heart-vision that can 'savour' truths beyond the physical senses, considered in particular by Shabistarī as the central factor in the Sufi theory of inspiration. The psychological detail of the great Rūzbihān Baqlī's (d. 606/1210) eloquent allegory of *dhawq,* whose theories, as Annemarie Schimmel notes, "form the basis for our understanding of most Persian poetry,"[629] merit citation in this regard:

> The first station experienced by lovers is the drinking from ocean-like goblets of mystical illumination *(tajallī).* As they contemplate the radiance of Divine intimacy in their hearts, redolent with fragrant breezes wafted from the Invisible Realm, the wide plains of the divine Qualities' illumination is revealed to them. As the transconscious ground *(asrār)* of their Spirits inclines towards intimacy with God, they realize the purity of creative intuition *(dhawq)* and experience the radiance of contemplative vision.[630]

It is this spiritual appreciation alone which allows one to recall the original sense of poetic metaphors, to rediscover the veridical meaning in physical imagery, to transcend the letter and understand the 'archetypal meaning'. Quite early on in the history of Sufism one finds the term *dhawq* employed with a similar technical theosophical connotation. One of its earliest appearances is in the work of Sulāmī (d. 412/1021);[631] later, in Qushayrī (d. 465/1072), one reads of the "taste, the direct perception of archetypal meanings" *(dhawq al-ma'ānī).*[632] Ghazālī also accords a special prominence to *dhawq,* describing it in his *Munqidh min al-ḍalāl* as "the most special characteristic of the highest Sufi mystics, and what is uniquely theirs, [this] can only be attained by taste, not by learning . . . [it is] like witnessing with one's own eyes and taking in one's own hands."[633]

In later Persian Sufism, the term becomes used routinely. Thus, we find that Rūzbihān in his *Commentary on the Paradoxs of the Sufis* comments that *"dhawq* is the beginning of *shurb* (drinking). Its reality consists in the heart finding the sweetness of purity during union."[634] 'Izz al-Dīn Maḥmūd Kāshānī (d. 735/1334), the author of an important manual of Sufi doctrine, accounts *dhawq* as the first of three stages of intoxication, the next two being respectively, *shurb* (drinking) and *rayy* (quenching the thirst).[635] His definition, in turn, was derived from Shihāb al-Dīn Suhrawardī's (d. 632/1234) statement in the *'Awārif al-ma'ārif*[636] that *dhawq* corresponds to faith *(imān), shurb* to knowledge *('ilm),* and *rayy* to ecstatic consciousness *(ḥāl).*[637] *Dhawq* is a fundamental element in the Sufi gnosticism of Ibn 'Arabī as well, according to whom "the knowledge of mystical conditions cannot be attained to save by *dhawq,* nor can the reason of man define it, nor arrive at any cognizance of it by deduction, as is also the case with the knowledge of the sweetness of honey, the bitterness of patience, the joy of union, love, passion or desire, which one cannot know unless one be qualified by it or taste *(dhawq)* it directly."[638] Tahānawī (d. 1745), the great encyclopedist of gnostic terminology, describes *dhawq* as "the first degree of contemplative vision *(shuhūd)* of God within God. It is accompanied by continual flashes of lightning occurring at short intervals. Whenever *dhawq* becomes excessive, it is transformed into the station of *shuhūd,* which is called *shurb.* The ultimate degree of *dhawq* is called *rayy,* which is experienced when one's innermost consciousness is freed from reflection on other than God."[639]

From these definitions, it appears that *dhawq* is the spiritual intuition without which the understanding of Sufi poetry is impossible. It is also the central concept in Shabistarī's aesthetics of poetry and Lāhījī's exegesis. In the term *dhawq* we encounter a theory of aesthetics in which the concept of artistic taste and appreciation is inseparably connected with the idea of drunkenness and the symbol of wine. Thus *dhawq* may be defined as a kind of wit within a spiritually intoxicated temperament, a concept much more psychologically sophisticated than mere creative intuition or artistic

'Taste'.[640] So the doctrine elucidated by Shabistarī in line 722 (see below) is reflected throughout all Sufi poetry:

The mystical significance unveiled,
Experienced by heart-savour *(dhawq),*
No philological interpretation reveals.

It is a fundamental theme in the ghazals of Shah Ni'matu'llāh (d. 833/1430), and Maghribī, and is even expressed by Shabistarī's great contemporary, the Sufi poet Humām-i Tabrīzī, in identical terms:

In a straitjacket of words and syntax
Spiritual savour's *(dhawq)* expressions can't be fitted;
Above and beyond speech and sound
The waystations of these intuitions are found.[641]

The concept of *dhawq* as *heart-savour,* rather than intellectual *taste* (as the Persian dictionaries define it) is originally Peripatetic. "In Aristotelian psychology," writes James Hillmann, "the organ of *aisthesis is* the heart, passages from all sense organs run to it; there the soul is 'set on fire' . . . This link between the heart and the organs of sense is not simple mechanical sensationalism; it is aesthetic. That is, the activity of perception or sensation in Greek is *aisthesis* which means at root 'taking in' and 'breathing in'—a 'gasp', that primary aesthetic response . . . 'Taking in' means taking to heart, interiorizing, becoming intimate with . . . interiorizing the object into itself; into its image so that its imagination is activated (rather than ours), so that it shows its heart and reveals its soul."[642] This archetypal psychology based on an aesthetics of the heart was picked up from Aristotle by Avicenna and then passed into Sufi theosophy. The heady ratiocinative bias of Western society, however, makes it very difficult for us to understand a concept so subtle and spiritual as heart-savour. In Hillmann's words:

> We are bereft in our culture of an adequate psychology and philosophy of the heart, and therefore also of the imagination. Our hearts cannot apprehend that they are imaginatively thinking hearts, because we have so long been told that the mind thinks and the heart feels. . . . If we would recover

> the imaginal, we must first recover its organ, the heart, and its kind of philosophy.[643]

According to Lāhījī,

> The humanity of a human being is in the heart *(dil)*. It is the locus of the particularization *(tafṣīl)* of the knowledge and perfections of the Spirit *(rūḥ)* and a manifestation of the transpositions of the Divine theophanies *(ẓuhūrāt)* through the creative acts of the Divine Essence. Hence, it is called 'that which changes '*(qalb)* . . . This heart every moment displays another effect and quality, and is transformed from quality to quality. A further reason why the heart is a transformer *(munqalib)* is that as one aspect of it faces God, another aspect of it is turned towards creation, so that it receives grace from God, and channels it back towards creation.[644]

Lāhījī furthermore notes that gnosis is situated in the heart, and, "just as one may see objects by means of a lamp at night, likewise in the darkness of multiplicity *(kithrāt),* vision of the Divine Unity *(waḥdat)* may be obtained only by means of the heart's purity."[645] In light of Hillmann's remarks on the heart's significance in Aristotle's aesthetics and Lāhījī's explanation of the heart in Shabistarī's thought, it is evident how cognitively significant, and psychologically precise—not merely ornamental—are terms such as breath', 'drinking' and 'heart' in Sufi poetry. Consider, for instance, the following ghazal by Shabistarī's follower, Maghribī:

*The Religion of the Heart*

Ah, with every breath, our heart
professes an inner taste anew,
Adopts anew a creed of faith,
confesses religion and rite anew.
With every breath the heart imbibes
another cup from the beloved's lip.
Each cup it takes, each glass it sips
it drinks down with another lip.
Never will the heart seek the same
theme or aim two breaths at once.
Each moment-breath the heart selects

a theme afresh to pursue.
The lovely witness of the heart, besides
this body, down, and mole and double chin,
Another body owns, another kind
of down and mole and double chin.
Each breath a soul arrives afresh
from the lip of the Oversoul, to bless
The heart. Each soul thus gained a frame
of flesh the heart receives again.
There is another sphere and sun
in the heavens of our heart;
Another earth and firmament and throne
and other stars and solar-systems shown.
Beyond this present day you see,
another day the heart possesses.
Beyond this night you know and sense
another night the heart intuits.
The heart's a cavalier that when
it strains to hear, on every side
it hearkens, senses, another steed
is mounted, dispatched upon the way.

The heart of Maghribī is like
the slate of fate and destiny
wherein the school of the Friend, it's etched—
"The heart another school does have."[646]

The form of 'anagogic' metaphor employed by a Shabistarī, or by Maghribī in the above verses is quite unlike the vague personalistic symbolism of the French Symbolist poets such as Baudelaire and Mallarmé.[647] The archetypal symbolism of Sufi poetry arises out of a practical, psychologically documented spiritual discipline *(sulūk):* it is not derived from purely personal emotions. In this regard, T. Izutsu has observed that "the frequent use of metaphors in metaphysics, is one of the characteristic marks of Islamic philosophy ... It must not be taken as a poetic ornament."[648] This "cognitively rigorous" use of metaphor, as Marcus B. Hester has termed it,[649] is characteristic of the imagery of both medieval European poets such as Dante and the seventeenth-century English metaphysical poets.[650] But it should be stressed that these anagogic metaphors and analogies are archetypal, envisioned by the heart, intuited only by adepts of the heart. For this reason Shabistarī in line 723 of the text below declares:

The archetypal meaning – the esoteric *sens*
Through analogies and correspondences
The heart's initiates may best explicate.

The *ma'nā/lafẓ* dichotomy: archetype versus type, significatio vs. sensory fact, intensity of signification vs. extension of expression – also permeates Shabistarī's aesthetic theory. "The poetic use of the terms *ma'nā, ma'nawī,*" writes Julie Scott Meisami (about classical Persian poetry) "suggests something similar to the *significatio* or *sen* referred to by the medieval European poets as the 'deeper meaning' underlying the surface of the poem."[651] *Ma'nā* signifies primarily the *archetypal meaning* of a poetic metaphor. *Ma'nā* may also be defined as the 'spiritual meaning' or 'ideal reality'[652] (when juxtaposed to its antonym: *ṣūrat* or appearance). Its rhetorical meaning in non-mystical Persian poetry however, refers to the non-physical traits of any expression (that is to say: its 'tenor') and the inner content of a metaphor. In this respect, it is antonymous to *lafẓ* (= word, the 'letter', phoneme, *verbum, lexis)* just as the English term *sense* is contrasted to *syntax*. The recent study by C.A.M. Versteegh on the influence of Greek thought on Arabic grammar, finds the concept of *ma'nā* in Islamic philosophy derived from several sources. The main source of the Sufi theories seems to be the Stoics, who "made a strict distinction between the phonetic and the semantic aspect of the linguistic sign . . . *Sèmaīnon* is the signifying, i.e. phonetic aspect (= *phônè)* and the *lekton* is its semantic correlate *(sèmainomenon)*. In Arabic grammar *lafẓ* and *ma'nā* are used exactly in the same way."[653] However, the concept of *ma'nā* elaborated by Shabistarī below seems derived from Avicenna who considered *ma'ānī* (pl. of *ma'nā)* as *"intentiones universales* in the objects, put there by Allāh, and forming the material for the thinking mind, . . . *ma'ānī* are those elements in the objects which are not perceived by the physical senses, but only by some sort of perceiving faculty of the mind (called by Ibn Rushd *quwwa mutafakkira* and by Ibn Sina *quwwa bāṭina)*.[654]

According to the Sufis, *ma'ānī* are transcendental, understood only when seen in Vision *(shuhūd)* or through theophany *(tajallī)*. Shabistarī's view of archetypal meanings, in lines 721 and 722 below for instance, bears a striking resemblance to C.G. Jung's later theory of archetypes:

> . . . The statements of the conscious mind may easily be snares and delusions, lies, or arbitrary opinions, but this certainly is not true of statements of the soul: to begin with they always go over our heads because they point to realities that transcend consciousness. These *entia* are the archetypes of the collective unconscious, and they precipitate complexes of ideas in the form of mythological motifs.[655]

Paul Piehler, in his study of medieval allegory: *The Visionary Landscape,* describes a concept similar to *ma'nā* in the poetic metaphysics of the Sufis, postulating that

> The mind can function as an organ for the perception of autonomous psychic powers, felt as external to the perceiver, but making their appearances chiefly in the perceiver's internal world—the world of vision and dream. They manifest themselves in the form of images drawn from the external world but enhanced and transfigured by an infusion of spiritual meaning.[656]

—This last sentence is an exact description of what constitutes *ma'ānī* as understood by Shabistarī/Lāhījī. The fact that archetypal meanings may only be understood by analogy, as Shabistarī in verse 723 below explains, also resembles Jung's view of the 'supra-personal' character of true symbolic poetry, whose images "have the value of genuine symbols, because they are the best possible expressions of something as yet unknown—bridges thrown out towards an invisible shore.[657]

In Sufi poetry, rhetoric without heart-savour, reason without inspiration (or as the Persians would say: the 'letter': *lafẓ,* without the 'spirit': *ma'nā)* is formally unacceptable. In fact, the only type of literary criticism to which the Persian Sufis condescended to lend their approbation was the hermeneutic exegesis *(ta'wīl)* of poetry.[658] Although *ta'wīl* originally referred to a method of symbolic, esoteric exegesis applied by the Sufis to the Koran,[659] it may also be applied to philosophical works, as Henry Corbin's study of Avicenna has shown.[660] In this respect, Lāhījī's commentary on the *Garden of Mystery* is fundamentally a *ta'wīl* of poetry, that is to say, a process of allegorical interpretation which leads the word or letter 'descended' *(tanzil)* into the sensible condition where it is trapped as a lexical item or phoneme, back to its origin' *(ta'wīl)* in the domain of archetypal meanings. Lāhījī insists that the original sense of poetic images can only be comprehended by *ta'wīl*. The necessity for *ta'wīl* to bridge the dichotomy between letter *(lafẓ)* and spirit *(ma'nā)* in Sufi theosophy has been expressed by T. Izutsu quite succinctly:

> The word belongs in the world of material and sensible things *(mulk)* while the meaning properly is of the world of immateriality *(malakūt)*. Compared with the vast field of meaning that lies behind each word, the latter is nothing more than an insignificant, tiny point. The word is but a narrow gate through which the human mind steps into a boundless domain of meaning. Moreover, the meaning is something that has, so to speak, its own life. It has no fixity. Quite independently of the word which indicates it, the meaning develops as it were of its own accord with amazing flexibility in accordance with the degree of depth of man's experience and consciousness. The meaning with such characteristics is poured into the ready-made mould of a word. By simply observing from outside the word thus employed, one could hardly judge the width and depth of the meaning that is intended to be conveyed by it. This is particularly true when the meaning that has been poured into the mould of a word happens to be backed by a profound mystical experience . . . For one is here required to use the given word as a springboard by which to dive into the depth of the meaning. As long as one remains trying to understand the meaning from the word, one can never hope to obtain it.[661]

From the merely literal interpretation or lexical exegesis *(ta'bīr-i lafẓī)* one must leap into the transconscious realm of archetypal meanings and from thence apprehend the spirit animating the letter.

Hence, no appreciation of this symbolist tradition in classical Persian Sufi poetry, or, indeed, any understanding of the other mystical poets under the sway of Shabistarī's aesthetic thought, is possible without consideration of the ideas expressed in the following text, which afer all, but recapitulate the classical Sufi outlook on the relation of poetic inspiration to metaphysical imagination.

## Translation of the Text – The Poetics of 'Archeypal Meanings'

*Question* (posed by Mīr Husaynī)

714 What does the man of spiritual sense signify
By poetical tropes and epithets as 'lips' and 'eyes'?
715 With down or marks-of-beauty, tresses' tips, what use
Is there for one who fares within the inner states
Of heart, engaged upon the stations of the Way?

*Response*

716 Whatever is plain to see in this world that's visible
Is all facsimile: a reflection cast by
That world's sun—yonder and invisible.
717 The world's like a line of down, or like an eyebrow,
A beauty-mark or curl: everything is perfect, beautiful
In its own proper place.
718 Because the theophanic light shines, sometimes through Wrath,
Sometimes with Beauty irradiates: the 'face' and 'tress'
Convey such sense, with all their sheen are arrayed.
719 Such sublime qualities that Reality does possess –
Aspects of benign beauty/violent majesty –
The female faces, the curls of beloved idols express.
720 Letters and words are sensible when heard at first:
To purely sensible things their primal assignation attests.
721 The *mundus archetypus* is endless, infinite,
Words quite unfit to interpret it,
No exegesis its ultimate extent can express.
722 The mystical significance unveiled,
Experienced by heart-savour
No philological interpretation reveals.
723 The archetypal meaning – the esoteric *sens*
Through analogies and correspondances
The heart's initiates may best explicate.

724 These objects, real to sense, are tenuous shadows,
shades
*That* world projects. The world an infant appears;
The world yonder acts the part of Wetnurse.
725 A more primordial sense to me these words instate:
Those archetypal meanings – although at first
Their designation did to sensible things relate.
726 Yet boorish, vulgar man just sensible things
understands.
What hope the common man should comprehend
The *sens, intentio,*[662] or Archetypal Meaning?
727 This sensible *nomen* was all the word of Vision
The adepts contemplated: words narrated, turns
Of speech from *kosmos noetos*[663] related. Then
728 As archetypal *sens* descended into *lexis*
Philosophers through Correspondence conformed Spirit
to letter.
729 Yet univeral correspondence[664] doesn't exist:
Abate your quest for it.
730 No one may controvert your inner taste
For *sens* or archetypal meaning – here the priest
And pontiff-of-the-Faith, only Truth itself may be.
731 However, beware, beware, if of any 'I-ness'
You are aware, if still with self you're prepossessed –
The outer word and sense of the *sharī'at* you profess.
732 Indulgence in speech is granted to initiates-in-heart
In three spiritual states only: Intoxication,
Lovelorn Infatuation – or else – Annihilation.
733 Only those mystics intimate with these three States
Initiate – realize words' application,
Will know their ultimate signification.
734 Since to you ecstasy is alien, rapture foreign
Beware, lest you, by dumb mimicry of gnostics,
become
In ignorant pretense an infidel as well.
735 Reality's spiritual states aren't fanciful
Figures of speech, the *arcana* of the Path
The common man can never understand.
736 O friend! inflated lies, hyperbole, gnostics
Never did preach; but heart-conviction, heart's vision
Alone to you this truth can teach.

737 Of both the vocal letter - archetypal *sens* –
Their primal imposition, later application
I've spoken in brief: attend until you understand.
738 Plumb the spirit's depth, the ultimate within *intentio*
Conceive. Within each simile, each analogy
Perceive therein the divine, unique anagogy.
739 Let metaphors you strike be types precise;
The anagogy you make of tropes concise;
In mode and type other analogies dismiss.[665]

### Shabistarī's Hermeneutics of Sufi Poetry

Mīr Ḥusaynī's question (lines 714-15 above) begs the value of symbolism, being an inquiry into the use of erotic imagery in mystical poetry. According to Shabistarī's explanation and Lāhījī's exegesis upon it, each bodily part is endowed with a 'real' ontological status (and hence 'Divine' according to believers in the principle of the 'unity of being': *waḥdat al-wujūd*).[666] Underlying Shabistarī's verses is the doctrine of the 'Metaphysics of Love and Beauty', first expoused in Persian Sufism by Aḥmad Ghazālī in his *Sawāniḥ*,[667] later to be given a post-Ibn 'Arabian exposition by 'Irāqī in his *Lama'āt*, and lastly, expounded by the poet himself in the *Ḥaqq al-yaqīn*. The following extract from the last-named treatise provides a perfect *mise en scène* for the fascinating ontology sustaining the poet's use of erotic poetic imagery in the above translation:

> *A Reality:* Multiplicity and the 'Many' are subsistent through divine Unity *(waḥdat)* which is the source of their conceptualization. Likewise, each of the degrees of multiplicity, when considered from a general and universal perspective, is encompassed by (another kind of) unity, such as genus *(jins)*, category *(faḍl)*, assignation *(mawḍū')*, and predication *(maḥmūl)*.
>
> Therefore, both inwardly and outwardly, multiplicity *is* Unity. Multiplicity is nothing but a pure insubstantiality *(i'tibārī)* and belongs to the subsidiary affairs of Unity, and 'differentiation' *(ikhtilāf)* which is one of the properties of multiplicity, is actually nonexistent *(amr-i 'adamī)*. The Divine unity is shown by [Koran LXVII: 3] "You do not see in the creation of the All-merciful any imperfection."

*A Reality:* The theophanic appearance of divine Unity in multiplicity is in proportion to the affinity *(munāsabat)* and compatibility *(muwāfiqat)* of the parts [of the corporeal receptacle] which is called 'Beauty' *(husn).* The mildness of disposition and the charming of hearts [exercised by Beauty] is caused by the concealment of the nonexistent individual determinations and the appearance of the reality of Being in divine Unity. This is a reality which occurs in each and every part of all beings, throughout every part of existence, for the chain of causality is linked to the One. "Our Lord is he who gave everything its creation" (Koran, XX: 50).

*A Reality:* Whereas the various parts of Being in the external world *(dar āfāq)* are divergent from each another, the various parts of Being in man converge together and unite. Hence, the leveling-out and harmonious straightening (of phenomena) which characterizes divine Unity has been revealed in him, and all the various degrees of universal perfection have become totally manifested *in actu* in him so that he is the terminal point of all species, being a complete corporeal receptacle for the theophanies of all being. "And [God] fashioned you and perfected your shapes" (Koran XL: 64 and LXIV: 3). Exalted is He, the best of creators!

*A Subtlety:* Romantic 'unreal' love *('ishq-i majāzī),* which constitutes an excess of loving-kindness *(maḥabbat),* cannot be configured except through the beauty of the epiphanic form of man/woman *(maẓhar-i insānī)*—for his/her heart's mirror (that heart which is endowed with spacious breadth of "My Heaven and earth contain me not, but the heart of my faithful servant contains me"[668]) is never absorbed (in the experience of romantic love) except by medium of a form of absolute beauty. Now, it is (only) this sort of love which, when overwhelmed by the figure of the human beloved *(ma'shūq-i majāzī),* enables the lover to burn away the delimiting individuality of form *(ta'ayyun)* so that, undisturbed by the illusory veils of 'other-than-itself' *(aghyār)*, of his own accord, he may engage in love's play. It is at this point that 'love' becomes Divine/Real *(ḥaqīqī).* "(God will bring a people) whom he loveth and they love him." (Koran V: 54)

> *A Reminder:* The mysteries of the degrees of this mystical state have been expounded in a treatise which we have named the *Treatise on the Theophanic Witness (Shāhid-nāma).* One should search for these matters in that work. "We will relate unto thee the fairest of stories." (Koran, Surah Joseph XII: 3)[669]

These passages explain the central role of human 'Beauty' in maintaining cosmic equilibrium. Human 'Beauty' is an *exempla* of divine Unity, for only within the 'Human Form Divine' is the Universal completely particularized. Although this idea also is treated in much detail elsewhere in the *Garden of Mystery,* for the sake of the present discussion, it enough to note that the poet endorses the Akbarian doctrine of the 'sacrality' of sexual love,[670] a notion which underlies Shabistarī's doctrine of the existence of metaphysical meaning in each of the Beloved's bodily parts. Commenting on verses 716 and 717 of Shabistarī's above response, Lāhījī elucidates this idea as follows:

> Because all the atoms of creation are manifestations of the Divine Names, Attributes, and Essence, which in turn cast their illumination upon the mirrors of the 'determined archetypes' of Possible Being [i.e. this world] – therefore everything visible and manifest in this world resembles a reflection of light cast by the sun of That World [i.e. of the Divine Essence, Names, and Attributes] . . .
>
> Now the Universal Human Form is an epitome and compendium of all the other forms of creation. In this form appear the features of 'eye', 'lip', 'curl', 'down', and 'mole', each of which contribute to human perfection. . . . Furthermore, each of these bodily parts is an exemplar and a theophanic form *(maẓhar)* embodying a particular meaning pertaining to the one true Divine Essence . . . thus he [Shabistarī] has declared that the world is like the curl, down, mole, and eyebrow. By the term "world," he indicates the respective degrees of beings and *it is these very degrees which are analogous to the curl, down, mole, and eyebrow. For each of these bodily parts is a pointer to and an exemplar of a particular sense of one of the Divine Names and Attributes . . .*
>
> While each of these bodily parts is utterly different and

> contrary to each other during human maturation, yet they are all intrinsically necessary to complete human growth and effectuate formal and spiritual perfection. Each of these bodily parts exhibits, in fact, to the extremity of its essence, the utmost loveliness, the absence of which part would certainly cause a blemish to man's outer form. Likewise, all such phenomenal physical forms serve as a witness and demonstration of those intelligible archetypal meanings *(ma'ānī ma'qūla)*. Even though they are realities of a heterogeneous nature, they are, on their respective levels, completely perfect and totally beautiful in themselves. When you contemplate them with 'the Eye of Certitude' *('ayn al-yaqīn)*, it is impossible to imagine anything contrary to their perfection [671]

Concerning line 718, Lāhījī comments:

> Lovely visages of moonlike beauty, proportionate to their grace, radiance, and gentleness, are analogous to a theophany of Divine Beauty *(tajallī-yi jamālī)*, while the tresses of coquettish, bewitching idols *(butān)*, proportionate to their darkness, turbidity, and hiddenness, resemble a theophany of Divine Wrath *(tajallī-yi jalālī)*. The visage and tress of loved ones are hence a veritable likeness and exemplar of Divine Beauty and Wrath, or rather, in actuality, they are utterly identical with these theophanies.[672]

Concerning line 719, Lāhījī observes:

> God Almighty possesses certain qualities of Clemency or Grace *(lotf)* – Gentleness, Light, Guidance, Nourishment, Life, and many others. He also possesses certain qualities of Constraint or Wrath *(qahr)* – Restriction, Constriction . . . etc. Hence it is that the tresses of 'moon-visaged idols' [see Maghribī's poem below], according to the comprehensive nature of their humanity, are endowed with these two contrasting qualities.[673]

It is quite significant that Lāhījī illustrates his exposition of this verse by citing the following five couplets from an eight line ghazal from Maghribī's *Dīwān*. Such citation of Maghribī's poetry demonstrates the fact that for Lāhījī, Maghribī's work furnishes explicit literary evidence of the veracity of Shabistarī's doctrine of the 'supra-sensible' and transcendent nature of Sufi poetic imagery. This relationship between Lāhījī, Shabistarī, and Maghribī is more than a literary influence, but rather is a conspicious example of what 'Abd al-Ḥusayn Zarrīnkūb has seen as a continuous link of symbolic theory and inspiration stemming from Rūmī.[674] As noted above (chap. IV, p. 121), one of Shabistarī's closest associates was a certain Isma'il Sīsī (d. 1383), who was, significantly, the initiator and master of Maghribī in Sufism. Thus, there is a unity to be seen in this Sufi tradition of symbolic poetry, based on an initiatory and oral tradition. The relevant verses from Maghribī's ghazal cited by Lāhījī are as follows:

Her face's epiphanic glory in the faces
   of every heart-bewitching beauty is clear:
Not just one way this glory appears;
   on every side it is clear.

Another moon-visaged beauty in every breath
   snares me with her curl's lasso, bears me off
Yet in every hairtip's snare it's clear
   to behold: it's only her hair.

What spell her magic eyes upon my eyes have fixed
   isn t obvious, yet to my eyes all that's clear
      are her eyes . . . bewitching eyes.

Her features' epiphanic glory led me on . . .
   How else could I have stumbled
      out of the darkness of her braids' tangles?

      Since only her eyebrow appears to me
      in the moonlike features of the fair
      my regard remains riveted, unrelaxed
      upon the eyebrows of the fair, the beauteous.[675]

Shabistarī's next verse (720) espouses the classical Sufi outlook on the origin of poetic images, the belief in the precedence of allegory to fable, a doctrine Shabistarī holds in common with Rūmī.[676] Lāhījī thus remarks:

> Literal poetic expressions *(alfāẓ)* such as 'face', 'tress', 'down', 'mole', 'eye', and 'eyebrow' are to be primarily defined with a sensible meaning since they are, in the first place, sense objects, sharing the common condition of sensibility. By *waḍ'* (assignation, designation) is implied the special designation of a word to be equivalent to a certain meaning, so that whenever it is read or heard, that same meaning is inferred from it . . . [677] In any case, these words were originally defined with these exclusively sensible meanings.[678]

Lāhījī views line 721 as confirming this standpoint of the initial 'sensibility' of poetic metaphors: the boundlessness of the domain of archetypal meanings being too immense to be comprehended by any verbal expression:

> The world of archetypal meanings *('ālam-i ma'nā)*—meaning the world of the Divine Essence, Attributes, and Names, which is of infinite nature—admits of no finite boundary. Each of these 'archetypal meanings' contains as well, within itself, an infinite variety of hierarchial degrees, and hence they can never be accommodated by any vessel fashioned of words *(lafẓ)*.[679]

The transcendence of poetic inspiration to ratiocination is the subject of verse 722, Lāhījī's commentary on which emphasizes the importance of creative intuition or heart-savour *(dhawq),* the result of contemplative vision *(shuhūd)* and interior revelation *(kashf).* Lāhījī's eloquent exegesis of verse 723 merits full citation:

> Whenever people of the heart *(ahl-i dil),* who have attained a realization of archetypal meanings *(ma'ānī)* and acquired gnosis through punfication and illumination of the heart, wish to interpret and express these meanings revealed to their heart, they never express them directly, because aspirants on the Sufi path, and others who are worthy are better instructed by indirect expression. Their praiseworthy custom, however, consists in inventing a suitable analogy and equivocation *(mushābihat)* as an intermediary between the intuited spiritual significance *(ma'nā)* and the sensible facts *(umūr-i maḥsūsa)* under consideration. The heart's adepts exhibit these archetypal meanings in the raiment of 'objects of the senses' for the perusal of

initiates and the contemplation of adepts. It is for this reason that the exoteric viewers – observing only the external facade, lacking the aptitude to apprehend the archetypal significance – interpret the symbolic allusions of the Sufis as mere bombast *(ṭāmāt)*[680] and through sheer ignorance and obstinacy, permit themselves to reject and ridicule the states and statements of the Sufis.[681]

The doctrine of indirect expression propounded by Lāhījī in this passage is a common theme in other neo-Platonic poetic and philosophical traditions, as has been shown by M.-D. Chenu's studies.[682] It was vigorously defended by John Bunyan in *The Pilgrim's Progress,* for instance.

By Metaphors I speak? were not God's Laws,
His Gospel-Laws, in olden times held forth
By Types, Shadows. and Metaphors? Yet loth
Will any sober Man be to find fault
With them lest he be found to assault
The highest Wisdom . . . [683]

At this point in his commentary, Lāhījī cites the following two verses by Maghribī which occur in the poet's autobiographical introduction to his *Dīwān*. (The entire poem to which these verses belong is fully translated at the conclusion of this chapter.) Once again, Lāhīj's citation of Maghribī's verses in his commentary communicates the presence of the archetypal and non-personalistic unity in Sufi poetry.

Oh, within each and every phoneme of mine
  a live soul resides,
within every *lexis,* an *animus* there is,
  a soul alive within each word,
in every letter a cosmos concealed

You should seek its spirit – its flesh reject,
  its noumenon pursue and Named-Essence adopt—
its phenomenon do not claim.[684]

These verses, which are not merely coincidentally composed in the same *baḥr-i hazaj* metre as Shabistarī's *Garden of Mystery,* appear as a kind of amplification and exegesis in Persian symbolic imagery of some Arabic verses by Ibn 'Arabī in his *Tarjumān al-ashwāq,* cited by Maghribī in the same autobiographical introduction to demonstrate his adherence to Ibn 'Arabī's philosophy.[685] In these lines the 'Greatest Shaykh' had spelled out the hermeneutics of his own erotic poetry.[686] By citing these particular verses by Maghribī, it would seem that Lāhījī is obliquely informing us that Maghribī's poetic practice and Shabistarī's poetic theory are, indeed, of an identical visionary and symbolic nature. Furthermore, these verses indicate that the understanding of Sufi symbolic poetry requires a process of hermeneutical exegesis *(ta'wīl),* as already explained above.

If we are to grasp the unity[687] in the Persian Sufi poetry—whether this be *qaṣīda, ghazal,* or other forms—we must recognize in it the existence of a hidden "presidency of meaning"[688] and in its imagery detect a series of symbols to be interpreted with a sense of the archetypal reality overlying it—the spirit, in Rūmī's words, hovering over the body of the poetic text:

> Words are only nests. Meanings *(ma'nā)* winged creatures
> aflight. Bodies are rivers,
> the Spirit their steady current.[689]

Maghribī's *Dīwān*, reappearing at this point in Lāhījī's commentary, reveals itself to be a manifesto of the theories of creative inspiration professed by the Sufi symbolists in mediæval Tabriz. Such an interfluence of ideas among metaphysical poets is, in fact, quite common. The reader may recall, for instance, the influence of George Herbert on Richard Crashaw.[690]

In his commentary on line 724, while employing the terminology of Ibn 'Arabī, Lāhījī explains that "the world of archetypal meanings *('ālam-i ma'nā)* is the basis of the realm of the senses which is mere form . . . Just as a shadow, which would otherwise be non-existent, is revealed by light, so the entire world is illuminated and revealed through the theophany *(tajallī)* and brilliance of the lights of the Divine Names and Attributes. The sensory realm is to be considered as an infant and the spiritual world as its Wetnurse, because all evolution and perfection in this world derives from That World."[691]

The epistemological debate briefly raised in line 720 concerning the sensible and physical versus the archetypal and metaphysical origin of Sufi poetic imagery, is examined in greater depth by Lāhījī in his exegesis of line 725:

> It is right to use words in general to refer to objects of the senses, as well as to refer to those archetypal meanings *(ma'ānī)* by way of hermeneutical exegesis *(ta'wīl)* ... However, in actual fact, these phonemes *(alfāẓ)* which were said to have been referred only allegorically *(ta'wīl)* to those archetypal meanings, were primarily and originally intended to refer to those meanings . . . For these archetypal meanings are, in fact, the primordial origin of Being itself, and sense objects stem from them in a merely derivative and secondary manner.[692]

The Platonic doctrine preached by Lāhījī in this passage[693] was first elaborated in the Latin West by Pseudo-Dionysius, whose doctrine is best described by M.-D. Chenu as "essentially a method of approach to intelligible reality, not an explanation of the world of sense by means of that reality. But for him this method was to be conceived as an ascent that began from the lowest material level, on which the mind of man found its connatural objects—objects whose value for knowledge, for sacred knowledge, lay not in their coarse material natures but in their symbolic capacity, their 'anagogy' ... This *anagoge,* this upwards reference of things was constituted precisely by their natural dynamism as symbols. The image of the transcendent was not some pleasant addition to their natures; rather, rooted in the 'dissimilar similitudes' of the hierarchical ladder, it was their very reality and reason for being."[694]

Swedenborg's theory of scriptural hermeneutics, elaborated in his *Arcana Coelestia* (2995) also resembles Lāhījī's doctrine and seems to be in this same neo-Platonic, Pseudo-Dionysian tradition:

> Since the people of the earliest church habitually saw something spiritual and heavenly in the details of nature (to the point that natural phenomena served them simply as concrete means of thinking about spiritual and heavenly realities) they were able to talk with angels and to be present with them in the Lord's kingdom in the heavens at the same time they were present in His kingdom on earth, the church. For them, natural things were so united with spiritual ones that they were utterly responsive. Further, nothing under any circumstances occurs in this created world that does not have a correspondence with things that exist in the spiritual world, and that does not there-

> fore in its own way portray something in the Lord's kingdom. This is the source and emergence of everything.[695]

In his exegesis of line 726, Lāhījī comments:

> The attribution of a purely sensual meaning to these words or expressions *(lafẓ)* related to objects of the senses, is a mode of expression pertaining to the slang of the vulgar. What do the vulgar understand of the meanings originally intended and established for these words? The vulgar understanding cannot fathom this depth, comprehension of that archetypal significance being reserved solely for adepts.
>
> One should realize that whenever a particular expression's original meaning is shifted to another meaning, and the former meaning becomes obsolete, then—providing that the speaker be giving utterance to the vulgar sense—it is designated as 'a narration of the vulgar' *(manqūl-i 'urfī).* An example of this is the word *dabba,* which originally referred to every moving creature on the earth's surface. The vulgar usage changed the meaning of this word and made it refer exclusively to quadrupeds, such as the horse, donkey, camel, etc.
>
> The Shaykh states that connecting these poetic words with these objects of the senses is typical of the vulgar usage and slang, and an unfortunate consequence of this vulgarization is that their *primary spiritual significance* has been now abandoned. The truth of the matter is when such folk who were unfamiliar with visionary experience *(ahl-i mukāshafa nabūdand)* heard these expressions related by the spiritually realized adepts acquainted with visionary insight and the divine self-disclosure *(ahl-i kashf wa shuhūd),* they totally misunderstood their implication and considered the connotation of these words to relate exclusively to sensory phenomena, using merely their own [limited] reasons, omitting their original meaning as 'obsolete'. However, to the realized adept *(muḥaqqiq),* these words still remain 'designated' to convey their original archetypal meaning.[696]

Those familiar with Coleridge, Shelley, and other of the English Romantic poets will have noted how similar Shabistarī's theory of *dhawq al-ma'nī* is to William Blake's conception of "Visionary Fancy, or Imagination." For Shabistarī, just as for Blake, "'vision' or 'Imagination' . . . is the sole aesthetic faculty."[697] Just as Lāhījī had stated, commenting on line 725, that "these archetypal meanings are the primordial origin of Being itself," so Blake asserted:

> The Nature of Visionary Fancy, or Imagination, is very little Known & the Eternal nature & permanence of its ever Existent Images is consider'd as less permanent than the things of vegetative and Generative Nature; yet the Oak dies as well as the Lettuce, but Its Eternal Image & Individuality never dies, but renews its seed; just so the Imaginative Image returns by the seed of Contemplative Thought.[698]

* * *

At this juncture, before proceeding to summarize the rest of Lāhījī's commentary on verses 714-739, it is best if we look elsewhere in the *Garden of Mystery* at some of Shabistarī's verses which themselves furnish an excellent example of his doctrine of the 're-assignation' of poetic images back to their original noumenal Object, giving us a vivid exposition of his own doctrine of the 'archetypal meaning' "hovering" (in Rūmī's words) over each of the human beloved's bodily parts. The following extract (with some of Lāhījī's comments being provided in notes), gives a good idea of the awesome visionary topography inspiring the sensual imagery of Persian poetry, revealing the primordial supra-sensible 'designation' of Sufi erotic imagery. In the seventeen couplets translated below, the poet provides his own esoteric exegesis, *ta'wīl,* of the anagogical meaning of poetic images such as the 'visage' (*rukh*), the 'down' (*khaṭṭ*),[699] and the 'beauty spot or mole', also touching on the metaphysical significance of the 'tress', 'cheek' and 'hair' in Sufi poetry:

### The Anagogic Sense of the Visage (*rukh*) and Down (*khaṭṭ*)

777 The image of the visage here portrays
a theophanic display of Divine loveliness.[700]
'Down' denotes the antechamber
of the August, the Awesome.[701]

778 She sketched upon her visage
the winsome line of her down,[702]
"I alone am good-looking;
Only my complexion is becoming."

779 The down came forth as the greensward
of the *mundus anima;*
Thence they named it
"homeland of Eternal life."[703]

780 Turn day to night
with her tresses' tenebrity.
Seek in her down
the fount of life.[704]

781 Seek the well springs of immortality
like her down's line.
Set forth like Khiḍr from that station
which no signals point to
and all traces are erased.[705]

782 When with true certainty
you see her face and down
you'll apprehend each feature
of Unity and multiplicity.[706]

783 From her tresses recognize
the world's laborious affairs
and from her down decipher
the puzzling *arcanum.*[707]

784 Amongst all those who see the down
upon that fair face flowering
my heart beholds that selfsame face
within that down's grace.[708]

785 Unless, alas,
her entire visage expresses
the sevenfold exordium of the Koran,
underneath whose every letter
seas of meaning lie submerged![709]

786 Thousands of oceans of gnosis
of the *mundus secretus*
found under each strand of her hair.[710]

787 Behold upon the waters
Mercy's Throne: the heart, upbourne
as upon her winsome cheek the down
of the soul's beloved blooms.[711]

The Anagogic Sense of the Mole or Beauty Spot *(khāl)*

788 Her beauty spot encompasses her face
as the point is the base
of the circle it surrounds.
789 From this 'mole' sprang a streak.
a line, sweeping through micro and macrocosmos:
the source and substance of the psyche and heart.

791 From her beauty spot stems
all the grief and blood that brims
within our hearts;
No way out, no exit
from this degree exists.
793 I know not if her beauty spot
is our heart's double, its projected image,
or the heart the image and facsimile
of her face's fascinating beauty spot.

794 Has the heart, as a reflection or facsimile
of that face come forth,
or was her image
therein projected so palpably?
795 Is the heart within her face
or her face within the heart?
An intricate enigma, ineffable, invisible
to me as well!

796 Yet if the heart merely duplicates her mole,
is an image of her mole reflected,
why this fickleness in every mood,
this discord, this disparity
in mystical states?[712]

Although these verses are couched in imagery which also appeals to the language of lyrical expression of the classical Persian poets who composed conventional love poetry, they are obviously intended to expound the aesthetic nuances of divine Unity and provide a symbolic portrait of the transcendental 'Beloved' as 'She/He' appears in the Human Form Divine. Shabistarī's *affaire de coeur* thus becomes an exposition of the mysteries of the psychology of the spiritual heart,[713] with the bewitching mole of the human beloved representing the Qualities of the One, Unique and Eternal Being.

* * *

With the above example of poet's own metaphysical application of erotic imagery in mind, we may now return to our study of Shabistarī/Lāhījī's hermeneutics of the 'archetypal meanings' of poetic imagery. Interpreting verse 728, Lāhījī asserts that suitable terms must be found to maintain the proper 'correspondence' *(tanāsub)* between the supra-sensual, 'real' realm of Vision, and the sensual, 'metaphorical' realm of erotic imagery. Shabistarī's aesthetics of poetry, one could say in our modern terminology, advocates the use of the 'cognitive' rather than the 'emotive' type of poetic metaphor.[714]

Concerning the following verse (729), Lāhījī comments that since the sensible and intellectual realms are at antipodes, a proper 'universal analogy' evocative of both is impossible to attain.[715]

Lāhījī finds in the following line (730) an allusion to the *tanzīh-tashbīh* dichotomy—the debate prevalent in Islamic theology between those who believed God is beyond all likeness and analogy, a Being inviolable *(tanzīh),* and those who claim to find His likeness *(tashbīh)* in creation. But, as Lāhījī reiterates, it is a fallacy to think that mystical states *(aḥwāl)*[716] can be adequately assessed in terms of such artificial theological concepts. The 'religion of love', found in 'Ayn al-Quḍāt Hamadhānī (d. 525/1131),[717] and later in the writings of Ibn 'Arabī,[718] transcends these scholastic dogmas, employs different, antinominian standards. To explain this doctrine, Lāhījī resorts to Rumi's renowned verse:

> Love's state is apart
> from religions and faiths;
> God is the lover's religion
> God is the lover's state.[719]

Interpreting this apparently libertine doctrine, Lāhījī however, admonishes

> That which is revealed to masters of mystical states by way of interior revelation is beyond the comprehension of reason, and religious duties only apply to people of reason. No one,

> however, has any authority to impose any religious duty upon those who have realized the station of mystical absorbtion *(istighrāq)* and selflessness . . . [720]

What appears on the surface to be an individualistic view of poetic inspiration, 'heart-savour' and mystical revelation, is clarified by Lāhījī's interpretation of couplet 731:

> Although the "pontiff-of-Faith *(ṣāhib-i madhhab)*" at this hierarchical level is exclusively God [or Truth], as long as the wayfarer remains self-conscious and his reason *('aql)* steadily balanced, he is prohibited from giving utterance to any words or expressions which contradict the religious law *(sharḥ)*.[721]

Albeit expressed in a entirely different context (that of exoteric Islamic theology), couplet 732 resembles Socrates' doctrine of poetry as a form of the 'Divine Madness', as stated in the *Phaedrus* (545A):

> He who knocks at the gate of poetry untouched by the madness of the Muses, believing that art alone will make him an accomplished poet, will be denied access to the Mystery, and his sober compositions will be eclipsed by the creations of inspired madness.[722]

However, putting this apparently Platonic doctrine in a Sufi context, Lāhījī explains that poetic expressions uttered in the subjective state of annihilation *(fanā')*, intoxication *(sukr)*, and infatuation *(dalāl)* differ from literal statements of ordinary consciousness. He interprets the term *dalāl* (infatuation, enticement) to mean a state of selflessness brought on by deep spiritual anxiety and aroused through an excess of love and heart-savour *(dhawq)* which affects the Sufi during contemplation. Hence, "he involuntarily cries out and announces whatever [truths] flash upon his heart . . . "[723] *Dalāl* is exemplified in the state of the shepherd (in Rumi's tale in the *Mathnawī,* II: 1720-1815) who was reproached by Moses for his blasphemous comparison *(tashbīh)* of God to a human beloved. God Himself later rebukes and chastises Moses for his meddling in lovers' affairs and for his objections, allowing Rūmī to comment, following the verse cited above, that the "religion of lovers" transcends the "religion of reasoners."

Commenting on the following three verses (733-35) Lāhījī cautions that,

> If you do not possess these three kinds of ecstatic states – beware, a hundred times over! – beware! – that you don't become an infidel by imitation of those who have realized them . . . All the scholars of the *Ṭarīqa* (the Sufi Path) and the *Sharī'a* agree that whoever utters such words without the corresponding mystical state is to be condemned for blasphemy as a matter of course.[724]

Lāhījī's exegesis of these verses shows that the science of Sufi symbolism is more an intuited experiential practice than a theoretical doctrine. Lāhījī recapitulates the purport of couplet 736 by asserting that the poetic imagery of the Sufis

> expresses without a doubt, a genuine spiritual state. No one should entertain the vain fancy that such allusions are mere poetical metaphors *(majāz)* or the product of a deluded mind, rather, they are true *(haqīqī),* expressing states of consciousness understood by the perfect beings, realized and manifested to them in revelation *(kashf)* and vision *(shuhūd).*[725]

Some of the ethical and spiritual qualities necessary to comprehend this spiritual state, Lāhījī enumerates as follows: innate aptitude *(qābiliyāt-i fiṭrī)*, a spiritual master's direction, mystical and ethical conduct or discipline *(sulūk),* ascetic self-restraint *(zuhd),* experiencing the spiritual stations acknowledged by the classical masters, God's grace, and spiritual strength, adding

> Many are the wayfarers –
> the wayknowers, the wayseers few;
> among one hundred thousand wayfarers
> but one man the road knew.

By "the *arcana* of the Path" *(asrār-i ṭarīqat),* the poet refers to esoteric states of Reality, the *ṭarīqat* being an introduction to the realization of the *Ḥaqīqat* (Reality). Just as the Sufi Path is the inner mystery of the *sharī'at* (religious law), so Reality is the inner mystery of the Sufi Path. Just as it is totally neurotic *(waswasa)* to follow the Sufi Path without the

> religious law, so it is utter blasphemy and heresy *(zandiqa wa ilḥād)* to contemplate Reality without the Sufi Path. However, those people whose minds are sound, whose reasons are fully developed will realize of course, that the masters of the Sufi Path have undergone severe austerities, and attained the total spiritual result thereof, for without taking such troubles no such result will ever be reaped.[726]

Lāhījī's exegesis of couplet 736 elaborates that there are two possible ways to understand Sufi symbolic poetry:

1. Either a person actually undergoes the spiritual discipline *(sulūk)* and perfect guidance of the Sufis, and so attains the station of interior revelation and contemplative vision, witnessing these states personally for himself, and thus comes to realize that whatever the Sufis have said, was the outcome of insight and observation, or else –
2. Through divine grace one attains to 'conviction of the heart' *(taṣdīq)*[727] concerning the sayings of the saints and gains certain realization that all that they have pronounced was by means of direct contemplative vision *('ayn-i shuhūd)*.[728]

Concerning the key term 'realized adepts *(ahl-i taḥqīq)*' in this line, Lāhījī had explained earlier in his commentary that the true Sufi poet is

> that perfect being unto whom the Reality of everything 'as it really is' is revealed. This archetypal meaning can only be comprehended by one who has realized the degree of divine revelation and with direct vision has seen that the reality of everything is God, and, except for One Absolute Being, no other being exists.[729]

In line 737, Shabistarī reconfirms his earlier statement that these archetypal meanings *(ma'ānī)* are not merely rhetorical metaphors, but contain an esoteric aspect which not everyone can grasp. One must plumb to the depths of the spirit to fathom these meanings, comments Lāhījī on the last two lines: 738 and 739, in order to distinguish just how far equivocation or making comparisons *(tashbīh)* is permissible, and how far God's inviolability *(tanzīh)* should be observed. There is a definite *sacra regula,* in short, to be followed in the Sufi manual of poetic theosophy.

In his commentary on the final couplet translated above (739), Lāhījī explains that "one should only employ metaphors in a particular style or mode [i.e. which evokes the archetypal and metaphysical origin of ordinary words]." The concept of the usage of "types precise" *(wajh-i khāṣṣ:* literally 'a special aspect') of striking similes, Lāhījī elucidates in particularly exact detail:

> In this verse, the poet implies that types precise should be employed which accord with the requirements of each of the levels of archetypal meanings in striking similes *(tashbīh),* and only use words which definitely denote that particular significance. Steer clear of all other aspects necessarily included in [the hierarchical and metaphysical nature of] these levels. For example, when one uses the word 'eye' *(chishm)* intending to express the (divine) Quality of vision *(baṣīrī)* – insofar as during the final degrees of the appearance of divine theophanies and revelation, vision demands an eye *(baṣar),* you should strike your simile *with this precise aspect* in mind and abstain from all other aspects, such as, for example, imagining that the eye is corporeal and thus subject to the conditions of corporeality.[730]

Finally, in order to overcome the *tashbīh-tanzīh* dichotomy, Lāhījī comments that whereas God totally transcends all the demonstrable meanings of words *(lafẓ)* and expressions *('ibārat)* on the level of the divine Essence, on the level of the descent of the divine Acts and Effects *(athār wa af'āl),* it is God who appears in the form of various things. He goes on to remark that making similes *(tashbīh)* and the annulment of all similes and comparisions *(tanzīh)* are notions which are still bound to the realm of illusion and material phenomena. "Since nothing actually exists but God, to what may one compare Him? From what, in fact, should His comparability with, be annulled?[731]

## Conclusion – The Hermeneutic Tradition

What is heart-savour – the realization of Archetypal Meanings;
Not preaching piety, nor issuing fiats.

– 'Aṭṭār, *Muṣībat-nāma*

Shabistarī's theory of aesthetics is based on a science of mystical states, rather than the study of rhetoric and prosody. Furthermore, as this chapter has shown, the separation made by many scholars of the school of Ibn 'Arabī from that of Rūmī, and their contrasting of the "discursive Sufism" of Ibn 'Arabī and his followers Ṣadr al-Dīn Qūnawī and Shabistarī, with the so-called "ecstatic and visionary Sufism" of Rūmī is highly artificial, and in fact, unfaithful to the spirit of the *Garden of Mystery*.[732] It is an aesthetics of intoxication, an awareness of the non-sensible and supranatural, the heart's own humour, an *aesthesis* and appreciation of beauty to which the external eye and ear are only a mute audience, rather than willing participants. Every word, phrase, or turn of speech in the lexicon of the Sufi symbolist poets conveys an intricate ecstatic 'taste' to the heart, and relays a subtle noetic light to the soul. It is necessary to be aware of the precise symbolic implications their metaphors contain. To trace the historical of such imagery, or to analyse their allusions from a purely aesthetic standpoint, is insufficient.[733] For the Sufis themselves such images function as a mystical mandala which are employed as a contemplative device to intuitively penetrate, by means of spiritual audition *(samā')*, the domain of archetypal meanings.[734] After the foregoing study of Lāhījī's commentary, it seems obvious how inaccurate is the following statement by E.J.W. Gibb in his still classic summary of Sufi theosophy, *A History of Ottoman Poetry:*

> The Sufi teachers have reduced their system to a science which bristles with a complicated and generally obscure terminology. Into this, it is unnecessary we should enter, as it has little direct bearing upon their poetry. The poet who is imbued, as most poets are, with the Sufiistic mysticism, pays scant heed to these technicalities.[735]

Rather, the reverse is true: Persian symbolist poetry is directly inspired by Sufism. The view expressed below concerning Ḥāfeẓ's poetry by Eric Schroeder is even truer in regard to the verse of symbolists such as Maghribī or Shabistarī:

> Hafez's Divan is permeated with Sufism, and the meaning of his life and work is primarily religious and metaphysical. Even an aesthetic critique of his verse which fails to show the intricacy of his metaphysical reference is aesthetically shallow.[736]

Perhaps the most comprehensive summary in classical Persian literature of this 'symbolist mentality' characteristic of poets of Shabistarī's school, are eighteen couplets written by Maghribī. These verses represent a kind of manifesto of the philosophy of Sufi symbolism. They are also cited by Lāhījī in the portion of his commentary here translated (see above, p. 192, commentary on line 722) to expound this philosophy. Never before translated or mentioned in any European language study of Sufi poetry, perhaps they may best communicate to us the feeling of this still living hermeneutic tradition.

*The Hermeneutic Tradition*

So if you see in this tome of verse
  name and sign of vintner and wine,
of rack and ruin,
  of 'haunters of taverns'
the legend of the Magus
  and Mazdaism, crosses and icons,
the tale of cloisters and totems,
  Christian rosaries, pagan cinctures,
hear a glass praised
  or enamel decanter discussed,
talk of wine, and 'witnesses
  in flesh' of what's divine;
If candle I cry
  praising chapels and cells,
speak of harp's whine,
  hail drunkard's clamour,
refer to wine and winehouses,
  to 'rogues of the Ruin',
or ascetics at prayer, declare
  I cupbearers adore
or an organ chord if I note,
  praising the flute's poignant cry,
summon a 'dawn-cordial' be served up,

mention 'pass round the cup'
or utter 'goblet', 'pitcher'
'vat', or 'cup', or 'vintner';
Of rites of drinking, comportment with wine
write, of fleeing mosques
of resting in taverns and taking refuge in pubs . . .

Should I ever say, "To wine myself I've pledged"
and profess to relinquish
this spirit and flesh
for love of wine,
or praise the parterre,
consort with flowers
of arboretums write,
reckon account of cypresses,
the dewdrop's tale recite,
the anemone's inner life,
trace the rain's tale,
yarn of the hail,
relate the hoarfrost's history . . .

Then of down and beauty-spots should I speak,
The eyebrow's bend and towering statures praise,
Take note of cheeks and cheekbone,
Impudent eyes, and teeth, lovely waists;
Of faces and braids should I sing
Or else of cuff and fist insist you listen –
At such idioms be flustered not;
Of their object inquire.
Of long and short feet,
Of my phrases' morphology don't ask
If with symbolists you'd be confident,
Into hermeneutics an initiate.

Rectify your eye
You'll see straight.
Perfect your insight –
You'll see right.
Reject the rind
The nut you'll find.

Unless the crust you reject
Howsoever will you become a Kabbalist?

O, within each and every phoneme of mine
  a live soul resides
within every *lexis,* an *animus* there is,
  a soul alive within each word,
in every letter a cosmos concealed.

You should seek its spirit, its flesh reject,
  its noumenon pursue and Named-Essence adopt;
its phenomenon do not claim.

Neglect no Minute Particular
If in the truths of the symbolists
You'd become adept.[737]

## Notes

[615] An abbreviated version of this chapter appeared under the title of "Shabestari's Garden of Mysteries: The Aesthetics and Hermeneutics of Sufi Poetry," in *Temenos: A Review Devoted to the Arts of the Imagination,* No. 10 (1989), pp. 177-207. Grateful acknowledgement is made to Dr. Kathleen Raine for permission to reproduce and for her efforts at editing the original essay.

[616] Rūmī, *Mathnawī,* II: 3292.

[617] Arberry's studies of Sufi poetry include: *Fifty Poems of Ḥāfiẓ* (Cambridge University Press, 1977 rpt.); "Orient Pearls At Random Strung," *Bulletin of thc School of Oriental and African Studies,* II (1948). In the first work, Sufism is dismissed as a "philosophy of unreason" and in the last, all mention of it is omitted! Michael Hillmann's main work is *Unity in the Ghazals of Ḥāfiẓ* (Chicago 1976). Annemarie Schimmel's works include a sensitive and refined study of Islamic poetry: *As Through A Veil: Mystical Poetry in Islam* (New York: Columbia University Press, 1982) and a comprehensive opus on Sufi philosophy and literature: *Mystical Dimensions of Islam* (Chapel Hill: University of N. Carolina, 1975), as well as her wide-ranging volume: *A Two-Colored Brocade: The Imagery of Persian Poetry* (Chapel Hill: University of N. Carolina, 1992).

This same purely aesthetic approach is also adopted by the works of Persian scholars such as 'Abd al-Ḥusayn Zarrīnkūb's *Naqd-i adabī* (2 vols.; Tehran 1976), except for a few pages on mystical inspiration (I, pp. 52-58) and Sufi poetic theory (I, pp. 251-55). Likewise, Dr. Kadkani's *Suwar-i khiyāl dar shi'r-i fārsī* (Tehran 1970) is also exclusively concerned with the aesthetic and social realm of Sufi poetic imagery.

[618] *Allegorical Imagery: Some Medieval Books and Their Renaissance Posterity* (Princeton University Press, 1966), Chap. 4.

[619] As, for example, Eric Schroeder's comparison of John Donne to Ḥāfiẓ, in his article "Verse Translation and Ḥāfiẓ," *Journal of Near Eastern Studies,* Vol. 7 (1948) or Annemarie Schimmel's view that Sufi poets, merely because of "the ambiguity of the experience of love," employed erotic symbolism, then imposed upon "a basic symbolism of earthly love" a gradual process of allegorization, until "eventually, the charm of a quatrain is lost in the heavy chains of a terminology stemming from Ibn 'Arabī." *Mystical Dimensions,* p. 301. It is highly questionable, in my opinion, whether the puritanical concepts of 'sacred' and 'profane' can be directly applied to Islamic poetry at all (a point brought out by A. Bouhdiba in his *Sexuality in Islam,* translated from the French by Alan Sheridan, London, 1985; chap. 8, "The sexual and the sacral," for instance). The whole endeavour of the Sufi poets seems more hierophanic (to use Mircea Eliade's term: *The Sacred and The Profane,* New York: 1961, p. 11) than strictly religious; it is an attempt to envision everything 'profane' as 'sacred' in terms of its being *(wujūd).* Vincent Buckley has argued convincingly, in my opinion, that there is no separate genre of religious or sacred poetry; observing, apropos of 16th and 17th-century English poetry, that "sacred poetry" as a completely separate category is something of a psychological monstrosity." - *Poetry and the Sacred* (London, 1968), p. 29.

[620] Rūzbhān Baqlī. *Le Jasmin des Fidèles d'Amour (Kitāb abhār al-'āshiqīn),* edited by Henry Corbin and M. Mu'īn (Tehran, 1981); Corbin's introduction, p. 5.

[621] Cf. S. H. Nasr's preface to *Fakhruddīn 'Irāqī: Divine Flashes,* translated into English by William C. Chittick and Peter Lamborn Wilson, p. xiii.

[622] On logopoeia, see Ezra Pound, *ABC of Reading* (London, Faber & Faber, 1979), p. 63.

[623] The works of these three scholars considered in this chapter are: Izutsu's "The Basic Structure of Metaphysical Thinking in Islam" in *Collected Papers on Islamic Philosophy and Mysticism,* edited by H. Landolt (Tehran, 1971), pp. 41-72, his "Mysticism and the Linguistic Problem of Equivocation in the Thought of 'Ayn al-Quḍāt Hamadhānī" in *Studia Islamica,* Vol. 31 (1970), pp. 153-70 and "The Paradox of Light and Darkness in the *Garden of Mystery* of Shabistarī," in Joseph P. Strelka (ed.) *Anagogic Qualities in Literature* ((University Park, Pa. 1971); S. H. Nasr's "Metaphysics, Poetry, and Logic in Oriental Traditions" in *Sophia Perennis,* Vol. 3, no. 2 (1977), pp. 119-28; and Henry Corbin's *Avicenna and the Visionary Recital,* translated firom French by W. R. Trask (London, Kegan Paul, 1961).

[624] Works such as the *Risāla-yi Mishwāq* by Mullā Muḥsin Fayḍ Kāshānī (in Rasūl Ja'fariyān, ed., *Dah risāla-yi al-Ḥakīm al-'Ārif al-Kāmal al-Fāḍil Muḥammad Muḥsin al-Fayḍ al-Kāshānī,* Iṣfahān: 1371 A.Hsh./ 1993; pp. 236-73) and the *Lāṭifa-yi ghaybī* by Muḥammad al-Dārābī (Shirāz: Kitāb-khāna-yi Aḥmadī, n.d.) are typical of examples of treatises devoted exclusively to discussion of the metaphysical presumptions

and theomonist doctrines underlying Persian Sufi poetry. A modern interpretation of the *Dīwān* of Ḥāfiẓ by S. Aḥmad Bihisthī Shīrāzī (*Sharḥ-i junūn,* Tehran: Intishārāt-i Rūzana 1371 A.Hsh./1993) illustrates the possibilites of a modern 'gnostic' interpretation of Sufi poetry in the tradition of Fayḍ Kāshānī and Muḥammad al-Dārābī.

[625] The importance of symbolism in Sufi poetry is exemplified in a unique dialogue between two great Tabrīzī Sufi poets and masters: Maghribī and Kamāl Khujandī, mentioned by Jāmī in his *Nafaḥāt al-uns,* ed. Mehdī Tawḥīdipūr, p. 613.

[626] Both Iranian literati and Western orientalists generally regard Sufi theories of poetic imagery as too far-fetched and esoteric to merit discussion. The most significant work in this field, after Ja'far Sajjādī's *Farhang-i lughāt wa iṣtilāḥāt wa ta'bīrāt-i 'irfānī* (Tehran 1960), is Javad Nurbakhsh's *Farhang-i Nūrbakhsh* of which ten volumes out of a proposed 15-volume series have so far been published in Persian. 9 volumes of this encyclopedia have been translated into English under the title of *Sufi Symbolism* (London: KNP 1984-94). Vol. I of this encyclopedia, entitled *Sufi Symbolism I,* translated by Leonard Lewisohn, (London: KNP 1984), treating the esoteric symbolism of the parts of the Beloved's body, and the allegorical meanings of imagery relating to wine, convivial gatherings, and ecstasy, still remains the only in-depth study of Sufi poetic symbolism in the English language.

[627] Maghribī's relationship to Shabistarī was discussed above in chapter 4, p. 121.

Lāhījī's commentary, in its new edition by Khāliqī and Karbāsī, runs to over 600 printed pages of small Persian type; his citations of Maghribī occur approximately every 14 pages, quoting from a total number of 40 different ghazals by Maghribī, which is to say that Lahiji, when extemporizing his commentary, had memorized almost all of Maghribī's Dīwān (= 200 ghazals). All references to Maghribī's Dīwān below are to Leonard Lewisohn (ed.) *Dīwān-i Muḥammad Shīrīn Maghribī.*

[628] These verses are also cited in full by Qāsim Ghanī in his pioneering work on Ḥāfiẓ: *Baḥth dar āthār wa afkār wa aḥwāl-i Ḥāfiẓ: Tārīkh-i taṣawwuf dar islām tā 'aṣr-i Ḥāfiẓ*, II, pp. 334-5, to illustrate the unique technical and symbolic style elaborated in Sufi poetry during this period.

[629] *As Through a Veil,* p. 54.

[630] From Rūzbihān's *Mashrab al-arwāḥ* (*The Fount of Spirits*), an encyclopedic work in Arabic on the spiritual stations in Sufism. Cited by Dr. Javad Nurbakhsh, *Farhang-i Nurbakhsh* (London: KNP 1984), II, p. 99.

[631] Sulāmī, *Kitāb Ṭabaqāt al-ṣūfiyya,* ed. J. Pedersen (Leiden 1960), p. 528.

[632] Qushayrī, *Risāla,* II, p. 220.

[633] Ed. F. Jabre, pp. 35, 44. For further discussion of Ghazālī's conception of *dhawq,* Eric L. Ormsby, "The Taste of Truth: The Structure of Experience in al-Ghazālī's *Al-Munqidh Min Al-Ḍalāl,*" in W.B. Hallaq and D.P. Little, *Islamic Studies Presented to Charles J. Adams* (Leiden: E.J. Brill 1991), p. 142.

[634] *Sharḥ-i shaṭhiyyāt,* edited by Henry Corbin (Tehran 1981), p. 627.

[635] *Miṣbāḥ al-hedāya wa miftāḥ al-kafāya,* ed. Jalāl al-Dīn Humā'ī, p. 134.

[636] *'Awārif al-ma'ārif,* (Beirut: Dār al-Kitāb al-'Arabī 1983). This book was partially translated into English (so ungracefully, however, as to be practically unreadable) by H. Wilberforce Clarke, under the title of *The 'Awārif-u'l-Ma'ārif,* (Calcutta 1891).

[637] *Miṣbāḥ al-hidāya,* p. 137n., cited by the editor.

[638] *Al-Futūḥāt al-Makkiyya* (Cairo 1329 A.H.), I, p. 31. Cited by R.J. W. Austin in his 1965 London University Ph.D. thesis: *The Spiritual Heart: Studies in the Māhiyat al-Qalb of Ibn al-'Arabī,* p. 42.

[639] *Kashshāf iṣṭilāḥāt al-funūn (A Dictionary of the Technical Terms Used in the Sciences of the Musalmans),* Edited by M. Wajih, 'Abd al-Ḥaqq, & Gholam Kadir, under the superintendence of A. Sprenger & W. Nassua Lees. (Calcutta 1862), I, p. 514. Cited in *Farhang-i Nūrbakhsh,* II, p. 98.

[640] Cf. "Taste" in A. Preminger (ed.) in the *Princeton Encyclopedia of Poetry and Poetics* (N.J.: Princeton University Press 1986; enlarged edition).

[641] *Dīwān-i Humām-i Tabrīzī,* ed. Dr. Rashīdī 'Aywaḍī, p. 68.

[642] *The Thought of the Heart* (Ascona: Eranos Foundation, 1981), pp. 31-32.

[643] *The Thought of the Heart,* p. 3.

[644] *Mafātīḥ al-i'jāz,* ed. Khāliqī & Karbāsī, p. 3. For a good discussion of the function of the heart in post-Ibn 'Arabī Sufism, see J.W. Morris, "Listening for God: Prayer and the Heart in the *Futūḥāt,*" *JMIAS*, XIII (1993), pp. 19-53.

[645] *ibid.*

[646] *Dīwān-i Muḥammad Shīrīn Maghribī,* (ed.), Leonard Lewisohn, p. 169, ghazal 80.

[647] Cf. C.M. Bowra, *The Heritage of Symbolism* (London: 1951), p. 12, and Kamal Abu Deeb, *Al-Jurjani's Theory of Poetic Imagery* (Warminster: Ans & Phillips, 1979), pp. 124-42. The function of anagogy in Western literature is discussed in great detail by Northrop Frye's *Anatomy of Criticism*, pp. 118-22.

[648] "The Basic Structure . . .", p. 59.

[649] *The Meaning of Poetic Metaphor* (The Hague, 1967), p. 14. Cited by Izutsu, *ibid.*

[650] See Paul Piehler, *The Visionary Landscape: A Study in Medieval Allegory* (London: 1971), pp. 42-45, 134. Also cf. Louis Martz, *The Poetry of Meditation: A Study in English Religious Literature of the 17th Century* (New Haven: Yale University Press, 1976, 6th rpt.), pp. 202-03, 342, 342.

[651] "Allegorical Gardens in the Persian Poetic Traditions," *International Journal of Middle Eastern Studies,* XVII/2 (1985), p. 259, n. 71.

[652] This resembles the traditional Christian outlook on poetic knowledge, which, according to Jacques Maritian, "is an emotion as *form,* which being one with the creative intuition, gives form to the poem, and which is intentional, as an idea is, or carries within itself infinitely more than itself. (I use the word 'intentional' in the Thomistic sense . . . which refers to the purely tendential existence through which a thing . . . is present, in an immaterial or suprasubjective manner) . . . an idea for

instance, which, insofar as it determines the act of knowing, is a mere immaterial tendency or *intentio* towards the object." – *Creative Intuition in Art and Poetry* (New York: Pantheon Books, 1953), Bollingen Series 35.1, pp. 119-20.

653 *Greek Elements in Arabic Linguistic Thinking* (Leiden: E.J.Brill, 1977), p. 185.

654 *ibid.*, p. 189.

655 *Answer to Job,* in *Collected Works of C.G. Jung,* II, p. 551; cited by Kathleen Raine, *The Human Face of God: William Blake and the Book of Job* (London: Thames & Hudson 1982), p. 270.

656 Paul Piehler, *The Visionary Landscape: A Study in Medieval Allegory,* p. 17.

657 From his "On the Relation of Analytical Psychology to Poetic Art" in *Contributions to Analytical Psychology* (London 1928), p. 244.

658 This point is eloquently argued by Prof. Zarrinkub, *Naqd-i adabī,* (Tehran: Amīr Kabīr 1361 A.Hsh./1982), I, p. 251.

659 See Paul Nwyia, *Exégèse Coranique et Langue Mystique* (Beirut: 1970), pp. 33, 59-61, 145-46.

660 *Avicenna and the Visionary Recital,* pp. 28-35 ("Ta'wīl as Exegesis of the Soul"). On the other hand, we may call the Sufi method of extracting meaning from a poetic image a *tafḥīm* as well, which, as Corbin notes elsewhere (referring to theomonistic thought of al-Jīlī), implies "in the strict sense of the word, a *hermeneutics,* an Understanding, which is here a truly existential hermeneutics, since the vision of the Divine Face epiphanizes the Face which the Godhead has in each being and which is the Holy Spirit of that being. ... The Godhead is this Form, and this Form is all this and nothing more: apparition. The theophanic event is twofold: there is the determinate form (this hair, this dress, these sandals) and there is the hidden meaning *(ma'nā)* which is not be sought within the context of general abstract truths or in human truths sublimated and applied to God, but in the irremissible connection between the Form seen and the being to whom God shows Himself in this form." *Creative Imagination in the Ṣūfism of Ibn 'Arabī,* translated from the French by R. Manheim, (Princeton: Princeton University Press 1969), Bollingen Series XCI, p. 378n. 4.

661 "Mysticism and the Linguistic Problem," pp. 158-59.

662 This Latin term, like *significatio* and *sen,* was often employed by mediæval European scholastic philosophers for *ma'nā.* Cf. Corbin, *Avicenna ... ,* p. 301n.

663 *Jahān-i 'aql:* the World of the Intellect.

664 Shabistarī's verse here contradicts Baudelaire's view (which is actually a misrepresentation of Swedenborg's doctrine of Correspondence) that "l'imagination est la plus scientifique des facultés, parce que, seule elle comprend l'analogie universelle, ou ce qu'une religion mystique appelle la Correspondance." Quoted by Kamal Abu Deeb, *op. cit.,* p. 125.

665 MAS, pp. 97-8; *Gulshan-i rāz,* edited by Dr. Javad Nurbakhsh, pp. 47-8. Whinfield's version seriously mistranslates lines 721,725, 727 (in MAS) above, which my translation has amended.

666 On this doctrine, see below, chap. 7, p. 240.

[667] Translated from the Persian by N. Pourjavady: *Sawānih: Inspirations from the World of Pure Spirits* (London: KPI 1986). Also cf. *idem.*, "Ḥusn wa malāḥat: baḥthī dar zībā'ī-shināsī-yi Ḥāfiẓ," in N. Pourjavady (ed.) *Barguzīda-yi maqālahā-yi Nashr-i Dānish* (Tehran: 1365 A.Hsh./1986), pp. 21-38.

[668] *Aḥādīth-i Mathnawī,* ed. Badī' al-Zamān Furūzānfar, no. 63. See also Javad Nurbakhsh, *Traditions of the Prophet,* I, p. 25.

[669] MAS, *Ḥaqq al-yaqīn,* p. 303.

[670] For further study, see Sachiko Murata, *The Tao of Islam: A Sourcebook on Gender Relationships in Islamic Thought* (Albany: SUNY 1992), chap. 6, and *idem.,* "Witnessing the Rose: Ya'qūb Ṣarfī on the Vision of God in Women," in Alma Giese & J-C. Bürgel, *God is Beautiful and He loves beauty: Festschrift in honour of Annemarie Schimmel* (Bern: Peter Lang 1994), pp. 349-61.

[671] *Mafātīḥ al-i'jāz,* ed. Khāliqī & Karbāsī, p. 465. Cf. Blake: "The head Sublime, the heart Pathos, the genitals Beauty, the hands & feet Proportion." (Proverbs of Hell)

[672] *Mafātīḥ al-i'jāz,* ed. Khāliqī & Karbāsī, p. 467. On 'Majesty' vs. 'Beauty', the masculine and feminine nature of these qualities and their effects on the soul, see Murata, *The Tao of Islam,* pp. 69-74.

[673] *Mafātīḥ al-i'jāz,* ed. Khāliqī & Karbāsī, p. 467.

[674] *Justujū,* p. 313.

[675] *Dīwān-i Muḥammad Shīrīn Maghribī,* p. 229, ghazal 110.

[676] *Mathnawī-yi ma'nawī,* ed. Nicholson, IV: 1359-72.

[677] The history of medieval Arabic grammatical terms such as *waḍ'* is discussed by Versteegh, *op. cit.,* pp. 29ff.

[678] *Mafātīḥ al-i'jāz,* ed. Khāliqī & Karbāsī, p. 468.

[679] *Ibid.*

[680] 'Abdu'llāh Anṣārī defines *ṭāmāt* as "a form of discourse that is incomprehensible or an allusive utterance that is obscure. It may be the expression of a state which one is experiencing or an indiation of what one imagines oneself to be experiencing." Cited by J. Nurbakhsh, *Sufi Symbolism VIII (Farhang-i Nūrbakhsh),* trans. by Terry Graham *et al,* London: KNP 1994), p. 75.

[681] *Mafātīḥ al-i'jāz,* ed. Khāliqī & Karbāsī, p. 469.

[682] See chap. 3: "The Symbolist Mentality," in Chenu's *Nature, Man, and Society in the 12th Century,* translated from French by J. Taylor and L.K. Little (University of Chicago Press, 1968).

[683] R. Sharrock (ed.), *The Pilgrim's Progress,* (London: Penguin Books 1987), p. 46.

[684] Leonard Lewisohn (ed.), *Dīwān-i Muḥammad Shīrīn Maghribī,* p. 7.

[685] *The Tarjumān al-ashwāq: A Collection of Mystical Odes by Muhyi'ddín Ibn al-'Arabí,* trans. and ed. by R.A. Nicholson (London: Theosophical Publishing House, 1978 rpt.), p. 13, (Arabic text), vv. 1-16.

[686] For a good discussion of which, see W.C. Chittick, "The World of Imagination and Poetic Imagery according to Ibn al-'Arabī," in *Temenos: A Journal Devoted to the Arts of the Imagination,* no. 10 (1989), pp. 99-119.

[687] Here, I refer to the long-standing debate concerning the unity of the

ghazal, for a good summary of which see: Frances W. Pritchett, "Orient Pearls unstrung: The Quest for unity in the Ghazal," *Edebiyāt,* NS IV/1 (1993), pp. 119-35.

688 Eric Schroeder, "Verse Translation and Hafiz," *Journal of Near Eastern Studies,* VII (1948), p. 220.

689 Rūmī, *Mathnawī* II: 3292.

690 In emulation of George Herbert's *The Temple*, Richard Crashaw entitled one of his collections of poetry *Steps to the Temple.* Other similar influences in seventeenth-century mystical poetry are discussed in Frank J. Warnke's introduction to his *European Metaphysical Poetry* (New Haven: Yale University Press, 1961).

691 *Mafātīḥ al-i'jāz,* ed. Khāliqī & Karbāsī, p. 469.

692 *Mafātīḥ al-i'jāz,* ed. Khāliqī & Karbāsī, p. 469-70.

693 The influence of Plato's thought on Arabic theories of *lafẓ* and *ma'nā,* especially the role of his dialogue: *Cratylus* (On the Correctness of Names), is discussed by Versteegh, *op. cit.,* pp. 173, 187. F.E. Peters places the *Cratylus* among the list od Platonic texts known to and studied by Islamic Neoplatonists such as Fārābī, and thus possibly known to Shabistarī as well. "The Origins of Islamic Platonism: The School Tradition," in P. Morewedge (ed.), *Islamic Philosophical Theology* (Albany: SUNY 1979), p. 29.

694 Chenu, *op. cit.*, pp. 82, 123.

695 From *Emmanuel Swedenborg, The Universal Human and Soul-Body Interaction,* edited and translated by G. Dole (New York: Paulist Press, 1984), pp. 39-41.

696 *Mafātīḥ al-i'jāz,* ed. Khāliqī & Karbāsī, p. 470.

697 Frederic Will, *Intelligible Beauty in Aesthetic Thought: From Winkelmann to Victor Cousin* (Tubingen, 1958). p. 37.

698 "A Vision of the Last Judgement," in *Blake: Complete Writings,* ed. G. Keynes, p. 605.

699 MAS, *Gulshan-i rāz,* pp. 99-100.

700 By the "visage" is signified, says Lāhījī, "the entire range of perfections of the divine Names and Attributes necessary for the Divine Essence." *Mafātīḥ al-i'jāz,* ed. Khāliqī & Karbāsī, p. 494.

701 This term is said to symbolize the threshold or antechamber *(janāb)* of Divine Glory, which signifies the world of disembodied spirits, which is the closest level in the hierarchy of being to the hidden realm of the Divine Selfhood. . . . It may also signify the theophany of Divine Majesty in spiritual manifestations. *Ibid.,* pp. 494, 466.

702 The winsome line of the down, says Lāhījī, symbolizes "all the subtle nuances and esoteric realities of Divine Beauty." *Ibid.*

703 The down appearing on the face or visage *(rukh)* represents the determined forms *(ta'ayyunāt)* of the world of the spirits gathered about the Divine Essence ... The term 'greensward' indicates the world of the soul *('ālam-i jān = mundus anima)* and symbolizes both the initial appearance of vegetative growth as well as the first level of the manifestation of spirits, being the isthmus *(barzakh)* between the Absolute Invisible and the Visible worlds." The term 'homeland' refers to the verse, "Indeed, the home of the Hereafter—that is Life, if they but

knew." (Koran XXIX: 64).

704 According to Lāhījī, *(ibid.,* p. 495), the "tresses of the Beloved" symbolize "Multiplicity on the level of the determined forms of the apparent and visible world *('ālam-i shahādat),* the superficial aspect of which is imagined to be 'day', although in the lexicon of the Sufis, it is actually a 'day-darkness' because it "obstructs the flow of information concerning the reality of Divine Unity for the seeker. Hence, the injunction to "turn day to night" simply means to dispell the gloomy shades of this multiplicity. One should not pause, like a grazing animal, in the darkness of the down (symbolic of the invisible world and the determined forms of the spirits) but seek out the 'Fount of Life': the Absolute Divine Essence.

705 Lāhījī, *(ibid.,* p. 496) explains that the eternal water of life or "wellsprings of immortality" *(āb-i zindigānī)* denotes the Divine Essence, from which the down (here equivalent to the determined forms of the world of the spirits) drinks (in Lāhījī's text, the verb 'to drink' is a variant reading of 'to seek'). The Prophet Khiḍr (whose name comes from the Arabic root meaning 'green') attained a legendary immortality by drinking from the water of life in a 'region of darkness', which is the 'Cloud of Unknowing' of the Divine Essence: expressed by the poetic metaphor "that station no signals point to" *(bīnishānī,* literally 'tracelessness').

706 The visionary poet's perception of 'the face' reveals it as a symbol of Divine Unity, perceived to be 'day' because of its luminosity. The 'down', on the other hand, reveals itself to the mystic as a symbol of 'night' and 'multiplicity', i.e. scattered conciousness, dispersed awareness, confusion and darkness.

707 The tresses and down of the Beloved are two images, says Lāhījī *(ibid.,* p. 496) to express the idea of multiplicity *(kithrat).* However, whereas the tresses represent the general multiplicty of the visible world, the down denotes the particular multiplicity on the level of the 'determined forms' of the world of the spirit, whose lore is of an esoteric and arcane nature.

708 Lāhījī *(ibid.,* p. 497) explains that the poetic image of the "down upon that fair face" refers to the contemplation of multiplicity within Unity, beholding the creature in the mirror of the Creator *(ḥaqq).* At this level, one is said to be 'a man of reason or insight' and given the name 'owner of reason' or 'possessor of intellect' *(dhu'l-'aql).* (On this term, see N. Safwat, trans., Qāshānī, *A Glossary of Sufi Technical Terms* [London: Octagon Press 1991], no. 503, p. 113). Shabistarī, asserting that his heart beholds 'the face in the down', implies that, because only God can be contained in his heart, he contemplates Unity through multiplicity, and views the Creator in the mirror of creation. One graced with this station is termed a 'man of insight' *(dhu'l-'ayn;* lit. 'possessor of an eye': see *ibid.).*

709 The exordium or Opening Surah of the Koran, called *al-Fātiḥa,* has seven verses. Lāhījī comments that just as *al-Fātiḥa* is a synopsis of the entire gnosis of the Koran, so the Beloved's visage *(rukhsar)* subsumes all Divine Names and Attributes. The visage is a symbol of

the Divine Essence and, as such, includes the seven 'Attributes of the Divine Essence': Life, Knowledge, Power, Will, Hearing, Vision, and Speech, just as *al-Fātiḥa* contains seven verses. Likewise all phenomena, viewed as theophanies *(ẓuhūr, tajallī),* insofar as they emanate and partake of the Divine Essence, contain an ocean of meaning just as do the seven verses of this Surah. This level is technically termed the 'hidden source of theophanies' *(sirr al-tajalliyāt).*

710 Lāhījī *(Mafātīḥ al-i'jāz,* ed. Khāliqī & Karbāsī, p. 498) explains that just as the Beloved's hair both veils and illuminates with beauty her visage, so the various theophanies of the Divine Names act like hair which both conceals and reveals entire "oceans of gnosis" of the Divine Essence (=Visage).

711 Shabistarī's imagery in this line, writes Lāhījī *(ibid.,* p. 498) is inspired by the Koran XI: 7, where God states that He "has placed his Throne upon the waters," and the Prophetic tradition that "the unbeliever's heart is the Throne of the Almighty." The metaphor extends to liken the cheek of the Beloved in its tenderness and delicacy to the 'waters', and the 'down', symbolic of the world of Spirits and the determined forms of things, to the heart—or throne—upon those waters.

712 MAS, *Gulshan-i rāz,* p. 100, vv. 788-96.

713 For a good interpretation of which (using Shabistarī/Lāhījī as illustration), see Dr. Javad Nurbakhsh, *The Psychology of Sufism,* trans. Terry Graham (London: KNP 1992), pp. 71-112.

714 On these terms, see Hester, *op. cit.,* p. 14.

715 Baudelaire's belief in the existence of such an *"analogie universalle,"* as he calls it, (see no. 664 above) involves, in fact, a confusion of synaesthesia (interfusion of sensory images) with 'Correspondence', characteristic of the Sufi use of poetic metaphors (Abu Deeb, *op. cit.,* pp. 124-34). It is to mistake, as T. Izutsu has defined it, the multidimensional "vertical polysemy" found in Sufi theosophy with our ordinary one-dimensional, and linguistically literal "horizontal polysemy." (Izutsu, "Mysticism and the Linguistic Problem of Equivocation . . . ," p. 159).

716 On *aḥwāl,* see Dr. Javad Nurbakhsh, *Spiritual Poverty in Sufism,* translated by Leonard Lewisohn, IV: 'Mystical States'.

717 'Ayn al-Quḍāt Hamadhānī, *Tamhīdāt,* ed. Afif Osseiran, (Tehran: 1962), pp. 21-6.

718 See W.C. Chittick, "Ebno'l-'Arabi as Lover," in *Sufi,* no. 9 (1991), pp. 6-9. For a brief treatment of this topos in classical Persian mystical poetry, see Shīrāzī, *Sharḥ-i junūn,* pp. 770-79.

719 *Mathnawī,* I: 1770.

720 *Mafātīḥ al-i'jāz,* ed. Khāliqī & Karbāsī, p. 471.

721 *Ibid.,* p. 472.

722 Cited by Anton-Hermann Chroust, "Inspiration in Ancient Greece," in E. O'Connor, *Charismatic Revival* (London: SPCK 1985), pp. 74-5.

723 *Mafātīḥ al-i'jāz,* ed. Khāliqī & Karbāsī, p. 473.

724 *Ibid.,* p. 475.

725 *Ibid.,* p. 476.

726 *Ibid..*

[727] This technical term is discussed in detail in chapter VIII, pp. 271ff.

[728] *Mafātīḥ al-i'jāz,* ed. Khāliqī & Karbāsī, p. 477.

[729] *Ibid.*, p. 52.

[730] *Ibid.*, p. 478.

[731] *Ibid.*

[732] This mistaken attitude is exhibited, for instance, by 'Abd al-Ḥusayn Zarrīnkūb's *Sirr-i nay: naqd wa sharḥ-i taḥlīlī wa taṭbīqī-yi Mathnawī* (Tehran: 'Ilmī 1367 A.Hsh./1988), I, p. 102.

[733] Our translation of Dr. Nurbakhsh's encyclopedia of Sufi terminology: *Sufi Syrnbolism I* has proven how barren and insipid such an approach is. Dr. Kadkani's now classic study of *Imagery in Persian Poetry (Suwar-i khiyāl dar shi'r-i fārsī),* aside from a short chapter on Nāṣir-i Khusraw, utterly ignores the metaphysical imagination which concerns the Sufi poets. Hence his discussion of imagination *(khiyāl)* is limited to its rhetorical meaning of 'phantasy' or 'fancy'. The difference between the archetypal imagination and fancy is discussed in Elemire Zolla's article: "The Uses of Imagination and the Decline of the West," *Sophia Perennis* I/1 (1975). Also cf. W.C. Chittick, "Revelation and Poetic Imagery," *Imaginal Worlds,* chap. 5.

[734] Cf. Jean During, *Musique et Extase: L'audition mystique dans la tradition soufie* (Paris; Albin Michel 1988), pp. 135ff.

[735] *History of Ottoman Poetry,* I (London: Luzac & Co. 1958 rpt.), p. 65.

[736] Eric Schroeder, *art. cit.,* p. 216.

[737] Leonard Lewisohn (ed.) *Dīwān-i Muḥammad Shīrīn Maghribī,* pp. 6-8.

# VII

# THE THOUGHT OF THE HEART

## Shabistarī's Doctrine of Contemplation

*Reflection is passing from the false to the Truth*
*And seeing the Universal Absolute within the part.*

### *Tafakkur* in Mediæval Sufi Doctrine

One of the most intriguing aspects of Sufi contemplative disciplines is the juxtaposition and symbiotic interaction of the two practices of 'remembrance of God/Prayer of the Heart' *(dhikr)* and 'contemplative thought'/reflection' *(fikr)*.[738] As can be found in the Koran,[739] these terms usually occur side by side in Sufi texts, and their relative virtues in terms of realization are a favourite subject of discussion. Although some mention of the practice of *dhikr* will be unavoidable in the study below, my focus will be on 'reflection'. Given the strong emphasis on 'reflection' in Shabistarī's teachings (over two hundred couplets of the *Gulshan-i rāz* being devoted to this practice[740]) it will be revealing to briefly examine the theosophical background and conception of *fikr* in the writings of a few important speculative mystics who flourished in the centuries and decades immediately preceding him, namely Abū Ḥāmid al-Ghazālī, 'Azīz Nasafī (d. circa 680-99/1281-99), Rūmī, and Ibn 'Arabī, before proceeding to discuss the poet's own views.

## Abū Ḥāmid al-Ghazālī on Reflection

After Ibn ʻArabī, the major source of Shabistarī's inspiration in the formulation of the doctrine of *tafakkur* found in the *Garden of Mystery* was Ghazālī's *Kitāb al-tafakkur* in the ninth book of the fourth quarter of the *Iḥyā' ʻulūm al-dīn.* In this chapter Ghazālī, drawing on the venerable genre of the *Kutub al-ʻaẓama,* a body of early Muslim literature concerned with the study of natural phenomenon whose primary intention was "to widen man's horizon through an increased knowledge of creation,"[741] Ghazālī delineates the function of reflection as having two goals: i.) to increase knowledge: *takthīr al-ʻilm* and ii.) the reappropriation of a knowledge that is no longer at hand: *istijlāb maʻrifa laysat ḥāṣila.* In the latter sense, reflection was defined as "the effort of refreshing one's memory, of re-creating an intellectual reality as effectively present in one's mind, even to the point of seeking a degree of identity with it."[742] As Anton M. Heinen has demonstrated, Ghazālī's use of reflection

> extends as far as the frontiers of macro- and micro-cosmos, i.e., over the whole of creation, but does not include the Creator Himself, His essence and nature. However, true to the religious and even mystical character of the *Iḥyā' ʻulūm al-dīn,* al-Ghazālī restricts the application of *tafakkur* to religious matters, such that in this case *tafakkur* is almost synonymous with "meditation." After him, the practice of *tafakkur* became almost completely appropriated by the Sufis, who recommended it warmly to their followers and often valued it higher than prayer or *dhikr,* the mystical remembrance of Allāh.[743]

In the second part of the *Kitāb al-tafakkur* Ghazālī presents "a painstaking analysis of the various modes of meditation and reflection, revealing the many rich varieties of this discipline. He distinguishes between *tafakkur* (reflection, meditation, contemplation), *iʻtibār* (considering, learning lessons), *tadhakkur* (mindfulness, recalling), *naẓar* (speculation or mental examination), *ta'ammul* (reflection), and *tadabbur* (pondering). The nature and benefits of each form of contemplation are analysed with the meticulousness characteristic of the author. *Tadabbur, ta'ammul,* and *tafakkur,* says Ghazālī, are almost synonymous terms. *Tadhakkur, iʻtibār,* and *nazar,* on the other hand, all connote a single process that of passing on from two related observations to arrive at a third cognition—but with different nuances. This process of extending one's cognition and understanding through disciplined and regular meditation ought to be a continual one, limited only by the length of one's life-span.[744] Ghazālī also stresses the pre-eminence of *fikr* over *dhikr*.

> The fruits of meditation, then, consist of varieties of knowledge, states and actions. The fruit specific to each, however, is nothing other than a form of knowledge. When knowledge is acquired within the heart, the state of the heart is altered. When the heart's state changes, the actions of the bodily members change. Thus action follows spiritual state, states follow knowledge, and knowledge follows meditation. Meditation is therefore the beginning of and the key to all action.
>
> What we have said thus far will show you how excellent a thing is meditation *(tafakkur)* and how it surpasses invocation *(dhikr)* and remembrance *(tadhakkur)*. For reflection *(fikr)* is *dhikr* with something else added. *Dhikr,* for its part, is better than any physical action: if an action be good, it is so by virtue of the *dhikr* accompanying it. Consequently, meditation is better than any other deed.
>
> Should you wish to understand how meditation transforms one's state, then take for example what was stated earlier about the Afterlife. Given that meditation upon it brings us the knowledge that the Afterlife is preferable [to the life of this world], once such knowledge is firmly rooted in our hearts as a matter of certainty, our hearts change, turning in longing for the Life Beyond and renunciation of worldly things. That is exactly what we mean by the term 'state' . . .
>
> . . . In this connection five separate stages can be distinguished. First: remembrance or invocation *(tadhakkur),* which consists in bringing to mind two cognitions. Second: meditation or reflection *(tafakkur),* which is the search for the cognition which one seeks to obtain from the two concepts already in mind. Third: obtaining the desired cognition, and the heart's illumination by it. Fourth: a change in the heart from its former state, by virtue of the illumination attained. Fifth: service performed for the heart by the bodily members in conformity with the new state prevailing within it.[745]

## Nasafī on Reflection

Discussing the differences between the paths of prayer and contemplative thought, 'Azīz Nasafī, one of the first exponents and interpreters of Ibn 'Arabī's theosophy in the Persian language,[746] comments that those who have realized the heights of the transcendental unity of being (whom he names the 'people of unity', *ahl-i waḥdat)* normally divide mystics into two categories: the "terrestrial wayfarers" and the "celestial wayfarers." To my knowledge, this division is quite unique to Nasafī and is found in no other author, preceding or following him. However, the very uniqueness of his views renders them worthy of interest. Here, we will consider only Nasafī's views on the "celestial wayfarers."

Nasafī gives precise information about the spiritual method, the principles and path pursued by these "celestial wayfarers," illuminating the role of reflection in Sufi spiritual practice. The celestial wayfarers mount the mythical "winged steed" *(burāq)*, the Pegasus of contemplative vision *(mushāhada),* which is a symbol of inspired reflection. This steed has four archetypal faculties represented by the image of its four "wings," by means of which it soars aloft in the hierocosmos of contemplation.

The first wing is *Correct audition,* which Nasafī describes as "hearing things perfectly, as the words are in their essence, as a wise man would hear them spoken." By this, he implies the perfection of the ear of the heart, the refining of the faculty of intuition.

The second wing is *Correct vision,* described as "seeing things as they actually are." Correct audition and vision are described as the wings which provide the mystic with a "manifest inspiration" *(waḥy-i jahr).*

'Reflection' itself is the third wing, and this is given profuse treatment by Nasafī:

> "Everyone calls reflection *(fikr)* by a different name. Some say it is a 'mystical state' *(ḥāl),* some say it is the condition [which the Prophet described when he remarked]: "I have a time with God"[747] some call it 'absence' *(ghaybat).* Now all these expressions imply that a person experiences within himself a certain mystical time *(waqt)* in which he is so immersed and absorbed in something that the activity of his external senses ceases, such that his inner being becomes completely concentrated upon that thing. For some people this

> mystical state lasts an hour, for others a day or several days, and in others it may even last up to ten days.[748] The experience of reflection causes others in the midst of ritual prayer to become abstracted from themselves. Others, in the midst of eating, may find themselves caught up in contemplative thought, remaining absorbed therein for up to one or two days, while holding a morsel of food in their hand or mouth![749]

Nasafī's definition of reflection is indeed extraordinary: it bears absolutely no relation to the process of reasoning or even 'meditation' on divine Qualities; instead, it is a definition of *contemplation* itself, a description of the experience of rapture and ecstasy *(ḥāl)*, – indeed, a purely 'celestial reflection'. However, even this type of experience is surpassed by the degree of *fikr*, 'thought' itself, still more advanced. This fourth and final degree or "wing" of contemplation is termed "inspiration" *(ilhām)* and, like reflection, is understood by different people to mean different things, being called by various names.

> Some call it an inspiration *(ilhām)*, others call it heralding *(adhina)*, others a passing thought *(khāṭir)*, but the meaning of all these diverse expressions is that it is a moment in which a certain knowledge appears in a person's heart, so that he becomes aware of the circumstances of the past and future, without prior reflection or having been informed by anyone.[750]

Nasafī considers the last two "wings"—reflection and inspiration—as constituting "a non-manifest inspiration," that is to say, as types of consciousness which belong to the innermost depth of contemplative thought or reflection.

From the above précis, we can deduce that the path of reflection, containing four hierarchical degrees: *audition, vision, reflection and inspiration,* all subsumed under the rubric, "reflection," constitutes the highest mode of contemplation and spiritual discipline utilized by the most advanced Sufi adepts. According to Nasafī's description, it is characterized by the sharpening of all the inner senses, the perfecting and spiritualizing of the faculties of audition and vision. By such immersion in 'reflection', consciousness of temporality and the spatial delimitation of the human condition is swept aside. (His view of reflection here appears to be similar to that of Plato and Suhrawardī Maqtūl,[751] both of whom described similar raptures as modes of 'reflection' rather than as types of meditation.) Reaching the final degrees of reflection, the celestial wayfarer is lent the "wing of inspiration," transporting him beyond time into the future, tearing aside the veil suspended before the *nunc aeternum.*

Now, Nasafī's view of the contemplative discipline of invocation or recollection as pertaining to beginners on the Path is completely contrary to that of Rūmī. We have already seen that according to Nasafī, reflection (or 'contemplation') is the crown of all spiritual practice, and that the aim of the Sufi is *to transcend recollection (dhikr)* and to realize the depths of reflection *(fikr):*

> When the wayfarer puts recollection behind him and when reflection presents itself and overwhelms him, he soars beyond the realm of the body and reaches the world of the spirit *('ālam-i arwāḥ).* When he transcends reflection, inspiration presents itself, which enables him to transcend the world of reason *('aql)* and reach the world of love *('ishq).* When he transcends the level of inspiration, contemplative vision *('iyān)* presents itself, whereupon he transcends the world of love and atttains to the spiritual station of stability *(tamkīn).*[752]

Having reached stability in all these disciplines, the mystic transcends all fluctuation and mutation *(talwīn)* and realizes total self-control in all his spiritual practices, such that

> if he wishes, he engages in recollection *(dhikr);* if he wishes, he occupies himself with contemplative thought, or else, he negates both of these practices in order to be receptive to inspiration *(ilhām),* and thus becomes informed of events bygone or yet to come. That is, he burnishes the mirror of his heart clean from the images of both the worlds, so that the image of whatever is happening in the world, either in the present or future, will be cast into his heart.[753]

## Rūmī on Reflection

In Rūmī's poetry, in contradistinction to Nasafī's writings, *fikr* (reflection, contemplative thought) appears as merely a preliminary stage and initiatory degree preceding remembrance of

God/recollection *(dhikr)*. To Rūmī, whereas *dhikr* may be likened to a rose in full bloom, *fikr* may be no more than a newly sprouted bud. The following lines from the *Mathnawī* illustrate this viewpoint:

> So much have we said:
> Go, engage in reflection on what's left unsaid.
> If reflection becomes blocked and frozen, apply recollection.
> Recollection rouses reflection to agitation
> Make recollection a sun to kindle congealed and frozen
> reflection.[754]

Contrary to Nasafī's view, Rūmī holds that the process of spiritual progression is from reflection to recollection *(fikr–>dhikr)*. This point of view is illustrated by Rūmī in the following quatrain:

> My poetic nature sprung to life
> with the apparition of reflection
> when within the nuptial chamber of recollection
> the bride of verse set foot.
> In every line of mine a myriad maidens
> are shown, like Mary, and all are virgins.[755]

Quite often, reflection *(fikr)* even has a negative connotation and value *vis-à-vis* recollection *(dhikr)*. Thus, in the fourth book of the *Mathnawī*, he draws a parallel between recollection of God *(dhikr)* and water in which the mystic takes refuge from the memory of 'the maddening crowd' and worrisome reflection *(fikr)*, which is compared metaphorically to a swarm of hornets. Rūmī counsels the mystic to:

> Be patient beneath the waters of recollection and hold
> your breath
> until you find emancipation from reflection and old
> temptation.[756]

Nonetheless, Rūmī does not ignore the positive nature of thought. Indeed, an oft-quoted maxim in the *Mathnawī* is a testimony to the high degree or importance which thought holds in the psyche: "O brother, you are your very thought—the rest is all but flesh and sinew. If your thought is rosy, you too are as a garden. If your thought is thorny, you too are fuel for the fire."[757] 'Inspired reflection' is thus viewed by Rūmī as the very essence of the mind.

Striking another simile, he compares the body to a guesthouse into which every morning a different guest enters. These "guests" symbolize passing or stray thoughts which must be treated with respect. Rūmī's allusion here is to the phenomenon of intuition or *firāsat,* in which the Sufi who exercises some degree of control over his thoughts, does not 'think' in the ordinary sense of the word: rather, thoughts come to him. "The gnostic, acquiescing in those thoughts of sorrow or joy, resembles a hospitable person who treats strangers with kindness, like Abraham, whose door was always open to receive guest with honour, whether they be infidels, Muslims, trustworthy or treacherous. To all such guests ('thoughts'), he acquiesced, he presented a cheerful face and a welcoming mien:"[758]

> O youth, this body is a like a guesthouse
> Every morning a new guest walks through the door.
> Beware, do not ask: "Why have I been afflicted with such
> a guest?"
> —For soon he will vanish into nothingness.
> Whatever passes through your heart from the invisible
> world
> is just a guest, so entertain and welcome it.[759]

* * *

> Every moment, like dear guests, another thought enters in
> your house
> Consider thoughts to be, oh friend, the same as persons
> for *people have value according to their thoughts.*[760]

Rūmī goes on to say that all thoughts are inspired by God, regardless of whether they be harbingers of grief or heralds of joy. Each thought when examined correctly leads you to the Creator-of-thought, who is God. The work of the Sufi is to have certainty of this psychological truth, to be able to see spring in the midst of winter, behold conviviality in the midst of mourning.

However, according to Rūmī, the precondition for correct reflection on, or recollection of, God, is selflessness. In one passage of the *Mathnawī* (VI: 210-48), Rūmī bewails his affliction with freewill and personal volition. "How long will you afflict me with this calamity. O Lord, torment me no longer. Give me a single creed to follow, not ten different creeds. I am a gaunt and weary camel; my back is sore and chafing under the weight of this pack-saddle of freewill." He concludes thus: "Everyone knows that this self-existence is a snare: *dhikr* and *fikr* based on freewill equals hell."[761]

## Ibn 'Arabī on Reflection

In his epistemology, probably echoing the traditional orthodox dislike for the Mu'tazilites' free use of *naẓar* (free-thinking speculation), Ibn 'Arabī explicitly rejects reason *('aql)* and speculation *(naẓar)* as valid authorities for the attainment of truth. He refers to his own mystical method as that of "unveiling" *(kashf),* "tasting *(dhawq),*" "opening *(fatḥ),*" "insight *(baṣīra),*" and "witnessing *(shuhūd, mushāhada).*" "We are not one to quote the words of philosophers," asserts the Shaykh in the *Futūḥāt al-Makkiyya,* "nor the words of anyone else, since in this book and in all our books we write only that which is given by unveiling and dictated by God."[762]

Stressing the unreliablity of *tafakkur,* the *Shaykh al-akbar* pronounces:

> The Folk of Allah do not follow the authority of their reflections, since a created thing should not follow the authority of another created thing. Hence they incline toward following God's authority. They come to know God through God, and He is as He says about Himself, not as meddlesome reason judges.[763]

> Sound knowledge is not given by reflection, nor by what the rational thinkers establish by means of their reflective powers. Sound knowledge is only that which God throws into the heart of the knower. . . . He who has no unveiling has no knowledge *(man lā kashf lah lā 'ilm lah).*[764]

Elucidating the knowledge of "unveiling," Ibn 'Arabī explains the difference between the two ways of ratiocination and gnosis as follows:

> The way of gaining knowledge is divided between reflection *(fikr)* and bestowal *(wahb),* which is the divine effusion *(fayḍ).* The latter is the way of our companions. . . . Two ways lead

> to knowledge of God. There is no third way. . . . The first way is the way of unveiling. It is an incontrovertible knowledge which is actualized through unveiling and which man finds in himself. He receives no obfuscations along with it and and not able to repel it. . . . The second way is the way of reflection and reasoning *(istidlāl)* through rational demonstration *(burhān ʻaqlī)*. This way is lower than the first way, since he who bases his consideration upon proof can be visited by obfuscations which detract from his proof, and only with difficulty can he remove them.[765]

Furthermore, Ibn ʻArabī firmly rejects reflection *(fikr)* based on reason *(ʻaql)* alone as a means of knowledge, remarking in the *Futūḥāt:*

> Is there anything which cannot be reached by way of unveiling and finding? We say that there is nothing, and we forbid reflection totally, since it makes its possessor heir to deceit and lack of sincerity. There is nothing whose knowledge cannot be attained through unveiling and finding. In contrast, occupying oneself with reflection is a veil.[766]

## The Concept of *Tafakkur* in Shabistari's Works

Although Shabistarī belonged to the generation of Persian Sufis immediately following Rūmī, and, as shown in chapter five, flourished in an intellectual milieu steeped in the philosophy of Ibn ʻArabī, his views on reflection are much closer to those of Nasafī than Rūmī. Nonetheless, unlike Nasafī, Shabistarī would not consider denying or debasing the important role played by *dhikr* in the mystical piety of the Sufis. However, neither Nasafī nor Shabistarī seem to have taken very seriously Ibn ʻArabī's own reservations about the utility of *tafakkur* as a means to acquire gnosis. In reality, the advocation of the uses of reflection on the part of Shabistarī and Nasafī is quite unique, such that one might say that no other two authors in the literary history of Persian Sufism provide us such a vast panorama of the inner life revealed through the contemplative discipline of reflection, and no other work in Sufi literary history, nor in fact in the literature of any Islamic language, resembles the *Garden of Mystery* in fulfilling the task of extolling the virtues of mystical thought with such thoroughness.[767] In fact, one of the most important accounts of the role and function of 'reflection' in mediæval Persian Sufism is that provided in the *Garden of Mystery,* the central theme of which is the 'path of reflection'.

Along with Ibn 'Arabī, Rūmī, Nasafī, and indeed, nearly all the major names among the Sufis of the Mongol and Timurid period, Shabistarī and Lāhījī both rejected the validity of pure reason *('aql)* as a means of acquiring gnosis. While the analytical sobriety of Shabistarī/Lāhījī's analysis seems to owe much to Ghazālī's spirit, their high appraisal of the value of reflection is more typical of the views of their fellow Kubrāwī Shaykh, 'Azīz al-Dīn Nasafī. Shabistarī's reflection-centred focus is apparent from the very first verse of the *Garden of Mystery*:

*ba nām-i ānkay jān rā fikrat āmūkht*
*chirāgh-i dil zay nūr-i jān bar afrūkht*

In the name of He who's taught the soul
to think and mediate,
who set aglow the heart
with the light of the soul . . .

This couplet is today a common invocation used by modern Iranian writers to open their essays or lectures on Islam or Sufism, replacing in a way, the Arabic *Bismi-Allāh al-Raḥmān al-Raḥīm,* in the contemporary literary doxology. Commenting on this verse, Lāhījī provides an illuminating rendition of the theological and philosophical background of *tafakkur.* In a definition reminiscent of Ibn 'Arabī's exposition of *tafakkur* written some two centuries earlier, he explains that there are two types of reflection. The first type of thinking pertains 'to the head': ratiocination or logical reasoning *(istidlāl)* and consideration *(naẓar),* which are modes or reason proper to the philosophical sages or *ḥukamā',* who are the "Elect."

The second type is a reflection 'of the heart', that is to say, an unveiling *(kashf),* which consists of the dual processes of "severance [from selfhood] and union [with God]" *(infiṣāl wa ittiṣāl).*

Although both methods are valid in their own spheres of reference and both are recognized as valid modes of *fikr* or forms of reflection, the process of unveiling is superior to ratiocination. Whereas the former is a 'contemplative' discipline, the latter is but a 'mental' derivative of intellection. Propounding the superiority of unveiling, Lāhījī states that

> *Fikr* (reflection) is in reality a spiritual journey from the Outward *(ẓāhir)* to the Inward *(bāṭin)* and from Form *(ṣūrat)* to Archetypal Meaning *(ma'nā)*. By "soul" is meant the human spirit *(rūḥ-i insānī)* which apprehends this idea, and is an inspirer of minds and a mentor of the divine sciences. . . . So the poet makes his invocation "In the Name of He" who has bestowed with such tremendous grace this gnosis by way of 'reflection' *(ma'rifat bi ṭarīq-i fikrat)*.[768]

Another basic definition of *tafakkur* is provided by Shabistarī a few lines later on in the *Garden of Mystery:*

> Reflection is passing from the false to the Truth
> And seeing the Universal Absolute within the part.[769]

Commenting on this couplet, Toshihiko Izutsu drew attention to the fact that Shabistarī's conception of "thinking" *(tafakkur)* "is of a totally different nature from its ordinary definition. What is meant by 'thinking' is *kashf,* 'unveiling', that is, an immediate intuitive grasp of Reality, as opposed to *istidlāl,* the process of reasoning by which one tries to arrive, on the basis of something known, at something unknown."[770] This verse also recalls Nasafī's definition of *tafakkur* as realization of a certain mystical time *(waqt)* in which the mystic is so immersed in something that the activity of his external senses ceases and his inner being becomes completely concentrated upon that thing. Shabistarī's couplet in this respect brings to mind Blake's immortal lines:

> To see a World in a Grain of Sand
> And a Heaven in a Wild flower
> Hold Infinity in the palm of your hand
> And Eternity in an hour.[771]

Attempting the task of interpreting the ontology of Shabistarī's doctrine of reflection as 'unveiling', Lāhījī explains:

> The meaning of *tafakkur* in the Sufi lexicon is that the mystical wayfarer travel *(sālik)* on a 'visionary' journey of unveiling *(sayr-i kashfī)* from multiplicity and the individual deter-

> minations [of Being which delimit the Absolute] *(ta'ayyunāt)* which are in reality false *(bāṭil)* – that is, nonexistent – towards the Truth, that is, towards the Absolute Unity of Being *(waḥdat-i wujūd-i muṭlaq)*. . . . This journey can be characterized as the realization by the wayfarer of the spiritual station of 'annihilation in God' *(fanā' fī'llāh)*, self-obliteration *(maḥw)* and thus the dissolution and disintegration of all the atoms of the universe in the irradiation of the light of the Unity of the divine Essence.
>
> . . . In the second hemistich of the couplet, the poet, speaking of the vision of the "Universal Absolute," alludes to the final perfection of gnosis of God *(ma'rifat)* which is "subsistence in God" *(baqā' bi'llāh)*. . . . In the lexicon of the adepts in Sufi symbolism *(arbāb-i ishārat),* reflection *(tafakkur)* which is a means of obtaining gnosis, signifies that the wayfarer on the Path find his own individual determination, as well as all the determined forms [of creation], so absorbed in the ocean of divine Unity, that, following this annihilation, he regains his essential nothingness, which is the realization of 'subsistence in God', and thus beholds all things, both in their invisible *(ghaybān,* i.e. spiritual) and visible *(shahādatān,* i.e. material) natures as theophanies of the One Reality. Then he recognizes that it is this Reality which appears in various forms and disguises throughout all the diverse manifestations of possible existence.[772]

In this passage, Lāhījī provides an eloquent summary of some of the key terms in the Akbarian lexicon upon which Shabistarī's couplet was based. He emphasizes that the process of reflection entails the loss of ego-consciousness *(bī-khudī,* as Lāhījī/Shabistarī call it) until the ephemeral nature of the apprehending self's 'determined form' is existentially realized. The consequent self-negation leads paradoxically to an affirmation of the continuity and subsistence of the divine being. This is the mystery of the *coincidentia oppositorum* of annihilation and subsistence *(fanā'/baqā'),* which, as Toshihiko Izutsu notes, is "an ontological and metaphysical experience of an extraordinary but neatly delineated nature, which occurs at the transcendental level of awareness."[773] 'Reflection' as a spiritual discipline is, hence, inseparable from 'recollection' *(dhikr),* since the loss of self-identity experienced by the mystic is itself a by-product of his practice of the 'remembrance of God' whose theophany overcomes his consciousness, drowning him in the ocean of divine Unity.

At this juncture in the *Garden of Mystery*, Shabistarī proceeds to examine the Peripatetic (also partially Platonic) doctrine of Reasoning – his poetic flights of thought being carefully recorded in precise and well-fashioned theological prose by his able exegete. According to Shabistarī, as well as Ibn 'Arabī,[774] correct ratiocination involves several stages. The first is 'conception' *(taṣawwur)* of an unknown object of knowledge. The second stage is the organization of this 'conception' into its principal constituent elements, which is called 'recollection' *(tadhakkur)*. Here, of course, Shabistarī draws close to the Platonic *anamnesis*, the 'unforgetting' of what we already know from eternity.[775] The third stage is actual ratiocination *(fikrat)* in which the process of syllogistic reasoning assumes control. The fourth stage is the 'inference' or 'moral' *('ibrat)* to be drawn from this entire process. Thus, "when known objects are arranged into their particular elements, by discernment of what is known, one can verify the unknown."[776]

Ultimately however, Shabistarī/Lāhījī reject this form of *tafakkur* as both too time-consuming and subject to doubt and error; thus, unreliable as an adequate method of obtaining Truth.[777] The only viable method of obtaining truth, of 'verifying' the results of reflection is through the "process of purification and illumination of the heart *(taṣfiya wa tajliya-yi qalb)*.[778] Commenting on the verse cited earlier on: "Reflection is passing from the false to the Truth/ And seeing the Universal Absolute within the part," Zarrīnkūb noted that this doctrine constitutes "the basis of the Sufi vision, as it expounds the difference between the Sufi concept of knowledge realized through 'unveiling' or 'visionary disclosure' *(kashf)*, and that of the philosophers which is obtained by logical methods."[779] Elucidating the spiritual method underlying this discipline, Lāhījī devotes a special chapter in his commentary to explaining why "True Gnosis cannot be Obtained by Logical Methods," stating:

> Success in the process of purification and illumination depends upon erasing everything but God from the slate of the heart. As long as the mystic has not scrubbed clean the iconography of 'other than God' from the slate of the heart with the water of recollection and reflection *(dhikr wa fikr)*, the emblem of true divine Unity cannot be etched thereupon. The way of ratiocination, or demonstration of the truth of something

> through adducing proofs and reasons, is contrary to the way of purification.
>
> Whereas according to the Reasoner, the proof is the locus of the lexical sense of what is demonstrated, the gnostic *('ārif)* considers the proof as a veil *(ḥijāb)* over the lexical sense of what is demonstrated. According to the latter standpoint, the more proofs that are adduced, the more hidden the object to be demonstrated becomes. In reality, the perfection of divine Unity consists in the negation of 'other-than-God' *(ghayriyyat)*. Hence, what serves as 'proof' for the scholar, is, for the gnostic, the objectively demonstrated Truth itself, and what is a veil for those who are veiled, is, for the visionary, a mirror reflecting the divine Beauty.[780]

A few pages on in the text, Lāhījī provides a classic definition of this second type of follower of the path of reflection: the so-called gnostic, who has realized the fruits of contemplative reflection. He explains that he is one to "whom the Divine has vouchsafed the level of the vision of the Essence and Names of his sublime Qualities, so that this station is disclosed to him directly as a 'mystical state' *(ḥāl)* and by revelation *(mukāshafa)*, not merely by learning, so that he personally realizes this gnosis."[781]

It is interesting to find that the most broadly-based definition of *tafakkur* in Shabistarī's works does not in fact occur in the *Garden of Mystery,* but in the *Sa'ādat-nāma,* in the eighth and last chapter subtitled "On the Benefits of Obedience to the Almighty." Here, he situates this contemplative discipline in the wider context of other Islamic devotional practices:

> The service and worship of God
> Is a dictate of the Merciful
> To every creature: man and jinn alike.
> And yet this order takes to task
> The most elect[782] – as God has said:
> —"I did not create the jinn and men
> for aught but they should worship Me."[783]
> Through worship man is brought to prayer;
> From prayer to mystic thought, and then from thought
> The flame of gnosis leaps, until he sees
> The truth with contemplation's inner eye.
> Such wisdom comes from altruistic love:

The latter is its fruit, the first the bough.
At last comes Love which ousts all else:
Love undoes all sense of 'two';
Love makes all One,
Until no 'mine'
Nor 'thine'
Remain.[784]

In the above lines *fikr* is placed within a hierarchy of seven spiritual stations or disciplines in ascending order. Thus, the following schema is obtained:

7. *'ishq* (Love, Eros)
↑
6. *maḥabbat* (Loving-kindness, altruistic love)[785]
↑
5. *ma'rifat* (Wisdom)
↑
4. *'irfān* (Gnosis, Mystical Knowledge)
↑
3. *fikr* (Reflection, Thought)
↑
2. *dhikr* (Recollection, Invocation, Prayer)
↑
1. *'ibādat* (Worship)

As we can see from this schema, the purpose of *fikr* (rendered as "mystic thought" in my translation) is to fan the flames of gnosis *('irfān)*. Shabistarī's schema here stands in line with a Sufi tradition going back to Rūzbihān (d. 606/1209), who also featured servanthood *('ubūdiyyat*, from which the term 'worship' or *'ibādat* is derived), as the first rung, *murāqabat* or meditation as the third rung, and *maḥabbat* or loving-kindness as the eleventh rung of his ladder of twelve mystical stations.[786] Rūzbihān's ladder of mystical ascent culminates in a higher, thirteenth station of universal love *('ishq-i kullī)*. Although in terms of mere quantity, Shabistarī's categorization lacks Rūzbihān's detail, the direction of ascent in both their schemas is the same, and most important of all, the first, third and last categories in both schemas are, to all purposes, identical. The resemblances become even more striking when one notes that Rūzbihān includes the discipline of *dhikr* as part of the practices pertaining to the level of servanthood *('ubūdiyyat),* and defines meditation as the control of random thoughts, both of which ideas Shabistarī follows closely.

Lāhījī expands on the exclusively mystical mode of reflection—'unveiling'—further on in his commentary on the *Garden of Mystery*, when interpreting Shabistarī's verse:

> Reason cannot tolerate
> the rays which irradiate
> from the light of that face;
> Another eye you must seek
> to behold it.[787]

The exegete is emphatic about the Sufi methodology which must sustain 'reflection' if it is to function as a proper contemplative discipline:

> One cannot behold the vision of God by the eye of ratiocination *(khirad ki 'aql ast),* for only the eye of the heart *(dīda-yi dil)*, which is known as the faculty of inner vision *(baṣīra)*, can one behold God. As long as you do not brighten this eye [i.e. sharpen its vision] with the collyrium of asceticism, spiritual conduct *(sulūk),* purgation of the soul *(tazkiya-yi nafs)*, purification of the heart *(taṣfiyya-yi qalb)* and illumination of the Spirit *(tajliyya-yi rūḥ)* you will be unable to witness the Friend's beauty in contemplation. All the masters of the Path *(ṭarīqat)* are in accordance that this reality can be realized only through the guidance of a Perfect Man who knows and contemplates God.[788]

Lāhījī's exegesis here both reflects the influence of Ibn 'Arabī's view that "occupying oneself with reflection is a veil," as well as the strong influence of post-Mongol Persian *ṭarīqa* Sufism, which dogmatically stressed as its spiritual discipline the necessity for 'methodical progress' *(sulūk)* on the Sufi Path under the supervision of the spiritual director *(pīr).*

Over the course of the next eight verses following this couplet, Shabistarī/Lāhījī conclude their review of the limitations of reflection by attacking various (non-Sufi) theologians—who advocated the use, or rather the abuse, of the faculty of reason to fathom God—as having defective vision. These include the Peripatetic thinkers who are described as "too squint-eyed *(aḥwal)* to behold the 'Unity of Being',"[789] philosophers upholding the doctrine of 'transmigration of souls' *(tanāsukh),* who are attacked as "one-eyed,"[790] the 'Islamic rationalists' *(Mu'tazila)* and the Muslim scholastic theologians *(ahl-i kalām),* whose outlook is pejoratively labeled as "congenitally blind," and hence, of no purpose or benefit,[791] and lastly, of course, the Sufis' age-old foes, the "people of outward appearances" *(ahl-i ẓāhir),* who are the exoteric clerics. Their eyes are sadly afflicted with "ophthalmia."[792]

Amīr Ḥusaynī's second question concerning the proper use of *fikr* immediately follows these diatribes: "What kind of 'reflection' is the *sine qua non* of the Path? Why is 'reflection' sometimes a sin, sometimes a moral duty?" he wonders. Shabistarī's reply adduces a variety of metaphysical, moral and theological principles underlying the doctrine of Sufi *tafakkur*.

112 The *sine qua non* of the Path is 'thought',
'reflection' on the blessings, boons
and benefits of God,
but meditation on the Truth's *Essentia*
is wholly wrong, an utter sin.
113 How vain, inane and void is thought
—to try to find the Essence of the Truth,
to probe the Real's Ipseity! What fallacy it is
to claim back goods you've always owned!

114 The signs of God are bright through light divine:
The Essence casts its beam on them—they shine.
The Essence, know for sure, will not be shown
by its own beam.
115 When by his light the world's made to manifest
How then should he be made distinct by it?
116 The *Lux essentiae* is not cut out
to fit the suit of Form's phenomena;
the August Light's too bright for that,
his Glory's Wrath subdues *materia.*
117 Be free of reason, wholly be with God—
his solar glare the eyes of bats can't bear to see.
118 For at this site where *Lux*
*divina* is your guide, what place
is left for the speech and homilies
declaimed by Angel Gabriel?

119 Though angel and seraph enjoy proximity
unto his court, they are not fit to know
that state of heart which spoke, "I have a time
with God no other prophet finds, nor angel knows,
much less the purest spirit—Gabriel."[793]
120 And since his light sets aflame the wings
of angels, reason too, toe to crown, it commits to
flames.
121 The lustre that dull reason has, before
that Fount of Lights, is like the beam cast by
the naked eye up at the orb of day,
122 so if the seer stare overmuch or stay
too close to it, his sight grows dim at once,
his cognizance becomes eclipsed.[794]

It will be revealing to examine Muḥammad Lāhījī's commentary on these verses in order of their appearance. The first verse (112) illustrates the fundamental importance of reflection in the context of Islamic piety, revolving around the Prophetic dictum *(ḥadīth)* which enjoins: "Reflect upon God's bounties and blessings *(ālā')*, but do not reflect upon his Essence."[795] Lāhījī lends a fresh gnostic twist to this Prophetic directive cited by Shabistarī when he interprets the term *ālā'* —translated above as "blessings, boons, benefits"—in verse 112 as referring to

> the Divine Names and Qualities which are the source of emanation of all outward and inward blessings. It is these Names and Qualities which have manifested existence *(ifāḍa-yi wujūd)*,[796] bestowing an infinite plenitude *(kamālāt)* upon the atomic particulars of all existent things *(dhārrāt-i mawjūdāt)*, so that by means of these blessings, everything has been brought from non-existence into existence, and each entity according to its aptitude has received the boon of divine grace in both a formal and a supraformal manner. Reflection on God's bounties is a condition of the Sufi Path because through such meditation a seeker is roused from heedlessness and brought to the spiritual station of wakefulness.[797]

Here, we should note that in Arabic the term faith *(īmān)* implies, by definition, the admission of thanks to the Creator and the expression of gratitude to God for his bounties, and in the Koran the term *kufr* (infidelity) often appears as the antonym of gratitude *(shukr)*.[798] To be an 'infidel' *(kāfir)* does not so much denote an intellectual position of an atheistic or anti-monotheistic nature as a psychological insensitivity and lack of appreciation for the ubiquitous presence of the divine bounties. More deeply considered, *kufr,* 'infidelity' means existential 'ingratitude'.[799] Therefore, Lāhījī defines infidelity *(kufr)* as a "refusal to acknowledge bounties as gifts of the Bountiful."[800] All worldly bounty *(ni'mat)* should be held up as a mirror reflecting God's infinitely bountiful Nature.

Reflection on the divine Essence is prohibited, asserts Lāhījī, because "the inclusiveness and permutation of the transcendent divine Essence [throughout creation] is so universally comprehensive and sublime that no other entity in the entire realm of being exists which might provide a means for understanding it."[801] In Shabistarī's words (v. 113):

> How vain, inane and void is thought
> —to try to find the Essence of the Truth,
> to probe the Real's Ipseity! What fallacy it is
> to claim back goods you've always owned![802]

The expression "claim back goods you've always owned"*(taḥṣīl-i ḥāsil)* indicates, in an epistemological sense, the pure impossibility of demonstrating that which itself is the cause of demonstration, or, as the nineteenth-century Persian philosopher Ḥajī Mullā Sabzawārī (d. 1878) expressed it—to "acquire what has already been acquired," or "to actualize what has already been actualized."[803] Shabistarī's doctrine of the impossibility of reflection on the divine Essence therefore should not be taken as a theological dogma, constituting, for instance, an Islamic counterpart to Calvin's prohibition of *curiositas,* of illicit speculation beyond that which God has revealed,[804] but rather as expressive of a metaphysical axiom.

Lāhījī provides the theological background to Shabistarī's epistemological theory, noting that "there is the type of apprehension which is existentially innate *(dhawāt-i fiṭrī* = belonging to man from pre-eternity) from the time when God asked the 'Children of Adam' whether he was their Lord and they replied affirmatively (referring to Koran VII: 172)." One cannot reflect upon this type of innate apprehension according to Shabistarī/Lāhījī because it is totally futile to attempt to realize the cause of realization *(taḥṣīl-i ḥāṣil)* itself. In fact, all reflection acts as but a veil over such perception."[805] Shabistarī elucidates this doctrine in the *Ḥaqq al-yaqīn* in the following manner:

> *A Reality:* The substance of innate apprehension [within man] *(idrāk-i fiṭrī)* —that is to say, universal-synthetic 'gnosis' *(ma'rifat-i basīṭ)*[806]— is beyond the powers of reflection *(tafakkur)* to grasp, because it is impossible to demonstrate that which itself is the cause of demonstration *(taḥsīl-i ḥāsil maḥāl ast)*. In fact, reflection here becomes a veil over the object of reflection. For this reason he [the Prophet] commanded: "Do not reflect upon the Essence of God." The proper site of reflection is the 'conscious apprehension' *(idrāk-i idrāk)*[807] by intermediary of the 'signs of God'; it is for this reason that reflection upon these 'signs' has been enjoined (in the Koran III: 191:) "[Those who remember God, standing and sitting and on their sides,] and reflect upon the creation of the heavens and the earth . . . "
>
> *A Reality:* Innate apprehension or gnosis *(ma'rifat)* is different from conscious apprehension or 'knowledge' *('ilm)*, for the former is synthetic and noncomposite *(basīṭ)* and the latter is composite *(murakkab)*. "You see them looking at you, but they do not see you." (Koran VII: 198)[808]

Since all knowledge in Islamic mysticism—epistemologically speaking—derives from what Mehdi Ha'iri Yazdi has called "knowledge by presence,"[809] apprehension is thus a kind of a divine gift, one of the 'signs' *(āyāt)* of God shown to all humankind. Human consciousness is preconditioned by the divine awareness of the human self, and the self's apprehension of God is considered to be prior to its knowledge of itself. As Shabistarī in the *Ḥaqq al-yaqīn* again explains:

> *A Reality:* Every individual[810] who exists, whether *in actu* or *in potentia*, necessarily apprehends *(mudrik)* his own existence (as the verse explains [Koran LXXV: 14]) "Nay, man shall be an eye-witness against himself."[811] This [self-apprehension] necessarily entails the apprehension of the Absolute Being *(hast-i muṭlaq)*, since the general is more evident than the particular. "[In the earth are signs for those having sure faith;] and in your own souls; what, do you not see?" (Koran LI: 20-21)

> *A Reality:* The apprehension of the existence of God *(hastī-yi ḥaqq)*—who is the most evident and known of all entities—precedes the soul's apprehension of itself, for the soul derives from the world of the divine Command *('ālam-i amr)*[812] and "God's command prevails over all." (Koran XII: 21) For this reason, becoming forgetful of God necessitates forgetfulness of oneself [or 'soul'], for forgetfulness comes after gnosis *(ma'rifat).* "[Be not as} those who forgot God, and so he caused them to forget their souls." (Koran LIX: 19)[813]

Reflection has its limitations, its own proper function and place. This proper place, as Lāhījī puts it, "is the 'apprehension of apprehension' by means of the signs of God, not the substance of apprehension itself *(idrāk-i idrāk-ast ba-wāsiṭa-yi āyāt; na nafs-i idrāk).*"[814] Shabistarī's eminent exegete here touches on one of the most essential empirical characteristics of mysticism, which, as William James was to define it, is "the problem of ineffability,"[815] about which Mehdi Ha'iri, analysing the ultimate incommunicable knowledge or ineffable experience of Sufism, observes:

> Mystical consciousness is the unitary simplex of the presence of God in the self, and the presence of the self in God. Belonging to the order of existence and not to the order of conception and representation, this unitary simplex is primarily incommunicable and therefore ineffable. Such is the case insofar as it remains nonintrospected and not reflected upon.[816]

The best overall interpretation of line 114 (serving as a hermeneutical summary of the message of couplets 116, 121 and 122 as well) is that composed by the poet himself in the third chapter of his *Ḥaqq al-yaqīn.* Here, Shabistarī offers a further interpretation of the impotence of man's powers of apprehension to grasp Reality directly, stating that

> "The intensity of the theophany of the Object-of-Apprehension *(ẓuhūr-i mudrak)* becomes an obstacle to apprehension itself, similar to the obfuscation which bedims the optical eye which attempts to behold the solar orb of day. (Hence, he who attempts to apprehend this theophany becomes) "one whom

> God lets go astray, knowingly [that his mind is closed to all guidance] (Koran XLV: 23)[817] Furthermore, 'conscious apprehension' *(idrāk-i idrāk)* cannot be exercised except by means of an internal or external agency, these being the 'signs of God displayed in creation and within the human soul *(āyāt-i āfāq wa anfus)*. "Surely in the creation of the heavens and earth and in the alternation of night and day there are signs for men of understanding." (Koran III: 190)[818]

The ultimate incommunicability of the knowledge of God is also expressed by Shabistarī in the *Sa'ādat-nāma,* where, citing the Koranic passage: "and He is with you wheresoever ye may be" (LVII: 4), he remarks:

> That present-existent Being who is hidden from all seeking cannot be perceived through labor and exertion. The obstacle on the path of understanding God is, if you only knew, your own 'knowledge of knowledge' *(dānish-i dānish)*. The knowledge of the Truth/Reality *(dānish-i ḥaqq)* is innate in the existent essences [of man] *(dhawāt);* but it is the 'knowledge of knowledge' *(dānish-i dānish)* to which 'reflection' pertains.[819]

At the same time, while it is this same self-conscious 'knowledge of knowledge', this limited egocentric conscious 'understanding' which prevents human consciousness from grasping the divine omnipresence, it is also to this finite knowledge that the faculty of human reason and 'reflection' pertains, according to Shabistarī. "Reason, or the ratio of all we have already have known," William Blake remarked in a similar context, "is not the same that it shall be when we know more. . . . He who sees the Infinite in all things, sees God. He who sees the Ratio only, sees himself only."[820] Shabistarī likewise laments that man has "lost God within his ego."[821]

Deepening his analysis of the impossibility of ever penetrating to the divine Essence, the poet goes on to comment that

114 The signs of God are bright through light divine:
The Essence casts its beam on them—they shine.
The Essence, know for sure, will not be shown
by its own beam.

Ultimately, the only possibility of realizing the essence of reflection is by direct contemplative realization, or mystical 'union' with the divine Essence itself, as Lāhījī informs us in his commentary on the above verse:

> According to the gnostics, whoever wishes to comprehend the divine Essence by means of the divine Names, Qualities and Acts is like a person who in a dream perceives some disordered images not corresponding to his waking experience, whereas whoever realizes the divine Names, Qualities and Acts *by means of the Essence* is one who pursues the path of contemplative vision *(shuhūd),* and attains to the station of the infinite divine Essence, and from thence descends back down, passing through the stages of the divine Names and Qualities. In this fashion, he perceives that it is the divine Essence whose perfection is manifest wherever the theophany of a divine Name or Quality appears. Such a person is like one who is fully awake, perceiving things and events as they unfold in their true objective actuality.[822]

Lāhījī here echoes the above-cited views of Ibn 'Arabī who, as noted above, severely criticized the limitations of the faculty of reflection in the *Futūḥāt*. In the same vein in the *Ḥaqq al-yaqīn,* following the *Magister maximus,* Shabistarī had observed that "intellectual matters in relation to what is understood by visionary disclosure *(mukāshafāt)* have the same position as purely imaginary mental matters *(i'tibāriyyāt)* have to pure intelligibles *(ma'qūlāt).*"[823]

Commenting on the next couplet (115), Lāhījī gives a succinct summary of the doctrine of 'theomonism', or the 'unity of being',[824] Considering that this doctrine is the substratum of Shabistarī's ontology, Lāhījī's own definition will be useful to peruse:

> The permanent archetypes *(a'yān)* of all possible existent beings are made bright and manifest by his Light—that is to say, by his theophany—and by means of this theophany which they have assumed, the forms of phenomenal things have become qualified with 'being'. However, in reality, there is no other 'being' than God *(ḥaqq*=Truth/Reality), for all things through Him have come into appearance, and since there is no 'other' (being) besides Him capable of acting as a medium

> of his phenomenal appearance, no 'thing' can be said to have caused his creative manifestation.[825]

As he turns to the analysis of the next couplet (116), Lāhījī grows ecstatic, insisting that no one can understand the least of the poet's allusions in this line except by way of visionary consciousness *(shuhūd wa ḥāl)* "To increase the certitude of sincere aspirants on this Path," he reflects, "it is appropriate to record here a visionary incident pertaining to the mystical states *(ḥālāt)* which I have experienced." To prove this point, he presents us with his interiorized vision of Shabistarī's poem, his own personal vision of the 'Light of the divine Essence':

> In the year 858 [=1454) during the time when I was isolated in a forty-day retreat *(arba'īn)* I experienced a state of rapture in which I became 'absent' from self *(ghaybat)*.[826] I saw myself travelling through the air and flying over a gigantic metropolis. The whole city was illumined by candles, lamps, lanterns and torches, and all the world likewise was filled with light in a manner impossible to describe.
>
> All at once the (lower) atmosphere in which I was flying itself soared heavenwards. I soared on with it. I reached the first heaven *(āsimān-i awwal)* and saw myself totally merge and become one with it, witnessing many marvels and wonders at that level. Again, from there I went to the second heaven where I merged and became totally one with it, and certain occult mysteries were revealed to me. In the same manner I fared on, entering all seven heavens, merging with each one, in each of which countless marvels and mysteries were disclosed to me.
>
> Then I saw myself flying in a subtle and luminous realm, where God was manifest *(ḥaḍrat-i ḥaqq tajallī namūda)* in the form of light without quantity or quality. Before the awesome grandeur of his luminous self-manifestion, all beings had been set on fire, and the whole world had been set aflame. That same fire then fell upon me, so that I burnt and became totally annihilated *(fānī-yi muṭlaq shudam)*.
>
> Next, I saw that I was still in that realm; however, I had regained consciousness and was drunk and selflessly ecstatic, crying and wailing, while singing this couplet:

*O my king who's set the world afire!*
*O my moon who's set my soul alight!*
*O you, my rule, my riot – my mêlée, my harmony!*
*When, when will I see you again?*

And then the Almighty, in his August Majesty, revealed himself in the form of light, and—just as on the previous occasion—before that awesome theophany, the world was again set afire and totally incinerated. This poor wretch *(faqīr)* also was totally burnt up and completely obliterated.

Again, I regained consciousness in that realm and was singing that verse as before. God once again revealed himself in a glorious theophany and the entire world was burnt down and this poor wretch *(faqīr)* also was totally burnt up. . . . These mystical states were vouchsafed me countless times.

When I recovered from that state I found myself overcome by such madness *(dīwānigī)* and self-bereft ecstasy *(bīkhwudī)* that I lost my reason. I rent my clothes and became selfless. This intoxication and rapture lasted several days until by the good guidance of the master of the age I recovered my sobriety from that drunkenness![827]

In couplet 117 Shabistarī compares the light of reason to the vision of a bat, using a simile that is of ancient provenance in Persian poetry, appearing in the works of both 'Aṭṭār and Rūmī where it "represents the ordinary benighted human thought which does not understand . . . the Sun of Truth."[828] Indeed, in the first chapter of the *Sa'ādat-nāma,*[829] Shabistarī had retold in verse the parable of the owls who denied the light of the sun, and the hoopoe who attempted—until blinded by them—to preach the 'doctrine of daylight' to them, a story first told in prose by the founder of the Theosophy of Oriental Illumination, Shihāb al-Dīn Suhrawardī Maqtūl.[830] Both parables, whether by the Ishrāqī theosopher or the Akbarian poet, illustrate the same moral: the blindness of natural reason to apprehend visionary experience. Practical reason, Lāhījī explains, "is just like the untrained ear and misshapen disposition of a person for whom the harmony of music or the rhythms of poetry are incomprehensible"[831]—the exegete, of course, here carefully following the doctrine of the poet himself, as presented in the *Ḥaqq al-yaqīn,* where he had explained that

> The situation of reason in regard to apprehension of this (mystical) vision can be likened to a palpable and sensible object which one sense tries to understand by medium of another sense, or like a congenitally blind person *vis-à-vis* colors, or a malformed and imbalanced disposition in relation to well-proportioned and harmonious things, such as poetry or the principles of music.[832]

Since the highest reaches of knowledge and visionary reflection are inexpressible, mystical realization becomes expressed in negative terms, becoming, in the words of St. John of the Cross, a *"no saber sabiendo . . . toda sciencia trascendiendo."* Certain passages in chapter two of the *Ḥaqq al-yaqīn* provide a prose counterpart to this same message of ineffability and inexpressiblity versified by Shabistarī in couplets 118-20. Here, the poet elaborates these same points with philosophical sobriety and a broad detail of scriptural references:

> *A Reality:* The summit of knowledge *('ilm)*—which is 'conscious apprehension' *(idrāk-i idrāk)*—is inapprehension *('adam-i idrāk),* for whereas the Real 'Object-of-Apprehension' *(mudrak)* is infinite, knowledge *('ilm)* is finite. This inapprehension is a type of apprehension without consciousness of either apprehension or inapprehension,[833] and at this point one finds dumbfounded stupor *(ḥayrat)* and absorption of the apprehending subject *(mudrik)* in the (divine) 'Object-of-Apprehension' *(mudrak).* Insofar as the perceiver is endowed with inapprehension, his condition resembles (ordinary) ignorance and heedlessness—although the possessor of this mystical state is, in fact, veiled from such [ignorance]. "You would have thought them awake, as they lay sleeping." (Koran XVIII: 18)
>
> *A Subtle Mystery:* After the experience of this state, all sense of 'relationship' *(nisab)*—for that pertains to the level of multiplicity and crypto-polytheism *(shirk-i khafī)*—is dissolved and the annihilation of the apprehending subject *(mudrik)* in the (divine) 'Object-of-Apprehension' *(mudrak)* objectively appears. At this point (the situation of) "Upon the day the earth shall be changed into other than the earth" (Koran XIV: 48) and "Upon the day when we shall roll up the heavens as a recorder rolls up a written scroll" (Koran XXI: 104), with

all its concomitants, such as the dissolution of the stars and the folding up of the sun, etc., takes place, and the pre-eternal and post-temporal summons of Reality, "Whose is the Kingdom today?" (Koran XL: 16) is addressed to the ear of the consciousness of the mind-bereft wayfarer, whereupon, from the emptiness of his true annihilation *(khalā'-i fanā-yi ḥaqīqī),* the answering cry returns: "It is God's, the One, the Omnipotent" (XL: 16).

... *A Hint:* It was due to the constraints of this condition that he (the Prophet) stated: "I have a time with God no other prophet finds, nor angel knows, much less the purest spirit—Gabriel."[834]

The lights of the Divine essence, Shabistarī states in this passage, erase the faculty of conscious awareness, creating an 'apprehension' which is actually 'inapprehension', since the illusory personality of the apprehending subject has become 'annihilated' in its divine Object.

The *ḥadīth* cited in the last "hint" was also used by the poet in couplet 119. From the point of view of comparative religion, it is quite interesting to note here that nearly all of Shabistarī's technical terminology, style of expression, and views on the ineffability of the mystical apprehension were to be echoed in identical terms some two centuries later in Spain by St. John of the Cross.[835] The following stanzas from his poem "Sobre Un Éxtasis de Harta Contemplación," for instance, provide a perfect Spanish *naẓīra* to Shabistarī's couplets 116-22.

Cuanto más alto se sube
tanto menos se entendía
que es la tenebrosa nube
que a la noche esclareciá;
por eso quien la sabía
queda siempre no sabiendo
toda sciencia trascendiendo.

Este saber no sabiendo
es de tan alto poder
que los sabios, arguyendo,
jamás le pueden vencer;
que no llega su saber

a no entender entendiendo,
toda sciencia trascendiendo.

Y es de tan alta excelencia
aqueste summo saber,
que no hay facultad ni sciencia
que le puedan emprender;
quien se supiere vencer
con un no saber sabiendo,
irá siempre trascendiendo.

Y si lo queréis oir
consiste esta suma sciencia
en un subido sentir
de la divina escencia,
es obra de su clemencia
hacer quedar no entendiendo
toda sciencia transcendiendo.[836]

In his commentary on couplet 119, Lāhījī offers an interesting defence of the poet's opinion that the proximity of the angel to the divine Being is inferior in degree to the more universal access attained by the Perfect Man. Since Shabistarī's view of reflection's limitations is based on the poetic simile comparing the divine luminosity which sets aflame the wings of angels with the supraformal light which overpowers reason, a brief digression into his angelology is required at this point.

Both the poet and his exegete here closely followed the opinions of Ibn 'Arabī who spoke of the superiority of the Perfect Man to the angels in the first chapter of the *Fuṣūṣ*,[837] as well as some of the Shaykh al-Akbar's later commentators, such as Farghānī.[838] However, within the framework of this essentially epistemological study, it will be impossible to contribute to that debate in any significant manner; it should suffice here to simply outline the parameters of this concept in Shabistarī's thought insofar as it relates to reflection.

Since these same subjects are discussed in depth by Shabistarī later on in the same second chapter of the *Ḥaqq al-yaqīn* cited above, it will be illuminating to compare Lāhījī's views on the sciences of angelology, prophetology and the concept of the Perfect Man and our author's pronouncements in the *Ḥaqq al-yaqīn* on these themes.

Expounding the distinction between the angel's nearness and the universal Perfect Man's proximity to God, Lāhījī remarks that 'Gabriel' – who is an "imaginalized form of reason, and a theophany of knowledge, has no access to the spiritual station of annihilation *(maqām-i fanā')*, because, at the degree of annihilation in God, all knowledge, reason, apprehension, discernment and other (human) qualities are obliterated."[839] He furthemore explains that:

> The term "proximity *(qurb)*" denotes either the removal of causal intermediaries between something and its source, or diminution in causal intermediaries (between them). Therefore, according to the order of created beings, although the angels—who are the celestial intelligences, the souls, spirits and human faculties[840]—may enjoy proximity to the divine court, but considering their pure simplicity *(basāṭat)* and immateriality *(tajarrudī)*, they have no access to the level of 'annihilation in God' which belongs to the Perfect Man.
>
> Although the degree of the angels is, indeed, as mentioned above, quite exalted, 'perfection' *(kamāl)*—which may be defined as total realization of all the divine Names and the spiritual truths of created beings *(ḥaqā'iq-i kawniyya)*—is reserved for the Perfect Man, since he is, from the point of view of this realization, more 'perfect' than the most intimate archangels, although from the standpoint of their diminution of causal intermediaries *(vis-à-vis* the divine) the archangels are nobler than the Perfect Man. It was due to his all-inclusive and comprehensive nature that the venerable Seal of the Prophets—peace be upon him—declared that: "I have a time with God no other prophet finds, nor angel knows, much less the purest spirit—who is Gabriel." This is because the 'archangel', who an epiphanic form of 'reason', 'knowledge' and 'discernment', has no access to the spiritual station of *fanā,* which is the apex of the journey towards human perfection. And, as mentioned above, knowledge and discernment, when juxtaposed to the pure condition of annihilation, only serve to obstruct union with God. So what room is there for an angel here? Even an appointed prophet *(nabī-yi mursal)*, such as myself, that is to say: 'Muḥammad', cannot be contained here, for 'Muḥammad' himself is but one self-determination *(ta'ayyun:* i.e. of the Absolute), and no formal determination has any place in that divine Presence.[841]

To understand the unusual-sounding doctrine of the preeminence of man to angel espoused by Shabistarī's loyal exegete, it is necessary to recall that according to Ibn 'Arabī's exposition in the opening chapter "on the Wisdom of Adam" of the *Fuṣūṣ,* the 'Perfect Man'—who is Adam—is considered to be the mirror of all the divine Qualities and Names. In relation to his form: "the angels were only certain faculties *(quwā)* of that form which was the form of the Cosmos, called in the terminology of the Sufis, the Great Man. In relation to it the angels are as the psychic faculties in the human formation."[842] And, as Gisela Webb pointed out, in Ibn 'Arabī's anthropology, "angels are on the level of faculties or powers within the universe, each having different functions, while man is the 'spirit' and unification of *all* elements that make up the 'worlds'. . . . The human creature, then, has the capacity for a type of knowledge *(jam'iyya,* 'general', comprehensive knowledge) to which the angels are not privy."[843] Thus, the higher levels of reflection are reserved for the transconsciousness of the 'Perfect Man', who, ascending beyond his own ratiocinative awareness and fictitious self-identity, beyond even the understanding of the angels, 'reflects' upon the divine being after the annihilation of his own ego-consciousness.

Shabistarī's discussion of these same themes in the *Ḥaqq al-yaqīn* centers around the relative merits of sainthood *(walāyat)* and Prophecy *(nabuwwat).* Although not directly related to our discussion of the epistemology of reflection, his views do have some bearing on the subject of the 'fruits of reflection' and the consequent realization of the ontological reality of *fanā'* on the gnostic's part. He claims that the gnostic who has reached "summit of knowledge", which he had called the conscious 'apprehension of inapprehension' in a passage cited above, basks in the lights of sainthood without any intervening medium, and may thus dispense with a spiritual guide:

> When the gnostic realizes this spiritual station [i.e. the 'summit of knowledge' wherein he perceives that 'conscious apprehension' *(idrāk-i idrāk)*—is inapprehension *('adam-i idrāk)]* he receives, without any mediation, effusions of light from the sphere of Sainthood *(walāya).*[844] He now becomes liberated from the need for any external master, for external magistracy is only necessary for the sake of disciplining the passions of the lower soul *(riyāḍat-i nafs),* while the temperment of the

gnostic's soul is as has been stated: "and their dog stretching out his paws on the threshold" (Koran XVIII: 18).

Furthermore, the function of the spiritual master *(murshid)* is to direct, guide, and stimulate moral development, but the mystical state of the gnostic is that of being astray and dumbfounded *(ḍalāl wa ḥayrat)* in the station of "I become his eye, so that he sees by me and his tongue, so that he speaks by me."[845] for "whomsoever God leads astray, you will not find for him a saintly master to guide him *(walīyān murshidān)* (Koran XVIII: 17).[846]

Therefore, we may say that in every sense of the word and in every hierarchical realm of being, whether pertaining to spiritual *magisterium cathedrae pastoralis* of the Sufi *ṭarīqat* or to the hierarchy of angel and seraphim, the Perfect Man's apprehension, based upon his experience of *fanā'*, represents the highest form of understanding in the cosmos. Whereas, on the one hand, the Perfect Man surpasses the angels in his comprehensive being and knowledge, he is also so supremely fulfilled in the rank of what Ibn 'Arabī called 'perfect servanthood' that he may dispense with the external figure of the guiding Shaykh.[847]

Shabistarī concludes his discussion of the higher reaches of visionary reflection with four couplets (126-29) on the doctrine of the 'Black Light', the symbol of the 'midnight sun' and theophany of the *Deus absconditus*. Since these subjects have already been analysed masterfully and meticulously by Henry Corbin in *The Man of Light in Iranian Sufism,*[848] they are omitted from our translation above and study below.

* * *

The above study has only analysed a mere 60 out of a total of 215 verses which Shabistarī devotes to the subject of 'reflection' (in work of 1004 verses). Hence, it would be well to summarize the rest of the poet's presentation, in order to provide a comprehensive view.[849]

For various sections of the remaining couplets (vv. 130-286) in his poem, both Shabistarī and Lāhījī provide short subtitles of the various "rules" or "principles" *(qā'ida)* of the types of reflection, such as i) the Principle of Reflection on the Heavens, ii) the Principle of Reflection on the Soul, iii) the Principle of Reflection on the divine Names of the Soul, and iv) the Principle of

Reflection on the divine Names in Creation. However, true to the Sufi spirit, Shabistarī notes that the terminus of reflection is bewilderment. The extensive range of philosophical concepts and subjects featured in the course of Lāhījī's commentary are assigned various headings, which in the order of their occurence may be listed as follows:

1. Theophany in the form of the immutable essences *(a'yān).*
2. The appearance of divine mysteries by means of man.
3. God's love and the devotee's love: their relationship.
4. The summation of the universal within the particular.
5. The theophany of the complementary divine 'Majestic' and 'Beautiful' Names within the heart.
6. The interdependence of all living beings and the precedence and subsequence of certain realities over others.
7. The ontological relativity of all the world's individual entities and the necessity for them to remain in the condition of possibility.
8. An exposition of the meaning of the terms: Sīmurgh, Mt. Qāf, Paradise, Hell and Purgatory.
9. The five universal worlds.
10. The quantity of orients and occidents and Ibn 'Abbās's words in this regard.
11. The intermediary resurrection and the greater resurrection and their effect upon raising human consciousness to the state of wakefulness.
12. The role of the spiritual master in the purification of aspirants.
13. Incitement of the mystic wayfarers to combat the passional drives of the ego *(nafs-i ammāra)* and to refrain from blind religious imitation *(taqlīd).*
14. A typology of theophanies.
15. Turning away the mystic wayfarer from the veils of light and darkness.
16. The theophany of Reality in the sensible forms of phenomena to Moses.
17. The ascension of the Prophet and that of the saints.
18. Explanation of the principle of the analogy between the book of the cosmos and the revealed Scripture.
19. The principle of reflection on the breadth of creation *(āfāq).*
20. The motion of the *primum mobile* and of the eight spheres.
21. The ten spheres and the twelve constellations.

22. The stations of the seven planets.
23. The stations of the moon and their diverse conditions.
24. The wisdom in the creation of the stars and planets.
25. The pre-determination and lack of independence of the heavenly spheres.
26. The four natural elements, the three vegetable kingdoms and their confession of servanthood to God.
27. The principle of reflection on the soul.
28. The meaning of man being called an "oppressor" and "foolish."
29. The situation of man in the world.
30. The divine Names and their relationship to the immutable essences *(a'yān-i thābita).*

Obviously, exhaustive coverage of all thirty items is impossible here. Only a few of them, which directly relate to problems of Sufi reflection, will be examined below.

### The Principle of Reflection on the Breadth of Creation

My translation of the phrase *fikr fī 'l-āfāq* as 'reflection on the breadth of creation' in the above subheading attempts to give an idiomatically meaningful translation in English of what in Arabic literally means "contemplating the horizons;" in fact, the phrase implies, by extention, 'to ponder on all the wonders which lie in vast distances of the cosmos, to ponder the marvelous breadth of creation which stretches to all the far corners of the earth, and the immense reaches and space of the heavens'. In Islamic mystical thought *fikr fī 'l-āfāq* is often contrasted with *fikr fī 'l-anfus,* the latter term literally meaning 'meditating upon the souls', but in this context implying 'to ponder one's own existence, to reflect upon Who am I?, to meditate upon the soul: its substance, its whither and wherefore'.[850] Both phrases feature as headings of a long series of verses in the *Garden of Mystery.*[851] Consider the following verse (211) from the *Garden of Mystery:*

Now, go and meditate upon the heavens,
    on how they're made,
So that you come to praise the Divine;
    then by these signs of him
        you'll be a panegyrist of Reality.[852]

Commenting on this verse, Lāhījī defines *fikr fī 'l-āfāq* as meditating on the vast extent of the heavens, a process which should lead one to ponder "in what fashion they have been created, with which kind of motion they continuously revolve, how each sphere differs from others in its orbit, and what diverse effects and influence they have upon earth."[853] Such 'reflections' necessarily will induce the piously attuned to magnify God's "signs" *(āyāt)*—referring, stresses Lāhījī, to the *āyāt-i Qurānī:* those Koranic passages which eloquently celebrate the panorama of creation. As a consequence of such *tafakkur,* "God will also praise *you,*" declares the exegete, "for as God himself has declared:

> Surely in the creation of the heavens and earth
> and in the alternation of night and day
> there are signs for men possessed of minds
> who remember God, standing and sitting
> and on their sides, and *reflect upon*
> the creation of the heaven and the earth:
> 'Our Lord, Thou hast not created this for vanity.
> Glory be to Thee! Spare us
> the chastisement
> of the Fire."[854]

Following Shabistarī's introduction of the topos of cosmological reflection come some forty verses which provide a concise yet intricately detailed summary of medieval astrology, discussing such matters as the relationship of the seven heavens to the heart of the Perfect Man, the effects of the zodiacal signs and the planets upon the sub-lunar realm, how divine Providence controls and guides the revolution of the Heavens, the inter-relationship of the four material elements (water, earth, fire and air), the *materia prima,* and the "three realms of nature" (animal, vegetable and mineral) to the Heavens. These aspects of *tafakkur* exemplify the "profound contemplative perspective" of Islamic cosmology—as S.H. Nasr, in reference to the *Gulshan-i rāz,* has termed it[855]—but properly belong to the field of astronomy and astrology. Since any qualitative translation or treatment of such verses would require extensive commentary beyond the scope of this study, they are omitted from the present discussion. Furthermore, Shabistarī's exposition, being modeled on the Ptolemaic system of concentric spheres, according to which "the sun comes to rest in the House of Leo," and "the fifth heaven is the place of Mars and in the fourth is our sun which adorns the world,"[856] from the standpoint of modern astrophysics is outdated, although that system, as Robert Darr has pointed out, "happens to make an ideal working metaphor for the relationship between humanity, the cosmos and God."[857] Ibn 'Arabī had also used the same geocentric system of the planetary world which subjectively situates man at its centre, as symbolic of "the central role of man in the cosmic whole, of which man is like the goal and the centre of gravity."[858]

Considered from a contemplative point of view the geocentric system then has definite advantages. The schemata of concentric spheres with earth situated at their centre, and the supreme spheres of the 'Divine Pedestal' and the 'Throne' – the former containing the skies and the latter englobing all things – can even be viewed, as Titus Burckhardt has noted, as marking "the passage from astronomy to metaphysical and integral cosmology."[859] This mystical approach to the 'Starry heavens' was also well understood by the visionary poet William Blake, who, notwithstanding his erudition in the heliocentric cosmology of Copernicus and Newton, in the early nineteenth century concluded that

> As to that false appearance which appears to the reasoner
> As of a Globe rolling thro' Voidness, it is a delusion of
> Ulro.
> The Microscope knows not of this nor the Telescope; they
> alter
> The ratio of the Spectator's Organs but leave Objects
> untouch'd.
> For every Space larger than a red Globule of Man's blood
> Is visionary, and is created by the Hammer of Los:
> And every Space smaller than a Globule of Man's blood
> opens
> Into Eternity of which this vegetable Earth is but a shadow.
> The red Globule is the unwearied Sun by Los created
> To measure Time and Space to mortal men every
> morning.[860]

For the purposes of deeper examination of the science of cosmological *tafakkur* it is more relevant if we look further down in the same section of the text at some verses which, as Lāhījī explains, are written "in evocation of the fact that contemplation of the positions of the heavenly bodies provokes the human soul to advance towards its ultimate perfection,"[861] where the poet says:

235 If you become a man who's reached perfection
by dint of meditation and practice of reflection[862]
you will admit as a matter of fact
there's nothing null and void about creation.
236 The Word of God declares just that:
beholding all as null and void, it states,
"is the surmise of those who hate the Truth."[863]
237 There's such a grand sagesse and lore
within a tiny gnat, why do you think
in Mars or Mercury there's less than that?
238 And if you look upon this cosmic task,
descry its source, *causa causans,* you'll see
the orbit of the spheres subject to an edict
of One Omnipotent.
239 All those astronomers who gaze aloft
were weak in faith from the start
and that is why they said: "effects of stars
on earth reflect the Heaven's odd designs."
240 They cannot see how Heavens' Wheel
revolves subject to God's edict and wish—
and just how subjugated its orbit is.

The science of reflection upon celestial affairs is conducive to realizing the rank of the 'Perfect Man', says Lāhījī in his exegesis on verse 235, for human pettiness becomes visible only in the mirror of divine Magnificence:

> If through the practice of reflection *(fikr)* you become a Perfect Man *(mard-i kāmil)* and reflect upon this [divine] handiwork and artifice in the required manner, you will behold how the grand plan of the spheres and stars—with all their grandeur, individual variation of motion, their infinite aspects and interaction—is formulated and based upon hermetic sciences *(ḥikmathā)* the understanding of which is beyond the scope of man. You will also perceive in what way the celestial influences and properties are produced in the sub-lunar realm—[as the verse indicates]: "It is God who has created the seven heavens, and of the earth an analogy thereof, between them

the divine commandment descending" [Koran LXV: 12]—and how their virtues are actualized, in what precise order their effects are determined, and in what manner they are a manifestation of "Every day he is upon some affair" [Koran LV: 29]. Therefore, certainly you will acknowledge that such things are 'not null and void *(bāṭil)*', for in each event is concealed a mighty wisdom.[864]

Shabistarī's teaching in couplet 236 is in line with the theosophy of his eminent contemporary, the Kubrāwī Shaykh 'Alā' al-Dawla Simnānī who, citing the same Koranic verse ((XXXVII: 27), stresses the teleological meaningfulness of everything in existence.[865] The final verse cited above (240) takes the sublime science of Sufi *tafakkur* out of the realm of cosmology and back to its mystical origins in the philosophy of the 'Unity of Being'. Here we encounter Lāhījī, commenting on how the celestial Wheel turns captivated, enslaved by Divine Dictate, presenting us with this Sufi maxim as a parting reflection: "There is no effectual power in existence except for God." *(Lā mu'aththir fī -'l-wujūd illā llāh).*

## The Principle of Reflection on the Soul

Shabistarī concludes his discussion of reflection in the *Garden of Mystery* with thirty-two couplets devoted to the most esoteric aspects of Sufi anthropology, the concept of Man as Microcosm, and specifically, to the Perfect Man who is 'Human Form Divine'. Since this concept has been treated elsewhere in this study (V, pp. 159-63) my treatment here will not be extensive.

Shabistarī's view of the psyche or soul *(nafs)* again is part and parcel of a traditional world-view in which spirit was considered inseparable from matter, soul from heart, prophetology from psychology, cosmology from anthropology and pneumatology from metaphysics. Here, I will cite only the opening passage from Lāhījī's commentary on this "psychological principle" of Sufi contemplative disciplines. Couched in Akbarian terminology, this passage illustrates how profound a spiritual experience was this engagement in mystical 'soul-search' for the mediæval Muslim mystic. Understanding the full purport of Lāhījī's exegesis here requires not only extensive mystical reflection but also familiarity with the terminology of Ibn 'Arabī. What is of central importance for the understanding of the concept of *reflection upon the soul* in Shabistarī's Sufism is that there is a unity between the 'Reality of Humanity' or the 'Perfect Man' and the 'Divine Presence' and that these two spiritual degrees are mutually related and absorbed within each other. As Lāhījī informs us:

> The principle of 'reflection on the soul' *(al-tafakkur fī 'l-anfas)* is devoted to the exposition of the macrocosmic Reality of Humanity *(jām'iyyat-i insānī),* and the inclusive presence and permeation of this reality throughout all the levels of being. It should be understood that the Essence of divine Unicity (or Exclusive Unity, *aḥadiyyat),* in accordance with its innate love of Self-manifestation and disclosure, requires the appearance of the First Entification *(ta'ayyun-i awwal)* which is the Universal Isthmus *(barzakh-i jāma'),* combining the 'concrete properties' *[aḥkām,* i.e. of the eternal prototypes of creation] and Necessary and Possible Being, encompassing all these directions [of Being].
>
> The First Entification is called variously: the Supreme Pen *(qalam-i a'lā),* the Almighty Spirit *(rūḥ-i a'ẓam),* the Universal Intellect *('aql-i kull),* the Source of the Scripture *(Umm al-kitāb)* and the Spirit of Muḥammad *(rūḥ-i Muḥammadī).* This level is also designated as the 'Reality of Humanity' *(ḥaqīqat-i insānī).* Between this Reality and the divine Presence there is no intermediary, so that whatever exists in the divine Presence is also found inscribed in the form of a 'comprehensive replica' *(nuskha-yi jāmi'a)* in this Reality. Many of the realized adepts *(muḥaqqiqān)* have considered the spiritual level of the divine Presence as essentially equivalent to that of the First Intellect *('aql-i awwal)* which is the 'Reality of Humanity' *(ḥaqīqat-i insānī),* and have held that they are completely identical.
>
> From the standpoint that this First Entification is the 'Living One *(ḥayy)*' and the Life of all beings derives from its mediation—it is named the 'Almighty Spirit *(rūḥ-i a'ẓam)*'. From the standpoint that all beings proceed through its mediation and by medium of it creation all beings have been 'dictated' into the Scripture [of creation]—that is to say, 'the world'—it is termed the 'Pen' *(qalam).* From the standpoint that it shows intelligence in conceiving and generating itself and all learning and science proceed from it, it is named 'Universal

> Reason *('aql-i kull)'*. From the standpoint that the delineation of the 'signs *[āyāt,* i.e. of creation]' and the 'words' of creation, in both their particular and general aspects, are contained within its essence, it is named the 'Mother of Scripture *(umm al-kitāb)'*. In relation to the fact that the effusion of the bounties of the lights of Prophecy *(nabuwwat)* from their supernal Source occurs by grace of its mediation[866] it is named the 'Muḥammadan Spirit *(rūḥ-i Muḥammadī)'*. The true noumenal form which is 'Allāh' *(maẓhar-i ḥaqīqī Allāh)* is, indeed, this Reality, and all other living beings are but phenomenal forms of its materialization.[867]

In this passage we encounter a kind of transcendental reflection in which the soul itself becomes "the macrocosmic Reality of Humanity" encompassing the entire span of being. One is reminded of George Herbert's metaphor of the *Anima Mundi:*

> The soul doth span the world, and hang content
> From either pole unto the center:
> Wherein each room of the well-furnisht tent
> He lies warm, and without adventure.[868]

Later on in his commentary, Lāhījī describes the heart as the organ of psychic perception and "the universal form of the Divinity which encompasses all of the divine Names."[869] This heart-centred basis of 'psychological reflection' is expressed quite directly by Lāhījī in the following passage:

> Since the human being is a comprehensive theophany *(maẓhar-i jāmi')* of all the divine Names and Qualities and has been created in the universal divine form, just as the divine Presence cannot be completely comprehended and understood in its essence, likewise knowledge cannot formally comprehend the human being who is a complete manifestation of that Presence, except at the point where the mystical wayfarer's particular knowledge *('ilm-i juzwī-yi sālik)* —upon realization of the spiritual station of 'Subsistence in God *(baqā' bi'llāh)'*—becomes the universal knowledge of God *('ilm-i kullī-yi ḥaqq)*, so that all the spiritual truths of things are understood by him through divine knowledge.[870]

With this admission of the impotence of human reason and reflection to encompass either itself or God, Shabistarī/Lāhījī pass onto the theory of the divine Names which enable the Sufi to acquire knowledge and gnosis of the soul. The role of the divine Names in overseeing the operation of created being, as well as their invocation as a means to mystical self-knowledge, is perhaps the most important and original concept in the theosophy of Ibn 'Arabī. Necessarily, Shabistarī's thought and Lāhījī's exegesis of his poem are so deeply imbued with this concept that psychology takes on a theological hue and appears to be merely a branch of the universal science of divine Names. "Everything is a theophany of one of the divine Names," writes Lāhījī, "such that its origin and ultimate goal of return is that very Name, so that it understands God through that Name of which it is itself an emanation."[871] Whereas each thing is a theophany of one particular Name, Man, however, is a theophany of *all the divine Names,* being a duplicate copy, image, or replica *('aks)* of the 'Named One': God. Man is an exemplar of all of these Names, containing and manifesting all of their opposing attributes: Mercy and Wrath, Beauty and Majesty, and for this reason, "sometimes man is obedient and sometimes a transgressor against God."[872] The contemplative discipline of *tafakkur* engenders awareness of these diverse theophanies, and this higher consciousness is the essence of the process of 'reflection'. The following verses are some of the most brillant blossoms on the subject of psychological reflection in the entire *Garden of Mystery:*

> All beings are ordained in origin and end-return—
> Each has its set delight and lot, its destiny assigned
> by Names divine and through these Names all things
> abide;
> their Names commune with God, extolling him in ceaseless
> litany.
> Because the genesis of every thing is from a Name
> upon return to God it takes that holy Gate again
> and makes its own debut and final fate the same;
> its exit from and entrance in to life by one passage.
> We errant men are vagabonds: you all must fare this course
> because through this you've known the Names, and all their
> lore
> is yours to grasp—that you are but a form, a silhouette
> that's cast on earth by he-who-named-all-things. By you

divine Command and Rule is shown; by you exposed to
view
his act of Will; by you, Fortune's soveriegn, O low devotee
by you his Science put on show! You are the Oratrix
and Seer, the Hearer too – for Life itself is you! Some
permanence
you have, but not from this you call your 'self'; it's from
Beyond;
your home is yon. Well done, oh man! You are that 'First'
whose source and archetype is 'Ultimate' and 'Last'.
You theorize about your 'I' all day and night—
but better not to know this 'self'—'self'-ignorance is best!
Now, since reflection's consummation is bewilderment,
Reflection's dialogue and thought's debate here terminate.[873]

As the above lines illustrate, Shabistarī's lengthy treatment of reflection concludes with the assertion of the inadequacy of reflection as a contemplative discipline independent of divine grace. Lāhījī's theosophical explanation of this view is again revealing:

> The ultimate end of reflection—as founded on the 'principle of reflection on the soul'—leads to bewilderment, due to the onslaught of theophanies of the divine Essence and Qualities, and the irradiation of flashes of the lights of the infinite divine Names upon the comprehensive human receptacle. Ultimately, this bewilderment results in inability to discern between the human condition of devotion/worship of God *('ubūdiyyat)* and the supernal condition of Divinity *(rubūbiyyat).*
>
> . . . At this degree, alpha and omega become one, and the discourse of reflection reaches its terminus and thinking is concluded, insofar as reflection is a means to and a cause of the realization of gnosis *(ma'rifa)*, whereas at the spiritual station of the unification *(ittiḥad)* of the corporeal receptacle of theophany *(ẓāhir)* and Theophany itself *(maẓhar),* there is no place left for duality and otherness. Here the gnostic, the Object of gnosis and gnosis itself are, in their being, one single entity.[874]

### Reflection from the Vista of Bewilderment

Due to the essential ineffability of the mystical experience and practice, the foregoing study of the concept of reflection in Shabistarī's *oeuvre* has, as a matter of course, focused upon the limitations, rather than the entire scope of possibilities found within the contemplative discipline of *tafakkur*. We have seen that Shabistarī's conception of *tafakkur* largely accorded with the views of his fellow Kubrāwī Shaykh 'Azīz Nasafī who had envisioned reflection as a kind of "celestial inspiration" on the wings of which the mystic soared beyond the realm of the body and reached the world of the spirit. Shabistarī's emphasis on the powers of reflection also evidently owed more to Ghazālī's views found in his *Kitāb al-tafakkur* than to the works of Ibn 'Arabī, for whom reflection, being something merely "created," could not serve to free one from the trappings of time and place.

To Shabistarī, reflection is the thought of the heart. It is the passage from vanity to Absolute Truth. Thus, as Lāhījī calls it, *tafakkur* is a "spiritual voyage." Founded on the practice of the remembrance of God *(dhikr), fikr* is a potentially dynamic discipline, which often transcends its original source. However, before the divine Essence which is beyond division and analysis, even such a mighty tool shows itself to be impotent. Likewise, because one cannot penetrate into the realm of that which is the cause of reflection itself, reflection is but a veil over the divine Essence. The cause of demonstation is, in itself, indemonstrable. Thus, the mystic must comprehend the Essence *by means of* the Essence, and from thence, through this *via illuminativa,* descend back down to the divine Names.

However, because reason before this vision is blind as a bat, this descent and revelation must be experienced, rather than merely analyzed. Thus, paradoxically, states Shabistarī:

> The summit of knowledge *('ilm)* —which is 'conscious apprehension' *(idrāk-i idrāk)*—is inapprehension *('adam-i idrāk),* for whereas the Real 'Object-of-Apprehension' *(mudrak)* is infinite, knowledge *('ilm)* is finite. This inapprehension is a type of apprehension without consciousness of either apprehension or inapprehension . . .

At this point, the wayfarer who pursued the spiritual Path methodically under the guidance of a Shaykh discovers that the only signpost marking the road to the Truth is a featureless map of bewilderment.

Reflection is also a tool for man to apprehend the cosmos directly from within his own soul. Even if Shabistarī's doctrine of cosmological reflection was based upon the geocentric Ptolemic model of a concentric hierarchy of celestial spheres, it was not limited by this schema, insofar as the real Object of reflection is the macrocosm within man. At this point, *fikr fī 'l-āfāq* becomes *fikr fī 'l-anfus*. His doctrine of psychological reflection, which emphasizes the unity between the level of the Perfect Man, the ontological Reality of Humanity, and the divine Presence, expresses this with even greater clarity. 'Reflection upon the soul' touches the very depth of that universal soul which 'spans the world'.

In the end, however, although reflection has proven itself a worthy tool, its limitations, like those of its feeble employer man, have gotten the better of it. Both employer and worker therefore have been forced into the sudden retirement of bewilderment. Our terminus thus appears very much like our commencement: the realization of human impotence before the Divine. No poet has expressed this condition to my mind better than Awḥadī :

> Gratitude enough you cannot render unto Him—that's *fikr*.
> Know His presence as always here—that's *dhikr*.
> Once this is known, you will become both deaf and mute;
> but if that's not then known to you,
> then who is it that you invoke?[875]

## Notes

738 For a good description of both these practices in Islamic mysticism see Muhammad Isa Waley, "Contemplative Disciplines in Early Persian Sufism," in L. Lewisohn (ed.), *Classical Persian Sufism: from its Origins to Rūmī*, pp. 497-548.

739 Cf. Surah III: 191, where *dhikr* and *fikr* occur together.

740 MAS, *Gulshan-i rāz,* pp. 69-78, vv. 70-286.

741 Anton M. Heinen, "*Tafakkur* and Muslim Science," in Maria Eva Subtelny (ed.), *Annemarie Schimmel Festschrift,* p. 105

742 *Ibid.,* pp. 109-10. See also Guiseppe Celentano, (trans.) *Al-Ghazālī: il libro della Meditazione,* (Trieste: Società Italiana Testi Islamica 1988), introduction, pp. 14-18.

743 Anton M. Heinen, "*Tafakkur* and Muslim Science," p. 107.

744 *Iḥyā', Bāb al-Tafakkur,* vol. 4, p. 412. Waley, "Contemplative Disciplines . . . ," p. 542.

745 *Iḥyā', Bāb al-Tafakkur,* vol. 4, pp. 412-3. Translation by M.I. Waley, "Contemplative Disciplines in Early Persian Sufism," p. 544.

746 See Isabelle de Gastines' (trans.) introduction to Nasafī's *Le Livre de l'Homme Parfait (Kitāb al-Insān al-Kāmil),* (Paris 1984), p. 10.

747 Alluding to a famous saying of the Prophet: "I have a time with God no other prophet finds, nor angel knows, not even the purest spirit—

who is Gabriel." This *ḥadīth* is cited below in my translation of couplet 119 from the *Gulshan-i rāz.*

748 *Kashf al-ḥaqā'iq,* ed. Aḥmad Mahdawī Dāmghānī (Tehran: B.T.N.K. 1965), p. 139.

749 *Ibid.*

750 *Ibid.*

751 For an interesting discussion of the relationship between Suhrawardī's myticism and epistomology, see Y.H. Hairi, "Suhrawardī's *An Episode and a Trance:* A Philosophical Dialogue in a Mystical Stage," in Parviz Morewedge (ed.), *Islamic Philosophy and Mysticism* (New York: Caravan Books 1981), pp. 177-89.

752 *Kashf al-ḥaqā'iq,* p. 141.

753 *Ibid.,* pp. 141-2.

754 *Mathnawī,* ed. R.A. Nicholson, VI: 1475-79.

755 *Kulliyyāt-i Shams yā Dīwān-i Kabīr,* ed. Badī' al-Zamān Furūzānfar (Tehran: 1976, 2nd ed.), VIII, no. 914, p. 155.

756 *Mathnawī,* IV: 437-8.

757 *Mathnawī,* II: 277-8.

758 From the caption of the first passage cited below.

759 *Mathnawī,* V: 3644-46.

760 *Mathnawī,* V: 3676-7.

761 *Mathnawī,* VI: 226.

762 *Futūḥāt al-Makkiyya,* (Cairo: Dār al-Ṣādir, n.d.), II: 432.8; cited by W.C. Chittick, *The Sufi Path of Knowledge*, p. xv.

763 *Futūḥāt* II: 298.2; Chittick, *The Sufi Path of Knowledge,* p. 166.

764 *Futūḥāt* II: 290.25; Chittick, *The Sufi Path of Knowledge,* p. 170.

765 *Futūḥāt* I: 319.27; Chittick, *The Sufi Path of Knowledge,* p. 169.

766 *Futūḥāt* II: 523.2; Chittick, *The Sufi Path of Knowledge,* p. 203.

767 This reflection-centred bias of the work was partially inspired by a book by Mīr Harawī (who had posed the questions to Shabistarī which prompted his *Garden of Mystery).* In his *Nuzhat al-arwāh,* composed in 711/1311, only six years prior to the *Garden of Mystery,* Harawī claimed his work to be an inspiration from the "sea of *tafakkur.*" See Najīb Māyil Harawī (ed.) *Nuzhat al-arwāh,* p. 193.

768 *Mafātīḥ al-i'jāz,* ed. Khāliqī & Karbāsī, p. 3.

769 MAS, p. 70, v. 71.

770 T. Izutsu, "The Paradox of Light and Darkness in the *Garden of Mystery* of Shabistarī," p. 303.

771 *Collected Poems,* ed. G. Keynes, "Auguries of Innocence," p. 431.

772 *Mafātīḥ al-i'jāz,* ed. Khāliqī & Karbāsī, p. 45.

773 "The Paradox of Light and Darkness . . . ," p. 291.

774 Cf. Chittick, *The Sufi Path of Knowledge,* p. 163.

775 Cf. Waley, "Contemplative Disciplines in Early Persian Sufism," p. 507.

776 *Mafātīḥ al-i'jāz,* ed. Khāliqī & Karbāsī, p. 54.

777 *Mafātīḥ al-i'jāz,* ed. Khāliqī & Karbāsī, pp. 48-9.

778 *Mafātīḥ al-i'jāz,* ed. Khāliqī & Karbāsī, p. 50, v. 5.

779 Zarrīnkūb, *Justujū,* p. 314.

780 *Mafātīḥ al-i'jāz,* ed. Khāliqī & Karbāsī, p. 50, vv. 5-11.

781 *Mafātīḥ al-i'jāz,* ed. Khāliqī & Karbāsī, p. 53, vv. 7-9.

782 Rashīd al-Dīn Maybudī in his famous Sufi Koranic commentary: *Kashf al-asrār wa 'uddat al-abrār,* ed. 'Alī Aṣghar Ḥikmat (Tehran: 1357 A.Hsh./1978), vol. 9, p. 323, cites the opinions of Al-Kablī and Al-Ḍaḥḥāk that "this verse [cited in the next two lines] pertains exclusively to the people of devotional works among those sects which are rightly guided," an opinion in agreement with Shabistarī's hermeneutics.

783 Koran LI: 56.

784 *Sa'ādat-nāma,* MAS, p. 238, vv. 1483-87.

785 On the psychology and symbolism of love in Sufism, see Carl Ernst, "The Stages of Love in Early Persian Sufism from Rābi'a to Rūzbihān," in L. Lewisohn (ed.), *Classical Persian Sufism,* pp. 435-55; Javad Nurbakhsh, *Sufi Symbolism II: Love, Lover, Beloved, Allusions and Metaphors,* trans.Terry Graham et al., (London: KNP 1987), part 1.

786 Rūzbihān Baqlī, *'Abhar al-'ashiqīn,* ed. Henry Corbin and Muḥammad Mu'īn, Bibliothèque Iranienne, 8 (Tehran: Institut Français d'Iranologie de Téhéran 1958), chapters 19-32. Also cf. Ernst "The Stages of Love," pp. 449-51.

787 *Mafātīḥ al-i'jāz,* ed. Khāliqī & Karbāsī, p. 66.

788 *Ibid.,* p. 66.

789 *Ibid.,* p. 68.

790 *Ibid.,* p. 70.

791 *Ibid.,* pp. 71-2.

792 *Ibid.,* p. 72.

793 A tradition of the Prophet. See *Aḥādīth-i Mathnawī,* p. 39.

794 MAS, *Gulshan-i rāz,* pp. 71-72, vv. 112-122.

795 *Aḥādīth-i Mathnawī,* p. 142.

796 A technical term in Ibn 'Arabī's vocabulary. As Prof. Izutsu notes: "The term 'emanation' *(fayḍ)* is for Ibn 'Arabī always synonymous with 'self-manifestation' *(tajallī).*" *A Comparative Study of the Key Philosophical Concepts in Sufism and Taoism* (Tokyo: Keio Institute 1966), p. 37.

797 *Mafātīḥ al-i'jāz,* ed. Khāliqī & Karbāsī, p. 76.

798 See W.C. Chittick, *The Faith and Practice of Islam,* p. 7. See also below, chap. VIII.

799 As Wilfred Cantwell Smith observed: "*Kufr,* rejection, is not lack of belief, not an intellectual position that holds that something is otherwise than is the case, and is certainly not mere ignorance. Rather it, too, like its correlative *īmān,* presupposes knowledge; for it is an active repudiation of what one knows to be true. That is why it is a sin, and indeed a (the) monstrous sin. It is the one final cosmic (or some would say, the one final human) wrong: the deliberate saying of "no" to what one knows to be right." "Faith as *Taṣdīq,*" in Parviz Morewedge (ed.), *Islamic Philosophical Theology,* (Albany: SUNY 1979), p. 109.

800 *Mafātīḥ al-i'jāz,* ed. Khāliqī & Karbāsī, p. 76.

801 *Mafātīḥ al-i'jāz,* ed. Khāliqī & Karbāsī, p. 77.

802 Our translation of the second hemistich of this couplet: "regain some goods you've always owned" also has a specifically logical connotation, as was conveyed by E.H. Whinfield's version of this hemistich: "Know it is impossible to demonstrate the manifest." E.H. Whinfield, *Gulshan i Raz: The Mystic Rose Garden of Sa'd ud Din Mahmud*

*Shabistari* (Lahore: Iran Pakistan Institute of Persian Studies; reprint, 1978), p. 12, v. 114.

803 See M.H. Sabzawarī, *Sharḥ-i Manẓūma,* part 1: Metaphysics, (ed.) M. Mohaghegh, T. Izutsu, (Tehran 1969), *Iṣṭilāḥāt wa Ta'bīrāt-i Sabzawārī,* p. 601.

804 Cf. Ch. Partee, *Calvin and Classical Philosophy,* Studies in the History of Christian Thought, 14 (Leiden: Brill 1977), pp. 110-5.

805 *Mafātīḥ al-i'jāz,* ed. Khāliqī & Karbāsī, p. 77.

806 The term *idrāk-i basīṭ* in Islamic philosophy refers to the innate knowledge which all existent beings have concerning their divine origin *(mabdā');* this is their 'noncomposite general knowledge' *('ilm-i basīṭ).* The term *basīṭ* (noncomposite, simple, general, universal) is contrasted to *murakkab,* meaning composite. The four elements and the heavenly bodies are considered to be 'simple', whereas the sub-lunary bodies are 'composite'. The divine Essence is beyond division and analysis, having no particulars which one could subject to analysis. For further discussion of the term *basīṭ,* see Ja'far Sajjādī, *Farhang-i 'ulūm-i 'aqlī* (Tehran: 1361 A.Hsh./1982), pp. 132-37.

807 Literally, "the apprehension of apprehension," but for Shabistarī *idrāk-i idrāk* means conscious knowledge or apprehension which is aware of its own apprehension, as opposed to the virtually 'unconscious' knowledge *(ma'rifat-i basīṭ)* which is innate and universally common to all beings.

808 MAS, p. 290, vv. 12-18. This verse is addressed to Muḥammad and concerns the unbelievers who ignored the message of Islam and instead 'looked the other way' when they heard the Koran.

809 *The Principles of Epistemology in Islamic Philosophy: Knowledge by Presence* (Albany: SUNY 1992). My reference to this work here is a considerable simplication of Yazdi's courageous attempt to construct a theory of religious experience on the basis of 'knowledge by presence'.

810 *Har nafsī:* literally, "every soul." The English word 'self' hardly conveys the complexity of traditional Islamic psychology, according to which, as (pseudo-)Shabistarī explains *(Mir'āt al-muḥaqqiqīn,* MAS, pp. 353-4), the soul is held to be a composite entity, encompassing various natural, psychological and supra-natural functions. The Human Soul (composed of five external + five internal faculties + anger + lust), also subsumes the Natural Soul, the Vegetable Soul and the Animal Soul.

811 The Koranic term for eyewitness here is *baṣīratin,* also meaning "a beholder. One who sees or understands himself." Cf. J. Penrice, *A Dictionary and Glossary of the Koran* (London: Curzon Press 1971), p. 17.

812 On the realms of being in Sufi metaphysics, see W.C. Chittick, "The Five Divine Presences from Al-Qūnawī to Al-Qayṣarī," *The Muslim World,* 72 (1982), pp. 107-28; Javad Nurbakhsh, *Sufi Symbolism IV,* trans. Terry Graham *et al.,* (London: KNP 1990), pp. 108-9. Lāhījī explains that "the divine Command *(amr)* is a world generated by the dictate of the Creatrix beyond matter and time, just as are the [celestial] intelligences and the [heavenly] souls *('uqūl wa nufūs),* and this world of divine Command is also known as the angelic world and the unseen world *(malakūt, ghayb).*"

*Mafātīḥ al-i'jāz,* ed. Khāliqī & Karbāsī, p. 13.

Lāhījī elsewhere describes the five 'worlds' of Being as consisting of: 1) the world of the divine Essence *('ālam-i dhāt),* 2) the world of the divine Qualities *('ālam-i ṣafāt),* 3) the angelic world *('ālam-i malakūt),* which is also known as the world of the Spirits, the world of the Divine Acts, the world of the divine Command, the world of Lordship, etc., 4) the world of sovereignity *('ālam-i mulk),* 5) the world of humanity *('ālam-i nasūt). Ibid.,* p. 114.

813 MAS, p. 287, vv. 11-17. *Mafātīḥ al-i'jāz,* ed. Khāliqī & Karbāsī, p. 114.

814 *Mafātīḥ al-i'jāz,* ed. Khāliqī & Karbāsī, p. 77. On apprehension of apprehension, see note 807 above.

815 William James, *The Varieties of Religious Experience* (New York 1936), pp. 371-2.

816 *The Principles of Epistemology in Islamic Philosophy,* p. 176.

817 My interpretation and translation of this verse follows Muhammad Asad, *The Message of the Qur'ān* (Gibraltar: Dar al-Andalus 1980), p. 768.

818 MAS, p. 296, vv. 3-7.

819 MAS, *Sa'ādat-nāma,* p. 160, vv. 157, 160-1. These lines are also cited by Lāhījī, *Mafātīḥ al-i'jāz,* ed. Khāliqī & Karbāsī, p. 77.

820 *Blake: Complete Writings,* ed. G. Keynes, pp. 96-7

821 MAS, *Sa'ādat-nāma,* p. 160, v. 165a.

822 *Mafātīḥ al-i'jāz,* ed. Khāliqī & Karbāsī, p. 78. It is interesting to note the similarities between Shabistarī's conception of the inability of human conceptualization and vision to enjoy the *visio dei* and the views of Pseudo-Dionysius, who cautions about "the rite of illumination" and beholding "the divine symbols" in connection with the sacrament of baptism: "Let no one who is uninitiated approach this spectacle. For no one with weak eyes can safely look upon the rays of the sun and there is risk for us when we handle what is above us." —*Pseudo-Dionysius: the Complete Works,* trans. Colm Luibheid & Paul Rorem (New York: Paulist Press 1987), p. 201.

823 MAS, *Ḥaqq al-yaqīn* p. 305, vv.s 11-12.

824 Henry Corbin, expounding this same passage in Lāhījī's commentary on the *Garden of Mystery,* remarked: "The famous expression *waḥdat al-wojūd* does not signify 'an existential monism' (it has no connection with Hegel or with Haeckel), but refers to the transcendental unity of being. The act of being does not take on different meanings; it remains unique, while multiplying itself in the actualities of the beings that it causes to be; an unconditioned Subject which is never itself *caused-to-be."* Henry Corbin, *The Man of Light in Iranian Sufism,* trans. Nancy Pearson (London/Boulder: Shambhala 1978), pp. 115-6.

825 *Mafātīḥ al-i'jāz,* ed. Khāliqī & Karbāsī, p. 78.

826 'See above, no. 582.

827 *Mafātīḥ al-i'jāz,* ed. Khāliqī & Karbāsī, p. 80.

828 Annemarie Schimmel, *The Triumphal Sun,* p. 111.

829 MAS, p. 159, vv. 140-155.

830 It had constituted a separate chapter in his treatise 'The Language of Ants'. See W. H. Thackston (trans.), *The Mystical & Visionary Treatises of Suhrawardī* (London: Octagon 1982), pp. 81-3.

831 *Mafātīḥ al-i'jāz,* ed. Khāliqī & Karbāsī, p. 81.

832 MAS, *Ḥaqq al-yaqīn,* p. 292, vv. 18-20.

833 The Persian original is: *Wa īn 'adam-i idrāk idrākī buwad bī-idrāk-i idrāk wa idrāk-i 'adam-i adrāk.*

834 MAS, *Sa'ādat-nāma,* p. 287, lines 7-17

835 On the many correspondences and cross-cultural influences between St. John of the Cross and Sufis such as Shabistarī, Ibn 'Arabī, Najm al-Dīn Kubrā, see Luce López Baralt's provocative study, *San Juan de la Cruz y el Islam: Estudio sobre las filiaciones semíticas de su literatura mística* (Puerto Rico: El Colegio de México 1985), pp. 199-244; esp. pp. 243-4. Unfortunately, further in-depth comparison between Shabistarī's symbolism of the 'bright night' and what Baralt calls "la irrupción de la elusiva noche sanjuanísta en la España del Siglo de Oro," *(ibid.,* p. 244) is precluded by the breadth of the topic. Also cf. Terry Graham, "The Sufi Origins of St. John of the Cross," *Sufi,* 25 (1995), pp. 5-9.

836 *Poesías Completas: San Juan de la Cruz,* ed. Cristóbal Cuevas (Barcelona: 1988), pp. 103-4.

837 *Fuṣūṣ,* ed. 'Afīfī, pp. 50-1.

838 See for a discussion of the later Ibn 'Arabī tradition's outlook on angelology, see Sachiko Murata, "The Angels," in S.H. Nasr (ed.) *Islamic Spirituality I: Foundations* (New York: Crossroad 1987), pp. 338-343.

839 *Mafātīḥ al-i'jāz,* ed. Khāliqī & Karbāsī, p. 81.

840 On the relationship between the angels and human psychology, see F. Jadaane, "La place des anges dans la théologie cosmique musulmane," *Studia Islamica* 41 (1975). On the connection between the angels, celestial intelligences and cosmology, see H. Corbin, *Avicenna and the Visionary Recital,* trans. W. Trask, chap. 2.

841 *Mafātīḥ al-i'jāz,* ed. Khāliqī & Karbāsī, p. 82.

842 R.J.W. Austin (trans.) *Ibn al-'Arabī: The Bezels of Wisdom,* p. 51; *Fuṣūṣ,* ed. Abū al-'Alā 'Afīfī, p. 49.

843 "Hierarchy, Angels and the Human Condition in the Sufism of Ibn 'Arabī," *The Muslim World,* LXXXI/3-4 (1991), p. 250.

844 On the concept of *walāya* in 13-14th century Sufism, see M. Molé, "Les Kubrawiya entre Sunnisme et Shiisme aux Huitième et Neuvième Siècles de l'Hégire," *Revue des études islamiques* (1961), p. 105ff. and H. Landolt, "Walāyah" in M. Eliade (ed.) *Encyclopedia of Religion.* Also cf. "The Sphere of Walāya" in Michel Chodkiewicz, *Seal of the Saints.* See also above, pp. 163-6.

845 These phrases are quoted from the famous *Ḥadīth-i qudsī* concerning *qurb-i farā'iḍ* and *qurb-i nawāfil:* "God says: 'My servant does not draw nigh unto Me by any means that pleaseth Me better than the performance of the obligatory duties of worship *(faā'iḍ)* which I have imposed upon him; and my servant does not cease to draw near to me by voluntary works of devotion *(nawāfil)* until I love him, and when I love him, I am his ear, so that he hears by me. and his eye, so that he sees by me, and his tongue, so that he speaks by me, and his hand, so that he takes by me." See Furūzānfar, *Aḥādīth-i Mathnawī,* p. 18; R.A.

Nicholson, Commentary on *The Mathnawí of Jalálu'ddín Rúmí,* I: 1938, p. 131.

846 MAS, p. 293, lines 16-21.

847 Describing the nature of the servant's annihilation in God and his loss of the sense of 'lordship' through witnessing his own servanthood, Ibn 'Arabī writes: "[The disciple] becomes disengaged from everything for God's sake just as the shaykh is disengaged. He trusts in God, not in the shaykh. Then he remains looking upon the shaykh to see what state God will cause to pass over him in respect of the disciple, such as speaking with a command or a prohibition or uttering knowledge which will benefit him. Then the disciple takes that from God on the tongue of the shaykh. The disciple knows in himself what the shaykh knows about himself: that he is the locus for the flow of the properties of lordship. Even if the shaykh should pass away, this disciple would not feel his loss at such, since he knows the state of his shaykh." Cited by W.C. Chittick, *The Sufi Path of Knowledge,* pp. 320-28, p. 324. This interiorization of the spiritual master's role is also typical of the Kubrāwī school (to which no doubt Shabistarī adhered), as Hermann Landolt (ed., *Correspondance Spirituelle, echanges entre Nuroddin Esfarayeni et Alaoddawleh Semnani,* (Tehran 1972), introduction, p. 10, has pointed out.

848 Trans. Nancy Pearson, pp. 110-20.

849 That is to say, the above study has omitted from its purview 156 couplets with Lāhījī's extended commentary (MAS, pp. 82-88, vv. 130-286), covering nearly a hundred pages (90-185) in the Khāliqī/Karbāsī edition.

850 Cf. Annemarie Schimmel, *Deciphering the Signs of God: A Phenomenological Approach to Islam* (Albany: SUNY 1994), p. 75.

851 For both headings see MAS, *Gulshan-i rāz,* vv. 210 and 259.

852 *Mafātīḥ al-i'jāz,* ed. Khāliqī & Karbāsī, p. 143.

853 *Ibid.*

854 Koran III: 191. Translation by A.J. Arberry, *The Koran Interpreted* (Oxford University Press 1983) with minor changes. *Mafātīḥ al-i'jāz,* ed. Khāliqī & Karbāsī, pp. 143-4.

855 S.H. Nasr, *An Introduction to Islamic Cosmological Doctrines* (Boulder: Shambhala 1978), p. 158.

856 Shabistarī, *Gulshan-i rāz,* MAS, p. 76, vv. 227, 230.

857 Shabistarī, *The Garden of Spiritual Mystery,* trans. Robert Darr (forthcoming), commentary on MAS, p. 76.

858 T. Burckhardt, *Mystical Astrology According to Ibn 'Arabī,* trans. from the French by Bulent Rauf (Sherborne: Beshara Publications 1977), pp. 10.

859 *ibid.,* pp. 13, 14.

860 *Blake: Complete Writings,* ed. G. Keynes, Milton: XXIX: 15-24, pp. 516-7. Similarly, Shabistarī also compares the entire cosmos to a single droplet *(qaṭra);* see MAS, *Gulshan-i rāz,* p. 88, vv. 500-4 (these lines were translated above, p. 156).

861 *Mafātīḥ al-i'jāz,* ed. Khāliqī & Karbāsī, p. 156, line 3.

862 Here both words in my translation (reflection, meditation) are references to the concept of *tafakkur.*

[863] An allusion to Koran XXXVII: 27. "We have not created heaven and earth and all that is between them without meaning and purpose, as is the *surmise of those who are bent on denying the truth:* but then, woe from the fire [of hell] unto all those who are bent on denying the truth!" (Translation by Muhammad Asad, *The Message of the Qur'ān,* Gibraltar: Dar al-Andalus 1980).

[864] *Mafātīḥ al-i'jāz,* ed. Khāliqī & Karbāsī, p. 156.

[865] See Simnānī, *Al-'Urwat li'l-ahl al-khalwat wa al-jalwat,* p. 243,

[866] Both editions of the *Mafātīḥ al-i'jāz,* (i.e. ed. Khāliqī & Karbāsī, p. 166, and K. Samī'ī, p. 195) read "occurs *without* mediation," which is obviously a *lapsus calami.*

[867] *Mafātīḥ al-i'jāz,* ed. Khāliqī & Karbāsī, p. 166, lines 9-22.

[868] "Content" in John Wall Jr. (ed.), *George Herbert: The Country Parson, The Temple* (London: SPCK 1981), p. 185.

[869] *Mafātīḥ al-i'jāz,* ed. Khāliqī & Karbāsī, p. 385.

[870] *Mafātīḥ al-i'jāz,* ed. Khāliqī & Karbāsī, p. 177.

[871] *Mafātīḥ al-i'jāz,* ed. Khāliqī & Karbāsī, p. 178

[872] *Mafātīḥ al-i'jāz,* ed. Khāliqī & Karbāsī, p. 179, line 9.

[873] Shabistarī, MAS, *Gulshan-i rāz,* p. 78, vv. 277-286.

[874] *Mafātīḥ al-i'jāz,* ed. Khāliqī & Karbāsī, pp. 184-5.

[875] *Dīwān-i Awḥadī Maraghī,* p. 600.

# VIII

# BEYOND FAITH AND INFIDELITY

## The Topography of Shabistarī's Visionary Ecumenism

*Whoever sees unveiled the real infidelity,*
*and face to face perceives the truth-of-heresy,*
*detests all rites, all forms of fake 'Islamic' falsity.*

*In this final chapter some of the theological and metaphysical ramifications of Shabistarī's unique and original interiorized vision of faith and infidelity will be examined. However, before expounding his doctrine, given the complexity of theological issues involved, it will be necessary to briefly examine the religious background of the concept of* īmān *in early Islam.*

### The Idea of Faith in Islamic Theology

Many recent studies of the notion of Faith *(imān)* in classical Islam by scholars such as Louis Gardet,[876] T. Izutsu,[877] Wilferd Madelung,[878] William C. Chittick,[879] and Wilfred Cantwell Smith,[880] have demonstrated that the dominant emphasis of both the scholastic theologians *(mutakallimūn)* and the Sufis was on the interior dimensions of faith—*niyya, taṣdīq*. The typical tripartite division of faith—equally espoused by both advocates of Kalām and the Sufis—consisted in the components of: verbal confession *(qawl),* works *('amal),* and intention *(niyya).* This division was based upon the saying of the Prophet: "Faith is a knowledge in the heart, a voicing with the tongue, and an activity with the limbs."[881]

It was the definition of the first-mentioned component, the interior dimension of faith, which became the main concern of most scholastic theologians, especially those of what became the dominant Sunni school in later Islamic history, the Ash'arite *madhhab.* Both the Sufis and the scholastic theologians in general disapproved of belief by blind imitation *(taqlīd)* and the Ash'arite and Shāfi'ite schools were especially quite severe on the deficiency of this type of religious commitment. As Louis Gardet has pointed out:

> The majority of the manuals of *kalām* regard as much superior to "faith by *taḳlīd*" faith based on knowledge (or science), *īmān 'an 'ilm:* an enlightened faith, which "proves" its object. The "proof" in question being understood as arising from the arguments and reasonings of the *mutakallimūn,* the "scientific" faith thus lauded was exposed to attacks by opponents, both Ḥanbalīs and *falāsifa.*"[882]

The Sufis, however, posited a higher type of faith, that realized by the heart's vision, or by illumination *(kashf wa shuhūd),* a concept which was also central in the thought of one of the greatest theologians in the history of classical Islam, Abū Ḥāmid al-Ghazālī.[883] Ghazālī, who believed that Sufism "represented the best way to the highest truth," maintained that there was "a third degree, higher than the preceding one, which he called the "faith of certitude" *(yaqīn).*[884] Here is probably to be seen an influence of both Shi'ism and Ṣūfism: this higher degree of faith, based on *yaqīn,* is, for Ghazālī, the only true faith, as was the "interior faith" for the Ikhwān al-Ṣafā'.[885]

Obviously influenced by Sufi mystical ideas, Ghazālī described this interior faith as a sort of 'unveiling', a visionary experience which, as we saw in the last chapter, was the central concept in the Sufi theory of knowledge.[886] He defined it as

> the knowledge of the nonmanifest domain *[al-bāṭin]* and the goal of all the sciences. . . . [It consisted in] a light that

> becomes manifest within the heart when the heart is cleansed and purified of blameworthy attributes. Many things are unveiled by means of this light. Earlier the person had been hearing the names of these things and imagining vague and unclear meanings. Now they become clarified. The person gains true knowledge of God's Essence, His perfect and subsistent attributes, His acts, His wisdom in creating this world and the next world, and the manner in which He makes the next world the consequence of this world: the true knowledge of the meaning of prophecy and the prophets, the meaning of revelation . . . [887]

For Ghazālī, only through the science of disclosure *('ilm al-mukāshafa)* can one "gain knowledge of the meaning of prophecy and the prophet, and of the meaning of revelation *(al-waḥy)*."[888] An important aspect of Ghazālī's contribution to later Persian speculative Sufism was his construction of a theological basis and framework for the language and the 'religion of the heart';[889] the 'heart' being to Ghazālī "the primary organ of perception," which "enables man to attain knowledge of God."[890]

According to the renowned *Ḥadīth* of Gabriel, the Prophet's religion is divided into *islām, īmān* and *iḥsān:* submission to God, faith and beneficence. The last two categories of belief were often considered to be the proper sphere of the science of Sufism and thus effectively to lie outside the jurisdiction of the Sharī'a-minded jurisprudents, as W.C. Chittick has revealed:

> The jurist as jurist can have nothing to say about faith or perfection *(iḥsān)*, since these belong to other dimensions of the religion. As Ghazālī puts it, 'The jurist speaks about what is correct and corrupt in *īslām* and about its preconditions, but in this he pays no attention to anything but the tongue. As for the heart, that is outside the jurist's authority *[wilāyat al-faqīh]*.[891]

This "para-mystical distinction" between Islam and *īmān* later became normalized as a kind of two-level faith identity in Islam, effectively distinguishing between the social and spiritual perspectives on the religious life, a division which was accepted, as Fazlur Rahman points out, "by orthodoxy, as expressing a distinction *within a whole,* between the spirit and the letter of the law, and not an absolute separation and disengagement of the two."[892] Making reference to the most significant verse in the Koran (XLIX: 14[893]) which delineates these two levels, the outer submission *(islām)* to God, which is but lip-service, and genuine interior faith *(īmān)*, Mahmoud Ayoub observes:

> The first level "is legal, cultural, and social, expressed in the individual's membership of the Muslim community. The framework of this identity is Islam as an institutionalized religion and legal system.
>
> The second is a deeper identity which is based on faith, or *īmān*. It belongs to God alone to decide as to the truth or falsity of this identity. . . . These two levels of identity stood side by side in the formative years of the Muslim community, and their legal and theological legitimacy is clearly affirmed in the Qur'ān and early *ḥadīth* tradition. Faith as a universal and primordial basis of true religious identity was not limited to the Muslims alone. Rather it extended to the Jews and Christians, as people of the Book, and to all those who have true faith in God.[894]

This second, interior dimension of faith was also known in Kalām theology as *taṣdīq*, which "designated truth at the personalist level of integrity"[895] in the words of Wilfred Cantwell Smith, insofar as it was beyond the definitive appraisal of dogmatic theology whose examination was based merely upon verbal *belief*. Derived from *ṣidq* (sincerity), *taṣdīq* meant to "authenticate" or "validate" religious truth. "Etymologically, faith *(īmān)* means verification *(taṣdīq)*," the early Persian Sufi 'Alī Hujwīrī stated categorically.[896] It definitely possessed an activist and moral connotation, being "the personal making of what is cosmically true come true on earth: the *actualization* of truth . . . More mystically, it is the discovery of the truth (the personal truth) of the Islamic injunctions: the process of personal verification of them, whereby, by living them out, one proves them and finds that they do indeed become true, both for oneself and for the society and world in which one lives."[897] Whereas *belief* is the mere *perception* of an external truth,

> *Taṣdīq* is the personal appropriation of that perception. It is the inner reordering of oneself so as to act in terms of it; the interiorization and implementation of the truth in dynamic

sincerity. *Taṣdīq* means not simply "to believe" a proposition but rather to recognize a truth and to existentialize it.[898]

Citing Taftāzānī's commentary on Nasafī's *'Aqā'id,* Wilfred Cantwell Smith furthermore underlines the existentialist and activist agenda of *Taṣdīq* in Islamic theology:

> Just as in English modern existentialists in order to express this notion turn to French, and borrow thence the terms *engagé* and *engagement,* so this medieval writer, in struggling to express the existentialist involvement that 'faith' connotes, turns to Persian and introduces into his Arabic a Persian term, *giravīdan* —which is virtually the precise counterpart of *s'engager,* since *girav* is the Persian for that for which *gage* is the French: namely, the stake of pawn or pledge that is put up as a warranty.[899]

According to Taftāzānī "the true nature of *Taṣdīq*" combines both the heart's assent to the veracity of the speaker's utterance, and an activist "yielding" and "surrender" to it, which is best expressed, he concludes, in Persian by *giravīdan,* or, as Smith expresses it, *s'engager.*[900] The Koranic concept of faith should be perceived as dynamic self-engagement rather than dogmatic 'belief'; in fact, the standard words for 'believing' in later Islamic scholastic theology, *(i'taqada, 'aqīdah, 'aqā'id)* do not even occur in the Koran, so one may speak of the "act of faith" rather than faith itself.[901]

Faith's locus is the heart, a subtle organ conceived of as "the center or essence of the human being . . . the place of intelligence, understanding, and every positive human quality."[902] Considering this 'cardiological' connotation of faith, which is actually its dominant meaning in early Christianity as well,[903] the term *taṣdīq* might best be translated as 'heart-conviction', since in Smith's words, *īmān* is a "self-engagement with truth . . . an interiorizing act of the heart whereby one's person finds inner serenity (mind and heart and bodily actions converging to obviate hypocrisy *[nifāq])* and outward realism (a living in accord with objective reality *[al-Ḥaqq]).*[904]

Unfortunately, while admitting that faith—in addition to verbal confession and physical works—was basically an 'act of the heart', Muslim theologians rarely managed to reach a consensus on precisely what the verbal catechism and oral profession of faith should consist in. Such was the deliberate ignoring or ignorance of

Muslim tradition that the many sayings of the Prophet emphasizing the interior dimension of the act of faith were conveniently ignored.[905] Ibn Ḥazm's (384/994-456/1064) description of the extremist Khārijite sect who followed Nāfi' ibn al-Azraq (d. 65/686), although somewhat exceptional in their bigotry, was unfortunately very characteristic of some of the excesses practiced in the name of 'keeping the faith clean' in later Islam:

> The Azraqites were of the opinion that, whenever they came across a Muslim who did not belong to their camp, they should ask him (at point of sword) as to his religious conviction. And if he said 'I am a Muslim' they killed him on the spot (because there could theoretically no Muslim outside their own camp), but they forbade killing anyone who declared that he was a Jew, or a Christian, or a Magian.[906]

The Azraqites exercised a sort of mind-control over the Islamic community in their day. As Ibn Ḥazm explained above, they would engage in 'interogation of personal beliefs' or *isti'rād,* a word which became a "symbol of terrorism and violence" in the seventh century—"a strange and ironical situation. Muslims were killed in the name of the purification of Islam, while the Jews, Christians and even the Magians were spared."[907] Among the fanatics of early Islam, as in certain modern-day interpretations, faith was measured by one's ability to read out the catechism and pass a religious test. From the second Islamic/eighth Christian century onwards, the phenomenon of the unrestrained application of *takfīr* (condemnation of one's co-religionists for heresy) as "a handy tool of party-politics"[908] often became common.

> In these circumstances a man could point to any one of his Muslim brethren and declare him an 'infidel' or even 'polytheist-idolater' on the slightest and most arbitrary ground . . . As theology developed gradually, *takfīr* came to be exercised freely and, apparently, without any compunction, in regard to the minute details of dogmatics."[909]

Although the heart was 'free' to practice *taṣdīq* in the oratory of private prayer, the tongue was still chained by the trite literalism of the dogmatics of the *Kalām* teachers and the jurisprudents. Examining the *ḥadīth* literature, one even finds the word *īmān* is appropriated for the purposes of factionalism, and theological party-politics.[910] Doctrinal rivalry to save souls is preached while the practice is acquisition of political power with the carrot of salvation and the stick of damnation.

> The polemical form that this took was the anathematization of opponents by the process of *takfīr,* "calling someone a *kāfir.*" The result of this trend was that certain theologians began to anathematize all Muslims who did not belong to their school. Such a step effectively restricted salvation to professional theologians adhering to the one correct doctrine.[911]

Of course, to the mystics, for whom faith and piety was, as dictated by the Prophet, "in the breast," the cathecisms and anathemas of the jurists were signs that the malady of hypocrisy had infected the entire Muslim body-politic. Turning upon themselves, many Sufis rejected the literal faith of the *faqīh*s, and transforming curses to compliments, laid the epithet of 'Infidel' like laurel upon their brows. Sufis, paradoxically, vied with each other in aspiration to the heights of 'praiseworthy infidelity', and to combat conceit, knowing the ego *(nafs)* to be "the worst of all enemies," in Hujwīrī's words, anathematized their pride. As Carl Ernst reveals:

> *Takfīr* practiced by the Sufis is quite different from the anathemas hurled at each other by rival theologians; spiritual *takfīr* is a process of purification that aims at the elimination of duality and hidden idolatry in oneself. It was in this sense that Shibli said, "Sufism is idolatry, since it is the safeguarding of the heart from the vision of that which is other (than God) and there is no other." All such denunciations can be considered as spiritual *takfīr*.[912]

The Sufis rejected the theologian's faith based on pure ratiocination as inadequate and instead admitted *their own interior infidelity of heart.* In this process of purification and interiorization, calling something heresy or "accusing of infidelity" became an integral aspect of Sufi doctrinal teaching concerned with the *ethics of the spirit,* and thus effectively removed from the realm of doctrinal squabbles. Here began what might be called the literary history of faith's interiorization, that 'unveiling' which is source of all those monuments of mystical poetry for which Persian Islam is renowned. This is the saga that has been told over many centuries[913] and is still being told in the heart, blood, and ink of Sufis everywhere in the Islamic world who are still undergoing persecution for practicing and preaching the primacy of the spirit of the Law over its Letter.

### The Faith of Ghazālī and 'Ayn al-Quḍāt Hamadhānī

In the early part of the eleventh century, shortly before Ghazālī's birth, it had become usual practice to condemn the belief of the common people as erroneous *(takfīr al-'ammah)* and as a consequence, "a good theory of *takfīr* had to be formulated on the solid basis of reason and logical persuasion," to check its abuses.[914] Ghazālī's answer to this problem was in accord with the anti-sectarian Sufi spirit which sought to establish a humane tolerance of differences of opinion among fellow Muslims in exploring the science of *tawḥīd.* Noting the absurdity of fanatical anathematization of co-religionists on the grounds of doctrinal differences, Ghazālī reflected:

> He is a downright fool who, when asked to give his definition of *kufr,* answers: "*Kufr* is anything that is opposed to the Ash'arite theory, or the Mu'tazilite theory, or the Hanbalite theory or indeed any other theory, (as the case may be)'. Such a man is more blind than a blind man, an uncritical follower of authority.[915]

Ghazālī condemned this narrow-minded bigotry, observing that "he who hastens without reflection to the *takfīr* of those who happen to oppose Ash'arī or anybody else is an ignorant and uncritical man."[916] And of those who would condemn the Islamic rationalists or Mu'tazilites, he wrote:

> It would be wise of you that you restrain your tongue as much as possible from condemning those who pray toward Mekka, and say: "There is no god but God and Muḥammad is His Apostle," without contradicting (by what they say and do) this confession of faith. The sin of leaving alive a thousand Kāfirs is far less grave than that of shedding just a few drops of blood of one Muslim.[917]

Even so, Ghazālī was quite harsh on followers of other religions and sects, condemning the Christians, Jews, Brahmins, the Dahriyya

(Materialists) and philosophers as infidels because their views, in varying degrees, refute the word of the Prophet.

Ghazālī's attitude towards religious diversity stood in sharp contrast to the liberal views of his contemporary admirer and intellectual disciple, the Sufi thinker 'Ayn al-Quḍāt Hamadhānī (d. 525/1131), one of the most insightful and original Sufi thinkers among his contemporaries.[918] Ghazālī's Sufism was far less radical than that of 'Ayn al-Quḍāt, and his thought, unlike the latter's, was as deeply legalistic as it was broadly mystical.[919] Thus, for Ghazālī, the essence of doctrinal infidelity is the antonym of *taṣdīq*, which is *takdhīb* or giving the lie to something. In this case, "*Kufr* is the *takdhīb* of the Apostle of God concerning any point of what he has told us." But faith "is to verify *(taṣdīq)* what he has told us."[920]

Contrasted with the opinions of Ghazālī, 'Ayn al-Quḍāt Hamadhānī's views were expressive of that pleasant extremity of religious tolerance for which Persian Sufism has ever been a byword,[921] and, in this sense, he anticipated the ecumenical spirit of Shabistarī's *Garden of Mystery*. 'Ayn al-Quḍāt was far more confident than Ghazālī in his own ability to convert the heretic, the lukewarm pietist, the sceptic or the apostate from infidelity, declaring:

> The members of each of the seventy-two religions are adversaries of each other, and for the sake of their respective national communities, struggle against one another. Yet if they could all come together and listen to the words of this wretch, they would reckon that they all adhere to one religion and one nation. People have been alienated from Reality by means of their erroneous conceptions and similitudes [about God]: "Most of them follow naught but conjecture. Surely conjecture can by no means take the place of truth." (Koran X 36) The names are multiple but the Essence and the Named Object is one.[922]

Elsewhere, stressing that terms such as 'Islam' and 'infidelity' had only nominal significance, being in themselves meaningless —insofar as the actual aim of all religious faith was to gain release from bondage of *shirk-i khafī* (crypto-polytheism) and from thralldom to the 'ego' which is the 'worst of infidels'—he remarked:

> I praise neither infidelity nor Islam. O friend, whatever brings a man to God is Islam and whatever debars a man on the path of God is infidelity. And the truth of the matter is that the mystical wayfarer can never put either infidelity or Islam behind him, for infidelity and Islam are two mystical states from which the seeker does not escape as long as he is 'with' himself. However, when freed from self, neither infidelity or Islam would ever be able to catch up with you should they come running after you.
>
> If in an idol temple I sense the sweet thought of my
> mistress
> Reason admits: circling the Ka'ba seems quite amiss,
> For without her scent, the Ka'ba is but a church;
> while church is the Ka'ba if graced
> with the fragrance of her presence.[923]

Even if he was 'Ayn al-Quḍāt's intellectual mentor, despite his Sufi leanings and sympathies, Ghazālī, like many other Muslim dogmaticians and Kalām theologians nonetheless failed to recognize the presence of any genuine spirituality in non-Islamic theological systems such as Buddhism and Christianity (at least in his exoteric works).[924] Many of the other classical Sufis, when it came to religious faith, in Wilfred Cantwell Smith's words, "stressed movement more than system, meaning more than form, person more than pattern," and more often than not took a cue from the tolerant outlook of the likes of Abū'l-Ḥasan Kharaqānī (d. 426/1034) who was known to advise his disciples not to ask traveling Sufis who visited his hermitage, "about their faith *(īmān),* but instead give them bread *(nān),*"[925] or from 'Ayn al-Quḍāt, who was convinced all the world could be converted by the sweet reason of his inspired rhetoric. For as Smith has noted, the Persian Sufi master was quite unique for his age in universalism, giving expression to "his humane – and divine – vision . . . with an eloquence and passion perhaps unmatched in any other literature. The [theological] systematizer, on the other hand, whether conceptually *(mutakallim)* or morally-legally *(faqīh),* has been largely exclusivist."[926]

This universalist and inclusivist attitude of the Persian Sufis, the interiorized vision of faith which beheld all religions as manifestations of one archetypal reality,[927] was still firmly rooted in the soil of the Islamic faith itself.[928] But both laborious scholarship as well as deep spiritual realization are necessary to fully comprehend this esoteric perspective, for, as 'Ayn al-Quḍāt was to comment: "These archetypal meanings *(ma'ānī)* only reveal themselves to one who has transcended the seventy odd religions/faiths *(madhhab)*. But how will someone who has not completely reviewed *one religion/faith* ever bridge the gap that exists between these words and himself?![929]

Admittedly, exploration of the deeper reaches of the concept of faith in Islamic thought (inclusive of its semantic boundaries, etymology and the development of its scholastic theology both in Kalām science and Sufi theosophy) has yet to be conducted. Even a critical history of the basic Sufi concepts of faith, as Smith laments, has not yet been written.[930] It is with the intention of making a slight rectification of this omission that the following discussion of the interiorization of faith in the thought of Maḥmūd Shabistarī has been undertaken.

## The Concept of Infidelity in Classical Sufism

Shabistarī's conception of 'real infidelity' *(kufr-i ḥaqīqī)* is a mélange of diverse ideas and conventions in Persian literature and Sufi theosophy, ranging from the symbolism of *kufriyyat* in Persian mystical poetry from the time of Sanā'ī down to Sa'dī, to the doctrine of 'real infidelity' *(kufr-i ḥaqīqī)* advocated by Ḥallāj, who was, as Carl Ernst calls him, "the real formulator of the mystical *topos* of faith and infidelity,"[931] a doctrine later elaborated by 'Ayn al-Quḍāt Hamadhānī, and lastly, differing etymological theories about the term *kufr*. Considering the antiquity and complexity in the genesis of this concept, it will be useful to briefly review these ideas before studying Shabistarī's own doctrine of *kufr-i ḥaqīqī*.

### The Literary Tradition of *Kufriyyāt*

The symbolism of infidelity *(kufriyyāt)*, employing metaphors drawn from non-Muslim religions—the praise of idols, Brahmins, Christians and Magians—has often been used as an excuse for the celebration of esotericism in Persian literature. In A. Bausani's words, such *kufriyyāt* should not always be taken literally but rather as "simply symbols of something contrasted with official Islam and, in lyrics, a symbol of a mystical reality deeper than any exoteric religion."[932] Shabistarī's advocation of infidelity, and his command to become "inimitable in infidelity," which are discussed below, can be seen to hark back to certain timeworn rhetorical conventions in Persian poetry which contrasted the way of Love *(eros)* to the way of the Law *(nomos)*. In this spirit, 'Ayn al-Quḍāt in his *Tamhīdāt* averred:

> A sign of love it is to throw away both soul and heart,
> to cast behind you all time and place and space;
> to be now infidel and now a pious man of faith
> and abide in both degrees unto eternity.[933]

Behind such verses lay the belief enunciated by many Persian Sufis that "in true *tawḥīd, kufr* and *īmān* (infidelity and faith) are basically unimportant because both of them are created, hence transient," as Annemarie Schimmel argues.[934]

Such verses also carried echoes of the theological doctrine known as the 'Transcendent Unity of God's Creativity' or the 'Oneness of Divine Action' *(tawḥīd-i af'ālī)*, a doctrine which surfaces in several passages of the *Sa'ādat-nāma* where Shabistarī asserts that anyone who refuses to believe that God creates every single event and act is a complete infidel *(kāfar)*.[935] Originating in al-Ash'arī's scholastic theology, the doctrine had been formulated by Sanā'ī of Ghazna (d. 525/1131) in a famous verse from the exordium to his *Ḥadīqat al-ḥaqīqat:*

> Both infidelity and faith
> upon his path run apace,
> united in their praise confess
> that "He is One without likeness.[936]

The doctrine was also maintained by Ibn 'Arabī and the Sufi thinkers of his school, such as 'Irāqī[937] and Shabistarī. In his commentary on the following verse from the *Garden of Mystery:*

> 'See One, say One, know One:' this axiom
> sums up the root and branches of *Imān*[938]

Lāhījī writes that the Sufi gnostic

> in every form should behold God's theophany manifest, whether this form be infidelity *(kufr)* or Islam. Verbally one should acknowledge that the only Real and True Being *(mūjūd ḥaqīqī)* is God, the Real *(Ḥaqq)* and thus everything which is, is Him. Make it your heart's firm conviction that all which exists, is God, and all else besides is pure nullity and non-existence.
>
> A further meaning of the couplet, may be expressed as follows: 'See One' in all activity, alluding to the Oneness of Divine Actions *(tawḥīd-i af'ālī);* 'Say One' [alone exists in creation] in quality, indicating the Oneness of Divine Qualities; and 'Know One' [throughout creation alone exists] in essence, referring to the Oneness of the Divine Essence. In short, the principles and derivatives of Faith in God culminate in Divine Unity *(tawḥīd)* and the science of Divine Unity is the root of all religious beliefs and gnostic certitudes.[939]

From the realization that God's action pervades all diverse "forms" of movement and rest—and hence, sustains all infidelity and faith—it was only a short step for the Sufi to dare to qualify himself with God's own universal comprehensiveness of both *kufr* and *īmān*. That is to say, to bravely envision the possibility of a transcendental faith in God which *included kufr* as well. An explicit example of just such an attitude is found, in fact, in the passage immediately preceding 'Ayn al-Quḍāt's verse cited above, where he states:

> Hearken to what that illustrious person said about these two stations: 'Infidelity and faith are two veils [drapped down from] beyond the divine canopy between God and the devotee'. A Man should be neither Muslim nor infidel! Anyone who remains in his individual faith or abides in infidelity is still behind these two veils, and the most advanced adept apprehends no other veil but 'God's August Glory and Essence' . . . "

The type of radical Sufi who could combine the contraries of faith and infidelity within himself, as Ayn al-Quḍāt had advocated, was represented by several pivotal terms in Persian mystical symbolism. References in Persian poetry to these terms—such as *qalandar* (a roving mystic unattached to religious formalities, the Persian version of the Hindu saddhu) *rind* (rogue) and *qallāsh* (rascal)—as J.T.P. de Bruijn has noted, "were traditionally subsumed under the heading *kufriyyāt.*"[940] Typically, the *qalandar*'s abode was the *kharābāt:* the Tavern of Ruin which ubiquitously encompassed good, evil, beauty, ugliness, and every kind of faith and infidelity (see above, IV, pp. 118-20). The definition of the *kharābāt* given by Abū'l-Mufākhir Yaḥyā Bākharzī, a contemporary of Shabistarī who was a major leader of the Kubrawī Order, uses *kufriyyāt* imagery drawn from Christianity to convey this point:

> The Tavern of Ruin *(kharābāt)* and Winehouse *(maṣṭaba)* are technical terms used by the Sufis to symbolize the overturning of traditional norms and natural habits, the elimination of self-righteousness, self-display, self-esteem, and ostentation, and finally, the transformation of one's merely human nature into the character of the people of love.
>
> I said to my heart, "O fierce heart,
> Seek your love in a monastery,
> Upon the carpet of prayer."
> My heart rejoined, "To the Tavern
> Of Ruin instead come round.
> If in the cloister nothing is found,
> seek truth there.[941]

Bākharzī's Sufi etymology of *kufr,* examined (p. 285) below, also highlights the central purpose underlying the usage of such heretical imagery by Sufi poets: the lampooning of shallow notions of faith based on pious dogmatism and religious formalism, rather than a personally introspected spiritual vision.

## The Hallājian Doctrine of *Kufr*

Although a detailed presentation of Manṣūr al-Ḥallāj's (d. 309/922) writings on 'real infidelity'[942] is beyond the scope of this study, a brief look at his pronouncements on the subject is unavoidable, since the entire doctrine of *kufr-i ḥaqīqī* in substance stems from his thought. Ḥallāj's doctrine of 'heretical faith' having already been subjected to a comprehensive monograph by Carl Ernst, it will only be considered briefly here.

Glancing over the later Ḥallājian corpus, Rūzbihān Baqlī's commentary on certain of Ḥallāj's ecstatic sayings in his *Sharḥ-i shaṭḥiyyāt* immediately strikes the eye as representative of the tradition underlying Shabistarī's doctrine of esoteric infidelity. Rūzbihān wrote:

> Ḥusayn [al-Ḥallāj] remarks in an ecstatic saying: "The knower *('ārif)* looks upon his initial mystical states and realizes that he does not have faith except after he becomes an infidel." They asked him for further exposition of this state. He commented, "In the beginning the poor man takes a position with respect to something. Then his position becomes advanced with respect to that thing. In the end he becomes an infidel. Don't you see that if he goes back on that, he has become an infidel?
>
> *[Rūzbihān's commentary:]* By this saying he implies that whoever converts himself to have faith *(īmān)* in God, yet still has in his heart awareness of the degrees and the intermediaries of divine grace, professes infidelity vis-à-vis the reality of divine unity *(ḥaqīqat-i tawḥīd)*, for even if initially he has faith in God, he becomes an infidel through his beholding of God's grace. Then at last he renounces all this, and becomes annihilated in God *(dar ḥaqq fānī shavad),* finding Faith.
>
> . . . O you who confess to God *(ay ḥaqq gūy),* know that God is Jealous. It is infidelity to profess faith in Unity because it is merely a created temporal being which acknowledges the Eternal Being *(īmān dar waḥdat kufr-ast zīrā kay ishārat ḥadath bi-qidam ast)*. And this acknowledgement only refers to external proximity with God, but is far from Reality. In respect to the Reality of divine Unity, infidelity is faith, because it is a confession to agnosis, and agnosis is the supreme truth of truths when it comes to created being. . . . Only after realization of 'gnosis' does one attain to bewilderment in 'agnosis'. So faith is the infidelity of infidelity and the infidelity of infidelity is faith.[943]

Ḥallāj's famous letter on real infidelity[944] also represents the spirit of these brave assertions about the esoteric doctrine of 'real infidelity'. In this letter we find the same doctrine, that "agnosis is the supreme truth of truths when it comes to created being," but here expressed with courageous fervour and unequalled frankness.

> In the name of God, the Merciful, the Compassionate, who manifests Himself through everything to whomsoever He wishes. Peace be unto you, my son. May God veil you from the exterior of the religious law, and may He reveal to you the reality of infidelity *(ḥaqīqat al-kufr)*. For the exterior of the religious law is a hidden idolatry, while the reality of infidelity is a manifest gnosis *(ma'rifah jaliyah)*. Thus, praise belongs to the God who manifests Himself on the head of a pin to whom He wishes, and who conceals Himself in the heavens and the earths from whom He wishes, so that one testifies that He is not, and another testifies that there is none other than He. But the witness in negation of Him is not rejected, and the witness in affirmation of Him is not praised. And the purpose of this letter is that I charge you not to be deceived by God, and not to despair of Him; not to covet His love, and not to be satisfied with not being His lover; not to utter affirmation of Him, and not incline towards negation of Him. And beware of affirming the divine unity! Peace.[945]

Comparing these words of Ḥallāj with the foregoing passages from Rūzbihān's commentary on his sayings, with the utterances of 'Ayn al-Quḍāt on the relativity of faith and infidelity, and lastly, with the statements by Bākharzī on the 'higher heresy' of the supra-formal 'Tavern of Ruin', it is evident that the Sufis, several centuries before Shabistarī, had already equipped themselves with a powerful lexicon of imagery to express their interiorized faith through non-Islamic and sometimes apparently anti-Islamic symbolism.

### Ibn 'Arabī's Semantic Re-orientation of the Concept of *Kufr*

Shabistarī's notion of infidelity is also a byproduct of several different etymological interpretations, both mystical and philosophical, of the technical term *kufr* over the course of many centuries. In the Koran *kufr* appears as a deliberate act of *agnosis,* a conscious self-deception, "certainly not mere ignorance," Wilfred Cantwell Smith has reminded us. "Rather, it too, like its correlative *īmān,* presupposes knowledge; for it is an active repudiation of what one knows to be true."[946]

The same idea of *kufr* as deliberate repudiation is further developed by Ibn 'Arabī, in whose school of Islamic gnosis the conventional connotation of 'infidelity' is superseded by "the root meaning of *kufr,* which is 'to hide, conceal',"[947] the very connotation which was to become its dominant meaning in post-Ibn 'Arabian Persian Sufism (as will be seen below). Of this later connotation of *kufr,* Toshiko Izutsu, interpreting Ibn 'Arabī's philosophical terminology, explains:

> The verb *kafara* in the Koran stands in opposition to *āmana* "to believe in," and signifies "infidelity" or "disbelief." But etymologically the verb means "to cover up." And for Ibn 'Arabī, who takes the word in this etymological meaning, *alladhīna kafarū* does not mean "those who disbelieve (in God)" but "those who cover and veil." Thus it is an expression referring to people who, by their "absence," conceal the Absolute behind the curtain of their own selves.
>
> The whole world, in this view, turns out to be a "veil *(ḥijāb)* concealing the Absolute behind it. So those who attribute Being to the world enclose the Absolute within the bounds of a number of determinate forms and thereby place it beyond a thick veil. When, for example, the Christians assert that "God is Messiah, Son of Mary" (V, 72), they confine the Absolute in an individual form and lose sight of the absoluteness of the Absolute. This makes them absent from the Absolute, and they veil it by the personal form of Messiah. It is in this sense that such people are Kāfirs, i.e., "those who cover up (→ those who disbelieve)."[948]

Given the complicated cognitive-semantic range and etymological polysemy of *kufr* in Persian and Arabic, W.C. Chittick goes so far (too far, I think) as to reject all previous orientalist tradition throughout his *Faith and Practice of Islam,* translating *kufr* as "truth-concealing" or "concealing the truth," thus discarding the normal academic renditions of 'unbelief' and 'infidelity'.[949] However, in his defence, it must be stated that by the time of Shabistarī, *kufr* had actually come to be considered by most Sufis as a type of psychological self-delusion and deliberate distortion of spiritual realities caused by egocentrism; the term was thus meant to imply a conscious 'covering up of the truth' rather than simply 'infidelity' or 'heresy'.

Living in an intellectual milieu totally steeped in the philosophy of Ibn 'Arabī (see chapter five), Shabistarī's works express as do no other Sufi writings composed during the Mongol period, the transformation undergone in Persian Sufism through the assimilation of the passionate Ḥallājian paradox of *kufr-i ḥaqīqī* into the difficult and complex metaphysics of al-Shaykh al-Akbar. The first thing noticeable about Shabistarī's outlook on infidelity and faith is that a significant shift in the former's meaning: from 'infidelity' or 'disbelief'—to 'concealing the truth', has taken place. This new—yet entirely traditional—semantic reorientation of the term is based on the original etymological meaning of the term *kufr* pioneered, though not invented, by Ibn 'Arabī, who popularized the original philological connotation of *kufr:* 'veiling', to connote 'veiling God by the self' or 'concealing Reality through consciousness of self'.[950] This semantic shift is also clearly reflected in the *Awrād al-aḥbāb*. Here, interpreting "certain expressions employed by singers during *samā',*" Bākharzī brillantly combines Ḥallāj's doctrine of *kufr-i ḥaqīqī* with a post-Ibn 'Arabian conception of the doctrine of 'infidelity's reality' as follows:

> In poetry, the term *kufr* does not signify religious 'infidelity' as opposed to 'Islam'. In Arabic *kufr* means to 'cover over'. . . . The letters KFR, pronounced *kafara,* denote 'veiling' in all their diverse conjugated forms in Arabic grammer, such as *kāfir, kaffārat, mukaffar, kaffār, kufūr,* and *makfūr*. The term *kufr* carries both blameworthy and praiseworthy connotations.
>
> In the blameworthy sense it refers to the continued existence of negative and immoral character-traits in a devotee. That is to say, as long as a devotee contemplates and concentrates on anything else but God in both the worlds or beholds any motion or activity without seeing God as the Agent thereof, or recognizes any other being besides God as worthy of worship—all of this is *kufr* and associating others with God *(shirk)* with its blameworthy significance in Sufi practice *(ṭarīqat).*
>
> However, in its praiseworthy sense, *kufr* is that you 'insulate' your heart from beholding either of the worlds (i.e. this world or the next), and thus become one who 'denies' or 'keeps under cover' the idol of the Infidel Selfhood *(kāfir-i ṭāghūt-i nafs-i khwud)* so that by the annihilation of its own attributes, it becomes eclipsed, and thus, when the existence of the selfhood is negated and annulled, its innate spiritual capacity is realized. At this point, the innermost core of the

Divine Selfhood is exposed and the Reality-of-Faith revealed. You become a true believer. As God Almighty declares:

> So whosoever rejects *(yakfur)*[951] false dieties
> and has faith in God
> has grasped a firm handhold
> which never will break.[952]

—That is to say, ["the firm handhold"] of divine unity *(tawḥīd)*. . . . When the sunlight of contemplative vision shines down on the arcanum of the revelation of infidelity, the stars of sensible things, intelligible ideas, imaginative concepts, created phenomena and legal formalities become masked and veiled to the eye of the heart.

> *Infidelity! Alas, the Magians may boast of you.*
> *Although your name they adore,*
> *Your essence they ignore.*

Blameworthy 'infidelity', on the other hand, is where the spiritual realities of religion become suppressed and veiled, causing the devotee to content himself with his obligatory religious duties, the performance of acts of devotion by rote and habituation, and worship through blind imitation.

However, the praiseworthy and 'real' infidelity is the interiorization of what is exoteric and the exteriorization of what is esoteric in its inwardness *(ẓawāhir bāṭin gardad wa bātin dar bāṭin ẓāhir shawad)*, so that the epiphanic light of spiritual realities beclouds and conceals the darkness of dogmatic imitation and conventional practice, obliterating the aspirant's personal character and self-identity. The 'infidelity', previously masked, becomes objectively visible[953] and the personal entity of the immutable archetypes *('ayn-i a'yān)*[954] and essences become covered up *(kufr gardad)*.

Shaykh Ḥusayn Manṣūr Ḥallāj wrote to his son: "My son! May God veil you from the exterior of the religious law, and may He reveal to you the reality of infidelity *(ḥaqīqat al-kufr)*. For the exterior of the religious law is a hidden idolatry, while the reality of infidelity is a manifest gnosis *(ma'rifah jaliyah) . . .* "[955]

In Bākharzī's interpretation of the concept of 'real infidelity' we may note both his boldness and his caution: boldness in defence of the doctrine of real infidelity *(kufr-i ḥaqīqī)* according to its original etymo-logical meaning, and caution in misquoting the addressee of Ḥallāj's letter, for these were weighty words of counsel for a mere disciple to bear, but for one so close of kin as a son, such frankness was evidently a tolerable indiscretion according to the mores of Islamic *adab*.

The above discussion of some of the central notions underlying the Sufi concept of mystical 'infidelity' reveals the recurrence of several different symbolic representations of the reality of *kufr* and *īmān*, which may be summarized as follows:

(a) *Kufriyyāt* symbolism was used by the Persian Sufi poets to celebrate their radically esoteric and eros-oriented mysticism as contrasted to normative exoteric and nomocentric theology.
(b) The exterior of the religious Law without attention to its interior dimension came to be considered a veil and cloud ("a hidden idolatry," Ḥallāj; "the darkness of dogmatic imitation and conventional practice," Bākharzī), a form of *kufr*.
(c) The faith observed by the pious rogue or inspired libertine *(rind, qalandar)* cannot be applied in an atmosphere where fanaticism and dogmatism prevails *(taṣdīq* being corrupted by ostentation), from which it follows that
(d) The spiritual degree of the poetic symbol of the 'Tavern of Ruin' excels that of the Mosque, the latter's conventional religious piety, based on self-display and ostentation, distorting the realization of the former's interior faith.
(e) The shocking rhetoric of anti-Islamic symbolism employed by Sufi poets should not be taken literally; rather (as will be seen from our study of Shabistarī/Lāhījī below), it has as its primary purpose salvation of the soul from bondage to blind imitation *(taqlīd)* and liberation from unreflective 'belief' without proper *taṣdīq*.

After this brief introduction into the theological background of the concept of faith in early Islam and the theosophical tradition of 'real infidelity' in classical Sufism, we now turn to analysis of Shabistarī's own approach to *islām, īmān, taṣdīq* and *kufr*.

## Muslim Infidel: The Faith of Maḥmūd Shabistarī

Shabistarī's own manifesto of the 'Faith of true infidelity' is based on several key topoi expounded throughout the *Garden of Mystery,* three of which, *viz.* i.) the doctrine of *kufr-i ḥaqīqī* espoused by Ḥallāj; ii.) Ibn 'Arabī's semantic reorientation of the term *kufr* to mean 'truth-concealing'; and iii.) the Persian literary tradition of *kufriyyāt*—have already been reviewed above, so no more need be added here. These topoi will also be seen to recur throughout the following pages.

However, there are two other interesting conceptions of *kufr* in Shabistarī's writings which will require some further introductory comment:

> iv. Persian poetic symbolism in which the bodily parts of the transcendental Beloved – specifically, the 'face' and the 'tress' – personify the divine Qualities of Beauty and Majesty, these Qualities being the imaginal source of 'Faith' and 'Infidelity' as defined by the world's religions.
>
> v. The transcendental ontology of the doctrine of *waḥdat-i wujūd,* or 'unity of being', wherein religion and blasphemy unite on common existential ground, as proteges of the opposites among the Divine Names which engender creation.

### The Eroto-Metaphysical Symbology of Infidelity and Faith

As was noted in chapter VI, the image of the Beloved's tress or curl *(zulf)* and her visage or face *(rukh)* as symbolic of infidelity and faith in Sufi poetry occupies a major portion of Shabistarī's poem. The usage of the visage and the tress of the Beloved as poetic symbols of Faith and Infidelity, which can be traced back to the poetry of Sanā'ī, 'Aṭṭār and 'Ayn al-Quḍāt,[956] is well expressed by this verse of Maghribī:

> Leave your infidelity and faith
> before her tresses and face
> Before her tresses and face
> say nothing of infidelity and faith.[957]

Here, faith and infidelity are revealed to be but masks, which when removed, expose the archetypal meaning therein. The Beloved's tress of infidelity appears as a poetic metaphor to express dispersion and darkness (revelation of God, however, by way of two divine Names: *al-Ḍārr,* the Punisher, and *al-Muḍill,* the Misleader), while faith is revealed to be a simile for vision of the *vultus divinus,* the divine Visage. The theosophical significance of these erotic images which portray divine Qualities is elaborated by Lāhījī in his interpretation of the following verses by Shabistarī:

> 766 If she left her two tresses free to fling
> In all the world no infidel would remain.
> 767 And if she left them always still
> not one true man of faith
> in all the world would remain.[958]

Lāhījī interprets the 'tress' in the first couplet (766) to refer to the 'determined forms' of multiplicity, and, more specifically, as symbolic of "the veils of light and darkness—the contrary divine Qualities of Beauty and Majesty *(jamāl – jalāl).*"

> Now if she were to shake her *two tresses* —here alluding to the determined forms of divine Majesty and Beauty—and leave them free to fling, thus rending apart the veil concealing [the Truth underlying] the determined forms and the multiplicity of phenomena, the Person hidden behind the veil of these determinations [of the Absolute] would be certainly exposed. The whole world would then witness the beauty of divine Unity. Having had their eyes opened to Oneness *(waḥdat),* not a single *'infidel'* would be left in the world; all polytheists would become monotheists and true Muslims, and the practise of infidelity itself would disappear.[959]

Here we may recall 'Ayn al-Quḍāt's citation of the mystic who claimed that "Infidelity and faith are two veils [drapped down from] beyond the divine canopy between God and the devotee." Underneath the dark curls of the divine Beauty and Majesty lies the secret divine Oneness veiled by the two tresses of the duality of the Qualities. But, if the *Deus absconditus* were to remain forever under wraps, notes Lāhījī in his interpretation of the next couplet, Faith as well would vanish from the world.

> If the veil of determined forms were never lifted from the visage of divine Oneness, not a single true believer *(mu'min)* would be left in the world to bear witness to the manifestation of divine Unity. Polytheism and infidelity *(shirk wa kufr)* would fill the world.[960]

## The *Coincidentia Oppositorum* of Infidelity and Faith in the Unity of Being

Utilizing the technical vocabulary of Ibn 'Arabī, Shabistarī affirms that the existence of infidelity is to be subsumed under the category of a necessary evil.[961] Furthermore, polytheism, idolatry and monotheism (according to the dictates of the orthodox Muslim religion) are, with respect to God's comprehensive 'General Mercy', but *one* in essence and being. Muḥammad Lāhījī elucidates this idea in the context of his commentary on this verse by Shabistarī:

> Since both faith and infidelity—both piety
> and blasphemy—in Being are always
> abiding and residing, thus idolatry
> and Unity are both but one essentially.[962]

– as follows:

> The poet implies that because blasphemy *(kufr)* and religion *(dīn)* are, regarding appearances at least, ideas of a contrary nature – nonetheless, they are both subsistent through Existence *(hastī)* and Being *(wujūd)*. Since the Absolute Existence is God, bearing witness to Divine Unity and profession of God's Oneness are thus, in source and essence, identical to idolatry. Indeed, it would be associating something else with God *(shirk)*, to regard blasphemy *(kufr)* and the idol as other than Divine in respect to their true reality. Holding such a view would make you an heretic to true Divine Unity *(tawḥīd-i ḥaqīqī)*. As the verse goes:
>
> There is no one else but you
> whom they adore in the pagoda
> Any person who bows down
> upon brick, stone, or wood.[963]

As Shabistarī in two other verses in the *Garden of Mystery* concerning the 'Perfect Man' makes clear, the perfect gnostic is in himself a *coincidentia oppositorum* of faith and infidelity, for

> 349 He makes the Law his cloak, the Path his undershirt,
> 350 The station of his inner essence know to be divine Reality:[964]
> *He integrates within himself both faith and infidelity.*[965]

The Perfect Man comprehends *(jāmi')* both sacred and profane, both faith and infidelity within himself because he has realized the transcendental ontological source of each, thus, as Lāhījī explains, "integrating and comprehending infidelity *(kufr),* which is a property which the Majestic Names of God require, and faith *(īmān)*, a property which the Beauteous Names of God require, within his own being."[966] However, this embracing of sacred and profane, as Lāhījī underlines, involves no toying with an antinominianism which might suspend the moral authority of the Law. Shabistarī's transcendental vision rests firmly on an *Islamic* basis. As if to underline this, apropos of verse 349, the exegete pronounces:

> Although from the philological point of view the term *Ṭarīqat* (Path) signifies *madhhab,* as a [Sufi] technical term it designates the voyage which is particular to the wayfarers on the Path to God who traverse the waystages of distance *(bu'd,* [from God]), advancing on through the stations of Proximity, thus passing from the temporal towards the Eternal. That is to say that the wayfarer on the Path to divine Reality *(ḥaqīqat),* following his ascension from the station of annihilation *(fanā')* to the station of subsistence *(baqā'),* should still (notwithstanding his realization of nearness to God and perfection) make the Law *(sharī'a)* —which is the religion *(dīn)* and way *(ṭarīqa)* of the Prophet Muḥammad, upon whom be peace—his cloak. In the same manner that he had fufilled all the necessary prescriptions of the Law in the beginning [of the Path], at the end [of the Path] he must observe the same respect, not neglecting even the least iota of it, so that he remain worthy of providing direction and guidance to others *(khilāfat was irshād).*[967]

In his commentary on couplet 350, Lāhījī reasons that the poet may also be alluding to the Perfect Man's comprehension of 'real infidelity' and faith within himself.[968] Since this concept is the central theme of this chapter, Lāhījī's interesting etymology of *kufr* which is based on Ibn 'Arabī's interpretation is worth citing here:

> By "infidelity *(kufr)* in this couplet [350], the poet may also be referring to 'real infidelity' *(kufr-i ḥaqīqī),* which can be defined as 'annihilation' *(fanā'),* and just as *kufr* literally means 'covering up', so 'annihilation', which signifies the dissolution of the illusion of self-existence *(hastī-yi majāzī),* is also the 'covering up' and eclipse—when confronted by the epiphany of divine Unity—of the personal fixed identity *(ta'ayyyun)* of the mystical wayfarer, which had been the cause of [his sense of] separation, duality and alienation.
>
> 'Faith' *(īmān),* on the other hand, can be defined as 'subsistence' *(baqā'),* insofar as the reality of Faith *(īmān-i ḥaqīqī),* which is the verification *(taṣdīq)* of God's Unicity, can only be obtained beyond all shadow of doubt after realizing the annihilation of the self *(fanā'-yi khwud)* and actualizing 'subsistence-in-the-One', whereupon in essence you *become* that One.[969]

To be a Muslim, states Shabistarī, you must respect other people's faith, enter into their belief-systems and try to comprehend their God, however alien to reality or your own concept of divinity this may be. In the opinion of Shabistarī, who was a product of the liberal religious culture of Mongol Persia, Faith *presupposes* inclusivism in the spirit of ecumenical tolerance of other religious traditions.[970] Lāhījī, in his commentary on these verses:

> If Muslims knew what idols were, they'd cry
> that faith itself is in idolatry.
> And if polytheists could just become aware
> of what the idols are, they'd have no cause to err
> in their beliefs. The graven image they
> have seen is but external handiwork and form,
> and so by Holy Writ their name is 'infidel'.
> No one will call you 'Muslim' thus, by the word of Law
> if you cannot perceive the Truth concealed therein,
> see the God within an idol hid.[971]

– hence boldly asserts:

> Just as the cause of the idolater's heresy, according to the Law of Islam, was his own shortsightedness and perception of the external created form of the idol, likewise, if you – who make claims to Islam and religious piety *(dīndārī)* – perceive naught but the idol's visible form and do not envision God hidden behind the veils of it's determined form—and it is this particular form which is a physical receptacle for God's theophany—you properly and legally *(dar sharḥ)* also cannot be called a Muslim. In fact, you are an infidel *(kāfar)* because you have veiled God's theophany appearing in the idol.

> O give not your hand to one who cannot tell
> the difference between the beloved's visage and her veil:
> I swear by Canon Law he is an infidel.[972]

The doctrine that every idol is, in reality, an icon, a transparent theophany of God, became quite common in later Persian and Indian Sufism. It is not particular or unique to Shabistarī. Shabistarī's views were even adopted and utilized by the Indian Emperor Akbar (d. 1605) when formulating his concept of 'Universal Religious Tolerance' *(ṣulḥ-i kull)* and the 'Divine Faith' *(dīn ilahī)* ideology under which he administered his empire,[973] and later, by the Mughal Prince and Sufi poet Dārā Shikūh (d. 1659).[974]

But more important for this study is that, immediately following the above cited verses, Shabistarī in a single verse makes perhaps the clearest statement about the relationship of the concept of mystical infidelity to Islam in the entire history of Persian Sufism:

> Whoever sees unveiled the real infidelity,
> and face to face perceives the truth-of-heresy,
> detests all rites, all forms of fake 'Islamic' falsity.

Commenting on this verse,[975] Lāhījī explains that the Sufis' faith is opposed to the notion, upheld by many theologians (the early Mu'tazilites for instance, and later, by Ibn Taymiyya, of course[976]) that "possible being is independent and separate from Necessary Being." On the contrary, asserts Lāhījī, true faith depends on vision of the 'Unity of Being':

> The very thesis of this question relates to certain assumptions entertained by some people concerning Islam, and in

> particular, the belief that the existence of possible things is separate and independent from the Necessary Being, so that each possible entity is held to be completely separate and independent from God. Such a person may wonder if the statement affirming that no one is an orthodox Muslim according to the *sharī'at* if he cannot contemplate God's theophany in an idol, isn't heretical and contrary to Islam. The author answers such a person by affirming that the idea that the Necessary and possible Being are absolutely separate from each other is merely a sort of 'metaphorical' or unreal Islam *(Islām-i majāzī),* not true Islam.
>
> . . . When a mystic realizes 'real infidelity' *(kufr-i ḥaqīqī)*—which connotes the covering up of the determined forms of multiplicity and existential diversity in the One True Existence—he becomes disillusioned with 'false metaphorical Islam' which is based on the premise that possible being is absolutely distinct and separate from Necessary Being, God. He will then perceive that it is, in fact, Necessary Being which reveals itself through the forms of possible beings and there is no other being besides this One Single Existence.[977]

In expressing the most esoteric truths of the Sufi faith with such clarity, Shabistarī was a legatee of the Mongols' patronage of diverse religious beliefs. Buddhism, Christianity and Shamanism, it should be recalled[978] were the faiths officially in favour in greater Persia during most of the poet's youth and for some seventy odd years of their reign (at least from 1221-1295). Muḥammad Lāhījī, in turn, was an heir of the Timurid princes' devotion to the free expression of mystical thought and respect for the Sufi Shaykhs.[979]

Shabistarī treats us to a unique philosophical articulation of religious inclusivism, but an inclusivism which is—unlike the inclusivistic "religious pluralism"[980] of contemporary scholars of religious mythology such as Mircea Eliade or of historians of religions such as Joseph Campbell—founded on an entirely theocentric metaphysics wherein 'Existence' implies God's Existence and is thus, the ultimate ontological fact.[981] His exposition of this metaphysical relativism of beliefs[982] however, is not simple to grasp, as Lāhījī's commentary of 601 printed pages of small Persian type on the *Garden of Mystery* illustrates. Even so, with the possible exception of the last-quoted lines, Shabistarī's views on faith and infidelity—his disdain and disregard for what Lāhījī calls "the fetters of infidelity and Islam" and advocation of the faith of 'real infidelity' versus the faith of 'false Islam'—are most clearly expressed in eleven couplets found in the last quarter of the *Garden of Mystery*. These couplets are translated below, followed by a study of Lāhījī's commentary upon them.

*The Muslim Infidel*

957 The Mosque in which you step to pray
is just a pagan temple
as long as you're engrossed in else than Truth,
958 but when that alien raiment is taken off
the temple's form becomes for you a Mosque.
959 I do not know . . . but still, whatever state you
possess,
combat the Infidel Selfhood: you'll then be free.
960 The 'Christian creed', the 'cincture', 'idol',
'churchbell'
are symbols for the loss of face, forgoing of fair
name.
961 If you would be a servant known for high degree,
a chosen bondsman, prepare to render pure devotion,
inure yourself to truthfulness.
962 Go – take this 'self' which bars the path;
each moment engage yourself in Faith anew.
963 Inside us all the lower soul's an infidel:
Rest not content with this Islam of outer form.
964 Each instant at heart regain your faith afresh.
Be Muslim, Muslim, Muslim, Muslim!
965 How many a faith there is – born of infidelity;
what strengthens faith is not infidelity.
966 Be free of shame and name – hypocrisy and
notoriety –
Cast off the dervish frock, tie on the cincture,
967 and like our master, be inimitable in Infidelity
if man you be: unto a Man commit your heart
entirely.[983]

In these couplets Shabistarī outlines the contours of the Sufi *regula* governing the consequences of the doctrine of 'real infidelity', delineating the moral boundaries and the theological limitations of this doctrine in a relatively systematic fashion. Although his exposition undoubtably hopes to convince by the logic of poetic eloquence as well as by appealing to common sense and reason, embedded in these verses are also four different mystical doctrines which are carefully illustrated in Lāhījī's exegesis.[984] These doctrines may be summarized as follows:

1. Liberty from bondage to the 'Infidel Selfhood' is only by entry into the 'Tavern of Ruin', a realm beyond sign and symbol, which hence, transcends both Faith and Infidelity.
2. Faith is actualized only by following the 'Path of Blame'; hence, Heresy is a symbolic statement of Faith.
3. Faith=*Taṣdīq* experienced by direct vision. Blind imitation *(taqlīd)* = blasphemy and infidelity.
4. Selfless gnosis of God is the Faith of 'Real Infidelity'.

### *1. The Doctrine of the'Infidel Selfhood'*

Interpreting line 959 above, Lāhījī emphasizes the psycho-spiritual origin of infidelity. *Kufr,* thus defined, is the illusion and the conceit of self-existence before the divine Being:

> The veil of egotism is the worst of all the veils. The source of all infidelity *(kufr),* dualism *shirk)* and outer and inner psycho-spiritual bondage is obedience to and concordance with, the lower soul, for "verily, the soul commands to evil." (Koran XII: 53). Thus, it is reported that "God said to Moses by way of inspiration, 'If you desire my satisfaction, then oppose your lower soul" In any case, whereas opposition to the lower soul is the crown-jewel of worship, and concordance with it is the cardinal principle of all sin . . . [985]

The same doctrine of the lower soul's moral 'infidelity' *(kufr-i nafs)* was also propounded earlier on in the *Garden of Mystery* in this verse (836):

> To 'haunt the tavern regularly' means liberty
> from self. Although it bear the look of piety,
> 'Selfhood' is pure infidelity.

Interpreting this couplet, Lāhījī emphasizes that the 'heresy of egocentricism' constitutes the central psychological attitude of an irreligious temperament:

> Occupation with the "selfhood" or egocentricism *(khwudī)* means to attribute an act or quality of Existence to oneself as an effective agent. Such an attitude is, in truth, pure infidelity *(kufr),* since infidelity denotes the covering up of Reality by the illusory existence of one's personal fixed identity *(ta'ayyyun-i hastī-yi khwud)* and other than God. That is to say that you ascribe, either qualitatively or actually, real 'being' to something else beside God *(ḥaqq),* and thus, you 'cover up' the Truth under the guise of something else.[986]

Although the practice of piety *(pārsā'ī)* is meritorious, if it causes one's own conceit to increase, it is in vain. One is still caught up in the fallacies of ego-consciousness; one is still inwardly an 'infidel', veiling God/Reality under the cloak of personal self-importance.[987]

The 'regulars' at the 'Tavern of Ruin' are described a few lines (843; see also p. 119 above) later on in the *Garden of Mystery* as being "neither faithful believers nor infidels." Their transcendence of faith and infidelity Lāhījī glosses as follows:

> They are a group of inspired libertines indifferent to worldly cares *(rindān-i lā-ubālī)*[988] who have made their abode the spiritual station of the 'Tavern of Ruin of divine Unity' *(maqām- kharābāt-i waḥdat),* having attained self-obliteration and non-existence . . . They are "neither faithful believers nor infidels" because they have realized the annihilation of their separative self-existence and personal fixed identity *(hastī-yi wa ta'ayyyun-i khwud).*
>
> *Now, determining whether someone professes 'infidelity' or 'faith' all depends upon whether a person has separative existence and determined identity! However, since these inspired libertines are deprived of all individual delimitation, of course, no pronouncement concerning their 'infidelity' or 'faith' may be given!*[989]

Faith and infidelity depend on the continuing consciousness of the subjective ego. On the supra-personal level of selflessness, however, faith and infidelity have only relative meaning, just as inside the precincts of the Ka'ba, no *qibla* is to be sought. The Sufi who experiences faith directly, becomes, paradoxically enough, bereft of both self and faith. Hence, as Ḥallāj said, the gnostic "does not have faith except after he becomes an infidel." Maghribī's verses illustrate this state:

Don't tell blindmen's tales to seers.
Recount no more *than this* before seers
of blindmen's circumstances,
    Be silent!

At Certitude's arrival, forego the stories of hypothesis;
cease to expound the legendary account of doubt.
When you behold her bare visage unveiled,
Then of philosophic proofs,
    Be silent!

Hand over blasphemy and belief
For infidels and the faithful to care for . . .
Stay drowned in her, totally obliterated and immersed;
Of all faith, of every infidelity,
    Be silent![990]

The ineffability of this experience of faith resembles Shabistarī's description in the *Ḥaqq al-yaqīn* (cited above, p. 243) of the supreme summit of mystical contemplation where "all sense of 'relationship' *(nisab)*—for that pertains to the level of multiplicity and crypto-polytheism *(shirk-i khafī)*—is dissolved and the annihilation of the apprehending subject *(mudrik)* in the (divine) 'Object-of-Apprehension' *(mudrak)* objectively appears."[991] Likewise, the exoteric form *(ṣūrat)* of belief dissolves into the unveiled meaning *(ma'nā)* of faith, an experience which can only be expressed in negative terms (recalling the *"no saber sabiendo . . . toda sciencia trascendiendo"* of St. John of the Cross).

For his own spiritual master, whom he describes as the *joie de vivre* of the 'Tavern of Ruin', Shabistarī reserves the highest encomium, for by his grace and guidance the poet has found release from bondage to the 'infidel selfhood':

One man from him becomes an 'infidel',
Another – pure and 'faithful'. It's he who fills

the world with such mêlée and misery,
from him come all these woes and ills.
The Tavern of Ruin blooms
with life and health from his lips;
his visage beams light and lustre
upon the mosque. Thus, everything for me
by him seems now easy because I see
through him the possibility of liberty
from this egocentric heresy: my soul-of-infidelity.[992]

### *2. The Faith of the Path of Blame*

In verses 960, 961 and 966 Shabistarī resuscitates the ancient tradition of the 'Path of Blame' in Sufism *(malāmatī),* a tradition which, from its inception among the mystics of 3rd/9th - 4th/10th century in the Khurasāni city of Nishapur, was closely linked to Sufi teachings.[993] The *malāmatī* teaching stressed conscious and public repudiation of external acts of piety in order to actualize *ṣidq,* sincerity, in practice and to behold the heart-truth *(taṣdīq),* otherwise veiled by piety put on public display. As Lāhījī comments on verse 960:

> Those Perfect Masters who discourse on idolatry, the tying on of the cincture, the practice of Christianity and ringing the churchbell, symbolically allude by usage of these images to the abandonment of personal name and honour. According to them, all decadence and error in religious belief stems from the wish to preserve one's personal 'fair name', 'honour' and 'reputation'. The thickest veil which beclouds people of high social position and status is their 'honour' and 'reputation'—for such folk it is easier to abandon the world than to lose their reputation.[994]

Stressing the depth of commitment to self-abasement which is required by Sufi discipline, Lāhījī—commenting now on couplet 966—deepens his analysis of this *malāmatī* strain in Shabistarī's poem:

> One should renounce hypocrisy *(riyā'),* which may be defined as acting with an eye to gaining the esteem of people (instead of God's favor), renouncing the pursuit of notoriety

> *(sam'a)*: of fame and public praise, and reputation *(nāmūs)* which is a sycophantic desire to be honoured and endowed with high rank by people. Instead, one should pursue pure devotion *(ikhlāṣ),* seeking obscurity from the public eye and statusless *(bī-ta'ayyunī),* casting off the dervish frock or *(khirqa),* which is a cause of self-display and status, from your shoulders, and gird your loins with the cincture of service to humanity, lest people become convinced of the truth of your sanctimonious show of piety. In this manner you will remain untainted by reprehensible qualities and vices such as hypocrisy, pride, conceited self-importance and the deluded belief in one's own virtue and reputation.[995]

Utter sincerity and truthfulness[996] are virtues alluding to the state of the soul in which "nakedness is my shield"—as the poet Theodore Roethke put it—or "to show yourself as one actually is," as Lāhījī elucidates:

> Truthfulness *(ṣidq)* is to show yourself to be whatever you actually are; and 'pure devotion' *(ikhlāṣ)* is to rid yourself of relationship with aught but God, the true Reality *(ḥaqq).* In reality, sincerity is – with God and society, in both your private and public life, and in heart and tongue – to be honest and upright. 'Pure devotion' is to keep God constantly before the face of your heart, with every deed you do, with each word you speak, never reckoning the good and ill opinion of people to be of any account or importance.[997]

### *3. Because Faith is* Taṣdīq, *Imitation is Infidelity*

According to Shabistarī, faith is more than an intellectual precept, mental construct, or theological dogma; it is a condition of being. Living faith springs from mystic vision, not from the dogmas and articles of a catechism. Faith is nothing less than its own actualization, comments Lāhījī on Shabistarī's verses 962, 963 and 964 above. Such a dynamic, *engagé* approach to faith demands constant opposition to the poetic and mystic vision's perpetual enemy, egotism.

> As long as the human soul has not realized the degree of serenity and peace and become controlled by its spiritual

> faculties, it is constantly being prodded to act improperly by the passions' wickedness, guile and temptation. Thus, he [Shabistarī] states that you should regain your faith anew every moment. The reason for this is that the lower soul *(nafs)* casts an evil act or thought into your imagination every moment, striving to cast you down into the abyss of pride, hypocrisy and egotism. Each moment thus demands that you overcome and repulse such evil thoughts and false conceptions, constantly regaining your faith afresh and reaffirming your belief, never imagining yourself safe from the lower soul's deceit, even for a second. Every fantasy which oppresses you—driving you to infidelity and being veiled *(kufr wiḥtijāb)*, casting you down from your sublime station into the deepest pits of passions and carnal nature—must be met and opposed with a fresh faith, lest the citadel of your religion to be destroyed by lasso of lust and the sabre of wrath. [For] . . . the soul is an infidel utterly devoid of faith, who, disguised as a Muslim, has turned thousands of other people into infidels, heretics and hypocrites; its artifice and guile is beyond all bound and measure . . . it is ceaseless in its subterfuge and disingenuity . . . [998]

Interpreting Shabistarī's mystical theology, Lāhījī provides a uniquely Akbarian perspective on the concept of *taṣdīq*. Commenting on couplet 964, he emphasizes the importance of faith's interiorization:

> 'Faith' may be defined as verification *(taṣdīq)* of the Prophet's (– Peace be upon him) mission. It is divided into numerous degrees. One degree is faith in the divine Essence and Attributes. According to Sufis endowed with gnostic realization *(muḥaqqiqān)*, the divine attributes are infinite in number; the divine Essence has, relative to each attribute and relationship,[999] a different manifestation and special theophany. Generally speaking, the divine theophanies are infinite and faith is required and fundamental in respect to all of these diverse divine theophanies.
>
> Thus Faith has a great many, if not an infinite, amount of degrees of differentiation, on each level of which a 'hidden polytheism' or 'tendency to associate others with God *(shirk-i khafī)*' exists. Some of this hidden polytheism relates to the

> divine actions, some to the divine attributes and some to the divine Essence. Thus, the poet enjoins you to renew your faith in God every moment, meaning that the mystic wayfarer should not remain in the same spiritual waystation for more than two hours at a time. Since the Known (God) is Infinite, likewise divine gnosis is infinite. Hence, every moment you must ascend from the spiritual station where you abide to a more advanced one and renew your faith and 'ascertainment-in-the-heart-of-the-Truth' *(taṣdīq)* through this process. The saying of the Prophet, "Such a darkness covers my heart that I turn and repent to God seventy times a day,"[1000] alludes to this.[1001]

The broadminded tolerance of the Sufi vision of faith is evident in Lāhījī's exegesis on couplets 964 and 965. In fact, the following passage reads as much like an Islamic hermeneutical exegesis on William Blake's *Everlasting Gospel* as a commentary on Shabistarī's couplet 965:

> As we have explained in the above passages,[1002] faith is increased by such objects as the 'idol', 'cincture' and the 'Christian faith'. In this sense, one of the principles of real divine unity *(tawḥīd-i ḥaqīqī)* is that the idol is a theophanic manifestation of divine unity. According to the same doctrine, the cincture refers to the contract of service, obedience and divine worship which one [as a true Sufi] vows to observe, while the 'Christian faith' is symbolic of divesting oneself of materiality *(tajrīd)*, severing one's attachments, and becoming liberated from the restraints, conventions, customs and imitative forms of religious devotion. Insofar as from these things [i.e. 'idol', 'cincture' and the 'Christian faith'] true faith is born—*God forbid that this 'infidelity', which stimulates an increase of faith, should be conceived of as heresy or infidelity per se! On the contrary, it is the most perfect form of Islam, although it appear in the guise of infidelity.*[1003]

### *4. Selflessness: the Truth of Faith and Reality of Infidelity*

At this juncture, one may well recall 'Ayn al-Quḍāt's exclamation that he praised neither faith nor infidelity since both are veils. Since faith is unattainable except by voluntary disgrace, and disgrace has the 'fragrance' of infidelity, is it not better for the sincerely committed devotee to embrace infidelity and disgrace rather than assume the outward garb of cleric, jurisconsult or Sufi? Referring to this dilemma, we should recall Lāhījī's remark that "all perversion in religion and error in belief derives from the notion of 'honour' *(nāmūs)* and for those who hold high positions and possess elevated status in society, no thicker veil than this 'honour' exists, such that, in their eyes, it is easier to renounce the world than to renounce their [false notion of] 'honour', since 'the last thing which leaves the head of the sincere man is the love of high position'."[1004] It follows from this that a faith which is but a facade erected to maintain the ego's false dignity is worse than blasphemy. It is for this reason that the greatest challenge to the existentialization of the Islamic faith through *taṣdīq* ("the interiorization and implementation of the truth in dynamic sincerity") is, as Shabistarī terms it (last couplet: 967), to become "inimitable in infidelity." Lāhījī elucidates this subtle doctrine as follows:

> Becoming "inimitable in infidelity" has two meanings. The first refers collectively to all the previously mentioned types of so-called 'infidelity': "idolatry," "donning the cincture," "practice of the Christian faith," "ringing the church bell," "being *ḥanīfī* and monk," "becoming a frequenter of taverns," and seeking after wine, candles and beautiful women *(shirāb, sham', shāhid)*. That is to say, if the mystic wayfarer who has attained union with God has not realized these qualities of perfection, he remains as yet imperfect in regard to being able to grant guidance and counsel [to other Sufis on the *via mystica*].
>
> The second meaning of becoming "inimitable in infidelity" alludes to the 'truth behind infidelity' or the 'real infidelity' *(kufr-i ḥaqīqī)*, in this context, the term 'infidelity' *(kufr)* denoting the 'concealing' or 'covering-over' *(kufr)* of multiplicity *(kithrat)* in divine Unity *(waḥdat)*. In this act one should be distinctive and individually inimitable, with the sense that one obliterates and annihilates all the formal impositions and plurality of phenomenally existent things—even one's own being and personal 'determined form' *(ta'ayyun;* i.e. one's illusory individuality or character)—in the ocean of the divine Exclusive Oneness *(aḥadiyyat)* of the divine Essence. At this point one realizes subsistence in God's Eternal Being and

actually attains to the 'illumination of the divine singularity *(tajallī-yi fardiyyat),* thus becoming one with Oneness, and 'individually inimitable and unique in 'infidelity'.[1005]

## Conclusion

*The Vision of Christ that thou dost see*
*Is my Vision's Greatest Enemy.*
*Thine is a friend of All Mankind*
*Mine speaks in parables to the Blind.*
*Thine loves the same world that mine hates,*
*Thy Heaven doors are my Hell Gates.*
*Both read the Bible day & night,*
*But thou read'st black where I read white.*

William Blake[1006]

From the above study of Shabistarī's concept of 'real infidelity', several conclusions come to mind. The first is that the Islamic conception of faith as espoused in both the Persian 'ecstatic' Ḥallājian School and the Akbarian tradition was radically anti-monolithic. It was, in fact, extremely liberal in outlook, based on a conception of prophecy and revelation understood not by the dogmatic theological analysis practised by the Kalām specialists but through a Ghazālian 'unveiling' *'ilm al-mukashafa* and sapiential 'taste' *(dhawq).*

Furthermore, it cannot be overemphasized that the Shabistarian conception of *kufr-i ḥaqīqī* has profoundly moralistic overtones; his intention was obviously not to advocate—nor even to flirt with—an antinominian view of Islam. His use of *kufriyyāt* symbolism stems from his own mystical realization, a realization grounded in the spiritual disciplines *(sulūk)* of Islamic Sufism. Through the ritual devotions of the *sharī'a,* by slowly traversing the psycho-spiritual stages *(maqāmāt)* of the Path, integrating "proofs of Reason, verses of the Koran, with the taste of Vision,[1007] into a highly sophisicated contemplative discipline, the Sufi finally experiences the selfless rapture and gnosis of 'real infidelity'. Even if all the rulings of the Law exclusively depend upon the subsistence of the 'self',[1008] this supreme realization of *kufr-i ḥaqīqī* is not to be used as an excuse for overriding the dictates of the *sharī'a,* asserts Shabistarī:

However, beware, beware, if of any 'I-ness'
You are aware, if still with self you're prepossessed –
The outer word and sense of the *sharī'at* you profess.
Indulgence in speech is granted to initiates-in-heart
In three spiritual states only: Intoxication,
Lovelorn Infatuation – or else – Annihilation.
Only those mystics intimate with these three States
Initiate – realize words' application,
Will know their ultimate signification.
Since to you ecstasy is alien, rapture foreign
Beware, lest you, by dumb mimicry of gnostics, become
In ignorant pretense an infidel as well.[1009]

The key role played by the Sufis in their advocation of what Muhsin Mahdi has called the "jurisprudence of the heart;"[1010] their fearless advocation of a purely spiritual ethics to counterbalance the dogmatic use of religious faith as a tool of party politics, seeking first to cast the mote out of their own eye (that is, the process of 'spiritual *takfīr*') and cleanse their own hearts of infidelity, rather than engage in the anathematization of fellow believers, also cannot be over-emphasized. The value of the interiorized perspective *vis-à-vis* a mere verbal belief or 'profession of faith' is immediately evident: to him faith was primarily a moral condition and secondarily a social phenomenon; a condition to be actualized and personally introspected rather than to be idealized and marketed abroad as a public commodity. According to our author, *religion is consciousness.*[1011] The very *raison d'être* of faith was the pursuit of the 'Path of the Heart', the traveling of which caused the devotee, in the words of the Koranic command, to "contemplate God's portents 'in yourselves' (LI 21).[1012] Any experience of 'religion' in absence of genuine inward realization and a higher 'heart-consciousness' was in his view merely a kind of spiritual solecism and *non sequitur*.[1013]

This is because all the 'proofs' of faith can only be established by the "interiorization and implementation of the truth in dynamic sincerity" in the heart, that is to say, by heart-conviction and verification *(taṣdīq)*. Religious faith, therefore, is far too subtle an issue to be determined by mere legal examination, for like love, its external form "cannot be comprehended but only apprehended;"[1014] its reality can only be expressed in paradoxes and by negation instead of affirmation. There seems to be an attempt in the passages from the *Garden of Mystery* discussed above to dissolve the tension which operates at the literal level between antinominian *kufriyyat* and nomocentric Islam by elevating the debate to the sphere of a set of transcendent spiritual symbols. Whereas on the literal level (that of the 'infidel selfhood'), there are beliefs but no Faith, truths but no Truth, facts but no Reality, confessional *islām* but no realized *īmān,* on the symbolic level, both faith and infidelity are beheld in embrace. Of course, as Lāhījī reminds us, the inspired libertine inhabiting the Tavern of Ruin, having experienced *fanā'* of his 'heretical selfhood', is deprived of all individual delimitation, and thus "of course, no legal ruling regarding his 'infidelity' or 'faith' may be passed." To paraphrase Tennyson:

> For nothing worthy proving can be proven,
> Nor yet disproven: wherefore thou be wise,
> Cleave ever to the sunnier side of doubt,
> And cling to Faith beyond the forms of Faith![1015]

—the Sufi gnostic "integrates within himself both faith and infidelity," this integration being conditioned by the clause that he also "makes the Law his cloak, the Path his undershirt." Such a mystic is literally 'beyond faith and infidelity'. Can this be one meaning of Rūzbihān's gloss of Ḥallāj cited above: "In respect to the Reality of divine Unity, infidelity is faith, because it is a confession to agnosis, and agnosis is the supreme truth of truths when it comes to created being. . . . Only after realization of 'gnosis' does one attain to bewilderment in 'agnosis'. So faith is the infidelity of infidelity and the infidelity of infidelity is faith." —?

Shabistarī's direct attempt to integrate Christian doctrine into Islam by expounding the esoteric symbolic significance of the Sufi poetic imagery relating to such non-Islamic faiths (as advanced in chapter III, pp. 86-92) also demonstrates considerable ecumenical awareness far beyond his day and age, making him one of the founders of comparative religion. Today, when the homologous outlook of mediæval traditional thought has been ruptured by the appearance and encounter of other spiritual traditions upon our own religious horizons,[1016] we can no longer afford to ignore the Sufi contribution to the faith of Islam—particularly when this mystical faith also embraces what appears as 'infidelity/heresy', bridging, in Marshall Hodgson's words, "the gap between Muslim and infidel."[1017]

The radical interiorization of the concept of faith by propositions such as *īmān=taṣdīq / kufr=taqlīd* (advanced by Shabistarī) also demonstrates an extraordinary depth of vision and highly refined psychological sophisication, and offers a useful antidote to the commonly held Western view of Islam as a religion of "fanaticism."[1018] The most important ramification of such insights, to my mind, is not only the obvious psychological one (—that is, that the 'Infidel Selfhood' is the only *de facto* 'heretic') but also a socio-religious one: that the doctrine of 'infidelity's reality', on the basis of this preliminary study, appears as the 'truth', the 'heart-core' 'essence' and inner identity of the Islamic practice of faith. Shabistarī considered himself, and is still considered by his countrymen, as a Muslim in the fullest sense of the word,[1019] that is, squarely within the central historical current of traditional Islam.[1020] The Islamic spiritual tradition proves, by its inclusion, acceptance, and even avocation, of doctrines of such latitude, its perennial ability to universalize its vision beyond the dogmatism of its nomocentric forms.

According to Shabistarī, without faith in this true infidelity, Islam as a conventional faith will ever act as a veil for its inspired source. Whether his creative understanding of religion—this personal *taṣdīq* and reinterpretation of faith based on 'taste' *(dhawq)* and vision *(shuhūd)* be subjected to the terrorist tactics of 'interrogation of personal beliefs' or *isti'rād,* as advocated by the extremist seventh-century Azraqites, or distorted by the fundamentalist myth of a "fideist minimalism . . . devoid of epistemic content, whose utterance is consumed immediately by its audience,"[1021] the form of Islamic 'faith' popular among the early Ḥanbalite theologians, or, as today, become the pawn of fanatical (so-called) 'hezbollahism' which uses Islam as a brand name and a slogan to promulgate its own personal ideologies and agendas—I think ultimately matters little. Religious fanaticism in all its diverse forms signals but one thing: the imposition of an ideology based on servile imitation *(taqlīd)* by a clerical hierarchy according to whom religion is not conscious servanthood to the Supreme Being, but rather a political matter of rendering blind obedience and unquestioning partisan support to unassimilated (=not interiorized) doctrines[1022]—conventional dogmas which appear, on close examination, to express an extremely narrow-minded interpretation of Islam's many-faceted intellectual, artistic, literary and philosophical traditions. Just like Christianity and Buddhism, Islam has always encompassed and assimilated a bewildering amount of forms,[1023] forms which, as shown above, need not be considered necessarily antithetical. The very fact that a doctrine such as *kufr-i ḥaqīqī* was espoused by—even accepted as an integral part of the piety of—medieval Persian Sufism, itself demonstrates the extreme religious tolerance of traditional Islam, a tolerance which modern Islam is going to have to reinstate if it wishes to 'keep the faith' or indeed, to survive in a world of constantly increasing cultural and religious diversity.

## Notes

876 See his study in EI[2,] s.v. "Īmān," pp. 1170-74.

877 See his *The Concept of Belief in Islamic theology: a semantic analysis of* īmān *and* islām (Tokyo: Keio Institute of Cultural and Linguistic Studies 1965).

878 See his "Early Sunni Doctrine concerning Faith as reflected in the *Kitāb al-Īmān* of Abū 'Ubayd al-Qāsim b. Sallam (d. 224/839)," in *Studia Islamica,* XXXII (1970), pp. 233-54.

879 See his *Faith and Practice of Islam: Three Thirteenth Century Sufi Texts* (Albany: SUNY 1992); and "Imān" in Sachiko Murata and William C. Chittick, *The Vision of Islam* (New York: Paragon House 1994), pp. 43-131.

880 See his *Faith and Belief,* (New Jersey: Princeton University Press 1979), chap. 3.; and "Faith as *Taṣdīq,*" in Parviz Morewedge (ed.), *Islamic Philosophical Theology* (Albany: SUNY 1979).

881 Cited by Chittick, *Faith and Practice,* p. 6.

882 EI[2,] s.v. "Īmān," p. 1173. On the development of the doctrine of *taqlīd* in Islam, see George Makdisi, "The Fathers and Doctors in Christianity and Islam," in Maria Eva Subtelny (ed.), *Annemarie Schimmel Festschrift,* pp. 179-83.

883 Cf. *Iḥyā',* i, 107-8.

884 Eric L. Ormsby, "The Taste of Truth: The Structure of Experience in Al-Ghazālī's *al-Munqidh min al-ḍalāl,*" p. 143.

885 EI[2,] s.v. "Īmān," p. 1173.

886 On which, also see W.C. Chittick, "Mysticism Versus Philosophy . . . ," pp. 87-104.

887 *Iḥyā'* 1:15. Cited by Chittick, *Faith and Practice,* p. 19; also translated by N.A. Faris, *The Book of Knowledge, Being a Translation with Notes of the Kitāb al-'Ilm of al-Ghazzālī's Iḥyā' 'Ulūm al-Dīn* (Lahore: Sh. Muhammad Ashraf 1962), pp. 46-8.

888 See N.A. Faris, *The Book of Knowledge,* p. 47; also N. Heer, "Abū Ḥāmid al-Ghazālī's Esoteric Exegesis of the Koran," in Leonard Lewisohn (ed.) *Classical Persian Sufism: from its Origins to Rūmī,* p. 247.

889 As Victor Danner comments: "Ghazālī has very severe reprimands for those pharisaical Muslims who would reduce Islam to the external form of the Law and banish the Ṣūfī Path altogether from the revealed

message." *The Islamic Tradition,* p. 108.

890 For further elaboration of which, see Ormsby, "The Taste of Truth," p. 150.

891 Chtttick, *Faith and Practice,* p. 3. The citation from Ghazālī is from N.H. Faris (trans.), *op. cit.,* p. 42. For an alternate translation of the same passage, see Muhtar Holland (trans.) *al-Ghazālī: Inner Dimensions of Islamic Worship,* (Leicester: Islamic Foundation 1992), p. 37.

892 *Prophecy in Islam: Philosophy and Orthodoxy* (Chicago: University of Chicago Press 1958), p. 64.

893 "The Bedouins say, 'We have faith.' Say [O Muhammad]; 'You do not have faith;rather, say, 'We have submitted;' for faith has not yet entered yours hearts."

894 "Islam and Christianity Between Tolerance and Acceptance," *Islam & Chritian-Muslim Relations,* II/2 (1991), p. 173.

895 "Faith as *Taṣdīq,*" p. 110.

896 *Kashf al-Maḥjūb,* trans. R.A. Nicholson, p. 286.

897 Smith, "Faith as *Taṣdīq,*" p. 106.

898 *Ibid.,* p. 110.

899 *Ibid.,* p. 111.

900 *Ibid.* Cf. Hujwīrī's usage of *giravīdan,* in *op. cit.,* p. 289.

901 Smith, *Faith and Belief,* p. 39.

902 Chittick, *Faith and Practice,* p. 6. Also, see above, chap. VI, pp. 178-9.

903 See A. Guillaumont, "Les sens des noms du coeur dans l'antiquité," *Le Coeur – Études Carmélitaines,* (Bruges: Desclée de Brouwer 1950), pp. 41-81.

904 Smith, *Faith and Belief,* p. 49.

905 Such as the *ḥadīth:* "Submission is public and faith is in the heart," when, pointing to his breast, the Prophet said, "Fear of God is here, fear of God is here." Cited by Carl Ernst in his *Words of Ecstasy in Sufism,* (Albany: SUNY 1985), p. 56.

906 *Al-Fiṣal fi al-milal wa al-ahwā' wa-al-niḥal,* (Cairo 1317-21), vol. 2, part 4, p. 189. Cited by Izutsu, *The Concept of Belief,* p. 13.

907 *Ibid.*

908 Izutsu, *The Concept of Belief,* p. 17.

909 *Ibid.,* pp. 17,19.

910 Ernst, *Words of Ecstasy,* p. 57.

911 *Ibid.*

912 *Ibid.,* pp. 66-67.

913 For a good description of the inquisitions conducted by legalists against Sufis, see Louis Massignon's *The Passion of al-Ḥallāj: Mystic and Martyr of Islam,* trans. H. Mason (Princeton: 1982), I, pp. 379-80.

914 Izutsu, *The Concept of Belief,* p. 25.

915 *Ibid.* From Ghazālī's *Fayṣal al-tafriqa bayna al-īslām wa-al-zandaqa,* ed. Sulayman Dunyā, (Cairo 1961), p. 175. This work has been translated into English by R.J. McCarthy as "Appendix 1" in his *Freedom and Fufillment* (Boston: G.K. Hall & co. 1980). For further discussion of Ghazālī's theory of *Takfīr* see Bello, *op. cit.,* pp. 9, 43.

916 Izutsu, *The Concept of Belief,* p. 26.

917 Izutsu, *The Concept of Belief,* p. 29.

918 On the place of ‘Ayn al-Quḍāt in classical Sufism see Leonard Lewisohn, “In Quest of Annihilation: Imaginalization and Mystical Death in the *Tamhīdāt* of ‘Ayn al-Quḍāt Hamadhānī” in Leonard Lewisohn (ed.) *Classical Persian Sufism: from its Origins to Rūmī* , pp. 285-336; also cf. A.J. Arberry’s introduction to his (trans.) *A Sufi Martyr: The* Apologia *of ‘Ain al-Quḍāt al-Hamadhānī* (London: Allen & Unwin 1969); Hamid Dabashi, *‘Ayn al-Quḍāt al-Hamadhānī: An Intellectual Portrait* (London: Curzon Press, forthcoming).

919 For instance, Ghazālī’s approach to the problem of ‘taxing with infidelity’ was coupled with a complicated attitude to legal issues such as consensus of the Muslim community *(ijmā‘)* and interpretation of the Koran *(ta’wīl)* such that he hesitated to charge any Muslim with infidelity except on matters pertaining to clear unbelief in the fundamentals of faith. On this, cf. Iysa Bello, *The Medieval Islamic Controversy between Philosophy and Orthodoxy:* Ijmā’ *and* ta’wīl *in the Conflict between Al-Ghazālī and Ibn Rushd* (Leiden: E.J. Brill 1989), pp. 59-61.

920 *Concept of Belief,* p. 28; for further discussion of Ghazālī’s views on infidelity, see Bello, *op. cit.*, pp. 59-64; on the relation of *kufr* to *takdhīb,* see Peter Antes, “Relations with Unbelievers in Islamic Theology,” in A. Schimmel and A. Falaturi, *We Believe in One God: The Experience of God in Christianity and Islam* (London: Burns & Oates 1979), pp. 104-06.

921 As H. Landolt argues, “Two Types of Mystical Thought in Muslim Iran: An Essay on Suhrawardī Shaykh al-Ishrāq and ‘Aynulquzāt-i Hamadhānī,” *The Muslim World,* vol. 68 (1979), p. 192.

922 ‘Ayn al-Quḍāt Hamadhānī, *Tamhīdāt,* edited with an introduction by Afif Osseiran (Tehran 1962), p. 339, no. 449.

923 *Ibid.,* p. 25.

924 On the problem of understanding the ‘real’ Ghazālī amidst the confusing views presented in his various treatises, see Fazlur Rahman, *Prophecy in Islam: Philosophy and Orthodoxy*, pp. 94-99 and H. Landolt’s study: “Ghazālī and ‘Religionswissenschaft’,” *Asiatische Studien,* XLV/1 (1991), pp. 19-72.

925 A special study to the related phenomenon of “accentuation of the interior dimension of the *Sharī‘a* over the exterior” has been made by Javad Nurbakhsh, “The Key Features of Early Persian Sufism,” in Leonard Lewisohn (ed.) *Classical Persian Sufism,* pp. xxxiv-xxxix.

926 Smith, *Faith and Belief,* pp. 50, 202n.40; 1. Also, cf. Hodgson, *The Venture of Islam,* II, p. 220. For a preliminary study of the tolerant vision of Persian Sufism, see my “Overview” to L. Lewisohn (ed.) *The Legacy of Mediæval Persian Sufism* (London: KNP 1992), pp. 38-41.

927 For further exposition of this concept, see L. Lewisohn, “The Transcendent Unity of Polytheism and Monotheism in the Sufism of Shabistari,” pp. 379-406; F. Schoun, *The Transcendent Unity of Religions* (London 1984).

928 “We are like compasses,” sings Sa‘dī ecumenically “—one foot set firm in the Sharī‘at; the other voyages throughout all seventy-two communities *(millat).*” Smith’s observation *(The Meaning and End of Religion,* London: SPCK 1963; p, 113) that “there are even passages [in the Koran]

where the exclusivism of boundaries or religious communities is attacked in the name of a direct and uninstitutional moralist piety," also underlines the scriptural origin of such cosmopolitan piety.

929 *Tamhīdāt,* pp. 304-05, no. 401. Granted that the term *madhhab* usually had an intra-Islamic significance as 'sect, teaching', referring in particular to the four Sunni legal schools, the Sufis had long since resisted subsuming their way under that label (as Carl Ernst, *Words of Ecstasy,* pp. 123-25, argues). In this passage, 'Ayn al-Quḍāt clearly stretches the meaning of the term to include the teachings of other seekers of God in other religions as constituting alternative soteriological 'spaces'; discussing, in fact, a few lines on in the same passage, the views of the Jews, Christians and Magians. It should also be underlined that the Judge of Hamadān in his legal capacity as a jurist professed himself a perfectly autonomous *mujtahid* who followed the 'religion of love' whose partisans "do not follow the *madhhab* of Abū Ḥanīfa or Shāfi'ī or anyone else; rather, they follow the religion of love and the religion of God *(madhhab-i 'ishq wa madhhab-i khudā." (Tamhīdāt,* pp. 115-16). The doctrine of the 'religion of love' is found both in Rūmī (cf. *Mathnawī,* II, 1770) and Ibn 'Arabī *(Tarjumān,* xi: 15) as well as Shabistarī.

Likewise, in his interpretation of Shabistarī's verse cited above (chap. III, p. 76; MAS, p. 90, v. 956), Lāhījī interprets the meaning of *madhhab* to include "a religious way *(ṭarīq)*" of followers of other religions (effectively extended to the Jews and Christians), who are treated as people of the Book. *(Mafātīḥ al-i'jāz,* ed. Khāliqī/Karbāsī, p. 577: 10-11), although elsewhere *(ibid.,* p. 197) *madhhab* seems to convey the usual exclusively intra-Islamic connotation.

930 Smith, "Faith as *Taṣdīq,"* p. 114-15n. 1; Carl Ernst's *Words of Ecstasy in Sufism* has, in fact, presented us with such a preliminary study of the history of the mystical dimensions of faith. The present essay attempts to focus on the transcendental ecumenism expressed in the doctrine of 'real infidelity' in Shabistarī, who was omitted from (being outside the chronological focus of) Ernst's study.

931 Ernst, *Words of Ecstasy,* p. 61.

932 "Any non-Islamic religion can serve this purpose," Bausani adds, "true, historical Zoroastrianism has nothing to do with it and it is not necessary to suppose a direct continuation. The constellation of concepts that could be called the *kufr*-motif also included Iranian elements, but it is present also in Arabic literature of that time and is strongly connected with the Malāmatī school of Sufism." "Muḥammad or Darius? The Elements and Basis of Iranian Culture," in (Ed.) S. Vyronis Jr., *Islam and Cultural Change in the Middle Ages* (Wiesbaden 1975), p. 53.

933 *Tamhīdāt,* p. 123. See also, Ernst, *op. cit.* ,p. 84.

934 Annemarie Schimmel, *As Through a Veil,* p. 62.

935 MAS, *Sa'ādat-nāma,* v. 1125; vv. 1170-71, 1126-29.

936 *Ḥadīqat al-ḥaqīqat,* ed. Mudarris Riḍawī (Tehran 1950), p. 4.

937 "The source of all activity is one, but everywhere displays new colors and is called by a different name . . . – Only if the secret of God created you and what you do (Koran XXXVII: 96) were to wink its eye at them, would they ever come to know perforce that all power, all activity is

ours only so much as HE is us." – *Fakhruddin 'Iraqi: Divine Flashes,* trans. W.C. Chittick/P.L. Wilson, pp. 103-04. See also W.C. Chittick, *The Sufi Path of Knowledge,* p. 208. For a discussion of the role of this doctrine in early Persian Sufism, see M. Abdul Haqq Ansari, "The Doctrine of One Actor: Junayd's View of *Tawḥīd," The Muslim World* (1983), pp. 33-56.

938 MAS, *Gulshan-i rāz,* p. 103, v. 879.

939 Lāhījī, *Mafātīḥ al-i'jāz,* ed. Khāliqī/Karbāsī, p. 543.

940 "The *Qalandariyyāt* in Persian Mystical Poetry, from Sanā'ī Onwards," in Lewisohn (ed.), *The Legacy of Mediæval Persian Sufism,* p. 85.

941 *Awrād al-aḥbāb wa fuṣūṣ al-ādāb,* p. 249.

942 For a preliminary study of which see Ernst, *op. cit.,* pp. 63-72.

943 Rūzbihān, *Sharḥ-i shaṭḥiyyāt,* edited by Henry Corbin (Tehran: Institut Francais d'Iranologie 1981), pp. 394-96. For a slightly different translation of these passages see Ernst, *op. cit.,* pp. 64, 92. Prof. Ernst is preparing a full translation (based on the original Arabic text) of Rūzbihān's commentary on Ḥallāj's sayings (Carl Ernst, letter to the author, Dec. 9, 1994).

944 This particular letter appears to have been a dominant inspiration to the development of the genre of *kufr*-prose and poetry in Persian for some seven centuries following his death. For example, it is cited by Abū'l-Mafākhir Bākharzī (d. 736/1336) in his commentary (translated below, pp. 285-6) on Sufi terminology in the *Awrād al-aḥbāb.*

945 *Akhbār al-Ḥallāj: Recueil d'oraisons et d'exhortations du martyr mystique de l'Islam,* edited by L, Massignon and P. Kraus, Études Musulmanes, IV, (Paris 1955), no. 41. The translation is by C. Ernst, *Words of Ecstasy*, p. 65.

946 "Faith as *Taṣdīq,"* p. 109, where Smith cites Koran II 146, VI 20, XXVII 14 and IX 74 in support of his thesis.

947 Mustansir Mir, *Dictionary of Qur'ānic Terms and Concepts,* (London/New York: Garland Publishing company 1987), p. 52; s.v. Disbelief.

948 *A Comparative Study of the Key Philosophical Concepts in Sufism,* p. 29.

949 *Faith and Practice of Islam,* p. 6; the same translation policy is also adopted in his (with S. Murata) *The Vision of Islam,* p. 42.

950 For examples of which, see Ibn 'Arabī's *Futūḥāt,* (Būlāq 1329 A.H.), I, p. 415; II, p. 511; III, pp. 27, 92, 406.

951 Here Bākharzī wishes to imply that the original etymological connotation of *yakfur* 'whosoever rejects' also conveys the idea of suppressing the self and 'blindfolding the idol of the self' and that this notion underlies the Koranic conception of 'one who rejects false deities', the worst 'false deity' being the ego.

952 Koran, II: 256.

953 Or, alternately: "The hiddenness of the hidden becomes visible and the personal entity of the determined prototypes and essences of Being concealed . . . "

954 In the terminology of Ibn 'Arabī, *'ayn-i a'yān* refers to the temporal essence of the determined forms or prototypes of being.

955 *Awrād al-aḥbāb wa fuṣūṣ al-ādāb,* ed. Īrāj Afshār, only vol. 2, pp. 252-3.

956 *Tamhīdāt,* p. 118-211 is devoted to this topos. On similar symbology used by Sanā'ī and 'Aṭṭār, see J. Nurbakhsh, *Sufi Symbolism I,* trans. L. Lewisohn, s.v. 'visage' and 'tress'.

957 *Dīwān-i Muḥammad Shīrīn Maghribī,* ghazal 146: 7.

958 MAS, *Gulshan-i rāz,* p. 99.

959 *Mafātīḥ al-'ijāz,* ed. Khāliqī & Karbāsī, p. 489.

960 *Ibid.*

961 MAS, p. 199, *Sa'adatnāma,* pp. vv. 932-33.

962 MAS, *Gulshan-i rāz,* p. 103, v. 864.

963 *Mafātīḥ al-a'jāz fī sharḥ-i Gulshan-i rāz,* edited by K. Samī'ī, p. 639; Lāhījī, *Mafātīḥ al-i'jāz,* ed. Khāliqī/Karbāsī, p. 537. The poem at the end of the paragraph is from Maghribī's *Dīwān* (ed. Lewisohn), p. 29, XI: 6. It is interesting to discover that some recent historians of religion have drawn conclusions identical to those formulated by our mediæval Persian Sufis. Thus, W.C. Smith propounds that "actually, no one in the history of man has ever worshipped an idol. Men have worshipped God – or something – in the form of idols. That is what idols are for. Yet that is quite a different thing. 'The heathen in his blindness', sang the nineteenth-century hymn, 'bows down to wood and stone'. Yet it is not the heathen who is blind, but the observer." *The Meaning and End of Religion,* pp. 140-41. For similar comments on idolatry's relativism, cf. Rex Ambler, "Idolatry and Religious Faith," in Dan Cohn-Sherbok (ed.), *Islam in a World of Diverse Faiths* (London: Macmillan 1991), pp. 33-40.

964 The first hemistich contains a reference to the famous triad: *Sharī'a, Ṭarīqa,* and *Ḥaqīqa,* based on the Prophet's *ḥadīth:* "The *Sharī'a* is my discourse, the *Ṭarīqa* is my action, and the *Ḥaqīqa* is my spiritual state." See Javad Nurbakhsh, *Traditions of the Prophet,* vol. I, translated by L. Lewisohn, p. 64.

965 MAS, *Gulshan-i rāz,* p. 81, vv. 349-50.

966 *Mafātīḥ al-i'jāz,* ed. Khāliqī/Karbāsī, p. 248.

967 *Ibid.,* pp. 246-47.

968 This doctrine is based, in turn, upon Ibn 'Arabī's doctrine of perfect gnostic who himself has become a *jam' al-aḍdād.* See *Futūḥāt,* III, p. 396: 19. Also cf. W.C. Chittick, *Imaginal Worlds: Ibn 'Arabī and the Problem of Religious Diversity*, pp. 62-4.

969 *Ibid.,* pp. pp. 248-49.

970 The same idea underlies Rūmī's theomonistic inclusivist vision, *Mathnawī,* III, 1259: "All differences, O essence of Being, between the Muslim believer, Magian and Jew, derive from their respective [religious] perspectives *(naẓargāh).*"

971 MAS, p. 103, vv. 879-882; cited above, pp. 70-71.

972 *Mafātīḥ al-a'jāz fī sharḥ-i Gulshan-i rāz,* edited by K. Samī'ī, pp. 642-3; *Mafātīḥ al-i'jāz,* ed. Khāliqī/Karbāsī, pp. 539-40. The poem is from Rūmī, *Mathnawī,* III: 4045.

973 See Shuja Alhaq, "The New World Order of Akbar the Great: Profile of a Mystic Ruler," *Sufi: A Journal of Sufism,* issues 22, 23 (1994). Part

2 of this article (issue 23) details the rites of initiation into the 'Divine Faith' which was espoused by Akbar. The following description of this Order by Dr. Alhaq *(Sufi,* issue 23, p. 25) clearly shows the influence of Shabistarī's thought: "Their 'Order' was called 'Divine Unity' *(tawḥīd-i ilāhī),* or the 'Divine Faith' *(dīn-i ilāhī).* Though open to anyone who wished to enter, a Muslim upon initiation was to pledge his allegiance to Reason and universal tolerance through the declaration that he was renouncing *Islām-i majāzī wa taqlīdī* (the formal figurative and traditional Islam inherited from his forefathers)." As can be seen below, the latter phrase clearly echoes Shabistarī's expression (v. 873) in the *Garden of Mystery.* See also Makhan Lal Roy Choudhury, *The* Din-i-Ilahi *or the Religion of Akbar* (New Dehli: Munshiram Manoharlal, 3rd Ed. 1985).

974 See S.A.A. Rizvi, *A History of Sufism in India* (New Dehli 1983), II, p. 144; also cf. Bikrama Jit Hasrt, *Dārā Shikūh: Life and Works* (New Dehli: Munshiram Manoharlal Publishers 1982), chapter 9.

975 MAS, *Gulshan-i rāz,* p. 103, v. 873.

976 See M.A.H. Ansari, *Sufism and Shari'ah* (London: The Islamic foundation 1986), p. 132.

977 *Mafātīḥ al-a'jāz,* ed. K. Samī'ī, p. 643; *Mafātīḥ al-i'jāz,* ed. Khāliqī/Karbāsī, pp. 540-1. My translation and interpretation of this verse is based on Lāhījī's *second* reading and interpretation of the Persian text as *agar kufr-i ḥaqīqī shud padīdār* (see *Mafātīḥ al-i'jāz,* ed. Khāliqī/Karbāsī, pp. 540-41) and *not* on the first reading, the interpretation of which is far from clear.

978 Cf. A. Bausani, "Religion under the Mongols," in J.A. Boyle (ed.), *The Cambirdge History of Iran,* V, pp. 538ff.

979 B. Manz, *The Rise and Rule of Tamerlane,* (Cambridge University Press 1989), p. 17.

980 Cf. John Hick, s.v. "Religious Pluralism," in M. Eliade (ed.), *Encyclopedia of Religion;* W.C. Smith, *Religious Diversity* (New York 1976) and Harold Coward, *Pluralism: Challenge to World Religions* (New York 1985); Ian Hamnett, *Religious Pluralism and Unbelief* (London: Routledge 1990); Mircea Eliade, "Methodological Remarks on the Study of Religious Symbolism," in M. Eliade and J.H. Kitagawa (eds.), *The History of Religions: Essays in Methodology* (Chicago: University Press 1959), p. 91.

981 For a study of Ibn 'Arabī's views on non-Islamic religions which were the dominant influence on Shabistarī doctrine in the passages cited immediately above and below, see W.C. Chittick, "Belief and Transformation: The Sufi Teachings of Ibn al-'Arabī," *The American Theosophist* 74/5 (1986), pp. 181-92; *idem., Imaginal Worlds,* chapters 8-10; Dom Sylvester Houédard, "Ibn 'Arabī's Contribution to the Wider Ecumenism," in S. Hirtenstein & M. Tiernan (eds.) *Muhyiddin Ibn 'Arabi: A Commemorative Volume*, pp. 291-306.

982 For a good exposition of this Akbarian doctrine, see Chittick, "Transcending the Gods of Belief," *The Sufi Path of Knowledge,* pp. 335-56.

983 *Gulshan-i rāz,* ed. Javad Nurbakhsh, pp. 61-2; MAS, *Gulshan-i rāz,* p. 103, vv. 863-80.

984 The discussion below, however, generally omits reference to doctrines relating to the 'unity-of-being' since the views of Lāhījī/Shabistarī on this notion have already been thoroughly discussed in my "The Transcendental Unity of Religions . . . ," in *The Legacy of Mediæval Persian Sufism,* pp. 394-96.

985 *Mafātīḥ al-a'jāz,* ed. K. Samī'ī, pp. 690-1; *Mafātīḥ al-i'jāz,* ed. Khāliqī/Karbāsī, p. 579.

986 *Mafātīḥ al-i'jāz,* ed. Khāliqī/Karbāsī, p. 525.

987 *Ibid.*

988 The term *rind,* "evokes a lively lucidity, a *savoir faire,* a refinement of action, a tact that goes all the way to compliance, a discretion in speech, which are neither craft nor hypocrisy, nor an affectation of mystery; but can, outside their context, become those very things, being reduced to insidous shifts, not to say dissembling and imposture. Again, the term denotes an interior liberty, an authentic detachment from the things of this world, suggesting the deliverance, in however small a measure, of the man who, shaking off his tawdry finery, lays himself open without sham, and naked to the mirror of the world; however, degenerated from its primitive context, this attitude can turn into one of exhibitionism, of posing and of mere libertinage." Daryush Shayegan, "The Visionary Topography of Hafiz," in *Temenos: A Journal Devoted to the Arts of the Imagination,* vol. 6 (1985), p. 224.

989 *Mafātīḥ al-i'jāz,* ed. Khāliqī/Karbāsī, p. 527.

990 See Leonard Lewisohn (ed.), *Dīwān-i Muḥammad Shīrīn Maghribī,* p. 298.

991 MAS, *Sa'ādat-nāma,* p. 287, lines 7-17.

992 MAS, *Gulshan-i rāz,* p. 107, vv. 977-79

993 See Sara Sviri, "Ḥakīm Tirmidhī and the *Malāmatī* Movement in Early Sufism," in L. Lewisohn (ed.) *Classical Persian Sufism: From Its Origins to Rumi,* pp. 583-613.

994 *Mafātīḥ al-a'jāz,* ed. K. Samī'ī, p. 691; *Mafātīḥ al-i'jāz,* ed. Khāliqī/Karbāsī, p. 579.

995 *Mafātīḥ al-a'jāz,* ed. K. Samī'ī, p. 695; *Mafātīḥ al-i'jāz,* ed. Khāliqī/Karbāsī, p. 582.

996 For a good discussion of these technical terms *(ṣidq, ikhlāṣ)* in the Sufi lexicon, see Javad Nurbakhsh, *Sufism V,* trans. T. Graham (London: KNP 1991) pp. 89-99.

997 *Mafātīḥ al-a'jāz,* ed. K. Samī'ī, p. 692; *Mafātīḥ al-i'jāz,* ed. Khāliqī/Karbāsī, pp. 579-80.

998 *Mafātīḥ al-a'jāz,* ed. K. Samī'ī, p. 692; *Mafātīḥ al-i'jāz,* ed. Khāliqī/Karbāsī, p. 580.

999 Lāhījī, like Shabistarī, was a follower of Ibn 'Arabī's doctrine that the divine Names belong to the world of possibility and therefore have no ultimate reality beyond being merely "relationships" *(nisbat)* between God and the world. Ibn 'Arabī replaces the term "divine attributes" *(ṣifat-i ḥaqq)* used by the scholastic theologians, with *nisba* or 'relationship'. He also considers the divine Names to be merely kinds of 'relationships' as well. For further exposition of this doctrine, see W.C. Chittick, *The Sufi Path of Knowledge,* p. 52.

1000 See Furūzānfar, *Aḥadīth-i Mathnawī*, no. 425.

1001 *Mafātīḥ al-a'jāz,* ed. K. Samī'ī, p. 693; *Mafātīḥ al-i'jāz,* ed. Khāliqī/Karbāsī, p. 581.

1002 Lāhījī 's reference is to his previous exegesis of certain verses in the *Garden of Mystery* concerning the symbolic meanings of these esoteric expressions. For an exposition of some of these expressions, see my "The Transcendental Unity of Polytheism . . . " in L. Lewisohn (ed.), *The Legacy of Mediæval Persian Sufism,* pp. 379-406.

1003 *Mafātīḥ al-'ijāz,* ed. Khāliqī & Karbāsī, p. 582.

1004 *Mafātīḥ al-a'jāz,* ed. Khāliqī & Karbāsī, p. 579; ed. K. Samī'ī, p. 691. The final clause is a *ḥadīth* (see Khāliqī & Karbāsī's annotations to this line, *Mafātīḥ al-a'jāz,* p. 702).

1005 *Mafātīḥ al-a'jāz,* ed. K. Samī'ī, p. 695-6; ed. Khāliqī & Karbāsī, pp. 583-4.

1006 *Blake: Complete Writings,* ed. G. Keynes, from "The Everlasting Gospel," p. 748.

1007 MAS, p. 152, *Sa'ādat-nāma,* v. 55; also cf. *Ḥaqq al-yaqīn,* MAS, p. 286.

1008 MAS, *Gulshan-i rāz,* p. 79, v. 303.

1009 MAS, *Gulshan-i rāz,* p. 79, vv. 731-34.

1010 "The Book and the Master as Poles of Cultural Change in Islam," in S. Vyronis Jr. (ed.), *Islam and Cultural Change in the Middle Ages* (Wiesbaden 1975), pp. 9-10.

1011 It may be more accurate to define such consciousness, which is actualized through *taṣdīq,* as "religiousness," rather than 'religion, as W.C. Smith in fact, argues. Religion, Smith observes, can be seen to consist of two components. The first is an historical culmulative tradition and the second is the personal faith of men and women. Maintaining that attention to the first component renders the term 'religion'—used either as a plural or with an article—false and meaningless, Smith proposes abandoning the term 'religion' in favour of 'religiousness' or 'piety': "God is the end of religion in the sense that once He appears vividly before us, in his depth and love and unrelenting truth all else dissolves, or at least the religious paraphernalia drop back into their due and mundane place, and the concept 'religion' is brought to an end." (*The Meaning and End of Religion,* p. 201).

1012 Cf. Ayn al-Quḍāt Hamadhānī, *Tamhīdāt,* p. 21.

1013 As W.C. Smith points out: "Faith lies beyond theology, in the hearts of men. Truth lies beyond faith in the heart of God . . . A theological statement cannot be baldly true in itself, but rather can become true in the life of persons, when it is interiorized and lived." *The Meaning and End of Religion,* pp. 185, 322n.14.

1014 W.C. Smith, *The Meaning and End of Religion,* p. 188.

1015 From "The Ancient Sage," Cited by J.M. Cohen (ed.), *The Rider Book of Mystical Verse* (London: Rider & Co. 1983), p. 137.

1016 Cf. S.H. Nasr, "Islam and the Encounter of Religions," *Sufi Essays,* (London: Allen & Unwin 1972), pp. 124-26.

1017 "Once a reasonably Sharī'ah-minded Sufism came to be accepted (more or less from the early twelfth century), all varieties of Sufism came to have a cloak, and in subsequent centuries even forms most alien to the Sharī'ah temper were given tacit recognition. . . . The whole body of the Muslim people came to be united in a common pattern of piety, which in its rich diversity could provide a home not only for mystics properly speaking, but for ascetics and for those whose chief interest was in esoteric speculation; for those who sought God through warm personalities. . . . Indeed, such piety tended to bridge the gap between Muslim and infidel." *The Venture of Islam,* II, pp. 218-22.

1018 See Thierry Hentsch, *Imagining the Middle East,* trans. F.A. Reed (Monréal: Black Rose 1992), p. 102ff.

1019 Shabistarī in the *Sa'adatnāma,* in MAS, vv.27-8, confesses his Sunnism by singling out Abū'l-Ḥasan al-Ash'arī (873-935) for special mention as the thinker "who laid firm the foundation of devotion to God, establishing the Sunni faith and supporting the catholic community of Islam *(jamā'at).*" See above, II, p. 33.

1020 That is, "traditional," in the sense intended by many contemporary Muslim scholars. In this regard, S.H. Nasr explains that "as far as Sufism or the Ṭarīqah is concerned, traditional Islam considers it as the inner dimension or heart of the Islamic revelation . . . The attitude of traditional Islam to Sufism reflects that which was current during the centuries prior to the advent of puritanical and modernist movements in the 12t/18th century." "What is Traditional Islam" in S.H. Nasr, *Traditional Islam in the Modern World* ( London: KPI 1987), p. 15.

1021 See Aziz al-Azmeh, "Orthodoxy and Ḥanbalite Fideism," *Arabica* (1988), p. 266.

1022 Demonstrating the liberal outlook of traditional Islamic piety, Hasan Askari persuasively repudiates this attitude. Commenting that the core of the *Sharī'a* is the *niyya,* the intention formed by the Muslim, he notes that such intention, "being the internal and central dimension of the *Sharī'a,* cannot possibly be controlled by the state . . . [an] 'Islamic state' is a contradiction in terms. It is something very difficult to notice, but as soon as one realises the nature of the tyranny of the abstraction, namely, the state, one sees . . . that 'islam' which is submission to God alone, cannot possibly be linked up with submission to an abstraction which is the source of all lordships of man over man. The prophetic dynamics in history is (sic.) a constant combat with what we now know as 'state', the source of the power of the finite over *man,* the addressee of the Infinite." "Religion and State," in Dan Cohn-Sherbok (ed.), *Islam in a World of Diverse Faiths,* pp. 181-2.

1023 As both Aziz al-Azmeh ("Orthodoxy and Ḥanbalite Fideism," p. 254) and Muhammad Talbi, ("A Community of Communities: the Right to be Different and the Ways of Harmony," in John Hick and Hasan Askari (eds.), *The Experience of Religious Diversity;* Hants, U.K.: Gower Publishing Co. 1985; pp. 66-90) have eloquently argued.

# BIBLIOGRAPHY


Abu Deeb, Kamal. *Al-Jurjani's Theory of Poetic Imagery*. Warminster: Ans & Phillips 1979.

Abu-Lughod, Janet L. *Before European Hegemony: The World-System A.D. 1250-1350*. New York/Oxford: OUP 1989.

Abu-Rabi', Ibrahim M. "Al-Azhar Sufism in Modern Egypt: The Sufi Thought." *Islamic Quarterly*. XXXII/4 (1988): 207-34.

Addas, Claude. *Quest for the Red Sulphur*. Translated from the French by Peter Kingsley. Cambridge, U.K.: Islamic Texts Society 1994.

Afshār, Īrāj. "Khānaqāh-hā-yi Yazd." *Sufi, Faṣl-nāma-yi Khānaqāh-i Ni'matu'llāhī*. VIII (1990): 11-14.

Algar, Hamid. "Some Observations on Religion in Safavid Persia." *Iranian Studies*. (1974): 287-93.

—— "Reflections of Ibn 'Arabī in the Early Naqshbandī Tradition." *Journal of the Muhyiddin Ibn 'Arabi Society*. X (1991): 45-66.

Alhaq, Shuja. "The New World Order of Akbar the Great: Profile of a Mystic Ruler." *Sufi: A Journal of Sufism*. XXII (1994): 22-28; XXIII (1994): 25-30.

Ansari, M.A.H. *Sufism and Shari'ah*. London: The Islamic Foundation 1986.

Anwār, Qāsim-i. *Kullīyāt-i Qāsim-i Anwār*. Edited by S. Nafīsī. Tehran: Kitāb-khāna Sanā'ī 1958.

Arberry, A.J. *Aspects of Islamic Civilization*. Ann Arbor: University of Michigan Press 1967.

—— "Orient Pearls At Random Strung." *Bulletin of the School of Oriental and African Studies* 2 (1948): 699-712.

—— *Classical Persian Literature*. 1994 ed. London: Curzon Press 1958.

—— *Fifty Poems of Ḥāfiẓ*. Cambridge: Cambridge University Press 1977.

Ardistānī, Jamāl al-Dīn. *Mirāt al-afrād*. Edited by Najīb Māyil Harawī. Tehran: Zawwār 1992.

Āriyān, Qamar. *Chihrah-yi Masīḥ dar adabiyāt-i fārsī*. Tehran: Intishārāt-i Mu'īn 1990.

Arjomand, Said Amir. *The Turban for the Crown*. Oxford: University Press 1988.

Aṭṭār, Farīd al-Dīn. *Ilahī-nāma*. Edited by H. Ritter. Tehran: Tūs 1980.

al-Azmeh, Aziz. "Orthodoxy and Ḥanbalite Fideism." *Arabica*. 1988.

'Ayn al-Quḍāt al-Hamadhānī. *A Sufi Martyr: The Apologia of 'Ain al-Quḍāt al-Hamadhānī*. Translated by A.J. Arberry. London: Allen & Unwin 1969.

al-Ḥakīm, Su'ād. *Al-Mu'jam al-ṣūfī*. Beirut: 1981.

Asad, Muhammad. *The Message of the Qur'ān*. Gibraltar: Dar al-Andalus 1980.

Aubin, Jean. "Le Patronage Culturel en Iran sous les Ilkhans: une Grande Famille de Yazd." *Le Monde Iranien et l'Islam*. III (1975): 107-118.

—— "La Propriété Foncière en Azerbaydjan sous les Mongols." *Le Monde iranien et l'Islam*. IV (1976-77): 79-132.

—— "Etudes Safavides. I. Sāh Ismā'īl et les Notables de l'Iraq Persan." *Journal of the Economic and Social History of the Orient* II (1959): 37-81.

Austin, R.J.W. *"The Spiritual Heart: Studies in the Māhiyat al-Qalb of Ibn al-'Arabī."* Ph.D. Thesis. London University 1965.

Awḥadī Maraghī. *Dīwān-i Awḥadī Maraghī*. Edited by Sa'īd Nafīsī. Tehran: Amīr Kabīr 1340 A.Hsh./1961.

Bākharzī, Abū'l-Mafākhir Yaḥyā. *Awrād al-aḥbāb wa Fuṣūṣ al-ādāb*. Vol. 2: *Fuṣūṣ al-ādāb*. Edited by Īrāj Afshār. Tehran: 1979.

Baqlī, Rūzbihān. *Le Jasmin des Fidèles d'Amour (Kitāb abhār al-'āshiqīn)*. Edited by H. Corbin and M. Mu'īn. Tehran: Anjuman-i Īrān-shināsī-yi Farānsa dar Tihrān 1981.

Baralt, Luce López. *San Juan de la Cruz y el Islam: Estudio sobre las filiaciones semíticas de su literatura mística*. Puerto Rico: El Colegio de México 1985.

Barthold, W. *Turkestan Down to the Mongol Invasion*. 3rd. ed. London: Luzac & Co. 1986.

Bausani, A. "Muḥammad or Darius? The Elements and Basis of Iranian Culture." *Islam and Cultural Change in the Middle Ages*. Edited by S. Vyronis Jr. Wiesbaden: 1975.

—— *The Persians: from the earliest days to the twentieth century*. Translated from Italian by J. Donne. London: 1971.

Bello, Iysa. *The Medieval Islamic Controversy between Philosophy and Orthodoxy: Ijmā' and ta'wīl in the Conflict between Al-Ghazālī and Ibn Rushd*. Leiden: E.J. Brill 1989.

Bigdilī, Luṭf 'Alī. *Atashkada*. Tehran: Amīr Kabīr 1957.

Binyon, L. & J.V.S. Wilkinson & B. Gray, *Persian Miniature Painting*. New York: Dover Books 1971.

Blake, William. *Blake: Complete Writings*. Edited by G. Keynes. London: OUP 1972.

Blois, Francois de. *Persian Literature: A Bio-Bibliographical Survey, Poetry to ca. A.D. 1100*. vol. V/2. London: Royal Asiatic Society 1992.

Bly, Robert. *A Little Book of the Human Shadow*. San Francisco: 1988.

Bosworth, C.E. *"Aḥrār." Encyclopedia Iranica*. I: 667.

Bouhdiba, A. *Sexuality in Islam*. Translated from the French by Alan Sheridan. London: KPI 1985.

Bowra, C.M. *The Heritage of Symbolism*. London: 1951.

Boyle, J.A. "Dynastic and Political History of the Īl-Khāns." *The Cambridge History of Iran*. vol. 5. Edited by J.A. Boyle. Cambridge: Cambridge University Press (1968): 303-421.

—— *The Mongol World-Empire 1266-1370*. London: 1977.

Brown, Peter. *The Cult of the Saints: its Rise and Function in Latin Christianity*. University of Chicago Press: 1981.

Browne, E.G. *A Literary History of Persia*. 4 vols. Cambridge: Cambridge University Press 1906-30.

Bruijn, J.T.P. de. "Maḥmūd Shabistarī." EI².

—— "The *Qalandariyyāt* in Persian Mystical Poetry, from Sanā'ī Onwards." *The Legacy of Mediæval Persian Sufism*.. Edited by Leonard Lewisohn. London: KNP in association with the SOAS Centre of Near & Middle Eastern Studies 1992: 75-86.

Burckhardt, Titus. *Mystical Astrology According to Ibn 'Arabī*. Translated from the French by Bulent Rauf. Sherborne: Beshara Publications 1977.

Bunyon, John. *The Pilgrim's Progress*. London: Penguin Books 1987.

Bürgel, J.C. *The Feather of Simurgh: The "Licit Magic" of the Arts in Medieval Islam*. New York University Press, 1988.

Cahen, Claude. *Pre-Ottoman Turkey: A General Survey of the Material and Spiritual Culture and History, c. 1071-1330*. Translated by J. Jones-Williams. New York: Taplinger Publishing Company 1968.

Chabbi, Jacqueline. "Remarques sur le développement historique des mouvements ascétiques et mystiques au Khurasan." *Studia Islamica*. XLVI (1977): 5-72.

Chabot, J.B. (tr.). *Histoire de Mar Jabalaha III . . . (1281-1317)*. Paris: 1895.

Chenu, D. *Nature, Man, and Society in the 12th Century*. Translated from the French by J. Taylor and L.K. Little. Chicago: University of Chicago Press 1968.

Chittick, William C. "The Perfect Man as the Prototype of the Self in the Sufism of Jāmī." *Studia Islamica*. 49 (1979): 135-57.

—— *Faith and Practice of Islam: Three Thirteenth Century Sufi Texts*. Albany: SUNY 1992.

—— "*Awāref al-Ma'āref*." *Encyclopedia Iranica*. III: 114-5

—— "Mysticism vs. Philosophy in Earlier Islamic History: The Al-Ṭūsī, Al-Qūnawī Correspondance." *Religious Studies* 17 (1981): 87-104.

—— *The Sufi Path of Love: The Spiritual Teachings of Rumi*. Albany: SUNY 1983.

—— "Belief and Transformation: The Sufi Teachings of Ibn al-'Arabī." *The American Theosophist* 74/5 (1986): 181-92.

—— "The Five Divine Presences: from al-Qūnawī to al-Qayṣārī." *The Muslim World*. 62/2 (1988): 107-28.

—— "The World of Imagination and Poetic Imagery According to Ibn al-'Arabī." *Temenos: A Journal Devoted to the Arts of the Imagination*. X (1989): 99-119.

—— "Ebno'l-'Arabi as Lover." *Sufi: A Journal of Sufism*. IX (1991): 6-9.

—— "Ibn 'Arabī and His School." *Islamic Spirituality II*. Edited by S.H. Nasr. New York: Crossroad (1991): 49-79.

—— *Imaginal Worlds: Ibn 'Arabī and the Problem of Religious Diversity*. Albany: SUNY 1994.

Chodkiewicz, M. *Seal of the Saints: Prophethood and Sainthood in the Doctrine of Ibn 'Arabī*. Translated from the French by Liadain Sherrard. Cambridge: Islamic Texts Society 1993.

Coomaraswamy, A.K. "Notes on the Philosophy of Persian Art." *Coomaraswamy: Selected Papers on Traditional Art and Symbolism.* Edited by Roger Lipsey. Bollingen Series 89. Princeton: Princeton University Press (1986): 260-5

Cooper, J. "Rūmī and *Ḥikmat:* Towards a Reading of Sabziwārī's Commentary on the *Mathnawī.*" *Classical Persian Sufism: from its Origins to Rumi.* Edited by Leonard Lewisohn. London: KNP (1993): 409-33.

Corbin, Henry. *Creative Imagination in the Ṣūfism of Ibn 'Arabī.* Bollingen Series XCI. Translated from the French by R. Manheim. Princeton: Princeton University Press 1969.

—— *Avicenna and the Visionary Recital.* Translated from the French by W.R. Trask. London: Kegan Paul 1961.

—— *Trilogie Ismaelienne.* Tehran/Paris: 1961.

—— *The Man of Light in Iranian Sufism.* Translated from the French by Nancy Pearson. London/Boulder: Shambhala 1978.

—— *Histoire de la philosophie islamique.* Paris: Editions Gallimard 1986.

Cruz, San Juan de la. *Poesías Completas: San Juan de la Cruz.* Barcelona: 1988.

Dabashi, Hamid. *Theology of Discontent: The Ideological Foundations of the Islamic Revolution.* New York University Press: 1993.

Daftary, Farhad. *The Ismā'īlīs: their history and doctrines.* Cambridge: Cambridge University Press 1992.

Danner, Victor. *The Islamic Tradition.* New York: Amity House 1988.

Dārābī, Muḥammad al-. *Lāṭifa-yi ghaybī.* Shirāz: Kitāb-khāna-yi Aḥmadī, n.d.

Dawlatshah Samarqandī. *Tadhkirat al-shu'arā'.* Edited by E.G. Browne. London: 1901.

—— *Tadhkirat al-shu'arā'.* Edited by Muḥammad 'Abbāsī. Tehran: Kitābfurūshī Bārānī 1958.

Dawlatābādī, 'Azīz. *Sukhanvarān-i Ādharbāyjān.* 2 vols. Tabriz: Intishārāt-i Mu'asasa-yi Tārīkh wa Farhang-i Īrān 1976.

Digby, Simon. "The Sufi Shaykh and the Sultan: A Conflict of Claims to Authority in Medieval India." *Iran: Journal of the British Institute of Persian Studies* 28 (1990): 71-81.

During, Jean. *Musique et Extase: L'audition mystique dans la tradition soufie.* Paris: Albin Michel 1988.

Eliade, Mircea. *The Sacred and The Profane,.* New York: 1961.

Ernst, Carl. *Words of Ecstasy in Sufism.* Albany: SUNY 1985.

—— "The Stages of Love in Early Persian Sufism from Rābi'a to Rūzbihān." *Classical Persian Sufism from its Origins to Rumi.* Edited by L. Lewisohn. London: KNP (1994): 435-55.

Ess, J. Van. "'Alā' al-Dawla Semnānī." *Encyclopedia Iranica.* I: 774-77.

Farghānī, Sa'īd al-Dīn. *Mashāriq al-darārī.* Edited by Jalāl al-Dīn Ashtiyānī. Tehran: 1357 A.Hsh./1978.

Feldman, Walter. "Mysticism, Didacticism and Authority in the Liturigical Poetry of the Halvetî Dervishes of Istanbul." *Edibeyat* NS 4 (1993): 243-65.

Fletcher, A. *Allegorical Imagery: Some Medieval Books and Their Renaissance Posterity.* Princeton University Press 1966.

Fragner, Bert. "Social and Internal Economic Affairs." *Cambridge History of Iran*. vol. 6. Edited by Peter Jackson. Cambridge: Cambridge University Press (1986): 491-567.
Frank, Richard. "Al-Ghazālī's Use of Avicenna's Philosophy." *Revue des Études Islamiques* 45-47/1 (1987-89): 271-85.
Franz, Marie-Louis von. *Projection and Re-Collection in Jungian Psychology*. Translated from the French by W.H. Kennedy. London: Open Court 1980.
Frye, Northrop. *Anatomy of Criticism: Four Essays*. Princeton University Press 1957.
Furūzānfar, Badī' al-Zamān. *Aḥādīth-i Mathnawī*. Tehran: Amīr Kabīr 1982.
Gairdner, W.H.T. "The Way of a Mohammanan Mystic." *The Moslem World*. II (1912): I: 170-81; II: 245-257.
Ghanī, Qāsim. *Baḥth dar āthār va afkār va aḥwāl-i Ḥāfiẓ: Tārīkh-i taṣawwuf dar islām az ṣadr-i islām tā 'aṣr-i Ḥāfiẓ*. 3rd ed. 2 vols. Tehran: 1977.
Ghazālī, Abū Ḥāmid al-. *The Book of Knowledge Being a Translation with Notes of the Kitāb al-'Ilm of al-Ghazzālī's Iḥyā' 'Ulūm al-Dīn*. Translated by N.A. Faris. Lahore: Sh. Muhammad Ashraf 1962.
Ghazālī, Ahmad. *Sawānih: Inspirations from the World of Pure Spirits*. Translated by N. Pourjavady. London: KPI 1986.
Gibb, H.A.R. *Whither Islam? A Survey of Movements in the Moslem World*. London: Victor Gollancz 1932.
Glünz, M. "Sufism, Shi'ism and Poetry in Fifteenth-Century Iran: The Ghazals of Asiri-Lahiji." *Timurid Art and Culture: Iran and Central Asia in the Fifteenth Century*. Edited by Lis Golombek and Maria Subtelny. Leiden: E.J. Brill 1992.
Gruner, G. Cameron (trans.). *A Treatise on the the Canon of Medicine of Avicenna*. New York: Augustus Kelley 1970.
Guillaumont, A. "Les sens des noms du coeur dans l'antiquité." *Le Coeur – Études Carmélitaines*. Bruges: Desclée de Brouwer 1950.
Habibi, Nader. "Allocation of Educational and Occupational Opportunities in the Islamic Republic of Iran: A Case Study in the Political Screening of Human Capital." *Iranian Studies*. XXII/4 (1991): 19-46.
Haining, Thomas. "The Mongols and Religion." *Asian Affairs* XVII/1 (1986): 19-31.
Ḥallāj, Manṣūr al-. *Akhbār al-Ḥallāj: Recueil d'oraisons et d'exhortations du martyr mystique de l'Islam*. Edited by L. Massignon and P. Kraus. Études Musulmanes, IV. Paris: 1955.
Hamadhānī, 'Ayn al-Quḍāt. *Tamhīdāt*. Edited by Afif Osseiran. Tehran: 1962.
Ḥamūya, Sa'd al-Dīn. *Al-Miṣbāḥ fī'l-taṣawwuf*. Tehran: 1983.
Harawī, Mīr Ḥusayn. *Nuzhat al-arwāh*. Edited by M. Harawī. Mashhad: Zawwār 1972.
Healey, J. *Jefferson on Religion in Public Education*. New Haven: Yale University Press 1962.
Hebraeus, Bar. *The Chronography of Geogory Abu'l-Faraj . . . commonly knonw as Bar Hebraeus*. Translated by E.A. Wallis Budge. Oxford/London: 1932.
Heer, N. "Abū Ḥāmid al-Ghazālī's Esoteric Exegesis of the Koran." *Classical*

*Persian Sufism from its Origins to Rumi*. Edited by L. Lewisohn. London: KNP (1994): 235-57.

Heinen, Anton M. "*Tafakkur* and Muslim Science." *Annemarie Schimmel Festschrift*. Edited Maria Eva Subtelny. *Journal of Turkish Studies*, vol. XVIII. Cambridge: Harvard University (1994): 103-10.

Herbert, George. *The Country Parson, The Temple*. London: SPCK 1981.

Hidāyat, Riḍā Qulī-Khān. *Tadhkira-yi Riyāḍ al-'arifīn*. Tehran: Maḥmūdī 1344 A.Hsh./1965.

—— *Majma' al-fuṣaḥā'*. Edited by 'Alī Aṣghar Ḥikmat. Tehran: 1957.

Hillmann, James. *The Thought of the Heart*. Ascona: Eranos Foundation 1981.

Hillmann, Michael. *Unity in the Ghazals of Ḥāfiẓ*. Chicago: 1976.

Hodgson, M. *The Venture of Islam*. 3 vols. Chicago/London: University of Chicago, 1974-77.

Houédard, Dom Sylvester. "Ibn 'Arabī's Contribution to the Wider Ecumenism." *Muhyiddin Ibn 'Arabi: A Commemorative Volume*. Edited by S. Hirtenstein & M. Tiernan. U.K.: Element Bks. (1993): 191-206.

Howorth, Sir Henry. *History of the Mongols*. 4 vols. London: 1876-1927.

Hujwīrī, 'Alī al-. *The "Kashf al-maḥjūb:" The Oldest Persian Treatise on Sufism*. Translated by R.A. Nicholson. Gibb Memorial Series, no. 17. 1911. Reprinted London: 1976.

—— *Kashf al-maḥjūb*. Edited by V.A. Zhukovskii. St. Petersburg 1899. Reprinted, Leningrad 1926.

Ḥuqūqī, 'Askar (ed.). *Sharḥ-i Gulshan-i rāz* by an anonymous author. Tehran: 1345 A.Hsh./1966.

Ibn 'Arabī. *Fuṣūṣ al-ḥikam*. Edited by A Affīfī. Beriut: Dār al-Kitāb al-Arabī 1946.

—— *Al-Futūḥāt al-Makkiyya*. Cairo: 1329 A.H..

—— *Ibn al-'Arabī: The Bezels of Wisdom*. Translated by R.J.W. Austin. New York: Paulist Press 1980.

—— *Futūḥāt al-Makkiyya*. Cairo: Dār al-Ṣādir, n.d.

—— *The Tarjumān al-ashwāq: A Collection of Mystical Odes by Muhyi'ddín Ibn al-'Arabí*. Translated by R.A. Nicholson. Reprinted London: Theosophical Publishing House 1978.

Ibn Baṭṭūṭa. *Riḥlat Ibn Baṭṭūṭa*. Beirut: Dār Ṣādir, 1964.

—— *The Travels of Ibn Baṭṭūṭa (A.D. 1325-1354)*. Translated by H.A.R. Gibb. 4 vols. Cambridge: University Press 1958.

—— *Safar-nāma-yi Ibn Baṭuṭṭa*. Translated into Persian by Muḥammad Muwaḥḥid. Tehran: BTNK 1337 A.Hsh./1958.

Ibn Karbalā'ī Tabrīzī, Ḥāfiẓ Ḥusayn. *Rawḍāt al-jinān va jannāt al-janān*. Edited by Ja'far Sulṭān al-Qurrā'ī. Persian Texts Series No. 20. 2 vols. Tehran: 1344 A.Hsh./1965.

'Irāqī, Fakhr al-Dīn. *Fakhruddin 'Iraqi: Divine Flashes*. Translated by W.C. Chittick and P.L. Wilson. London: SPCK 1982.

Izutsu, Toshiko. "Mysticism and the Linguistic Problem of Equivocation in the Thought of 'Ayn al-Quḍāt Hamadānī." *Studia Islamica* 31 (1970).

—— "The Basic Structure of Metaphysical Thinking in Islam." *Collected Papers on Islamic Philosophy and Mysticism*. Edited by H. Landolt. Tehran: 1971.

—— ( 1965). *The Concept of Belief in Islamic theology: a semantic analysis of īmān and islām.* Tokyo: Keio Institute of Cultural and Linguistic Studies 1965.

—— *A Comparative Study of the Key Philosophical Concepts in Sufism and Taoism–Ibn 'Arabī and Lao-Tzu.* Tokyo: 1966.

—— "The Paradox of Light and Darkness in the *Garden of Mystery* of Shabistarī." *Anagogic Qualities in Literature.* Edited by Joseph P. Strelka. University Park, Pa. (1971): 288-307.

Trimingham, J.S. *The Sufi Orders in Islam.* Oxford: OUP 1973.

Jackson, Peter. "Abū Sa'īd Bahādor Khān." *Encyclopædia Iranica.* I: 374-76.

—— "Arğūn Khan." *Encyclopedia Iranica.* II: 400-04.

—— "Aḥmad Takūdār." *Encyclopedia Iranica.* I: 661-62

Jadaane, F. "La place des anges dans la théologie cosmique musulmane." *Studia Islamica* XXI. 1975.

Jahn, K. "Rashīd al-Dīn as a World Historian." *Yādnāma-yi Jan Rypka.* Prague (1967): 79-87.

Jāmī, Nūr al-Dīn 'Abd al-Raḥmān ibn Ahmad al-. *Nafaḥāt al-uns.* Edited by Mihdī Tawḥīdīpūr. Tehran: Intishārāt-i Kitābfurūshī Maḥmūdī 1336 A.Hsh./1957.

—— *Naqd al-nuṣūṣ fī sharḥ Naqsh al-Fuṣūṣ.* Edited by W.C. Chittick. Tehran: Imperial Iranian Academy of Philosophy 1977.

Juwaynī. *The History of the World-Conqueror.* Translated by J.A. Boyle. 2 vols. Manchester: 1985.

Jūzjānī, Minhāj al-Dīn. *Ṭabaqāt-i Nāṣirī.* 2 ed. 2 vols. Edited by 'Abd al-Ḥayy Ḥabībī. Kabul: 1963-4.

—— *Ṭabaqāt-i Nāṣirī: A General History of the Muḥammadan Dynasties of Asia, including Hindūstān.* Translated from the Persian by H.G. Raverty. London: Gilbert & Rivington 1881.

Kadkānī, S. *Suwar-i khiyāl dar shi'r-i fārsī.* Tehran: 1970.

Karbalā'ī, Ḥāfiẓ Ḥusayn Ibn. *Rawḍāt al-jinān wa jannāt al-janān.* Persian Texts Series No. 20. Tehran: 1965.

Kāshānī, 'Izz al-Dīn Maḥmūd. *Miṣbāḥ al-ḥidāya.* Edited by Jalāl al-Dīn Humā'ī. Tehran: 1946.

Kāshānī, Mullā Muḥsin Fayḍ. "*Risāla-yi Mishwāq.*" *Dah risāla-yi al-Ḥakīm al-'Ārif al-Kāmal al-Fāḍil Muḥammad Muḥsin al-Fayḍ al-Kāshānī.* Edited by Rasūl Ja'fariyān. Iṣfahān: 1993.

Kazārgāhī. *Majālis al-'ushshāq.* Oxford: Bodleian Library MS. Add. 24

Khujandī, Kamāl al-Dīn. *Dīwān-i Kamāl al-Dīn Khujandī.* Edited by 'Azīz Dawlatabādī. Tehran: 1958.

Khujandī, Kamāl al-Dīn Mas'ūd. *Dīwān-i Kamāl al-Dīn Mas'ūd Khujandī.* Edited by K. Shidfar. Moscow: 1975.

Khwandamīr. *Ḥabīb al-siyar.* Tehran: Khayyām 1993.

Khwārazmī, Tāj al-Dīn Ḥusayn ibn Ḥasan. *Sharḥ-i Fuṣūṣ al-ḥikam.* 2nd ed. Edited by N.M. Harawī. Tehran: Intishārāt-i Mawlā 1989.

Kirmānī, Khwājū. *Dīwān-i Khwājū Kirmānī.* Edited by A.S. Khwānsārī Tehran: Kitāb-furūshī Maḥmūdī 1957.

Kiyānī, Muḥsin. *Tārīkh-i khānaqāh dar Īrān.* Tehran: Ṭahūrī, 1369A.Hsh./1991.

Knysh, Alexander. "Ibn 'Arabī in the Later Islamic Tradition." *Muhyiddin Ibn 'Arabī: A Commemorative Volume*. Ed. S. Hirtenstein & M. Tiernan. Dorset: U.K.: Element Bks. (1993): 307-27.

Koran. *The Koran Interpreted*. Translated by A.J. Arberry. Oxford: OUP 1983.

Lambton, A.K.S. "Mongol Fiscal Administration in Persia." *Studia Islamica* LXIV (1986): 79-99; LXV (1987): 97-123.

— *Continuity and Change in Medieval Persia: Aspects of Administrative, Economic and Social History, 11th-14th Century*. London: I.B. Tauris, 1988.

Landolt, Hermann. "Two Types of Mystical Thought in Muslim Iran: An Essay on Suhrawardī Shaykh al-Ishrāq and 'Aynulquẓāt-i Hamadānī." *Muslim World*. 68 (1978).

— "Walāyah." *Encyclopedia of Religion*. Edited by M. Eliade.

— "Simnānī on *Waḥdat al-Wujūd*." *Collected Papers on Islamic Philosophy and Mysticism*. Edited by M. Mohaghegh and H. Landolt. Tehran: 1971.

— *Nūruddīn Isfarāyinī: Le Révélateur des Mystères*. Paris: Verdier 1986.

— "Ghazālī and 'Religionswissenschaft'." *Asiatische Studien* XLV/1 (1991): 19-72.

Lewisohn, Leonard. "The Life and Poetry of Mashriqī Tabrīzī (d. 1454)." *Iranian Studies*. XXII/ 2-3. (1989): 99-127.

— "Muḥammad Shīrīn Tabrīzī." *Sufi: A Journal of Sufism*. Issue 1 (1988-89): 30-35.

— (ed.) *The Legacy of Mediæval Persian Sufism*. London: KNP in association with the SOAS Centre of Middle Eastern Studies 1992.

— (ed.) *Dīvān-i Muḥammad Shīrīn Maghribī*. Persian text edited with notes, introduction, and index. Wisdom of Persia Series XLIII. Tehran: McGill Institute of Islamic Studies, Tehran Branch; London: SOAS 1994.

— "Overview: Iranian Islam and Persianate Sufism." *The Legacy of Mediæval Persian Sufism*. Edited by Leonard Lewisohn. London: KNP in association with the SOAS Centre of Near & Middle Eastern Studies. (1992): 75-86..

— "The Transcendental Unity of Polytheism & Monotheism in the Sufism of Shabistarī." *The Legacy of Mediæval Persian Sufism*. Edited by Leonard Lewisohn. London: KNP in association with the SOAS Centre of Near & Middle Eastern Studies. (1992): 75-86.

— "In Quest of Annihilation: Imaginalization and Mystical Death in the *Tamhīdāt* of 'Ayn al-Quḍāt Hamadhānī." *Classical Persian Sufism: from its Origins to Rūmī.*. Edited by L. Lewisohn. London: KNP 1993.

— "The Life and Times of Kamāl Khujandī." *Annemarie Schimmel Festschrif*. Ed. Maria Eva Subtelny. Cambridge: Harvard University 1994.

Lings, Martin (Abu Bakr Siraj al-Din). *The Book of Certainty: The Sufi Doctrines of Faith, Vision and Gnosis*. New York: Samuel Weiser 1970.

Loeffler, Reinhold. *Islam in Practice: Religious Beliefs in a Persian Village*. Albany: SUNY 1988.

Lāhījī, Muḥammad ("Asīrī"). *Dīwān-i ash'ār wa rasā'il-i Asīrī Lāhījī*. Edited by B. Zanjānī. Wisdom of Persia Series XX. Tehran: McGill Institute of Islamic Studies, Tehran Branch: 1978.

— *Mafātīḥ al-i'jāz fī sharḥ-i Gulshan-i rāz*. Edited by Muḥammad Riḍā

Barzgār Khāliqī and 'Iffat Karbāsī. Tehran: Zawwar 1371 A.Hsh./1992.
— *Mafātīḥ al-'ijāz fī sharḥ-i Gulshan-i rāz*. Edited by Kaywān Samī'ī. Tehran: Kitāb-furūshī Maḥmūdī 1337 A.Hsh./1958.
Madelung. "Early Sunni Doctrine concerning Faith as reflected in the *Kitāb al-Īmān* of Abū 'Ubayd al-Qāsim b. Sallam (d. 224/839)." *Studia Islamica* XXXII. 1970.
Maghribī, Muḥammad Shīrīn. *Dīwān-i Muḥammad Shīrīn Maghribī*. Persian text edited by Leonard Lewisohn with notes, introduction, and index. Wisdom of Persia Series XLIII. Tehran: McGill Institute of Islamic Studies, Tehran Branch; London: SOAS 1993.
Mahdi, Muhsin. "The Book and the Master as Poles of Cultural Change in Islam." *Islam and Cultural Change in the Middle Ages*. Edited by S. Vyronis Jr. Wiesbaden: Otto Harrassowitz (1975): 3-15.
Malamud, Margaret. "Sufi Organizations and Structures of Authority in Medieval Nishapur." *International Journal of Middle Eastern Studies*. XXVI/3 (1994): 427-42.
Manz, Beatrice. *The Rise and Rule of Tamerlane,*. Cambridge University Press: 1989.
Maqrīzī, al-. *Al-Khiṭaṭ al-Maqrīziyya*. Lebanon: Dār Iḥyā' al-'ulūm, n.d.
— *Kitāb al-sulūk li-ma'rifat duwal al-mulūk*. 2 vols. Edited by M.M Ziyāda. Cairo: 1956.
Maritian, Jacques. *Creative Intuition in Art and Poetry*. New York: Pantheon Books 1953.
Martz, Louis. *The Poetry of Meditation: A Study in English Religious Literature of the 17th Century*. 6 th rpt. ed. New Haven: Yale University Press 1976.
Mashkūr, Muḥammad Javād. *Tarīkh-i Tabrīz ta pāyān-i qarn nuhum-i hijrī*. Tehran: Intishārāt-i Anjuman-i Āthār-i millī 1973.
Massignon, Louis. *The Passion of al-Ḥallāj: Mystic and Martyr of Islam*. Translated from the French by Herbert Mason. 4 vols. Princeton: Princeton University Press 1982.
Maybudī, Rashīd al-Dīn. *Kashf al-asrār wa 'uddat al-abrār*. 10 vols. Edited by 'Alī Aṣghar Ḥikmat. Tehran: Intishārāt-i Dānishgāhī, 1952-60.
Mazzaoui, Michel M. *The Origins of the Ṣafawids: Šī'ism, Ṣūfism, and the Ğulāt*. Wiesbaden: Franz Steiner 1972.
McCarthy, R.J. *Freedom and Fufillment*. Boston: G.K. Hall & Co.: 1980.
Meier, Fritz. "The Problem of Nature in the Esoteric Monism of Islam." *Spirit and Nature: Papers from the Eranos Yearbook*. Edited by Joseph Campbell. New York: 1954.
Meisami. "Allegorical Gardens in the Persian Poetic Tradition: Nezami, Rumi, Hafez." *International Journal of Middle Eastern Studies*. XVII/2 (1985): 229-60.
Melville, Charles. "Cobān." *Encyclopedia Iranica*. V: 875-78.
— "Historical Monuments and Earthquakes in Tabriz." *Iran: Journal of the British Institute of Persian Studies*. XIX (1981): 159-77.
— The Itineraries of Sultan Öljeitū 1304-16." *Iran: Journal of the British Institute of Persian Studies*. XXVII (1990): 55-70.
— "*Pādishāh-i Islām:* the Conversion of Sultan Maḥmūd Ghāzān Khān."

*Pembroke Papers I: Persian and Islamic Studies in honour of P.W. Avery*. Edited C. Melville. Cambridge: University of Cambridge (1990): 159-77.

—— "The Year of the Elephant" Mamluk-Mongol Rivalry in the Hejaz in the Reign of Abū Sa'īd (1317-1335)." *Studia Iranica*, XXII/2 (1992): 197-214.

—— "Abū Sa'īd and the Revolt of the Amīrs in 1319." *L'Iran face à la Domination mongole*. Ed. D. Aigle. Damascus/Paris: 1995.

Meskoob, Shahrokh. *Iranian Nationality and the Persian Language 900-1900: The Roles of Court, Religion and Sufism in Persian Prose Writing*. Translated from Persian by Michael Hillmann. Washington, D.C.: Mage 1992.

Middle East Watch. *Guardians of Thought: Limits on Freedom of Expression in Iran*. Washington, D.C./New York: 1993.

Minorsky, Vladmir. "Tabrīz." EI[1].

Mir, Mustansir. *Dictionary of Qur'ānic Terms and Concepts*. London/New York: Garland Publishing company 1987.

Mir-Hosseini, Ziba. "Inner Truth and Outer History: the Two Worlds of the Ahl-Ḥaqq of Kurdistan." *International Journal of Middle Eastern Studies*. XXVI (1994): 267-85.

Molé, Marijan. "Les Kubrawiya Entre Sunnisme et Shiisme Aux Huitième et Neuvième Siecles de l'Hégire." *Revue des études islamiques* 52 (1961): 61-141

Morgan, David, (ed.). *Medieval Historical Writings in the Christian and Islamic Worlds*. London: SOAS Publications 1982.

Morris, J.W. "Ibn 'Arabī and his Interpreters. Part II: Influences and Intrepretations." *Journal of the American Oriental Society* 106/4 (1986): 539-51, 733-56; 107/1 (1987): 101-19.

—— "Listening for God: Prayer and the Heart in the *Futūḥāt*.." *Journal of the Muhyiddin Ibn 'Arabi Society*. XIII (1993): 19-53.

Munzawī, Aḥmad. *Fihrist-i nuskhahā-yi khaṭṭī-yi Fārsī*. 2 vols. Tehran: 1348 A.Hsh./1969.

Murata, Sachiko. "The Angels." *Islamic Spirituality I: Foundations*. Edited by S.H. Nasr. New York: Crossroad (1987): 324-57.

—— *The Tao of Islam: A Sourcebook on Gender Relationships in Islamic Thought*. Albany: SUNY 1992.

—— "Witnessing the Rose: Ya'qūb Ṣarfī on the Vision of God in Women." *God is Beautiful and He loves beauty: Festschrift in honour of Annemarie Schimmel*. Edited by Alma Giese & J-C. Bürgel. Bern: Peter Lang 1994.

Murtaḍawī, Manūchihr. *Masā'il-i 'aṣr-i Īl-khānān*. Tehran: 1991.

Mustawfī, Ḥamd Allāh. *Tāriīkh-i guzīda*. Edited by 'Abd al-Ḥusayn Nawā'ī. Tehran: 1983.

Mustawfi Qazwīni, Ḥamd-Allāh. *The Geographical Part of the Nuzhat al-Qulūb composed by Ḥamd-Allāh Mustawfī of Qazwīn in 740 (1340)*. London: Luzac 1095.

Mīnuwī, M. "*Rawshanā'ī-nāma*-yi Nāṣir Khusraw wa *Rawshanā'ī-nāma*-yi Manẓūm-i mansūb ba ū." *Yād-nāma-yi Nāṣir Khusraw*. Mashhad: 1976.

Nasafī, 'Azīz. *Le Livre de l'Homme Parfait (Kitāb al-Insān al-Kāmil)*. Translated by Isabelle de Gastines. Paris: 1984.

—— *Kashf al-ḥaqā'iq*. Edited by Aḥmad Mahdawī-Dāmghānī. Tehran: Ṭahūrī 1985.

Nasr, S. H. "Metaphysics, Poetry, and Logic in Oriental Traditions." *Sophia Perennis* III/2. 1977.

—— *An Introduction to Islamic Cosmological Doctrines*. Boulder: Shambhala 1978.

—— "Sufism and Spirituality in Persia." *Islamic Spirituality II*. Edited by S.H. Nasr. New York: Crossroad (1991): 206-222.

—— "Persian Sufi Literature: its Spiritual and Cultural Significance." *The Legacy of Mediæval Persian Sufism*. Edited by Leonard Lewisohn. London: KNP in association with the SOAS Centre of Near & Middle Eastern Studies. (1992): 1-10.

—— "Spiritual Movements, Philosophy and Theology in the Safavid Period." *The Cambridge History of Iran*. vol. 6. Cambridge: Cambridge University Press (1986): 656-97.

—— *Sufi Essays*. London: Allen & Unwin 1972.

Nawā'ī, Mīr 'Alīshīr. *Majālis al-nafā'is*. Edited by 'Alī Asghar Ḥikmat. Tehran: Manūchirī 1363 A.Hsh./1984.

Niffarī, Ibn Abdī 'l-Jabbār al-. The *Mawāqif* and *Mukhātabat* of Muḥammad Ibn Abdī 'l-Jabbār al-Niffarī with other fragments. Edited with translation by A.J. Arberry. E.J.W. Gibb Memorial Trust. London: Luzac & Co., 1978. Reprint of the 1935 edition.

Niẓāmī. *Makhzan al-asrār*. Tehran: Ibn Sīnā 1956.

Nurbakhsh, Dr. Javad. *Spiritual Poverty in Sufism*. Translated by Leonard Lewisohn. London: KNP 1984.

—— *Traditions of the Prophet*. vol. I. Translated by Leonard Lewisohn. New York: KNP 1981.

—— *Jesus in the Eyes of the Sufis*. Translated by Leonard Lewisohn, Terry Graham. London: KNP 1983.

—— *Ma'ārif Ṣūfiyya*. 7 vols. London: KNP 1983.

—— *Sufi Symbolism II: Love, Lover, Beloved, Allusions and Metaphors*. Translated by Terry Graham *et al*. London: KNP 1987.

—— *Sufi Symbolism IV*. Translated by Terry Graham *et al*. London: KNP 1990.

—— *Sufism V*. Translated by Terry Graham. London: KNP 1991.

—— *The Psychology of Sufism*. Translated by T. Graham. London: KNP 1992.

—— "Two Approaches to the Principles of the Unity of Being." *The Legacy of Mediæval Persian Sufism*. Edited by Leonard Lewisohn. London: KNP in association with the SOAS Centre of Near & Middle Eastern Studies. (1992): ix-xiii.

—— "The Key Features of Early Persian Sufism." *Classical Persian Sufism from Its Origins to Rumi.*. Edited by Leonard Lewisohn. London: KNP (1993): xv-xxxix.

—— *Sufi Symbolism VII: Contemplative Discipline, Visions and Theophanies, Family Relationships, Servants of God, Names of Sufi Orders*. Translated by Terry Graham et. al. London: KNP 1994.

—— *Sufi Symbolism VIII*. Translated by Terry Graham *et al*,. London: KNP 1994.

Nwyia, Paul. *Exégèse Coranique et Langue Mystique*. Beirut: 1970.

Ormsby, Eric L. "The Taste of Truth: The Structure of Experience in al-Ghazālī's *Al-Munqidh Min Al-Ḍalāl.*" *Islamic Studies Presented to Charles J. Adams*. Edited by W.B. Hallaq and D.P. Little. Leiden: E.J. Brill 1991.

Palāsī al-Shīrāzī, Ḥasan al-. *Tadhkira-yi Shaykh Muḥammad Ibn Sadīq al-Kujujī*. Translated into Persian from Arabic by Najm al-Dīn Ṭāramī. Tehran: Chupkhāna Packitchi 1947.

Peters, F.E. "The Origins of Islamic Platonism: The School Tradition." *Islamic Philosophical Theology*. Edited by P. Morewedge. Albany: SUNY (1979): 14-45.

Petrushevsky, I. P. "The Socio-Economic Conditions of Iran under the Īl-Khāns." *The Cambridge History of Iran*. vol. 5. Cambridge: Cambridge University Press (1968): 483-537.

Piehler, Paul. *The Visionary Landscape: A Study in Medieval Allegory*. London: 1971.

Pietmonese, Angelo. "La Leggenda del Santo-Lottatore Pahlavān Maḥmūd Xvārezmī 'Puryā-ye Vali'." *Annali dell'Istituto Universitario Orientale di Napoli*. 15. Nuova Serie (1965): 167-213.

Polo, Marco. *The Travels of Marco Polo*. Translated by Ronald Latham. London: The Folio Society 1958.

Pound, Ezra. *ABC of Reading*. London: Faber & Faber 1979.

—— *Literary Essays of Ezra Pound*. Edited by T.S. Eliot. London:: Faber & Faber 1985.

*Princeton Encyclopedia of Poetry and Poetics*. N.J.: Princeton University Press 1986.

Pritchett, Frances W. "Orient Pearls unstrung: The quest for unity in the Ghazal." *Edebiyāt* NS IV/1 (1993): 119-135.

Pseudo-Dionysius. *Pseudo-Dionysius: the Complete Works*. Translated by Colm Luibheid & Paul Rorem. New York: Paulist Press 1987.

Qushayrī, 'Abū'l-Qāsim al-. *The Principles of Sufism by al-Qushayri*. Translated by B.R. Von Schlegell. Berkley: Mizan Press, 1990.

—— *Al-risāla fī 'ilm al-taṣawwuf*. Cairo: 1912.

—— *Tarjama-yi Risāla-yi Qushayrī*. Edited by Badī' al-Zamān Furūzānfār. Tehran: 1345. A.Hsh./1982. Persian translation of the *Risāla* by Abū 'Alī Ḥasan ibn Aḥmad al-'Uthmānī.

—— *al-Risāla al-Qushayriyya*. 2 vols. Cairo: 1966.

Rahman, Fazlur. *Prophecy in Islam: Philosophy and Orthodoxy*. Chicago: Midway Reprint 1979.

Raine, Kathleen. "Yeats and Kabir." *Temenos: A Review Devoted to the Arts of the Imagination* V. 1984.

—— *The Human Face of God: William Blake and the Book of Job*. London: Thames & Hudson 1982.

—— *Defending Ancient Springs*. Suffolk: Golgonoonza Press 1985.

—— *Yeats the Initiate: Essays on certain themes in the writings of W.B. Yeats*. London: Dolmen Press 1986.

Rajā'ī, Aḥmad. *Farhang-i ash'ār-i Ḥāfiẓ*. 2 ed. Tehran: 1364 A.Hsh./1985.

Ram, Haggay. "The Myth of Early Islamic Goverment: The Legitimization of the Islamic Regime." *Iranian Studies* XXIV/1-4 (1991): 37-54.

Rāzī, Najm al-Dīn. *Mirṣād al-'ibād*. Translated by Hamid Algar: *The Path of God's Bondsmen from Origin to Return*. Delmar, N.Y.: Caravan Books 1982.

Richard, J. "La conversion de Berke et les debuts de l'islamisation de la Horde d'Or." *Revue des études islamiques* 35 (1976): 173-79.

Ridgeon, Lloyd. "The Life and Times of 'Azīz Nasafī." *Sufi: A Journal of Sufism.* XXII (1994): 31-35.

Rizvi, S.A.A. *A History of Sufism in India.* 2 vols. New Delhi: Mundshiram Manoharlal, 1978-83.

Roux, Jean-Paul. "La Tolérance Religieuse dans les Empires Turco-Mongols." *Revue de l'Histoire des religions.* CCII-2 (1986): 131-68.

Rúmí. *The Mathnawí of Jalálu'ddín Rúmí.* Gibb Memorial Series N.S. Translated and edited by R.A. Nicholson. 8 vols. London: E.J.W. Gibb Memorial Trust 1924 –40.

Rypka, Jan. "Poets & Prose Writers of the Late Saljuq and Mongol Periods." *The Cambridge History of Iran.* vol. 5. Edited by J.A. Boyle. Cambridge: Cambridge University Press (1968): 550-625.

Rūzbihān al-Baqlī al-Shīrāzī. *Tafsīr 'arā'is al-bayān.* Lucknow: Nawal Kishōr 1983-4.

—— *Kitāb mashrab al-arwāḥ.* Edited by N.M. Hoca. Istanbul: Maṭba'at Kulliyyāt al-Ādāb 1973.

—— *Sharḥ-i shaṭḥīyyāt.* Edited by H. Corbin. Bibliothéque Iranienne 12. Tehran: Departement d'iranologie de l'Institut Franco-iranien 1966.

—— *Le Jasmin des fidèles d'amour ('Abhar al-'āshiqīn).* Edited by H. Corbin and M. Mu'īn. Bibliothéque Iranienne, 8. Tehran: Institut Français d'Iranologie de Téhéran 1958; reprinted, 1981.

Sabzawarī, M.H. *Sharḥ-i ghurar al-farā'iḍ* or *Sharḥ-i Manẓūma.* Part 1: "Metaphysics." Translated into English by T. Izutsu and M. Mohaghegh. Tehran: 1983.

Sabzawarī, Muḥammad Ibrāhīm ibn Muḥammad 'Alī. *Sharḥ-i Gulshan-i rāz.* Tehran: lithograph edition 1330 A.Hsh./1951.

Sajjādī, Ja'far. *Farhang-i lughāt wa iṣṭilāḥāt wa ta'bīrāt-i 'irfānī.* Tehran: 1960.

—— *Farhang-i 'ulūm-i 'aqlī.* Tehran: 1982.

Ṣarrāf, M. (ed.) *Rasā'īl-i Jawānmardān.* Tehran: 1370.

Savory, Roger. "Some Reflections on Totalitarian Tendencies in the Safavid State." *Der Islam.* LII (1976): 226-241.

Schimmel, Annemarie. *Mystical Dimensions of Islam.* Chapel Hill: University of N. Carolina Press 1975.

—— *The Triumphal Sun: A Study of the Works of Jalāloddin Rumi.* London: Fine Books 1978.

—— "Turk and Hindu: A Poetical Image and its Application to Historical Texts." *Islam and Cultural Change in the Middle Ages.* Edited by Speros Vryonis Jr. Wiesbaden: Harrassowitz 1975: 107-25.

—— "Poetry and Calligraphy: Some Thoughts about their Interrelation in Persian Culture." *Highlights of Persian Art.* Edited by R. Ettinghausen & E. Yarshater. Colorado: Westview Press 1979.

—— *As Through A Veil: Mystical Poetry in Islam.* New York: Columbia University Press 1982.

Schroeder, Eric. "Verse Translation and Hafiz." *Journal of Near Eastern Studies.* VII/4 (1948): 209-221.

Shabistarī, Maḥmūd. *Gulshan-i Raz, The Mystic Rose Garden, the Persian*

*Text, with an English Translation and Notes, chiefly from the Commentary of Muhammad bin Yahya Lahiji*. Translated by E.H. Whinfield. Reprint of the 1880 London edition ed. Lahore: Islamic Book Foundation 1978.

—— *Ḥaqq al-yaqīn*. Edited by Dr. Javad Nurbakhsh. Tehran: Intishārāt-i Khānaqāh-i Ni'matu'llāhī 1975.

—— *The Garden of Spiritual Mystery*. Translated by Robert Darr. Forthcoming.

—— *Gulshan-i rāz*. Edited by Dr. Javad Nurbakhsh. Tehran: Intishārāt-i Khāniqāh-i Ni'matullāhī 1976.

—— *Gulshan-i rāz, surūda-yi Shaykh Maḥmūd Shabistarī, bā kashf al-abyāt wa arjā' ba dah sharḥ-i chāpī wa farhang-i Gulshan-i rāz*. Edited by Aḥmad Mujāhid, Muḥsin Kiyānī. Tehran: 1371 A.Hsh./1992.

—— *Majmū'a-i āthār-i Shaykh Maḥmūd Shabistarī*. Edited by Ṣamad Muwaḥḥid. Tehran: Kitābkhāna-i ṭahūrī 1986.

Shayegan, Daryush. "The Visionary Topography of Hafiz." *Temenos: A Journal Devoted to the Arts of the Imagination*. VI/1985.

Shīrwānī (Mast 'Alī Shāh), Zayn al-Dīn. *Riyāḍ al-siyāḥa*. Tehran: 1334 A.Hsh./1955.

Shīrāzī, M.M. *Tarā'iq al-ḥaqā'iq*. Edited by Muḥammad Ja'far Maḥjūb. 3 vols. Tehran: Kitābfurūshī Bārānī 1960.

Shīrāzī, Rukn al-Dīn Mas'ūd. *Nuṣūṣ al-khuṣūṣ fī tarjumat al-Fuṣūṣ*. Edited by R.A. Maẓlūmī. Wisdom of Persia Series XXV. Tehran: Institute of Islamic Studies 1359 A.Hsh./1980.

Shīrāzī, S. Aḥmad Bihisthī. *Sharḥ-i junūn*. Tehran: Intishārāt-i Rūzana 1993.

Simnānī, 'Alā al-Dawla. *Correspondance Spirituelle, echanges entre Nuroddin Esfarayeni et Alaoddawleh Semnani*. Edited by Hermann Landolt. Tehran: 1972.

—— *Al'Urwat li'l-ahl al-khalwat wa'l-jalwat*. Edited by N.M. Harawī. Tehran: Intishārāt-i Mawlā 1362 A.Hsh./1983.

—— *Chil majlis yā Risāla-yi Iqbāliyya*. Tehran: 1987.

—— *Divān-i kāmil-i ash'ār-i fārsī u 'arabī-yi 'Alā' al-Dawla Simnānī*. Edited by 'Abd al-Rafī' Ḥaqīqat. Tehran: 1985.

Smith, Grace Martin. *The Poetry of Yūnus Emre, a Turkish Sufi Poet*. University of California Press 1993.

Smith, Wilfred Cantwell. "Faith as *Taṣdīq*,." *Islamic Philosophical Theology*. Edited by Parviz Morewedge. Albany:: SUNY 1979.

Soucek, P. "Iranian Architecture: The Evolution of a Tradition." *Highlights of Persian Art*. Ed. E. Yarshater & R. Ettinghausen. Boulder: Westview Press 1979.

Spuler, B. *History of the Mongols, Based on Eastern and Westen Accounts of the Thirteenth and Fourteenth Centuries*. Translated from German by Stuart & Helga Drummond. Berkeley: University of California Press 1972.

Subtelny, Maria Eva. "Socioeconomic Bases of Cultural Patronage under the Later Timurids." *International Journal of Middle Eastern Studies*. XX/4 (1988): 479-505.

Suhrawardī, Shihāb al-Dīn Abū Ḥafṣ 'Umar. *The "Awārif al-ma'ārif*. Translated by H. Wilberforce Clarke. Calcutta: 1891.

—— *'Awārif al-ma'ārif*. Beirut: Dār al-Kitāb al-'Arabī, 1983.

Suhrawardī (Shaykh al-Ishrāq), Shihāb al-Dīn. *Opera Metaphysica et Mystica*. Edited by Henry Corbin. 3 vols. Tehran and Paris 1952-70.

Sulamī, ʻAbd al-Raḥmān. *Kitāb Ṭabaqāt al-ṣūfiyya*. Edited by N. Sharība. Cairo: 1953.

Sviri, Sara. "Ḥakīm Tirmidhī and the *Malāmatī* Movement in Early Sufism." *Classical Persian Sufism: from Its Origins to Rumi*. Edited by L. Lewisohn. London: KNP (1993): 583-613.

Swedenborg, Emmanuel. *The Universal Human and Soul-Body Interaction*. Translated by G. Dole. New York: Paulist Press 1984.

Swietochowski, Sussan Babaie and M.L. *Persian Drawings in the Metropolitan Museum of Art*. New York: 1989.

Tabrīzī, Humān-i. *Dīwān-i Humām Tabrīzī*. Edited by R. Aywaḍī. Tabriz: 1970.

Tahanawi, al- *Kashshāf iṣṭilāḥāt al-funūn (A Dictionary of the Technical Terms Used in the Sciences of the Musalmans)*. Edited by M. Wajih, Abd al-Haqq, G. Kadir & Nassau Lees. 2 vols. Calcutta: Asiatic Society of Bengal 1862.

Takeshita, M. *Ibn ʻArabī's Theory of the Perfect Man and its Place in the History of Islamic Thought*. Tokyo: 1987.

Tarbiyat, Muḥammad ʻAlī. *Dānishmandān-i Ādharbāyjān*. Tehran: 1935.

Taymiyya, Ibn. *Majmūʻ al-rasāʼil*. Cairo: 1905.

Theisen, Finn. *A Manual of Classical Persian Prosody*. Wiesbaden: Otto Harrassowitz 1982.

Vaṣṣāf. *Taḥrīr-i Tāʻrīkh-i Vaṣṣāf*. Edited by ʻAbd al-Muḥammad Āyatī. Tehran: Mūʼassisa-yi Muṭālaʻāt wa Taḥqīqāt-i Farhangī 1372 A.Hsh./1993. This book is an abridged version of Vaṣṣāf's own work *Tajziyat al-amṣār wa tazjiyat al-aʻṣār*. Edited by M.M Iṣfahānī. Lith. Bombay 1269/ 1852.

Versteegh, C.A.M. *Greek Elements in Arabic Linguistic Thinking*. Leiden: E.J. Brill 1977.

Vicente Cantarino, ( 1975). *Arabic Poetics in the Golden Age*. Leiden: E.J. Brill 1975.

Walbridge, John. "A Sufi Scientist of the Thirteenth Century: the Mystical Ideas and Practices of Quṭb al-Dīn Shīrāzī." *The Legacy of Mediæval Persian Sufism.*. Edited by Leonard Lewisohn. London: KNP (1992): 323-42.

Waley, Muhammad Isa. "Najm al-Dīn Kubrā and the Central Asian School of Sufism." *Islamic Spirituality II*. Ed. S.H. Nasr. New York: Crossroad 1991.

—— "A Kubrawi Manual of Sufism: the *Fuṣūṣ al-ādāb* of Yaḥyā Bākharzī." *The Legacy of Mediæval Persian Sufism*. Edited by Leonard Lewisohn. London: KNP in association with the SOAS Centre of Near & Middle Eastern Studies (1992): 289-310.

—— "Yaḥyā Bākharzī on Service in the *Khānaqāh*." *Sufi: A Journal of Sufism*. XX (1993): 12-20.

—— Waley, Muhammad Isa. "Contemplative Disciplines in Early Persian Sufism." *Classical Persian Sufism: from its Origins to Rūmī,*. Edited by Leonard Lewisohn. London: KNP (1993): 497-548.

Watt, W. Montgomery. *The Faith and Practice of al-Ghazālī*. London: 1952.

Will, Frederic. *Intelligible Beauty in Aesthetic Thought: From Winkelmann to Victor Cousin.* Tubingen: 1958.

Winkel, Eric. "Ibn 'Arabī's *Fiqh:* Three Cases from the *Futūḥāt.*" *Journal of the Muhyiddin Ibn 'Arabi Society.* XII/1 (1993): 54-74.

Yarshater, Ehsan. *Sha'r-i fārsī dar 'ahd-i Shāh-rukh.* Tehran: Danishgāh 1955.

—— "Some Common Characteristics of Persian Poetry and Art." *Studia Islamica.* XVI. 1962.

Young, T.C. (ed.). *Near Eastern Culture and Society.* Princeton: Princeton University Press 1951.

Yazdi, Mehdi Ha'iri. *The Principles of Epistemology in Islamic Philosophy: Knowledge by Presence.* Albany: SUNY 1992.

—— "Suhrawardī's *An Episode and a Trance*: A Philosophical Dialogue in a Mystical Stage." *Islamic Philosophy and Mysticism.* Edited by Parviz Morewedge. New York: Caravan Books 1981.

Zarrīnkūb, 'Abd al-Ḥusayn. "Sayrī dar Gulshan-i rāz." *Naqshī bar āb.* Tehran: Intishārāt-i Mu'īn 1989.

—— *Naqd-i adabī.* 2 vols. Tehran: 1976.

—— *Sirr-i nay: naqd wa sharḥ-i taḥlīlī wa taṭbīqī-yi Mathnawī.* Tehran: 'Ilmī 1988.

—— *Farār az madrasa: dar bāra-yi zindigī wa andīsha-yi Abū Ḥāmid Ghazālī.* Tehran: 1369 A.Hsh./1990.

—— *Justujū-yi dar taṣawwuf-i Irān.* Tehran: Amīr kabīr 1978.

Zolla, Elemire. "The Uses of Imagination and the Decline of the West." *Sophia Perennis* I/1 (1975): 33-59.

# INDEX